Refugee Protection and the Role of Law

Sixty years on from the signing of the Refugee Convention, forced migration and refugee movements continue to raise global concerns for hosting states and regions, for countries of origin, for humanitarian organisations on the ground and, of course, for the refugee. This edited volume is framed around two themes which go to the core of contemporary 'refugeehood': protection and identity. It analyses how the issue of refugee identity is shaped by and responds to the legal regime of refugee protection in contemporary times.

The book investigates the premise that there is a narrowing of protection space in many countries and many highly visible incidents of *refoulement*. It argues that 'protection', which is a core focus of the Refugee Convention, appears to be under threat, as there are many gaps and inconsistencies in practice.

Contributors to the volume, who include Erika Feller, Elspeth Guild, Hélène Lambert and Roger Zetter, look at the relevant issues from the perspective of a number of different disciplines including law, politics, sociology and anthropology. The chapters examine the link between identity and protection as a basis for understanding how the Refugee Convention has been and is being applied in policy and practice. The situation in a number of jurisdictions and regions in Europe, North America, South-East Asia, Africa and the Middle East is explored in order to ask the question: does jurisprudence under the Refugee Convention need better coordination and how successful is oversight of the Convention?

Susan Kneebone is Professor of Law at the Faculty of Law, Monash University, Australia.

Dallal Stevens is Associate Professor of Law in the School of Law, University of Warwick, UK.

Loretta Baldassar is Professor in the Department of Anthropology and Sociology at the School of Social and Cultural Studies at the University of Western Australia.

Routledge Research in Asylum, Migration and Refugee Law

Refugee Protection and the Role of Law

Conflicting Identities

Edited by

Susan Kneebone, Dallal Stevens and Loretta Baldassar

Routledge
Taylor & Francis Group

LONDON AND NEW YORK

First published 2014
by Routledge
2 Park Square, Milton Park, Abingdon, Oxon, OX14 4RN

and by Routledge
711 Third Avenue, New York, NY 10017

Routledge is an imprint of the Taylor & Francis Group, an informa business

British Library Cataloguing in Publication Data
A catalogue record for this book is available from the British Library

Library of Congress Cataloging-in-Publication Data
Refugee protection and the role of law : conflicting identities / edited by
Susan Kneebone, Dallal Stevens, Loretta Baldassar.
     pages cm. — (Routledge research in asylum, migration and refugee law)
Includes bibliographical references and index.
ISBN 978-0-415-83565-7 (hardback)— ISBN 978-0-203-48801-0 (ebk)
1. Refugees—Legal status, laws, etc.   2. Convention Relating to the
Status of Refugees (1951)   I. Kneebone, Susan, editor of compilation.
II. Stevens, Dallal, editor of compilation.   III. Baldassar, Loretta,
1965-editor of compilation.
KZ6530.R425 2014
341.4'86—dc23   2014005386

ISBN: 978-0-415-83565-7 (hbk)
ISBN: 978-0-203-48801-0 (ebk)

Typeset in Baskerville
by Keystroke, Station Road, Codsall, Wolverhampton

Disclaimer
Every effort has been made to trace and contact copyright holders prior to
publication. If notified, the publisher will undertake to rectify any errors or
omissions at the earliest opportunity.

Contents

Notes on contributors

Maurizio Ambrosini is Professor of Sociology of Migration at the University of Milan, Department of Social and Political Sciences, and *chargé d'enseignement* at the University of Nice-Sophia Antipolis (France). In his Department, he has contributed greatly to the advancement of L.I.M.eS. (Laboratory of Immigration, Multiculturalism and Society). He is also the editor of the journal *Mondi Migranti*, the first Italian journal in this field, and is the academic coordinator of the Centre Medì-Migrations in the Mediterranean, Genoa, as well as the Italian Summer School of Sociology of Migrations. He is a member of the editorial committee of the *Journal of Immigrant and Refugee Studies* and of several Italian sociological journals and collections. His main interests cover immigrants in the labour market, ethnic entrepreneurship, migration policies and refugees studies. He is the author of more than 150 books, articles and essays in these fields. His handbook, *Sociologia delle migrazioni*, is adopted as the textbook in many Italian universities. His most recent book is *Irregular Immigration and Invisible Welfare* (Palgrave, 2013). He was a consultant for the Italian Parliament and member of the National Advisory Board for the Integration of Immigrants at the Ministry of Social Solidarity. He was coordinator of the Italian Unit in the European project ACCEPT Pluralism (7th Framework Programme of the EC).

Loretta Baldassar is Professor and Discipline Chair of Anthropology and Sociology at the University of Western Australia and Adjunct Principal Research Fellow, School of Political and Social Inquiry, Monash University. Baldassar has published extensively on transnational migrants, families and caregiving including, *Transnational Families, Migration and the Circulation of Care: Understanding Mobility and Absence in Family Life* (with Merla, Routledge Transnationalism Series, 2014) and the landmark study *Families Caring Across Borders* (with Baldock and Wilding, Palgrave, 2007), as well as many journal articles and book chapters on this subject. She is a leading authority on Italian migration to Australia, and has written extensively in this area including the award-winning book, *Visits Home* (Melbourne University Press, 2001); *From Paesani to Global Italians* (with Pesman, UWAP, 2005) and *Intimacy and Italian Migration* (with Gabaccia, Fordham University Press, 2011). She is Regional

Editor for Oceania of the journal *Global Networks* and Board Member of Research Committee (31) Migration of the International Sociological Association. Baldassar served a term as Director at the Monash University Centre in Prato, Italy (2009–11), where she began new research projects on Chinese immigration. Baldassar is currently editing a volume *Chinese Migrants in Europe* (with Johanson, McAuliffe and Bressan, Palgrave, forthcoming) and a special journal issue on transnational families and ICTs.

Alexander Betts is University Lecturer in Refugee Studies and Forced Migration at the University of Oxford. His research focuses on the international politics of refugees, migration and humanitarianism, with a focus on sub-Saharan Africa. His recent books include *Protection by Persuasion: International Cooperation in the Refugee Regime* (Cornell University Press, 2009), *Refugees in International Relations* (with Gil Loescher, Oxford University Press, 2010), *Global Migration Governance* (Oxford University Press, 2011), *UNHCR: The Politics and Practice of Refugee Protection* (with Gil Loescher and James Milner, Routledge, 2012) and *Survival Migration: Failed Governance and the Crisis of Displacement* (Cornell University Press, 2013). He has worked as a consultant to UNHCR, OCHA, UNDP, IOM, UNICEF and the Council of Europe, and received research grants from the MacArthur Foundation, the Leverhulme Trust, and the Economic and Social Research Council. He has also held teaching and research positions at Stanford University and the University of Texas at Austin. He is Director of the Humanitarian Innovation Project.

Ulla Björnberg is Professor of Sociology, Chair in Family, Gender and Society at the Department of Sociology and Workscience since 1996; Emerita since 2011. Her expertise is in family sociology, gender and family, and family policy. She has been engaged in several cross-national projects on family policy and family life in Europe and has several publications covering aspects of the field. In her studies she has focused on the reconciliation of employment and family life from the perspective of gender and class, lone motherhood, negotiations and conflicts in couples within marriage, and family policy. She was Program Director of an interdisciplinary research project on the health and well-being of asylum-seeking children and parents, with a specific focus on the impact of various aspects of asylum reception on resilience and coping in the everyday life of children and parents. Most recent publications include 'Caught between a Troubled Past and an Uncertain Future: The Well-being of Asylum-seeking Children in Sweden', in Almudena Moreno Minguez, Ulla Björnberg and An Magritt Jensen (eds), *Social Indicators Research Series*, special issue on family well-being: European perspectives (2012); 'Immigration, Children and Families', in Ulla Björnberg and Mai Heide Ottosen (eds, 2013), *Challenges for Future of Family Policy in the Nordic Countries* (Institute for Social Research, 2013).

Erika Feller is an honours law graduate from Melbourne University, and holds an additional degree in the humanities, specialised in psychology. She is an academically acknowledged authority on refugee law, has published widely in journals, is co-editor with Volker Türk and Frances Nicholson of a book entitled *Refugee Protection in International Law* (Cambridge University Press, 2003) and has contributed to other publications, including the *Max Planck Encyclopaedia of Public International Law*. Feller held the post of Assistant High Commissioner – Protection (2005–13), one of the four top management positions of the UNHCR. Her professional career included three international postings with the Australian diplomatic service, followed by senior appointments with UNHCR, both in Geneva and the Field. As the High Commissioner's Representative in Malaysia, Singapore and Brunei, she concurrently serves as UNHCR's Regional Coordinator for Status Determination for the Indo-Chinese refugee outflow. Among her accomplishments, Feller initiated and managed the 2001–2 Global Consultations on International Protection, which generated the Agenda for Protection, an internationally endorsed multi-year 'road map' for global refugee protection. Her responsibilities have ranged from running refugee camps to undertaking many protection advocacy, negotiation and oversight missions to major refugee emergencies. As Assistant High Commissioner, Feller had personal oversight of age, gender and diversity mainstreaming and accountability throughout UNHCR's global programmes. She has recently been appointed a Fellow of the Australian Institute of International Affairs.

Donald Galloway is Professor of Law at the University of Victoria, Canada. He specialises in immigration law, citizenship law and refugee law. He is the author of *Immigration Law* (Irwin Law, 1997), and co-author of *Immigration and Refuge Law: Cases Materials and Commentary* (Emond Montgomery, 2006) and *Migration Law in Canada* (Kluwer, 2013). He has served as a member of the Immigration and Refugee Board (1998–2001) and as a member of the Executive Committee of the Canadian Association of Refugee Lawyers (2011–13). He was the founding President of the Canadian Association of Refugee and Forced Migration Studies.

Elspeth Guild is a Jean Monnet Professor ad personam in law at the Radboud University, Nijmegen, Netherlands and Professor of Law at Queen Mary University of London. She is also a senior research fellow at the Brussels-based think tank, the Centre for European Policy Studies. She retains her affiliation as a partner at the London law firm Kingsley Napley. She regularly advises EU institutions on migration and asylum-related matters including the Council of Europe's Commissioner for Human Rights. Her recent publications include: Didier Bigo, Sergio Carrera and Elspeth Guild (eds), *Foreigners, Refugees or Minorities? Rethinking People in the Context of Border Controls and Visas* (Ashgate, 2013); Guild and P. Minderhoud (eds), *The First Decade of EU Migration and Asylum Law* (Martinus Nijhoff, 2011); Didier Bigo, Sergio Carrera, Elspeth Guild and R. B. J. Walker (eds), *Europe's 21st Century Challenge* (Ashgate, 2010); *Security and Migration in the 21st Century Polity* (Policy Press, 2009).

Martin Jones is a Lecturer in international human rights law at the Centre for Applied Human Rights, an interdisciplinary research and teaching unit of the University of York. Martin previously taught and served as a visiting researcher at institutions in Canada, the USA, Egypt and Australia. He has published widely in refugee law and policy and international human rights law. Martin's research examines the role of the law and the legal profession in refugee protection, primarily in the Middle East and Asia. He has a lengthy and ongoing engagement with refugee legal aid organisations and refugee policy makers, serving as an adviser to and external reviewer of legal aid programmes in more than a dozen jurisdictions and has acted as adviser to the governments of Canada, Egypt, Hong Kong, Indonesia and Taiwan and to UNHCR about refugee policy. Before his academic career, Martin practised as a refugee lawyer in Canada. Since then, he co-founded and serves as the vice-chairman of the Egyptian Foundation for Refugee Rights, the largest provider of legal aid to refugees in Egypt. He was the founding chair of the Legal Aid Working Group of the Asia Pacific Refugee Rights Network, a network of more than 100 organisations working on refugee issues in the Asia Pacific, and currently serves as an adviser to its Steering Committee. He is presently a member of the Steering Committee of the Southern Refugee Legal Aid Network, a global network of refugee legal aid providers in the Global South.

Susan Kneebone is a Professor of law and Emeritus Associate of the Castan Centre for Human Rights Law, Faculty of Law, Monash University, Australia. She has published widely and teaches in the areas of forced migration, human trafficking, citizenship and migration law and refugee law. Her recent publications include: *Transnational Crime and Human Rights: Responses to Human Trafficking in the Greater Mekong Subregion* (Routledge, 2012) (with Julie Debeljak); and *Refugees, Asylum Seekers and the Rule of Law: Comparative Perspectives* (Cambridge University Press, 2009). Kneebone is currently Secretary of the International Association for the Study of Forced Migration. She is the leader of the Asia Pacific Forced Migration Connection, established as an Institutional Partner with the Refugee Research Network, Refugee Studies Centre Canada. Kneebone is recipient of a number of research grants funded by the Australian Research Council, including most recently: 'Towards Development of a Legal Framework for Regulation of International Marriage Migration'.

Hélène Lambert is Professor of International law at the University of Westminster, London. She has written extensively on international and European refugee law. Her particular interest lies in the globalisation of legal norms, international relations theory and human rights. Her publications include *The Global Reach of European Refugee Law* (edited with Jane McAdam and Maryellen Fullerton, Cambridge University Press, 2013); *The Limits of Transnational Law: Refugee Law, Policy Harmonization and Judicial Dialogue in the European Union* (edited with Guy S. Goodwin-Gill, Cambridge University Press, 2010); *International Refugee Law* (ed., Ashgate, 2010); *International Law and*

International Relations (co-authored with David Armstrong and Theo Farrell, 2nd edn, Cambridge University Press, 2012); *The Position of Aliens in relation to the European Convention on Human Rights* (3rd edn, Council of Europe, 2006); and *Seeking Asylum: Comparative Law and Practice in Selected European Countries* (Martinus Nijhoff, 1995). She is also author of numerous articles in the *International and Comparative Law Quarterly*, the *International Journal of Refugee Law* and the *Refugee Survey Quarterly*. Lambert is currently writing a research paper on the overlap between statelessness and refugee status. She is also working in the interdisciplinary area of international law and international relations on a project that looks at armed conflicts, civilians and courts. She has acted as a consultant for the Council of Europe and UNHCR on numerous occasions, and is a member of the editorial board of the *Refugee Law Reader* and the *International Refugee Law* Book Series.

Maria O'Sullivan is a Lecturer in the Faculty of Law and an Associate of the Castan Centre for Human Rights at Monash University, Australia. Her teaching and research interests are international refugee law and administrative law. Her research work focuses on interpretative issues arising from the Refugee Convention and comparative analysis between Australia, Canada and Europe. Maria has published a number of book chapters and journal articles on these issues, including: 'Territorial Protection: Cessation of Refugee Status and Internal Flight Alternative Compared', in S. Juss (ed.), *Research Companion to Migration Theory and Policy* (Ashgate, 2013); 'Non-state Actors of Protection in Refugee law' (2012) 24(1) *International Journal of Refugee Law* 1–26 and 'Article 1C' (co-authored with Susan Kneebone) in A. Zimmerman (ed.), *The 1951 Convention Relating to the Status of Refugees and its 1967 Protocol: A Commentary* (Oxford University Press, 2011). In 2012 she completed her doctoral thesis on Article 1C(5) of the Refugee Convention, dealing with cessation of refugee status. She has made a number of submissions to parliamentary inquiries on refugee law issues and is a regular contributor to media commentary on asylum in Australia.

Dallal Stevens is Associate Professor of Law at the University of Warwick. Her expertise is in the fields of refugee and asylum law. Much of her work has revolved around the construction of the asylum seeker within a contemporary perspective, although she has also examined the plight of the refugee in a historical context. She is author of *UK Asylum Law and Policy: Historical and Contemporary Perspectives* (Sweet & Maxwell, 2004). A particular focus of her research has been the law's treatment of asylum seekers in the UK and Europe. Her work adopts a contextual and, at times, comparative approach, and is concerned with highlighting the tension that exists between asylum law and human rights protection in this contentious area. She is currently researching asylum and refugee policies in the Middle East, and has written on Iraqi refugees in Jordan as well as the Israeli asylum policy. Stevens has acted as an adviser to a number of national bodies, including the Home Office and Parliament. She has served as a trustee for the former immigration law advisory agency in the UK – the Immigration Advisory Service – and for the Electronic Immigration Network. She is on the Editorial Board of *Immigration, Asylum and Nationality Law Journal*; *Law and Humanities*; and, formerly, *Butterworths Immigration Law Service*.

Roger Zetter is Emeritus Professor of Refugee Studies, University of Oxford, retiring as the Director of the Refugee Studies Centre in September 2011. He was Founding Editor (1998–2001) of the *Journal of Refugee Studies*. With research interests in sub-Saharan Africa, the EU and Middle East, his research, teaching and consultancy over a 35-year-long career has covered many aspects of forced displacement and has been conducted for many governments and international organisations: UNHCR, UNDP, World Bank, UNHABITAT, UNFPA, IOM IFRC, Swiss Agency for Development and Co-operation, OXFAM and Brookings-Bern Project; the governments of the UK, NZ, Denmark, Norway and Switzerland, and the EC. Recent research and consultancy has focused on three areas: the causes and consequences of European deterrence and restrictionism; the environmental impacts of climate change on population displacement; the economic impacts and costs of forced displacement. He was lead consultant for the IASC 2011 Strategy for Managing Humanitarian Challenges in Urban Areas and editor of the IFRC *World Disasters Report 2012* – themed on forced migration and displacement. He is currently undertaking a large-scale assignment for the Swiss Federal Commission on Migration entitled 'State of the Art Review of Current and Future Protection Needs and Protection Policies for Forcibly Displaced People'.

Preface

The chapters that comprise this volume are drawn from papers presented at a workshop held at the Monash University Centre, Prato, Italy, 2–3 May 2011 entitled 'Refugees and the Refugee Convention 60 Years on: Protection and Identity'. The workshop, organised by the editors of this book, was endorsed by the United Nations High Commissioner for Refugees (UNHCR) as an activity to mark the sixtieth anniversary of the 1951 Convention Relating to the Status of Refugees ('Refugee Convention').

Sixty years on, the need for a Refugee Convention is as pressing as ever. Refugee protection continues to be a major concern of the UNHCR and its many government and non-government partners. However, the goal of protecting refugees seems regularly to be eclipsed by the associated issues of refugee management and control. In the complex political and politicised contexts of refugee protection, it is not surprising that identifying refugees – and therefore, 'refugee identities' – has become the focus of concern. This edited collection draws on interdisciplinary perspectives to analyse how refugee identities are shaped by and respond to the legal regime of refugee protection and, in particular, how protection and identity are interconnected.

The chapters in this book highlight how the social and political tensions surrounding refugee protection go directly to the heart of contemporary global debates about the international movement of people and 'belonging', along with the associated issues of integration, citizenship, culture and identity. We use the sixtieth anniversary of the Refugee Convention as an appropriate moment to reflect on the importance and limitations of this most significant legal instrument, and the legal, political and social categories of persons seeking protection that it created. By highlighting the uniqueness of the refugee category and the significance of the Refugee Convention, in particular the processes and practices through which it confers status and identity, this volume offers a fresh and insightful approach to an understanding of how the law shapes responses to refugees.

As editors, we are extremely grateful for the enthusiastic, incisive and open engagement of our contributors and participants at the workshop in examining this issue from a diversity of disciplines and methodological approaches. We would like to thank, in particular, Katherine Carpenter and Mark Sapwell of Routledge, Warwick University Law School, the Law Faculty Monash University and the Monash Prato Centre for their generous support of the workshop and production of this book.

Susan Kneebone, *Law School, Monash University*
Dallal Stevens, *School of Law, University of Warwick*
Loretta Baldassar, *Anthropology and Sociology, University of Western Australia*
January 2014

Part I

Refugee law and protection: fit for purpose 60 years on?

1   Conflicting identities, protection and the role of law

Susan Kneebone, Loretta Baldassar and Dallal Stevens

> [L]ife and epistemology do not imitate legal categories. Instead, legal categories most often seek to 'discipline' life and knowledge to realize dominant interests in society.[1]

The Refugee Convention was thought to be a beacon of hope to emerge from the horrific aftermath of the two World Wars, which left millions of people displaced from their home countries and unable to return. Born of this historical moment, the Convention defined a 'refugee' as a person who:

> owing to [a] well-founded fear of being persecuted for reasons of race, religion, nationality, membership of a particular social group or political opinion, is outside the country of his nationality and is unable or, owing to such fear, is unwilling to avail himself of the protection of that country; or who, not having a nationality and being outside the country of his former habitual residence as a result of such events, is unable or, owing to such fear, is unwilling to return to it.[2]

The Convention reflected an emerging human rights culture in the post-Second World War period, evident in the references to the 1948 Universal Declaration of Human Rights (UDHR) in the Preamble to the Convention, and the principle of non-discrimination on the basis of 'race, religion or country of origin' in Article 3 of the Convention.[3] Yet it is precisely the pervasiveness of such discrimination against refugees in contravention of Article 3 that fuelled our concerns in the 60th anniversary year of the Refugee Convention. In contrast to the recognition of the need for protection which guided the making of the Refugee Convention, today industrialised receiving states have restrictive practices and policies which actively discriminate against asylum seekers[4] looking for refuge. In particular, over the last two decades protection has been weakened through a range of measures adopted by states, including non-entrée measures, interceptions, interdictions, offshore processing, restrictive application of the refugee definition and application of 'safe third country' concepts. Refugees have evolved from being a protected class at the end of the Second World War, to being discriminated against as 'irregular' international migrants; through notions such as the asylum–migration nexus that focuses on the 'mixed flows' of migrants and irregular status, rather than on the specific protection needs of certain categories of migrants.

Our starting point is that the cornerstone of refugee identity is the legal and normative framework of protection enshrined in the Refugee Convention. This definition is also the basis for the international response to refugees as part of the phenomenon of 'forced migration'.[5] And although, as explained below, different disciplines view the refugee category and the meaning of protection in different ways, the Refugee Convention remains a constant and central reference point. The Refugee Convention (and its definition) is 'one of the most widely accepted international norms, and probably one of the few to have penetrated the public consciousness'.[6] Arguably, it has a unique role in contrast to general human rights law in conferring a status on an individual[7] and hence in the construction of 'refugee' identity. As Feller commented at the Prato Workshop, the existence of such a Convention is a historical feat in itself; the international community would be unlikely today to develop a collectively agreed upon definition – thus its continuing and central importance.[8] Further, as we show in this volume, even in regions and countries where the Refugee Convention is not formally in place, responses to refugees are shaped by it, either as a deliberate rejection of its normative framework or as an attempt to adapt it to the local situation.[9] For this reason we place the Refugee Convention at the centre of our analysis to investigate: 'The Refugee Convention at 60: still fit for purpose?'.

In effect, the Refugee Convention produced a new legal category of person – the refugee[10] – seeking refuge in another country from 'persecution', which includes torture or 'inhuman and degrading treatment' and 'severe violation of basic human rights'.[11] While this was a 'compassionate' response to persecution, the Convention also created a new legal entitlement to a status in international law but left it to states to determine how to implement the rights of the refugee. As the chapters in this volume illustrate, states consistently deny refugees the rights owed to them under international law. The quintessentially legal identity of 'the refugee', clashes with the desire of states to control the composition of their communities on the one hand, and the 'humanitarian' objectives of the Convention, on the other. But in the 'securitised' context of international migration, it is not surprising that the identification of refugees is no simple matter and has become increasingly a fraught and much contested process, characterised by distrust of the refugee.[12]

In this volume, we consider the role of law and policy in making and unmaking the refugee category through an interdisciplinary lens, to explore how refugee identity is shaped by the particular legal, political and social processes that surround asylum-seeking. That is, although the Refugee Convention creates a concept of 'refugee', there are a number of refugee *identities* central to this analysis. As the chapters in this volume illustrate, the legal, political and policy contexts are intertwined, and influence the attribution of identity to refugees.

While much has been written about the refugee definition, a focus on the role of law (and the policy behind it) in creating and shaping the identities of persons defined as legal refugees has been surprisingly limited. In order to benefit from the protection promised by the Refugee Convention, people need to qualify, or meet the requirements of the law, to gain the legal status of refugee. This legal process sets up myriad social and personal dynamics, many of which are unintended and harmful. Most alarmingly, the onus to prove 'a well-founded fear' results in a 'guilty until proven innocent' scenario, evident in issues around the believability and credibility of applicants for legal refugee status.[13] In this volume, we examine both the intended and unintended consequences of the political, legal and social constructions of refugee identities. Indeed, one of the more complex issues that is addressed in a number of chapters in the volume is how the legal construction of refugee identity is influenced by state and global policy approaches to refugee protection.

Refugee law and protection: fit for purpose 60 years on?

This chapter is organised to reflect the structure of the volume and to contextualise the key themes of the chapters. We explore the key concepts of refugee 'protection' and 'identity' by analysing the link between these two concepts. This is done through overlapping lines of enquiry. First, we look at how individual and group identities are 'ascribed' and how this *process* is linked to law and to institutional power. As explained by Zetter in Chapter 2, the interplay between processes and institutional power 'not only plays a complex role in *describing* an identity but also, by presenting and (re)presenting that identity, it is instrumental in *making* an identity'. Second, we examine the *power* of the law and its institutions to make the point about the role of law as an instrument for making and unmaking the refugee category or identity.

Part I, which includes chapters by Zetter, Galloway and Feller, sets up the volume's central questions and main themes about the continuing relevance and effectiveness of the Refugee Convention definition and its role in shaping legal and social refugee identities. Complementing the chapters by Zetter and Galloway, Feller explains the significance of the international refugee protection regime, which influences the way that individual states respond to the Refugee Convention and formulate refugee policy. In Part II, chapters by Stevens, Kneebone and O'Sullivan explore the way implementation and interpretation of the Refugee Convention has shaped current understandings of refugee identity. This historical and comparative discussion prepares the way for the second half of the volume which examines how well the Refugee Convention has stood the test of time and whether it continues to be 'fit for purpose' today.

Part III examines the macro, formal and state-oriented perspectives and approaches to refugee protection, their role in creating and maintaining refugee identities, and especially the power, including institutional power, that operates under the rule of law to shape refugee identities. It includes contributions by Guild, Betts and Lambert that deal, broadly, with the policy behind legal processes. For example, Guild explains the role of law as an instrument of power, drawing on Foucault's concept of 'governmentality', in contradistinction to the role of law as a formal legal instrument. Betts, applying an international relations perspective, uses the notion of 'regime stretching' to explain how six states in Africa stretch the Refugee Convention definition to incorporate people at the margins of the formal legal definition, but fail to adapt it in other contexts. Lambert analyses the role of the European Union as a transnational actor in shaping refugee protection. To further deepen our analysis, Part IV examines micro, social, individual and politically oriented perspectives and approaches to refugee protection and their role in creating and maintaining refugee identities. Björnberg discusses the unintended negative consequences of well-meaning and highly organised integration policies for refugees in Sweden. In contrast, Ambrosini discusses Italy's ad hoc and mostly hostile formal response to asylum seekers, highlighting some of its unexpected positive outcomes. Jones, in his chapter, brings a different perspective, discussing the role of civil society in South-East Asia as protectors in opposition to the state. Once again, these contributions reveal the role of institutions and legal and policy processes in identity construction.

In Chapter 2 of Part I, Zetter reflects on how the individual asylum seeker negotiates the legal process, and considers the way individuals and groups may 'self-describe' or construct their own identities to bring themselves within the definition and grounds of the Refugee Convention. Galloway, conversely, explains how the Canadian government has reconfigured and reconceptualised 'the refugee' as an indirect beneficiary of government 'largesse' rather than as a 'rights-bearer'. In Canada, this means that the government doubts the ability of the refugee to 'self-assess'. Zetter, in a further contrast, focuses on the processes embedded in the concept of refugee under the Refugee Convention, some of which are very familiar to us. For example, we know that refugee applicants need to tell their story so as to conform to the dominant 'narrative' of a refugee. The refugee must narrate a story in which, as Zetter describes, their 'case' is delinked from their 'story', in order to 'conform to a prescribed identity which is normalised and granted materialist meaning though its institutionalisation'. In this process, refugees 'negotiate within a framework of legal designation, state practice, and political and everyday language, on the one hand, and their own accounts, on the other'.[14] For example, the refugee applicant, and particularly refugee women,[15] battle against the preconception of a refugee as someone persecuted for reasons related to civil or political status, rather than for social or economic rights. The core of the refugee definition, the very notion of 'persecution' has spawned competing interpretations about the extent to which the state's role is relevant to a finding of a 'well-founded fear'.[16] The process is critiqued as embodying a 'post-colonial' narrative,[17] formulated and dominated by 'Western' concepts and interests.[18]

The law at the national or state level determines the details of this 'ascriptive' process in some very important ways. The hearing process generally depends upon the administrative framework and powers that are conferred on the institution. For example, the extent to which the institution takes account of psychological and cultural factors[19] varies between jurisdictions. Issues of standard of proof and credibility play an important part in refugee status determination. But the neutrality of the legal process is called into question.[20] Zetter suggests that the role of law is 'inevitably partial', that it is highly 'instrumental in shaping and constraining that identity and the experiences of those so categorised'. Zetter argues that identity is linked through this role to institutional power – as he expresses the overlap between process and power, 'identities are *situated* not narrated'. As Donald Galloway explains in Chapter 3, new legislation in Canada effectively ensures that the refugee claimant 'no longer controls the agenda in the hearing room'.

The 'gatekeeper' role of the law demonstrates the power of the institution which may decide not to hear the applicant at all.[21] This is an example of the overlap between process and power, which Audrey Macklin describes as keeping the asylum seeker 'out of earshot'.[22] Zetter refers to this as a 'contestation over access to identity and . . . exercise of power over its characteristics':

> [T]he discursive shaping of identity is not the negotiated outcome of different narratives: rather it is a contestation over access to identity and the exercise of power over its characteristics.

Zetter describes the 'ascribed' identity as a constructed one which largely serves the needs of states, and suggests that refugees do not easily fit into the seemingly clear-cut categories and criteria of the refugee definition. Indeed, Betts in Part III argues that the term 'survival migrants' is a better term with which to describe the identity of contemporary refugees who are the product of new types of forced migration.

Another major plank of Zetter's and Betts's analyses, both of which show the overlap between process and power, is the argument that individual and group identities are ascribed in a similar way. For this aspect of his analysis Zetter draws on Goffman,[23] and links the construction of identity, as a personal and social process, to the instrumentality of institutional power by highlighting how refugees are seen as a security threat, and thus as a threat to state power. So, for example, the 'asylum–migration nexus' was designed by Western states to highlight the large 'mixed' flow of economic migrants and asylum seekers, and to promote policies to regulate migration. As a number of chapters in this collection demonstrate, refugees are racially defined in state laws and policies as 'risky' groups, as criminalised aliens, and as a burden on state resources, or as a threat to labour markets. The argument that individual and group identities are ascribed in a similar way highlights the role of states and of legal systems in making and unmaking refugee identity and protection. Refugee identities are determined by the processes and power which the legal system endorses.

Chapter 4 by Erika Feller, former Assistant High Commissioner for Protection, which concludes Part I of the book, makes the link between individual and group identities by highlighting the importance of global refugee policy. Feller discusses the current global protection challenges under the international refugee protection scheme, which the UNHCR is mandated to oversee. Her analysis demonstrates the connection between restrictive refugee policy on a global level and individual state policy (and in turn upon individuals, as discussed above). It demonstrates the domino effect of restrictive refugee policies, and their constraining effect, a point which is also made by Betts in Chapter 9.

Feller identifies the gaps in current protection needs at the international level, from UNHCR's perspective, and measures them against the provisions of the individualised refugee definition in the Refugee Convention. She discusses the possibility of providing different standards of protection for different cohorts of refugees, and suggests that protection outcomes ought to respond to the particular needs and 'identity' of the refugee cohort. An example of one such gap is evident in the development of the Refugee Convention itself. An essential feature of the definition that was provided in the Convention in comparison to previous instruments[21] was that it referred to an individualised 'well-founded' fear of persecution. Yet under the instrument by which the UNHCR was established by the UN General Assembly in 1950, the Statute of the Office of the United Nations High Commissioner for Refugees,[25] the UNHCR was granted a mandate in relation to both individuals and groups of refugees. Paragraph 6 of the Statute largely adopted the Convention definition of a refugee, but Paragraph 2 provided as follows:

> The work of the High Commissioner shall be of an entirely non-political character; it shall be humanitarian and social and shall relate, as a rule, to groups and categories of refugees.

Thus, it has been suggested that the UNHCR Statute contains an 'apparent contradiction'.[26] On the one hand, it applies to groups and categories of refugees, but it also provides an individualised definition in similar terms to the Refugee Convention. This 'apparent contradiction' between the perception of the refugee as a persecuted individual, and refugees as a part of a group or community (national or international) 'problem to be solved'[27] and as the object of *humanitarian* protection[28] has shaped the perception of *the* refugee and of *refugees* in international refugee policy over the past six decades. While the refugee is constructed in national (and supranational) or state law under the individualised definition of the Refugee Convention, the policies and laws that determine that construction take on the perception of refugees as a global 'problem to be solved'.

Indeed, the UNHCR Statute has a solution-oriented approach which reinforces the perception of refugees as a global problem. UNHCR's mandate has evolved over the past six decades in direct response to large-scale crises, to cover both refugees and other categories of displaced persons in regions of origin, asylum seekers in destination states and stateless persons, who are collectively referred to as 'persons of concern' in the UNHCR's collection of statistics. This mandate exists alongside the legal framework provided by the Refugee Convention, which grants *states* the right to determine refugee status. In short, as discussion in this volume illustrates there are contradictions in the international legal framework that created the concept of international refugee protection. These contradictions are well illustrated by Feller's and Betts's chapters.

Refugee identities and protection – historical shifts

As is made clear by a number of chapters in this book, the 'refugee problem' and responses have changed over the course of the last century. Stevens and Kneebone in Chapters 5 and 6 of Part II, explain how the focus on individualised protection under the 1951 Refugee Convention contrasts with the protection accorded in the pre-1951 period, which applied to groups of refugees.[29] The refugee problem was then associated with statelessness and its practical implications. The Convention had a specific type of protection in mind – as set out in its provisions – and sought to encourage naturalisation and assimilation of refugees into the host community (Article 34). But in response to contemporary concerns over increasing evidence of the 'forced' nature of refugee 'migration', including mass influxes, and some uncertainty as to the meaning of 'protection', attention is turning to the nature of protection as a legal concept and to the adequacy of the concept of individualised protection in the 1951 Convention.[30]

The contemporary nature of the refugee problem, which includes 'protracted refugee' and 'urban refugee' situations, as well as 'trafficked persons'[31] and 'smuggled migrants'[32] highlights the fact that the refugee category has multiple identities. Further, as Betts explains, there are new drivers of refugee movements and forced migration including generalised violence, environmental disaster, food insecurity, and state fragility, which frequently interact. Thus the protection needs of displaced persons are more complex. Such truths force us to confront the key challenges to, and limitations of, the 1951 Convention.

This leads to the tricky question, central to our argument: *what is protection?* How has it been interpreted in different jurisdictions, and social and historical contexts? Over a period of 60 years, as we have explained, the perception of refugees and the meaning of refugee protection have evolved. In 2008, largely in response to the problem of 'protracted refugee situations', the UNHCR decided to drop the language of the 'asylum–migrant nexus', and to concentrate instead on 'refugee protection and durable solutions in the context of international migration'.[33] In this reframing of the refugee 'problem', asylum seekers were seen as 'actors of development' with agency in relation to solutions to the problem (such as through being able to gain employment, or in bringing skills to the host country). As already discussed above, Zetter (Chapter 2) explains that refugee identity has been 'elaborated and continually reshaped' – through the prism of 60 years of protection – 'into a complex and multilayered identity by the interests of states and humanitarian actors and mediated by the distinctive social worlds of the refugees themselves'.

The importance of a well-grounded historical perspective and understanding is illustrated in this volume by Stevens in Chapter 5 ('Shifting conceptions of refugee protection: European and Middle Eastern approaches'), which addresses the creation of refugee identity and the nature of protection in a regional context.

Following consideration of the European origins of refugee protection and identity, Stevens discusses the contrasting case of the Middle East, where states tend not to be signatories to the Convention. She shows how, in the Middle East, immigration law, refugee law and traditional notions of Arab hospitality compete in creating multiple identities. Stevens describes how ascribed identities, whether by the state or the UNHCR, can come into conflict with one another as well as with the individual's perception of self. In this region, the link between identity and protection is clearly evident, and the protection provided is based on a mixture of human rights that are promoted by the UNHCR and accepted or endorsed by the state; as such, it closely resembles the 'law of asylum' advocated by Jones in relation to South-East Asia (Chapter 13). Though the state's goal is often temporary protection, the outcome tends to be a semi-permanent solution.

In similar historical context, Kneebone argues in Chapter 6, that over a period of time, the 'statist' approach to refugee law of the 1951 Convention has led to a 'surrogate protection'[34] interpretation, and a much diminished concept of protection. Under this approach refugee law has shifted from a position whereby, as per the refugee definition, a refugee is 'a person who' 'is *unable, or* owing' to fear of persecution, is '*unwilling* to avail himself' of the protection of the country of his nationality, to one whose entitlement to protection under the Refugee Convention depends on the ability and willingness of the *state* (or its agents) to provide protection. Kneebone's analysis shows that legal approaches are broadly divided between what can be called a protection or 'rights' approach and a 'status' or state-centred approach. Kneebone explains through a comparative study of former Commonwealth jurisdictions, how state law and policy has developed 'transnationally'. This endorses the observation that refugee law and constructed identities reflect state interests. As O'Sullivan also points out in relation to Australian policy, legally constructed identities largely reflect state interests, which compete with those of the UNHCR, civil society and of the individual, often with serious implications for the concept of 'protection'.

Kneebone and O'Sullivan also both raise the issue of the overlap between the Refugee Convention and human rights norms. This point is taken up again by Hélène Lambert in Chapter 10 ('Transnational law and refugee identity: the worldwide effect of European norms)'. Lambert suggests that the norms of refugee protection which are evolving under European Union law and policy are affecting the norms of the 1951 Refugee Convention. She echoes the views of Durieux, in her argument that 'the EU concept of asylum induces the phenomenon of a "vanishing refugee", whereby the central character of the 1951 Convention regime, namely the refugee, is blurred, marginalized or ignored'.[35]

To summarise Part II, it is clear that current refugee law constructs refugee identity as a reflection of state interests. The shifts in legal approaches to refugee protection over the last century demonstrate that state interests have become increasingly the dominant factor. Yet this conflicts with the fact that refugee status has been sought by asylum seekers because it affords them protection, this is what they need most; this is what they seek. The defining characteristic of the refugee experience is their act of fleeing persecution, their escape from violence[36] and breaches of human rights. Today that protection is sought in receiving Western countries primarily under the Refugee Convention, which provides a refugee identity that is shaped by refugee law. Concurrently, refugee identity shapes the form of protection received. But that identity is described in different ways by different scholars within and across disciplines. For example, Steinbock suggests that the key concept is 'protection of the innocent';[37] other lawyers by contrast are inclined to describe refugees as persons whose human rights have been violated.[38] The emergence and use of these broader concepts under human rights instruments also raises the issue about their effect on the primacy of the Refugee Convention. As the discussion of historical shifts in this volume reveals, the scope of refugee protection has been eroded since the Refugee Convention was formulated. In the second half of the volume, different perspectives are contrasted to provide a more comprehensive analysis of the nexus between refugee law and identity.

Law, power and refugee identity: macro and state perspectives

The chapters that comprise Part III of the volume explore the macro, legal, state-based responses and approaches to refugee protection and identity. As explained above, this section is concerned with the power of the law and policy, and its ability to shape refugee identity. We show that the meaning of 'protection' is dependent not only on context, but also on the approach to the issue. For example, the legal scholar Andrew Shacknove[39] describes the 'core' of 'refugeehood' as the loss of the bond between citizen and state; the refugee seeks restoration of the severed bond through protection under the Refugee Convention. However, the Convention does not prescribe one standard of protection, but rather a number of graduated rights, many of which depend upon the level of attachment that the refugee has to the country of asylum.[40] That is, protection is provided according to the intensity of the new bond created with the country of asylum, and according to the laws of that country. The minimum standard of protection provided by the Refugee Convention is the *non-refoulement* principle, the 'negative' right *not* to be returned to the frontiers of a territory where 'life or freedom would be threatened'.[41] Indeed, it is often contended that the *non-refoulement* principle goes to the heart of refugee protection. Further basic rights are included in the Convention; for example: Article 26 – freedom of movement within the state's territory – Article 32 – the right not to be expelled save on national security and public order grounds – and Article 31, which prohibits states from imposing 'penalties' upon refugees 'on account of their illegal entry or presence'.

Aleinikoff argues that 'any complete analysis of causes and solutions could not be wholly indifferent to the forms and structure of political power'.[42] This is illustrated by the chapters in Part III. The political scientist and scholar of international relations is concerned about 'protection' in terms of power relations, between individuals and states, and between states and with the role of other institutions such as the UNHCR. The political scientist seeks explanations for the political ramifications of protection regimes, whether in ethics[43] or other norms or structures of regimes and governance. For example, in his book *North–South Impasse: The International Politics of Refugee Protection*, Alexander Betts discusses the ways in which states contribute to refugee protection. His key concerns are with the extent to which states confer asylum (a right which does not exist in the strict sense under the Refugee Convention) and upon burden-sharing between states. He asserts that the two norms in the international refugee regime are asylum and burden-sharing.

Working somewhat against human rights perspectives on protection is the fact that the power of the state is enhanced by the Refugee Convention. The Convention is limited in its powers over states because it respects, supports and upholds the power of states to determine who may be admitted into its borders (and hence avail themself of the protection of its sovereignty). Refugee law does not therefore guarantee state membership in a new host state, nor does it impose a duty to offer citizenship (only, as stated above, a duty to 'facilitate'). As Aleinikoff notes: 'Recognizing the fundamental international law norm that states have complete control over the entrance of aliens into their territory, the Convention carefully fails to establish any duty upon states to admit refugees.'[44]

Another significant feature of state control is the granting of status. In contrast to other categories of 'persons of concern' under UNHCR's mandate, refugee protection under the Refugee Convention confers a unique advantage that arises from the operation of law.[45] But as Kneebone explains in Chapter 6, this has led to the notion of 'surrogate' protection which the courts in some jurisdictions have interpreted as imposing an extra-high burden of proof on refugee applicants. The notion of 'surrogate' protection reflects the fact that until recently, states have assumed that refugee protection leads to a permanent status in the host country, a view encouraged by Article 34 of the Refugee Convention.[46] But in Chapter 4, Erika Feller, former Assistant High Commissioner for Protection, UNHCR, argues that the nature of this status has been misunderstood; that legal status is not to be confused with permanence, or with asylum which can be of a temporary nature. In line with this approach, some states no longer provide refugees with an indefinite right to remain, but resort instead to limited leave – for example, since 2005, refugees in the UK are granted permission to enter and stay for an initial period of five years. Thus today, protection of refugees is ultimately the province of states and state structures, including legal institutions, and is often temporary.

The paradox of protection, the fact that the Refugee Convention definition and processes throw up many conflicting and self-contradictory elements, has the effect of destabilising the legal categories – and identities – of refugee and asylum seeker. In Chapter 8 ('Conflicting identities and securitisation in refugee law: lessons from the EU'), Guild points out that many states appear 'Janus faced' on issues of refugee policy: 'On the one hand, statements of commitment to refugee protection are plentiful, on the other, mechanisms are adopted which aim to exclude the refugee even from being heard.' This 'Janus-faced' approach to refugee issues ensures that refugees have conflicting identities in law and policy. In a nutshell, they are both objects of protection and of fear, as the chapters in

Part IV show. Because of the respect and indeed faith by which policies and institutions supported by laws are viewed, we decided to investigate the role of law in both creating and in responding to this paradox.

Guild employs Foucault's concept of 'governmentality' to examine the Janus-faced nature of European state practice. She explains law as an instrument of power as distinct from law as a formal instrument. In particular, Guild analyses the Procedures Directive in the context of European policy under the Common European Asylum System (CEAS), to explain how its provisions relating to access to refugee status determination procedures are examples of the law being used to discipline asylum seekers who present incoherent narratives and 'complex identities'. The refugee who fails to present a coherent narrative may be disciplined by being granted lesser international protection in the form of subsidiary protection under the Qualification Directive. Further, Guild explains how refugee policy is shaped by biopolitics through requirements of the CEAS to 'inform the state about all aspects of their existence'. For example, through the Frontex arrangement, an institution that is 'cut free from the state' was created to conduct surveillance and punishment of the asylum seeker population.

Guild describes aspects of the Procedures Directive which enable states to categorise and manage asylum seekers (as an example of biopolitics) through concepts that deal with them collectively, rather than as individuals. These concepts which are mirrored in other legal systems include the safe first country of asylum and safe third-country mechanisms. In the same vein, policies of containment in regions of origin, which have led to the deliberate creation of new categories of 'internally displaced persons' and 'protracted refugee situations', unsettle and destabilise the legal and normative framework of protection enshrined in the 1951 Refugee Convention.

In his contribution to this volume, Betts, in Chapter 9, makes evident the notion of governmentality in his description of the legal regime as an 'arbitrary' instrument. Betts describes how the six African countries which are the subject of his study have 'stretched' the legal regime, to suit their interests. He discusses the discretionary responses of six host states in Africa, and he examines the involvement of UNHCR in influencing the protection outcomes in these jurisdictions. Betts explains that the responses of host states in Africa have been shaped by the interests of *elites* within the governments of host states. Betts also examines the involvement of UNHCR in determining the protection outcomes in these six African states, to show how it contributes to 'shaping' the refugee category. The lesson of Betts's discussion is that in 1951 states came together to provide international protection to groups of refugees, because of the destabilising effects of the 'refugee problem'. It seems that 60 years later that lesson needs to be remembered for a meaningful response to the current global refugee crisis.

In Chapter 10, Lambert examines the impact of the Common European Asylum System (CEAS) on the development of refugee law. She draws on scholarship from international relations and sociology to specify pathways and processes whereby European law and practice on refugee protection spreads or may spread worldwide, and be selectively adopted by non-EU states. In this way, she continues the analysis in Chapter 6 (Kneebone) of how refugee identities are constructed judicially and transnationally. Lambert focuses on the key role of the EU as an 'agent of normative change' in the area of refugee law. Similar to Betts – and Jones in Part IV – Lambert 'drills down' into how 'the state' is comprised and leaves us to reflect on whether EU norms could have implications for the construction of refugee identity by courts beyond the EU.

These chapters illustrate collectively that other policies, institutions and factors operate outside the strict parameters of states and refugee law and that they are important in shaping refugee protection and identity. The chapters that comprise Part IV of this volume explore the relationship between the legal apparatus of protection and refugee identity from the perspective of the individuals involved.

Refugee identities and protection: micro, social and individual perspectives

The social scientist is concerned with the ways in which refugee protection policy constructs and constrains individual and social identities and it is this perspective that forms the focus of Part IV of the volume. Importantly, Paragraph 2 of the UNHCR Statute (set out above) supports this approach when it refers to its work as being 'humanitarian and social' and as relating, 'as a rule, to groups and categories of refugees'. This description challenges the legal view of 'refugeehood' as pronounced by Shacknove as concerned with the legal bond between state and individual. In contradistinction, humanitarian (and more generally, social science) definitions of protection tend to focus on the substantive needs and lived experiences of the individuals with a view to safeguarding their human rights. In 1992 Aleinikoff, who is now Deputy High Commissioner of the UNHCR for Refugees, suggested that:[17]

> From a sociological perspective, refugees are broadly conceptualized as involuntary migrants – persons forced to leave their habitual places of residence because of conditions that make life intolerable . . . [W]hat is significant about social science conceptualizations is that notions of statehood, sovereignty, and boundaries play subsidiary roles in defining persons in need of assistance.[18]

Aleinikoff was critical of legal scholars for writing from a 'state-centred perspective' or for their 'membership bias' which he said 'has been developed (and, in fact, imposed) by the lawyers and the legal system with little consultation with the refugees themselves'.[19] He argues:

> Lawyers seem to view membership as a coat that can be taken off and replaced rather than as a constitutive part of identity; and the law's unexamined preference for membership rarely considers the serious consequences it poses for refugees – frequently to make return far more

difficult ... The law ... forces refugees to (re)construct their identities in order to gain the status that the law determines is most appropriate for them. It is at least plausible that refugees might prefer an ambiguity and flexibility that does not compel an immediate consideration of identity questions and that keeps options open for future return or resettlement.[50]

As we demonstrate in this volume, the concept of protection creates a paradox arising from conflicting identities conferred through legal, political and social processes. In legal terms, there is a conflict between the Refugee Convention refugee as a bearer of rights, and the state's perception of them as objects of a humanitarian discretion. There are conflicts between the notion of a refugee as a person with a legal status, and the political and social constructions of a refugee. Returning to the ideas of law as *process* and law as *power* as discussed above, we could speak of a double jeopardy for the refugee – they have no option but to try to obtain formal refugee status, but as 'refugees' they may end up as persons without the 'right to have rights' (and hence, ironically, in many ways without protection).[51] In other words, nation states themselves seek protection from refugees through policies that discriminate against them, through detention regimes and other forms of restriction. In addition, assuming the identity of the refugee often impacts negatively on their lived experiences, by defining their life-worlds in the eyes of the community in very rigid, limited, and sometimes violent ways.

From a sociological (as opposed to a legal) perspective, in a world defined by nation states and border controls, refugees are 'matter out of place', to draw on anthropologist Mary Douglas's famous thesis that dirt, when understood as 'matter out of place', simultaneously implies both the existence and the contravention of an established order or system and that this in turn establishes dirt as symbolic.[52] We could extend this analogy further. Phyllis Palmer has written that dirt is 'a principal means to arrange culture'.[53] Similarly, the refugee, as 'matter out of place' is a social identity that does not fit easily into, or is not easily permitted to belong to, national cultural imaginaries or 'identities'. By definition, the refugee is someone outside the nation, an alien or outsider seeking refuge. The refugee's identity is not easily transformed into one who belongs or who is even a potential insider.

In this view, the refugee thus needs to be contained or re-contained (in camps or detention centres) within borders in order to protect the natural order of things.[54] The refugee poses a threat to sovereignty, to belonging and to the proper order of things. Nation states demand to be protected from 'illegal asylum seekers', from refugee 'influxes' and from irregular migration in general. Hence, Hathaway argues that 'Refugee Law as it exists today is fundamentally concerned with the protection of powerful states'.[55] National governments exploit the supposed threat represented by refugees to further safeguard their borders and national identities. It is a sad indictment of our times that refugee identity in today's world is more likely to conjure images of threat and fear than of compassion and sympathy. The politicisation of refugee protection as a divisive social issue has become a global phenomenon. Aleinikoff's statement in 1992 is still valid 20 years later: 'Refugee law has become immigration law, emphasizing protection of borders rather than protection of persons'.[56]

What emerges from this volume as a most disturbing trend is the apparently increasing negative light in which refugees are portrayed and viewed, in particular those most in need of protection – so-called 'illegal' asylum seekers[57] who may appear in the guise of undocumented or 'irregular' migrant workers,[58] including women with dependent children, many of whom may suffer discrimination on account of their ethnicity and/or religion.[59] It is precisely because of these social and political tensions surrounding refugees that we look to the law, to the courts and to international and national legal institutions for justice, guidance and objectivity. Given the deeply politicised nature of this issue and the serious social tensions that surround it, the role of the law is particularly important.[60]

But a central theme explored in the chapters that comprise this volume is the way the law and the Refugee Convention definition creates and constructs identities that are inherently fraught. That is, the law holds up a mirror to the conflicted sociological view of the refugee as someone 'out of place' and as a threat to society, and as the person simultaneously in need of protection. This is the focus of Part IV of this volume.

In Chapter 11 ('Ambivalent policies, uncertain identities: asylum seeking families in Sweden)', Björnberg analyses the social integration of asylum seekers in Sweden and their coping strategies during the wait for a permit of stay. Coping is linked to the period of transition, which is understood as the full process of leaving the home country, reception and application for asylum, and appeals for new trials after negative outcomes. The transitional process can be described as a social state or phase characterised by great ambiguity, in which one's position, identity and social belonging are no longer clearly defined. This ambiguity results in a general lack of trust on both the part of the asylum seekers towards the people with whom they come into contact, and vice versa. Björnberg concludes that 'mistrust is a built-in part of the organisation of the asylum process'. The asylum seekers' position is frequently one of dependency, where the absence of trust by others and lack of social recognition diminishes their sense of self-confidence. This leads to a basic lack of trust among asylum-seeking adults and children, which prevents them from building social capital during the transition period to refugee status. Not cultivating social relationships, however, can also be looked upon as a matter of self-protection. Keeping a low profile functions as a resilience strategy, helping to reduce the risk of experiencing shame and humiliation in the strained economic circumstances and poor housing conditions typical of the asylum seekers' situation upon arrival in the host country.

Björnberg reinforces the central point of this collection, that institutional power is an instrumental factor in shaping refugee identities. During the period of transition, in which an asylum seeker's position, identity and social belonging are no longer clearly defined, when they are, as Zetter would say, 'disempowered', the asylum seeker is confronted by many institutional experiences. Björnberg's contribution reveals that the status of refugee can impose another kind of violence on asylum seekers who fear being identified as refugees in hostile host society settings. The result includes high levels of anxiety and a general withdrawal from social engagement, which is doubly problematic for refugees who are often in need of social supports. Björnberg is especially attentive to the unintended consequences this can have on refugee children who try to hide or camouflage their refugee identities at school. In contexts where uncertainty over legal status pertains, ambiguous or flexible identities become rational choices by those wishing to regain some control of their futures, rather than cede to state or UNHCR objectives.

The identification of asylum seekers with risk and danger is also present in Italy's response to asylum seekers which is conflicted between Italy's legal obligations as a Member State of the EU and a party to the Dublin Regulation, and Italy's sensitivities regarding its national sovereignty. In Chapter 12 ('Better than our fears? Refugees in Italy between rhetorics of exclusion and local projects of inclusion'), Ambrosini portrays the Italian position as vacillating between law and politics, and describes the forms of support and protection that are given to asylum seekers, often through the services of religious and non-government organisations. Furthermore, many asylum seekers are given de facto migrant worker status on account of regularisation laws implemented by their employers. The Italian case shows that refugee identities are shaped in conflicting ways by different actors: the EU, the state and faith and non-governmental organisations, through the use of state and non-state power. Ambrosini concludes that conflict arises from an unresolved tension between 'fear and reception' of asylum seekers. His findings support Björnberg's thesis that flexible, ambiguous and multiple identities often best serve the interests of the individual asylum seeker and yet these attributes are an anathema to legal and state processes, which tend to focus on achieving a discrete, fixed and singular status.

The role of legal and state processes in 'containing' refugee identities is highlighted by Jones in Chapter 13 ('Moving beyond protection space: developing a law of asylum in South-East Asia'). He examines the concept of protection in South-East Asian countries where the state tends to 'discipline' refugees rather than treat them as persons to be protected. In particular he examines the respective roles of civil society organisations and the UNHCR, in order to refute the argument that countries in South-East Asia provide protection to refugees as persons who are in a 'humanitarian protection space'. He argues that such an approach privileges international interests, fora and the UNHCR as the negotiator, and that it does not reflect the actual reality of refugee protection which is often negotiated by civil society. Jones reveals how the identity of refugees in the region is shifting from a person who is the object of the exercise of sovereign discretion as a 'humanitarian entrant', to one who is the bearer of human rights. He thus expands our understanding of the way norms and institutions are instrumental in ascribing identity and what this means for the individual. Jones raises the important question about the potential power of civil society, and, by implication, individuals to redefine legal frameworks. While we have argued in this volume that the legal regime is the dominant defining force in creating refugee identities, we also, particularly in Part IV, explore the individual and collective acts of resistance to these processes.

Conclusion

The focus of this volume on the link between refugee protection and refugee identity was inspired by the paradox of 'protection'. That is, it arose from concern about conflict between legal, political and social conceptualisations of refugees and the effect of such conflict upon the notion of refugee identity. Not only are there conflicting concepts of protection, there is also conflict between the conception of individual refugee status as defined by the Refugee Convention and the humanitarian objectives of refugee protection. Thus, there are unintended consequences inherent in the process of being recognised as a refugee, in other words, in refugee *identities*. Is, then, the Refugee Convention 'still fit for purpose'?

While the aim of the Refugee Convention is to confer protection against persecution at the state or national level by bestowing a specific refugee status, and indeed to confer protection against persecution on the ground of difference,[61] being a refugee itself may lead to further discrimination and persecution. Persons who seek protection on the basis of persecution arising from their ethnicity or religion may find that they are denied full refugee status and rights to integration to which they are entitled under the Refugee Convention, precisely because of such ethnicity or religious beliefs.[62] As evidence of this, Feller, in Chapter 4, points to the fact that in host countries, 'refugees can become a cause of social tensions and a divisive political issue'.

As a number of the chapters in this collection demonstrate, the link between the construction of identity, as a personal and social process, and the instrumentality of law and institutional power, has become more complex. In this volume, we assess both the processes by which refugee identity is ascribed and the power of the law to make and unmake the refugee category. We pay close attention to the intersections of the legal, political and social processes in reflexive and multiple disciplinary approaches. This volume attempts to respond to these pressing issues by unpicking the role of law in shaping refugee protection policy, to look between the seams at both the intended and unintended consequences of 'being' a refugee and the resultant conflicting identities.

In addressing these issues this volume considers the following questions:

- 60 years after the creation of the Refugee Convention, is refugee law fulfilling the protection needs of the world's refugees?
- How have refugee identities and protection changed in this period?
- What are the macro and state perspectives on law, power and refugee identity?
- How do micro, social and individual perspectives affect identity construction and protection?

Notes

1 B. S. Chimni, 'The Birth of a Discipline: From Refugee to Forced Migration Studies' (2009) 22 *Journal of Refugee Studies* 11, 12.

2 Convention relating to the Status of Refugees, Geneva, 28 July 1951, 1989 UNTS 137, supplemented by the Protocol relating to the Status of Refugees, 31 January 1967, 19 UST 6223, 6257 ('Refugee Convention'), Art. 1A(2).

3 Art. 3 states: 'The Contracting States shall apply the provisions of this Convention to refugees without discrimination as to race, religion or country of origin.'

4 An 'asylum seeker' is a person seeking asylum from persecution who has yet to be recognised as a 'refugee' as defined in Art. 1A(2) of the Refugee Convention. But note that the United Nations High Commissioner for Refugees takes the view that a person who satisfies that definition is a 'refugee' without the need for a determination to that effect. This is known as the 'declaratory' theory – see UNHCR, *Handbook on Procedures and Criteria for Determining Refugee Status under the 1951 Convention and the 1967 Protocol Relating to the Status of Refugees*, HCR/IP/4/Rev.1, 1979, re-edited, Geneva, January 1992 ('UNHCR Handbook') (28).

5 Daniel Steinbock, 'The Refugee Definition as Law: Issues of Interpretation', in Frances Nicholson and Patrick Twomey (eds), *Refugee Rights and Realities: Evolving International Concepts and Regimes* (Cambridge University Press, 1999), ch. 1.

6 Ibid. 13. There are 147 states party to one or both of the Convention and the Protocol.

7 See Chapter 6 in this volume.

8 See, for historical context, Chapters 5 and 6 in this volume.

9 See Chapters 9 and 5 in this volume.

10 In everyday parlance a 'refugee' is a person in flight, a person seeking refuge. However, in international law a 'refugee' is a person who comes within the definition in Art. 1A(2) of the Refugee Convention and the Protocol relating to the Status of Refugees, New York, 31 January 1967, in force 4 October 1967, 19 UST 6223, 6257 ('Refugee Protocol').

11 See, for example, Art. 9(a) of Council Directive 2011/95/EU of 13 December 2011 on standards for the qualification of third-country nationals or stateless persons as beneficiaries of international protection, for a uniform status for refugees or for persons eligible for subsidiary protection, and for the content of the protection granted.

12 See Chapters 3 and 6 in this volume.

13 Ibid.

14 See Chapter 2 in this volume, pp. 25.

15 See generally on gender Heaven Crawley, *Refugees and Gender: Law and Process* (Jordans, 2001); Deborah Anker, 'Refugee Law, Gender, and the Human Rights Paradigm' (2002) 15 *Harvard Human Rights Journal* 133.

16 Chapter 6 in this volume.

17 Chimni, above n. 1.

18 Patricia Tuitt, *False Images – The Law's Construction of the Refugee* (Pluto Press, 1996); see also Chapters 5 and 9 in this volume.

19 Cecile Rousseau, Francois Crepeau, Patricia Foxe and France Houle, 'The Complexity of Determining Refugeehood: A Multidisciplinary Analysis' (2002) 15 *Journal of Refugee Studies* 43; Jane Herlihy and Stuart W. Turner, 'The Psychology of Seeking Protection' (2009) 21 *International Journal of Refugee Law* 171.

20 Tuitt, above n. 18.

21 See also Audrey Macklin, 'Asylum and the Rule of Law in Canada: Hearing the Other (Side)', in Susan Kneebone (ed.), *Refugees, Asylum Seekers and the Rule of Law* (Cambridge University Press, 2009), ch. 2.

22 Ibid., 78; see also Chapter 8 in this volume, which describes techniques used in the EU system to prevent access to hearings.

23 Erving Goffman, *Stigma: Notes on the Management of Spoiled Identity* (Penguin, 1963); Erving Goffman, *Asylums* (Penguin, 1982).

24 The Refugee Convention also included in the definition of refugee persons who had been considered refugees under earlier international agreements: Art. 1A(1). James Hathaway, 'A Reconsideration of the Underlying Premise of Refugee Law' (1990) 31 *Harvard International Law Journal* 129.

25 UNGA Res. 428(V), Annex, 14 December 1950; see also Chapter 5 in this volume.

26 Guy Goodwin-Gill and Jane McAdam, *The Refugee in International Law* (Oxford University Press, 2007), 23.

27 T. Alexander Aleinikoff, 'State-Centred Refugee Law: From Resettlement to Containment' (1992)14 *Michigan Journal of International Law* 120–1.

28 Susan Kneebone, 'Refugees and Displaced Persons: The Refugee Definition and "Humanitarian" Protection', in Sarah Joseph and Adam McBeth (eds), *Research Handbook on International Human Rights Law* (Edward Elgar, 2010), ch. 9.

29 Under the 1933 Convention Relating to the International Status of Refugees; see also James Hathaway, 'The Evolution of Refugee Status in International Law: 1920–1950' (1984) 33 *International and Comparative Law Quarterly* 348.

30 See generally Dallal Stevens, 'What Do We Mean by Protection?' (2013) 20 *International Journal of Minority and Group Rights* 233–62.

31 Susan Kneebone, 'Protecting Trafficked Persons from *Refoulement*: Re-examining the Nexus', in Satvinder Juss and Colin Harvey (eds), *Contemporary Issues in International Refugee Law* (Edward Elgar, 2013) Chapter 5; Susan Kneebone, 'The Refugee-Trafficking Nexus: Making Good (the) Connections' (2010) 29 *Refugee Survey Quarterly* 137.

32 See Chapter 7 in this volume.

33 Jeff Crisp, UNHCR New Issues in Research, Research Paper No. 155 April 2008, 'Beyond the Nexus: UNHCR's evolving perspective on refugee protection and international migration'; UNHCR, Discussion Paper 'Refugee protection and durable solutions in the context of international migration', UNHCR/DPC/2007/Doc. 02, 19 November 2007.

34 Susan Kneebone, 'Moving beyond the State: Refugees, Accountability and Protection', in Susan Kneebone (ed.), *The Refugees Convention 50 Years on: Globalisation and International Law* (Ashgate, 2003), ch. 11.

35 Jean-François Durieux, 'The Vanishing Refugee: How EU Asylum Law Blurs the Specificity of Refugee Protection', in Hélène Lambert, Jane McAdam and Maryellen Fullerton (eds), *The Global Reach of European Refugee Law* (Cambridge University Press, 2013), 228.

36 Arstide Zolberg, Astri Suhrke and Sergio Aguayo, *Escape from Violence – Conflict and the Refugee Crisis in the Developing World* (Oxford University Press, 1989).

37 Steinbock, above n. 5, 20.

38 Michelle Foster, *International Refugee Law and Socio-Economic Rights* (Cambridge University Press, 2007), 39

39 Andrew Shacknove, 'Who Is a Refugee?' (1985) 95 *Ethics* 274.

40 See Chapter 7 in this volume.

41 Refugee Convention, Art. 33.

42 Aleinikoff, above n. 27, 122.

43 Matthew Gibney, *The Ethics and Politics of Asylum* (Cambridge University Press, 2004).

44 (1992) 14 *Michigan Journal of International Law* 120, at 124.

45 Jane McAdam, 'The Refugee Convention as a Rights Blueprint for Persons in Need of International Protection' in Jane McAdam (ed.), *Forced Migration, Human Rights and Security* (Hart, 2008), ch. 10, 267.

46 'The Contracting States shall as far as possible facilitate the assimilation and naturalization of refugees. They shall in particular make every effort to expedite naturalization proceedings and to reduce as far as possible the charges and costs of such proceedings.'

47 Aleinikoff, above n. 27.

48 Ibid. 121–2.

49 Ibid. 136.50

50 Ibid.

51 Hannah Arendt, *The Origins of Totalitarianism* (Harcourt, Brace and Jovanovich, 1968), 177.

52 Mary Douglas, *Purity and Danger: An Analysis of the Concepts of Pollution and Taboo* (Ark Paperbacks, 1966), 35.

53 Phyllis Palmer, *Domesticity and Dirt: Housewives and Domestic Servants in the United States, 1920–1945* (Temple University Press, 1989), 139.

54 Leon Gordkenker makes a similar point when he argues that: 'In a world that abhors the presence of un-administered spaces or people, the presence of forced migrants must be treated as abnormal. Government authorities invariably react to refugee situations by trying first to contain them and later to eliminate them' (*Refugees in International Politics* (Columbia University Press, 1987), 125).

55 James Hathaway, 'Reconceiving Refugee Law and Human Rights Protection' (1991) 4 *Journal of Refugee Studies* 113–14.

56 Aleinikoff, above n. 27.

57 Fiona McCleod, Samantha Thomas and Susan Kneebone, '"It Would Be Okay If They Came through the Proper Channels": Community Perceptions and Attitudes toward Asylum Seekers in Australia' (2012) 25 *Journal of Refugee Studies* 113; Fiona McCleod, Samantha Thomas, Kate Holland, R. Warwick Blood and Susan Kneebone, '"AIDS Assassins": Australian Media's Portrayal of HIV-Positive Refugees Who Deliberately Infect Others' (2011) 9 *Journal of Immigration and Refugee Studies* 20.

58 This is the terminology used in the International Convention on the Protection of the Rights of All Migrant Workers and Members of Their Families (ICRMW), opened for signature 18 December 1990 (entered into force 1 July 2003), GA Res. 45/158.

59 See for example, on the UK and EU, Vicki Squire, *The Exclusionary Politics of Asylum* (Palgrave Macmillan, 2009); Paul Stratham, 'Understanding Anti-Alien Rhetoric: Restrictive Politics or Racist Publics' (2003) 74 *Political Quarterly* 163.

60 Kneebone (ed.), above n. 21.

61 Steinbock, above n. 5, 21.

62 Note that the UNHCR can apply the definition of 'refugee' as contained in its own Statute (largely the same as the Refugee Convention definition but without the ground of 'membership of a particular social group'); the definition contained in the Refugee Convention where it conducts Refugee Status Determination on behalf of a signatory state; or the expanded definition of 'refugee' under the UNHCR's international protection mandate: persons who are 'outside their country of origin or habitual residence and unable to return there owing to serious and indiscriminate threats to life, physical integrity or freedom resulting from generalized violence or events seriously disturbing public order'.

2 Creating identities, diminishing protection and the securitisation of asylum in Europe

Roger Zetter

Introduction

This chapter explores the interplay between the formation of refugee identity and the process of seeking protection. The core argument is that refugee identities are politically 'situated' not personally 'narrated' and that the practice of expropriating identity has profound implications for how refugee protection is enacted.

The chapter commences by outlining some practical and conceptual challenges in shaping identities. It then illustrates how the cornerstone of refugee identity has been established in the legal and normative framework of protection enshrined in the 1951 Refugee Convention,[1] exploring how that identity has been made, remade and given social and political meaning by the institutional context and processes that surround it.

The chapter then focuses on European Union Members States (EUMSs) to illustrate these concepts and processes. Confronted with the increasing diffusion and complexity of refugee movement, EUMSs have deployed an agenda of securitising asylum which has formed and transformed a refugee identity in ways which conform to and legitimise narrower obligations and commitments to protection. At the same time, transcending these self-fulfilling objectives, identifying refugees and asylum seekers as a security threat has reinforced the wider 'European project' of developing the European Union (EU) as a space of freedom, justice and security for its citizens.

Who do you think you are? Constructing a refugee's identity

I start this chapter with an anecdote to highlight some of the challenges in shaping an understanding of the situated and narrated identity of refugees. A few years ago I had a postgraduate student who would sit outside my office reading *Corriere della Sera* or *Gazzetta della Sport* while waiting for tutorials. He spoke English with an Italian accent and dressed in elegant Italian clothes. He was, however, a black Italian – a novel conjuncture of identities because only recently has Italy become a country of immigration not mass emigration; and unlike some other European countries, public acknowledgement of a new reality as a multicultural society is still highly contested terrain.

My stereotypes were also challenged by these disjunctive characteristics. Was he a refugee? What was his nationality? I needed to give him a label and an 'identity'. But what identity (or identities) could I ascribe to him. And how did he identify himself? What other factors mediated his identity and what were the potential consequences for him?

He had been ascribed (or had he chosen?), at least six 'identities'. Sequentially over the last few years he has been/is:

- a Somali (by birth)
- an asylum seeker (by civil war)
- a refugee (by the 1967 Protocol, in need of protection)
- an Italian citizen (by the not un-accidental historical legacy of Italy's imperial interests in the Horn of Africa in the 1930s)
- a UK resident with his family (by the Single European Act, 1986 permitting free movement of EU citizens)
- a diaspora Somali (by the social obligations of hawala)

I put these changing institutionalised identities in series, as a life narrative and a sequence of events. For him I suspect these are multiple identities which overlap and coexist. Coinciding with and reinforcing each other, for him they are replete with profoundly different meanings and consequences for his self-representation. They are not taken for granted, relatively stable and, to an extent, predetermined; rather, they are necessarily fluid and a highly instrumental part of his survival and that of his family. And of course these imposed identities say little about his social world of home and belonging, settlement and return, nation and locality, social norms and family aspirations.

Not surprisingly, his identity embraced complex and often contradictory meanings. There is an ascribed identity of a refugee and then an integrated migrant with his citizenship and nationality homogenised through European and government rhetoric. From this perspective he seemed to conform to the functionalist terms of European Commission policies for refugee integration: he appeared to validate the label 'integrated refugee' and, self-evidently, he is the archetypal mobile 'European citizen', at home, so to speak, in Italy or the UK. But another identity suggests a 'plurality of affiliations, and the coexistence of cohesion and separateness',[2] as he occasionally travelled back to Somalia and subscribed to his normative social obligations. Like many minority communities in the UK, he appeared to 'manage these multiple identities quite comfortably'.[3] Yet, this apparently 'here-and-there' belonging fitted uneasily with an identity of a refugee, exiled from his country, relabelled (like a well-travelled suitcase) by increasingly draconian legislation found in many EUMSs, whose need for protection might quite possibly have been undermined by the 'securitisation of asylum', perhaps motivated by a myth of return. Instead, he was one of millions of members of a networked, transnational society[4] and a smaller transnational social network of forcibly displaced people.[5] No longer was he contained in an atomised cluster of co-ethnic and co-national refugees, but part of a virtual community of globalised migrants, whose members are selectively distributed around the world across many exilic locations, who may never see each other but are bound by and in touch with a shared, but in some senses deterritorialised 'home'.[6]

In other words, in each of his six 'identities', the stereotypical and ascribed label fails to capture his rich and multilayered 'identity' or, indeed, that of any one of the millions of forced migrants seeking the identity of 'refugee' in Europe over the last decades. Like them, his identity is determined less by what he is but more by perceptions of what he might be.

Narrating and situating an identity

How can we make sense of these disjunctive characteristics? We like to think that we determine our own identity and that we are the instruments of our own self-representation; but we are as much the product of how others see us, the characteristics they attribute to us and the expectations they have of us. These ascriptive qualities are rooted in many aspects of our personal, behavioural and social development which shape and constrain who we are. Ascribed identities may challenge or reinforce our self-image; they may reflect some aspects of our identity but not others; they may pre-exist our persona or they may derive from social interaction. We are not free to choose what others attribute to us, but we can and do respond to these imputed identities in an iterative process – conforming, complying, acceding, mediating, challenging, denying, ignoring.

The same ascriptive processes which selectively shape individual identity also apply to social groups. In his classic studies of asylum in-patients and those who carry physical stigma, Goffman shows how selected attributes of their identities become normalised or stereotyped so that 'deviants' conform to and fulfil the expectations which others attach to these identities, behaving not as they are but how others would wish to see them.[7] But Goffman's work not only reminds us that group identities are ascribed in much the same way as for the individual. Also, in his concern to understand how we create the 'other' – in this case those who are symbolically confined to the margins of society – his work speaks powerfully to the notion that marginality is a socially constructed identity. These are groups whose identity is defined and reinforced by selected attributes which are perceived to be less desirable or problematic and are frequently discounted in the eyes of others. This ascriptive process, therefore not only plays a complex role in describing an identity but also, by presenting and (re)presenting that identity, it is instrumental in making an identity.

Significantly, these are partial accounts of an identity: intrinsically they are both exclusionary and homogenising in their simplification of complex stories and histories. Almost inevitably, they will have severe consequences for the self-identity of those subjected to these practices. And rejecting an imposed identity, or creating a counter-identity, carries with it the prospect of further exclusion.

Goffman's work provides the link between the construction of identity, as a personal and social process, and the instrumentality of institutional power. We live in an institutionalised world and the processes of identity formation in our personal and social world also hold true in this wider context. Just as at a personal level we are dealing with the negotiation between the narrated self and the situated self, the narrated identity or situated identity, so too this broader, institutionalised context frames negotiation between the narrated identity of the group and the situated identity which is constructed by institutions and bureaucracies and, of course, governments.

In this milieu, identity is discursively and rhetorically constructed and, in theory (but rarely in practice), may be much more open to discussion and interpretation than for the individual. Like other groups, therefore, refugees negotiate within a framework of legal designation, state practice, and political and everyday language, on the one hand, and their own accounts, on the other. It is the interplay between the formation of the narrated identity of the group and the situated identity produced by institutional and bureaucratic power that is the central concern here.

Goffman's 'pre-Foucauldian' observations, of course, resonate with other contemporary scholarship at that time which elaborated the instrumentality of social and institutional mechanisms in controlling social identity through the practices of governmentality. From this perspective, the discursive shaping of identity is not the negotiated outcome of different narratives; rather, it is a contestation over access to identity and the exercise of power over its characteristics. Enacted through documentation, certificates, legal and normative practices, technical vocabulary, how identity is conferred and who is doing the 'identifying', are crucial to how we recognise or identify specific groups. The construction of identity reveals the subjective exercise of power institutionalised and legitimatised through what often seem to be objective criteria and practices.

Elsewhere, I have portrayed this contestation as a process of delinking 'case' from 'story'.[8] In other words, individuals or groups, particularly those whose needs are greatest, usually do not and frequently cannot identify themselves through their stories – in all their rich complexity and diversity – but only as cases which fit the prescription of how others wish to see them. They conform to a prescribed identity which is normalised and granted materialist meaning through its institutionalisation. Refugees and asylum seekers are such a group whose identity is materialised or constructed (and denied) around the concept of protection and how that is enacted through state policies and practices. But forced displacement also creates new spaces of experience, contestation and transformation, which have their own momentum and impart new meanings to refugee identity. And, as perceptions of refugee identity have changed, so too the instruments and practice of protection have been transformed, narrowing down the rights and needs associated with that identity – their 'case'; the outcome is to further marginalise their 'story' and thus to limit their status as refugees.

Thus, while the refugee label, constructed around the need for protection, plays a crucial role in constructing an identity, the often misconceived or misappropriated assumptions on which that identity is constructed have profound and disempowering consequences both for those who successfully reconcile 'case' and 'story' and especially for those who do not. Albeit without prejudice, my creation of my student's identity was a microcosm of this process.

Refugees, refugee identity and protection

From the start, refugee identity has been largely ascribed, grounded in law and, as such, it is inevitably partial. The 1951 Convention relating to the Status of Refugees proposed a designation constructed around the core and intertwined principles of: (a) a well-founded fear of persecution; (b) outside the country of origin; and thus (c) in need of a defining attribute – international protection. A legal definition of a refugee established on these explicit and unique criteria was a construct of its time which, as Long has argued, separated the distinct category of 'refugee' from 'migrant' by reifying protection over other claims and needs.[9] Of itself it did not make an 'identity' but it framed the parameters of an identity in terms of specific social membership (the five grounds of persecution), spatial displacement (across an international border), and a claim (protection). In the succeeding six decades this definition of refugee, initially framed around these legal and normative conditions, has been elaborated and continually reshaped into a complex and multilayered identity by the interests of states and humanitarian actors and mediated by the distinctive social worlds of the refugees themselves.

Yet, the power of this original legal definition (and the definers) in ascribing certain defining characteristics to the category of refugee, has been highly instrumental in shaping and constraining that identity and the experiences of those so categorised. Whether or not the three conditions are necessary components of a refugee identity they are certainly insufficient of themselves. There are a number of tensions in the way this identity has been formed and its focus on protection.

First, although the international convention has produced a constructed identity which largely serves the needs of states, refugees do not easily fit into these seemingly clear-cut categories and criteria. While a focus on protection leads to the conclusion that this is the essential need – a right, perhaps even a privilege – it has always been assessed in relation to the two other criteria. Yet refugees are the product of complex social and economic conditions which precipitate conflict and violence and which may cause people to flee. An identity framed around these rather constrained legal requirements of space and membership of a specific social group reveals little about the micro and macro processes and the political economy which predispose or propel people to leave their homes, the extent of volition or compulsion, and the different typologies and multiple causes of forced migration.[10] Even if the need for protection is the defining feature of refugee identity, understood in the terms of the Convention, this may or may not be among the main expectations or requirements of refugees who have fled their homes.

Second, persecution, flight from country of origin and thus the need for protection is, arguably, too prescriptive a ground for claiming refugee identity in the contemporary world. This is because it is not only people who are exposed to specific forms of tyranny (persecution) who may need, or wish, to claim protection and thus a refugee identity, but also those who are exposed to generalised violence or conflict perpetrated by armed non-state actors often in so-called fragile or failed states. Moreover, today, far fewer people who are persecuted in these specific or generalised terms have crossed an international border than remain in their country of origin. Indeed, the need for protection may not be contingent on displacement at all. Conceptually, a refugee identity defined in terms of the need for protection might be better defined, as Shacknove has pointed out, in relation to the breakdown in political relations between a citizen and state and the extent to which certain fundamental rights are no longer safeguarded or protected – irrespective of the extent or destination of displacement.[11] Shacknove here draws on Arendt's arguments on the exceptionality of the refugee as someone who is both 'rightsless' and 'stateless'.[12] An ascribed identity fails to acknowledge these conditions, instead normalising refugees with an identity which decreasingly fits their own perceptions of their identity or their prevailing needs and experiences.

Third, protection framed around an individual claim has complicated implications for the formation of refugee identity. While an individual may claim protection, this status is determined not as a right but as a series of, usually contested, entitlements in a host country. This contestation produces different entitlements and levels of protection and thus different identities. There is a further paradox. Social groups are a key marker of identity and, indeed claims for protection on grounds of persecution are privileged to the five specific groups. But the proof of membership of one of these persecuted groups – an identity – is judged (that is, ascribed) not by the individual but by institutionalised procedures in the country of asylum. Arguably, the procedural and institutional processes of refugee determination, almost reverse the principles by which the 1951 Convention sought to achieve certain universalistic markers of refugee identity. These paradoxes highlight the dichotomy between 'case' and 'story', between narrated and situated identity.

Fourth, while international law, norms and institutions have come to ascribe and structure a particular identity of a refugee, at the same time they do not predetermine that identity and social world in absolute terms. Like others, refugee lives are indeed structured and mediated by these institutions and norms. But governmental and institutional structures frame social relations and social and economic capacities across time and space in a two-way process. These provide opportunities and resources to draw on, such that people are neither entirely dictated to by the social structures in which they find themselves, nor entirely independent of them. Refugees exercise agency; they both frame their identity within these structures but also negotiate that identity albeit within increasingly narrow limits. Successfully challenging an imposed humanitarian-driven identity of vulnerable and dependent victim demonstrates the power of refugee agency (and of course their advocates who ascribed them a different identity) in the 1980s and 1990s.

However, under contemporary conditions of global displacement, the boundaries structuring refugee agency have both shifted and narrowed in contradictory ways. Thus, on the one hand, refugee identity is conflated with broader policies and practices designed to regulate immigration as a whole in which the distinctive identity of the refugee story is lost. On the other hand, the claim to refugee identity is less and less valorised by humanitarian precepts and principles of protection but narrowed to highly specific and regulated granting of rights-based entitlements. In this ironic reversal of the original conditions of the 1951 Convention, the paradox is that a normative and idealised view of refugee identity is increasingly used to deny them protection. The multiple identities that a refugee may hold of herself are now constrained to a singular variable. With declining space to exercise agency, refugees now have less room to manoeuvre and thus to narrate and 'prove' their social identity.

Securitising asylum and controlling migration in Europe

I now illustrate how these dynamics of identity formation and protection are reflected in one aspect of European asylum and immigration policy and practice – the 'securitisation of asylum'. The core of the argument is this. Within the context of the globalisation of migration, identifying who is a refugee has become an increasingly complex and challenging process, both conceptually and in practice. Changing forms of persecution, and the changing processes and spatial scales of forced and voluntary migration are, as we have seen, some of the factors which underscore these challenges. In response to these transformations, the discursive practices of the receiving states in Europe (and, indeed, in all developed countries), are reconstructing the refugee identity, sometimes in seemingly contradictory ways,[13] as the much less privileged 'asylum seeker' whose rights to protection are highly circumscribed and whose identity is consequently perceived to be potentially more threatening.

Globalisation of migration, first as an economic process now as a security concern, has profoundly affected the political landscape of Europe. Its political saliency is arguably disproportionate to the overall scale of the migrant population (including refugees) which is barely 3 per cent of the world's population. Nevertheless, neo-liberal economic imperatives have increasingly been challenged first by European sovereign states and then EU-wide resistance to migration, animated by political concerns about the domestic social and economic consequences of large numbers of people on the move and the perceived threats to 'cohesion' and national identity.[14] More specifically aimed at refugees and asylum seekers, national and EU-wide discourses on 'securitisation and migration' and 'human security and migration' have intersected this ambiguous political-economy discourse on migration to drive what Guild has called the 'Europeanisation of Europe's Asylum Policy'.[15] Indeed, the objective to manage migration in the EUMSs is now driven as much by the perceived need to 'securitise' national populations (underpinned by the 'fear of the other'), as it is by a rationale to sustain 'good community relations' among an increasingly diverse mix of ethnicities, or the economic imperatives to manage domestic labour markets, or still less the protection of refugee claimants.[16]

These discourses have substantially reinforced the negative identity of refugees seeking asylum in the EU and diminished the scope and quality of protection, paradoxically so, since asylum seeking has dramatically declined in Europe in the last decade.

Of the competing conceptualisations of human security, a distinction is often drawn between its narrow and broad definitions as proposed in the Human Security Report.[17] In the former definition, the primary goal of human security is individual protection, a formulation closely linked to rights-based expectations: the broader and more malleable interpretation subsumes and embeds the protection of individuals within a framework of protecting larger entities such as the nation state and its value systems and securitising them from existential threats.[18] As Buzan *et al.* also note,[19] the existential danger evoked by the securitisation of a potential risk need not necessarily have to be real, only that there is a perception that current structures, polities, values and the like are threatened. Moreover, the intensity and persistence of the 'threat' is usually correlated to the institutionalisation of responses: precisely what has occurred with dramatic effect at national and supranational levels within the EU.

Beyond the broader socio-economic challenges posed by international migration, it is these security-based concerns which define how EUMSs have responded to immigration in general and asylum seeking in particular: the latter is increasingly portrayed as a key vector of the existential threat of terrorism to the agenda of European cohesion.[20] The legitimacy of securitising asylum in this context was confirmed, in the minds of European policy makers, by 9/11, the Madrid and London bombings in 2004/2005 and civil disorder involving ethnic minority migrant communities in for example the UK, France, the Netherlands and Italy in recent times.

How do both the conceptualisation, and the real experience of security threats, play out in European asylum and migration policy? The interweaving of economic, social and security ambitions into migration policy has significant implications for that category of migrants with special rights and claims on the international community – asylum seekers and refugees.

Of course, the imputed links between asylum seeking and terrorism is one facet of a broader discourse of multiculturalism and immigration which has pervaded national level policy making in Europe for many decades.[21] But the machinery of migration management, largely developed to safeguard national economic and social interests, finds a new and enhanced purpose to protect the national and personal security of European citizens and residents in the context of refugees and asylum seekers. Now a dominant feature of European political discourse, refugee-identity-as-security-threat is played out in ways that construct and institutionalise identities which, because they are perceived to threaten, enable EUMSs to diminish the claim for protection.

An obvious starting point is that many of the countries producing the largest numbers of refugee claims lodged in EUMSs such as Afghanistan, Iraq and Iran, are often those whose religious affiliations and 'lack of security' are identified as being the most threatening to national security in Europe. Yet, ironically, it is precisely these same challenges to human security – fragile governments and a limited ability to protect the rights of individuals from persecution and violence – which constitute the normative basis for a well-founded claim for protection through refugee status. However, being ascribed a 'threatening identity' because of these origins greatly diminishes the strength of the claim for asylum in EUMSs. Those most in need of protection from their own states find it increasingly hard to assert these claims precisely because their ascribed identity – their case – is constructed from selected markers of their country of origin.

Another dimension of this identity-forming discourse within the EUMSs has been the deeply problematic migration–asylum nexus and the perceived threat this constitutes. This is exemplified by the way EUMSs have attempted to distinguish between, and then regulate, the complex yet fluid motives, patterns and processes of contemporary international migration. Paradoxically, differentiation and conflation may often go hand in hand.[22]

The principal outcome of this process, in the present context, has been the Common European Asylum System (CEAS) (discussed below) which has established standardised procedures and regulations. Considerable energy has gone into narrowing down and codifying the conditions for refugee status determination in Europe over the last decade.[23] This has enabled the EUMSs to strengthen immigration policies and practices, while simultaneously enabling them to transform and politicise labels which suit an agenda of regulation and restrictionism against bogus 'asylum seekers'.[24] But, simplifying identities and stories into specific cases and statuses prescribed by political agendas, such as securitisation, has profound implications.

Creating the identity of the illegal migrant – less pejoratively, irregular or undocumented migrants – provides a linked but additional example of the way an ascribed identity reinforces the agenda of securitisation. As Ruhs and Anderson confirm,[25] the simple doxic of illegal/legal is not clear in practice: they identify more than 80 or so different entry categories to the UK alone. Nor does it conform to the migrants' own conceptions of their status and their agency. The conflation of different categories serves the securitisation agenda by reinforcing the existential threat represented by migrants who are perceived to be abusing rights of sanctuary, protection and welfare support.

Yet 'illegality' is a constructed concept, not an *a priori* or objective condition. Asylum seekers who enter 'illegally' are not increasingly criminal per se, as the ascribed identity implies. However, tightening entry routes, visa requirements and the machinery of deterrence have created conditions where even those who have a powerful claim for protection risk being identified as 'bogus asylum seekers' or economic migrants and go underground.[26] We want asylum seekers to be constructed as stereotypical victims, but when their identity does not conform to this stereotype and they use their agency to arrive 'illegally', we designate them opportunists with no call on our moral obligations. Thus, notions of the asylum seeker as 'illegal', as clandestine and criminalised, resonate powerfully with a public rhetoric on migration and asylum seeking which is increasingly politicised and managed as a 'securitisation' threat.

A third dimension pertains to Europe's securitisation and migration management agenda which has its own political logic and momentum, but it is not unidirectional. At times it has also been instrumental, and conveniently if selectively utilised, to promote the European 'project' of supranational economic integration and communitarian identity over sovereign state hegemony. At other times is has posed problems for the European project. Boswell, among others, has noted both the tension, but also the opportunism, created by the economic liberalisation and freedom of movement in an enlarged EU and the 'protectionist political discourse on migration in most European states'.[27]

A borderless Europe, enacted by the Schengen Agreement 1985 and principally in the Single European Act 1987 (SEA) and the Maastricht Treaty in 1993, came into being just when a steep rise in spontaneous asylum seeker applications in Europe in the late 1980s propelled asylum, somewhat accidentally, to the foreground of immigration policy. The Dublin Convention 1990 was the response to these unprecedented trends which subverted protection norms established in the 1951 Convention. And, by criminalising a right enshrined in the Convention – pejoratively labelling the process as 'asylum shopping' and thus by implication undermining the claims of 'legitimate' refugees – these European instruments both diminished the quality of human security available to asylum claimants and reinforced a perception that asylum was somehow a security threat to EUMSs.

By switching immigration and asylum to First Pillar status, the Treaty of Amsterdam 1997 (subsequently setting in train the sequence of the 1999 Tampere Programme,[28] Dublin II in 2003 and the Stockholm Programme 2010–14) was a decisive point of transition in supranational convergence on immigration policy and, specifically, the point of transition in developing, through the CEAS, a coherent and much more restrictive EUMS policy framework on refugees and asylum seekers. Making these issues as matters of Community competence and setting them in a seemingly more robust normative framework of a European Union of freedom, justice and security,[29] added coherence and legitimacy to the development of a common asylum and immigration system in which free intra-European movement of citizens is buttressed by key instruments such as secure borders, and tighter immigration and asylum controls largely to the detriment of the protection and human security of refugees.[30] Locating migration control at the heart of the dualistic link between freedom and security, Europe had come full circle to TREVI which first associated migration with illegality and criminality and thus an identity of the migrant as a security threat.

The high-profile extremist attacks in London and Madrid were decisive in shifting European policy making to the securitisation of its citizens and against the human security of refugees. They reinforced, in a profound way, the need to institutionalise the cardinal principle of securitising Europe by strictly regulating migration and the seemingly compelling logic of tighter border controls, extra-territorial processing and the like. But in identifying asylum and immigration as the threat, the greatest cost has been the diminution of protection and human security of refugees and asylum seekers by more sophisticated policies and practices to deter, regulate and remove them. A largely compliant media has simultaneously fed public anxiety and racism in Europe and supported the political rhetoric by constructing an identity of asylum seekers as the 'threat' to security. The media have highlighted instances where those apprehended as actual or putative 'terrorist bombers' are asylum seekers or refugees. All are tainted because one or two may be guilty. Securitisation demands that any asylum seeker could be identified as a terrorist.[31] Moreover, policies which simultaneously deter and restrict refugees and asylum seekers by identifying them as a threat to 'notions of a cohesive national identity',[32] yet promote cohesion and assimilation of migrant communities, also produce uncertainty and confusion.

Reframing and stigmatising asylum seekers as a threat to a secure and free Europe conveniently ignores the fact that these same governments concurrently turned a blind eye to undocumented economic migrants, including 'illegal' asylum seekers, who filled large-scale labour market gaps for unskilled workers in a period of economic prosperity 'without publicly admitting the need for unskilled migration'.[33] Ironically, in times of recession, what was invisible now becomes highly visible and the target of renewed hostility and demands for removal.

At times conflating and eliding the identity and the threat of immigration and asylum, at other times separating the two migratory processes to tackle the complexities of the asylum–migration nexus, EUMSs have further diminished the separate and unique claims of refugees by conveniently reformulating them as a single issue of protecting Europe from large-scale and spontaneous inward population movements.

Balancing freedom and security has thus fully permeated European policy making and discourse for almost two decades (far longer if one reverts to TREVI in 1975), first to overcome the Europe-wide 'security deficit' post SEA 1987, then to reinforce borders and migration control with the Accession 10, and finally to keep abreast of the ever-changing nature of asylum seeking. For more than two decades, the situated 'identity' of the refugee not as someone in need of protection but as an asylum seeker and a potential threat to security, has been a crucial element in motivating these objectives.

More so than in the past, when the rights and claims of refugees were subsumed in a wider migration policy discourse of exclusion and regulation related to economic and social impacts, now their identity and their claim for protection is increasingly hostage to the much more insidious political rhetoric and policy apparatus of securitisation. The latent processes which ascribe and situate identity within highly selected attributes of national conditions or religious affiliations (which are perceived to be undesirable or problematic), or which stigmatise as a criminal act the often desperate means by which people search for protection, denies another identity – that of the refugee and further diminishes the scope of protection.[34]

Conclusions

Focusing on just one policy variable – European securitisation – I have attempted to show how the situated 'identity' of refugees has been symbolically expropriated, reconstructed and institutionalised to exploit anxieties and perceived threats to another loosely constructed 'identity' of Europeanness, even if these fears are only tangentially related to migration.[35] The risk is conceived partly as the violation of physical security, but mainly in terms of an imprecisely defined but more insidious threat to value systems and ideologies. In this way managing migration and the identity of the asylum seeker are part of a wider Europe project serving to position and define the EUMSs and the Union as a whole in relation to the 'other' – the migrant – and thus in relation to particular understandings of what the (European) Community is and what it is not.

Yet at the same time, problematising immigration, and in particular asylum seeking, with connotations of illegality and misrepresenting the identity of the individual refugee claimant as a security threat to the host citizens, in some sense becomes a self-fulfilling project. This is achieved by fragmenting and fractioning that identity in relation to the complex motives, patterns and processes of refugee migration. This disaggregation of identity is materialised by systematically delegitimising and disqualifying the refugee's story which diminishes access to protection and reinforces the denial of asylum. In fact the 'refugee' has largely disappeared behind the asylum seeker as the focal interest of European policy; it is not without significance that the acronym CEAS, contains the word 'asylum' but not refugee.

In addressing the competing agendas of securitisation of nationals or human security and protection for asylum seekers and refugees, the EUMSs have firmly opted for the former. The outcome has been the progressive subordination of the human security and protection of that most easily identifiable minority of migrants – vulnerable asylum seekers and refugees – whose identity has been formed, transformed and politicised in more than three decades of European policy making.

Notes

1 Convention relating to the Status of Refugees, Geneva, 28 July 1951, 1989 UNTS 137, supplemented by the Protocol relating to the Status of Refugees, 31 January 1967, 19 UST 6223, 6257 ('1951 Refugee Convention').
2 Roger Zetter, David Griffiths, Nando Sigona, Don Flynn, Tauhid Pasha and Rhian Beynon, *Immigration, Social Cohesion and Social Capital: What Are the Links?* (Joseph Rowntree Foundation, 2006) <www.jrf.org.uk/publications/immigration-social-cohesion-and-social-capital-what-are-links>.
3 Ibid.

4 Manuel Castells, *The Rise of the Network Society* (Blackwell, 1996); Stephen Castles, 'Towards a Sociology of Forced Migration and Transformation' (2003) 37 *Sociology* 13; Stephen Castles and Mark J. Miller, *The Age of Migration: International Population Movements in the Modern World* (Palgrave Macmillan, 2006).

5 Khalid Koser and Charles Pinkerton, *The Social Networks of Asylum Seekers and the Dissemination of Information about Countries of Asylum*, Research Development and Statistics Directorate (Home Office, 2002).

6 Daniel Warner, 'Voluntary Repatriation and the Meaning of a Return to Home' (1994) 7 *Journal of Refugee Studies* 160; Liisa H. Malkki, *Purity and Exile: Violence, Memory and National Cosmology Among Hutu Refugees in Tanzania* (Chicago University Press, 1995).

7 Erving Goffman, *Stigma: Notes on the Management of Spoiled Identity* (Penguin, 1963); Erving Goffman, *Asylums* (Penguin, 1982).

8 Roger Zetter, 'Labelling Refugees: Forming and Transforming a Refugee Identity' (1991) 4 *Journal of Refugee Studies*, 39; Roger Zetter, 'More Labels, Fewer Refugees: Making and Remaking the Refugee Label in an Era of Globalisation' (2007) 20 *Journal of Refugee Studies* 172.

9 Katy Long, 'When Refugees Stopped Being Migrants: Movement, Labour and Humanitarian Protection' (2013) 1 *Migration Studies* 4.

10 Bridget Hayden, 'What's in a Name? The Nature of the Individual in Refugee Studies' 19 (2006) *Journal of Refugee Studies* 471–87; IFRC, *World Disasters Report 2012, Focus on forced migration* (IFRC, 2012) <www.ifrc.org/wdr>.

11 Andrew E. Shacknove, 'Who Is a Refugee?' (1985) 95 *Ethics* 274.

12 Hannah Arendt, *The Origins of Totalitarianism* (Harcourt Brace, 1951); Hannah Arendt, *The Human Condition* (Chicago University Press, 1958).

13 Roger Zetter, 'More Labels, Fewer Refugees: Making and Remaking the Refugee Label in an Era of Globalisation' (2007) 20 *Journal of Refugee Studies* 172.

14 Ibid.; Roger Zetter, David Griffiths and Nando Sigona, 'Social Capital or Social Exclusion? The Impact of Asylum Seeker Dispersal on Refugee Community Organisations' (2005) 40 *Community Development Journal* 169.

15 Elspeth Guild, 'The Europeanisation of Europe's Asylum Policy' (2006) 18 *International Journal of Refugee Law* 630.

16 Andrew Geddes, *Immigration and European Integration: Towards Fortress Europe?* (Manchester University Press, 2000); Andrew Geddes, *The Politics of Migration and Immigration in Europe* (Sage, 2003); Sandra Lavenex, *The Europeanisation of Refugee Policies: Between Human Rights and Internal Security* (Ashgate, 2001); Sandra Lavenex and Emek M. Uçarer (eds), *Migration and the Externalities of European Integration* (Lexington Books, 2003).

17 Human Security Report Project, *Human Security Backgrounder* (Simon Fraser University School for International Studies, 2005) <www.humansecurityreport.info/index.php?option=content&task=view&id=24&Itemid=59>.

18 Barry Buzan, Ole Weaver and Jaap De Wilde, *Security: A New Framework for Analysis* (Lynne Rienner, 1998), 27.

19 Ibid.

20 European Commission, *Unity, Solidarity, Diversity in Europe, its People and its Territory: Second report on economic and social cohesion adopted by the European Commission on 31 January 2001* (European Commission 2001) <www.inforegio.cec.eu.int/wbdoc/docoffic/official/reports/conclu32_en.htm>.

21 Ironically, as we review the contemporary dominance of the securitisation of migration and asylum processes, it was security concerns which first motivated EC thinking about migration under the disarmingly named TREVI Group (Terrorism, Radicalism, Extremism and Violence International), in 1975 responding to terrorism in the Middle East and in Europe (then West Germany and Italy). Interestingly, these European-level foundations for an overtly 'security-led' policy initiative based on judicial cooperation then lay effectively dormant for nearly three decades.

22 For example, seven of the UK Acts on these issues since 1993 contain immigration and asylum in their titles (only the word order changes), although recently nationality has been added to reinforce the concept of the migrant 'other'.

23 European Council, Council Directive 2003/9/EC of 27 January 2003 laying down minimum standards for the reception of asylum seekers: OJ 2003 No. L31/18 (Reception Conditions Directive) <http://eur-lex.europa.eu/LexUriServ/LexUriServ. do?uri=OJ:L:2003:031:0018:0025:EN:PDF>. European Commission, Qualification Directive, Council Directive 2004/83/EC (2004): OJ 2004 No. L304/12 (Qualification Directive) <www.homeoffice.gov.uk/documents/cons-2006-asylum-qual-directive/ eu-directive.pdf?view=Binary>. European Council, Council Directive 2005/85/EC of 1 December 2005 on minimum standards on procedures in Member States for granting and withdrawing refugee status: OJ 2005 No. L326/13 (Procedures Directive) <http://eur-lex.europa.eu/LexUriServ/LexUriServ.do?uri=OJ:L:2005:326:0013:00 34:EN:PDF>. European Parliament and of the Council European Directive 2011/95/ EU of the European Parliament and of the Council: OJ 2011 No. L337/9, 20 December 2011 (Recast 2011 Qualification Directive) <http://eur-lex.europa.eu/ LexUriServ/LexUriServ.do?uri=OJ:L:2011:337:0009:0026:EN:PDF>.

24 Zetter, above n. 13.

25 Martin Ruhs and Bridget Anderson, *Semi-Compliance in the Labour Market*, COMPAS Working Paper No. 30 (COMPAS, 2006).

26 Alice Bloch, Nando Sigona and Roger Zetter, *No Right to Dream: The Social and Economic Lives of Young Undocumented Migrants in Britain* (Paul Hamlyn Foundation, 2009), <www.jrf.org.uk/publications/immigration-social-cohesion-and-social-capital-what-are-links>.

27 Christina Boswell, *European Migration Policies in Flux: Changing Patterns of Inclusion and Exclusion* (Blackwell, 2003), 25.

28 The Tampere Programme (1999–2004) – the outcome of a special EU Council summit – is a critical 'hinge point' in this process because it marks the inception of the policy of promoting Europe as an area of 'Freedom Security and Justice', an initiative which simultaneously gave birth to the creation of the Common European Asylum System (CEAS).

29 Boswell, above n. 27, 18.

30 Geddes, above n. 16. For example, common reception procedures for asylum seekers; Europeanising the asylum claim process through the 2005 Procedures Directive covering a comprehensive range of access, examination and determination matters (Council Directive 2005/85/EC of 1 December 2005 on minimum standards on procedures in Member States for granting or withdrawing refugee status) – see above n. 22; Dublin II; the substantial stiffening of national status determination procedures such as fast-tracking measures, increased use of detention; extra-territorial processing; forced dispersal and curtailment of welfare benefits; expedited deportation and extradition (e.g. Frontex and the Italian–Libyan accords).

31 Mary Bosworth and Elspeth Guild, 'Governing through Migration Control: Security and Citizenship in Britain' (2008) 48 *British Journal of Criminology* 703.

32 Zetter *et al.*, above n. 2.

33 Castles, above n. 4, 16.

34 Space does not permit discussion of how refugees and asylum seekers have attempted to reconceive and reshape their identities, their sense of belonging and relationship with a host society, and their aspirations in relation to these state and practices.

35 Castles, above n. 4, 23.

3 Rights and the re-identified refugee: an analysis of recent shifts in Canadian law

Donald Galloway

Introduction

In 2012, two statutes came into force that modify the processes of refugee determination in Canada, reduce the benefits enjoyed by those seeking protection and impose additional hardships on some individuals found to be refugees. Neither the Balanced Refugee Reform Act,[1] nor the Protecting Canada's Immigration System Act[2] purports to introduce radical change. One can infer from their titles alone that their authors and sponsors presented them as attempts to shore up rather than to redefine the values underlying the immigration and refugee regime.

In the following pages, I argue that, despite the tone of modesty that has been used to articulate the objectives of the amendments, one can evince from the details of these two statutes, as well as from accompanying ministerial statements, strong evidence that the government is attempting to introduce into Canadian law a radical reconfiguration or reconceptualisation of refugee status which will have a serious impact on how refugees experience their position within Canadian society.

This reconceptualisation is being executed obliquely in so far as it has neither been proposed nor defended as an alternative to the existing, well-entrenched legal doctrines that have shaped refugee status. Instead, the new model is being introduced by implication. I argue that the very coherence of the recently introduced procedural changes is dependent on this set of implied substantive underpinnings. I do *not* argue that the Canadian government is covertly introducing a new definition of a refugee, one that is inconsistent with that found in the 1951 Convention Relating to the Status of Refugees ('Refugee Convention').[3] However, I do suggest that by somewhat furtive, elliptical means, the legal concept of a refugee is being altered as radically as it would be by substantive redefinition.

It is not only through legal amendments that the government has altered the terrain for claimants and refugees. In addition, in its political communications, it has projected a generic image of refugee claimants, constructed from statistical data, but bearing an unabashedly ideological imprint, to defend and justify the procedural changes and to validate its implied reconfiguration of the legal status.

Refugee claimants are now being profiled on the basis of a variety of suspect, overly broad traits and characteristics. The government claims that it is these generic traits that have necessitated the legal changes. The results of this profiling will have a strong bearing on whether refugee claims will be successful while further altering the social and legal implications of gaining refugee status. In effect, the profiled claimants will be carrying a prefabricated identity into the hearing room, and will be required to live with this imposed image even if found to be refugees.

For both claimants and refugees, the cumulative impact of these procedural, substantive and rhetorical measures is likely to be profound. The procedural changes will increase the difficulties for all claimants who are attempting to navigate the channels that lead to the determination of their status, with some being singled out to face additional burdens. As outlined below, one's country of origin and one's mode of arrival become important determinants of the processes that must be negotiated. In addition, the two-way interplay between the reconceptualised legal status and the social representation of refugee identity will have an impact in diverse social contexts. Even successful claimants will find it difficult to escape the generic identity traits that are being attributed to them. It is reasonably foreseeable that as their experience within the hearing room becomes more precarious so is it likely to become in other social contexts as well.

My central contention is that whereas the refugee was previously conceived as a rights-holder, whose interest in not being returned to face persecution was understood to be the ground of a governmental duty to provide protection, the recent amendments invert the relationship with the government: it is the government's many duties that are now regarded as the more basic element. Operating as vectors pulling in different directions, governmental commitments and policies will give rise to benefits whose content will be shaped by the strength of the various pulls. The refugee is now being reconceived as the indirect beneficiary of governmental decision making rather than its driver. The claimant appears at a hearing as a supplicant and as but one source of relevant information rather than as a person claiming the opportunity to show that they have a status that is defined entirely by their fundamental rights.

One of the keys to understanding the new model is that while refugees are still conceived as individuals whose interests should figure in government decision making, they no longer control the agenda within the hearing room. While they are not merely seeking government largesse, any obligation owed to them is regarded as defeasible and contextual and instead of being grounded on fundamental rights, its ambit will depend on a number of factors that take account of social and political concerns that may relate only tangentially to the particular claimant.

The process of refugee status determination is thus no longer to be conceived as an inquiry into facts that might establish an individual's rights against the government. Instead, it is being reshaped as an inquiry into facts that will form part of an assessment of the adequacy of the various possible governmental responses to the individual's arrival. Essentially, the refugee is being reconfigured as primarily a migrant whom the government may have reason to select.

From the government's perspective, because the hearing is no longer conceived as an inquiry into the claimant's fundamental rights, it is regarded as being only partially about the experiences of the particular claimant. Its primary aim will be to balance a variety of governmental concerns. Having redefined the aim, the government is then able to re-identify the optimal source of information. No longer is the claimant to be regarded as the best-qualified source of relevant evidence. This is a radical and revisionary shift in refugee law and the process of status determination. That it is the model that underlies the new amendments is confirmed by the fact that they blatantly deny to some refugees some substantive benefits formerly regarded as entitlements. The denial of these benefits – in seeming contravention of the mandatory provisions of the Refugee Convention – reaffirms the idea that the Canadian government is in the process of modifying the pre-existing image of the refugee as a rights-holder. Not only is it developing a reduced status for refugees within Canada, it is also reshaping the relationship between international obligations and domestic law.

Finally, I suggest that the reduced status that is now to be accorded to both refugee claimants and to refugees reveals an attempt to develop and implement a new social ethos with both communitarian and neoliberal dimensions that is intended to replace the liberal rights-respecting vision that has endured for approximately sixty years and that underpins the Refugee Convention. Underlying the amendments to refugee law, one can identify the development of a new conception of legality that has serious implications beyond immigration and refugee law for all individuals whose social status is precarious.

Recent amendments to Canadian refugee law

Designating countries and individuals

The passage of the two Acts through Parliament was a stormy one. The Balanced Refugee Reform Act was originally introduced when the government held a minority of seats in the House of Commons. Before it received royal assent, the opposition parties were able to force a number of important concessions and amendments aimed at tempering the harshness of the impact of the legislation on claimants and refugees. However, before the Act came into force, the government obtained a majority of seats in a general election. It then introduced the Protecting Canada's Immigration Act which, as well as introducing new measures, amended the Balanced Refugee Reform Act by returning it to the original blueprint.[1] The message was loud and clear: the harshness of the impact was one of the core elements of the new law and regarded as a component vital to the success of the government's aims.

Two of the many modifications introduced by the legislation stand out as being of particular significance. First, borrowing from other jurisdictions, such as the UK, the government has adopted the practice of designating countries of origin that are regarded as safe. The important characteristics of a designated country of origin (DCO) and the proposed treatment of claims of those who originate there are outlined as follows:

> DCOs are countries that do not normally produce refugees, respect human rights and offer state protection. The ability to designate such countries and accelerate the processing of refugee claimants from those countries provides the government with a tool to respond to spikes in claims from countries that do not normally produce refugees.
>
> The aim of the DCO policy is *to deter abuse of the refugee system* by people who come from countries generally considered safe. Refugee claimants from DCOs would have their claims processed faster. This would ensure that people in need get protection fast, while those with unfounded claims are sent home quickly through expedited processing. [emphasis added][5]

The underlying idea appears to be that increased statistical probability that a particular claim is unfounded, adjudged by the number of unsuccessful refugee claimants from that country, justifies devoting fewer resources to it, and processing it through the system more quickly. This is calculated to have the long-term effect of attracting fewer claims from these countries, which, in turn, will ensure that claimants from other countries (who are more likely to need protection) will be processed more promptly. A statement from the UNHCR, that accelerated procedures are justifiable when dealing with claims from safe countries of origin, has been cited to justify this approach.[6]

Designation brings with it a number of serious consequences. Claimants from a DCO are accorded a hearing that is scheduled earlier than those for claimants from other countries,[7] thus allowing less time to collect documentary evidence, arrange for interpretation of documents and instruct legal counsel.[8] In addition, claimants from a DCO do not have access to a newly established appeal process.[9] Furthermore, their removal from the country is not automatically stayed while they seek judicial review of a negative decision. Various other negative measures are also attached in order to deter people from a DCO from seeking protection in Canada.[10]

The designation of a country is made by ministerial order after consultation with other government departments. Two sets of factors can trigger a designation:

> The proposed triggers for a review are based on rejection rates, withdrawal and abandonment rates. A rejection rate (which includes abandoned and withdrawn claims) of 75% or higher would trigger a review. Similarly, an abandonment and withdrawal rate of 60% or higher would trigger a review.

For claimants from countries with a low number of claims, a qualitative checklist [is] established in legislation. The qualitative criteria checklist . . . include:

- the existence of an independent judicial system;
- recognition of basic democratic rights and freedoms, including mechanisms for redress if those rights or freedoms are infringed; and
- the existence of civil society organizations.[11]

The quantitative trigger is based on the rate of rejection, abandonment and withdrawal rather than on the low number of successful claims. It would seem that a country can be designated even though it produces a large number of refugees, as long as they are overshadowed by an even larger number of failed claimants.

The qualitative trigger has been equally controversial. Originally, the minister was granted the power to designate a country only after consultation with a panel of human rights experts. This requirement was removed in the final version of the Act that ultimately came into force,[12] leaving open the possibility that political factors may influence whether a designation will or will not be made.

Thus far, the minister has designated two lists of countries. The inclusion of Hungary in the first list and Mexico in the second has also sparked controversy.[13] Both have been source countries for a large number of claims,[14] and many of the claims from each have been abandoned or rejected, yet there is widespread concern that many nationals of both countries face significant dangers therein and have good reason to flee. In February 2013, barely two months after the Acts came into force the government declared the DCO implementation an unqualified success on the ground that the weekly rate of claims had decreased by 70 per cent from the equivalent period in earlier years. Moreover, claims from Hungary had decreased by 98 per cent.[15]

The second significant change introduced in the new legislation involves another mode of designation. A foreign national may gain the status of Designated Foreign National (DFN) if he or she is identified to be part of a group that is itself designated as arriving irregularly. The group designation is again made by ministerial order – in this case the Minister of Public Safety – and may be made when having regard to the public interest, the minister is of the opinion that:

- the examinations of the persons in the group, particularly for the purpose of establishing identity or determining inadmissibility of the persons involved in the arrival, and any related investigations concerning person in the group, cannot be conducted in a timely manner;
- or there are reasonable grounds to suspect that, in relation to the arrival of the group, there has been or will be, a contravention of subsection 117(1) related to organized human smuggling, for profit, or for the benefit of, at the direction of, or in association with a criminal organization or terrorist group.[16]

A person who is part of such a group is deemed to be a DFN. The consequences are severe. DFNs (including children older than 15) are subject to mandatory detention, with limited opportunities for judicial review. In addition, like those from a Designated Country of Origin, DFNs who are denied refugee status are also denied access to an appeal of the decision. Where DFNs are found to be Convention refugees or persons in need of Canada's protection, they will not be entitled to apply for permanent resident status for a period of five years. Nor are they entitled to an international travel document.[17]

General aims

Concurrently with the passage of the legislation through Parliament, the government published a number of policy papers and backgrounders[18] that aim to defend the changes. In these publications, one finds a catalogue of dysfunctions that are intended to reveal both the problematic disequilibria within refugee law and the serious threats faced by the immigration system. Four general themes are outlined in these explanatory texts.

First, the government expresses the opinion that unacceptably high levels of fraud and abuse have pervaded the refugee system, and refers to the high number of negative decisions, abandoned claims and withdrawn claims as evidence of this dishonesty.[19] The 'bogus refugee', a term transplanted from other jurisdictions and not employed frequently by previous governments, figures prominently and frequently in media releases[20] and joins an ever-growing cast of villains who have been presented as threatening the integrity of Canada's borders over the last decade. The eradication of fraud and abuse has become a dominant objective of the Canadian immigration regime and during this extended time-frame has given rise to an unprecedented number of amendments to both statutes and regulations. Others who figure prominently in government policies are the 'spouse of convenience', the 'birth tourist', the 'crooked immigration consultant' and the 'human smuggler'. Cumulatively, this cast of characters is cited to justify the need for widespread governmental intervention to preserve the integrity of the immigration regime. The government has subjected the human smuggler, in particular, to sustained denigration. When introducing the Protecting Canada's Immigration System Act, the Minister of Public Safety announced:

> Human smuggling is a dangerous and despicable crime – it puts lives at risk and threatens the integrity of Canada's immigration system as well as the security and safety of Canadians. That's why we've taken action to make Canada a less attractive destination for these criminal ventures. This [legislation] sends a clear message to criminal organizations contemplating human smuggling ventures that Canada will take strong, targeted action to prevent abuse of our generous immigration and asylum systems.[21]

In this statement, the minister appears initially to show concern for the safety of individuals who use the services of smugglers. However, by the conclusion he reveals a different reason for action: smugglers threaten the integrity of our selective immigration practices. We learn from other sources that they do so not only by bringing undeserving refugee claimants to Canada but also by coaching their cargo on how to manipulate to their advantage the refugee determination system by providing manufactured stories.[22] In short, the 'bogus refugee' and human smuggler operate as an organised team that threatens the integrity of immigration processes.

Closely connected to the concern about fraud and abuse is a second theme developed by the government that emphasises the costs and inefficiencies of the pre-existing determination processes. The lowering of these costs is advanced as a primary aim. The social and health benefits claimed by those awaiting status determination, the costs of legal counsel, interpreters and the required decision-making infrastructure have all been cited as factors that justified the streamlining of procedures. However, the delays and complexities in the system and the ever-increasing inventory and backlogs have been given special mention and have instigated specific changes. Thus, while previously it could take 18 months before a person found eligible to make a refugee claim was accorded a hearing, the new legislation mandates that a hearing be scheduled between 30 and 60 days after eligibility is determined.[23] By February 2013, the government was projecting that implementation of the changes would save $2 billion.[24]

Third, despite the proposed cutbacks, the government has also maintained that the new processes are nevertheless fair. As noted, it has relied heavily on statements from the UNHCR to provide the necessary moral authority for this position,[25] while also drawing comparisons between the new processes and analogous measures already adopted by other jurisdictions (and downplaying or ignoring any unique aspects of the Canadian system.)

The commitment to fairness is significant. The government promotes the view that the value of fairness is neither in tension with nor competes against the goals of avoiding excessive costs and deterring abuse. Instead, it implies that the assessment of the fairness of a process will always take into account the social costs incurred and the pervasiveness of and susceptibility to abuse and fraud. Due process, in other words, can be consistent with the implemen-tation of a two-tier or multi-tier hearing process, one stream of which may offer more cursory protections, on the ground that it deals with a larger proportion of costly or fraudulent claims. I argue below that this stance provides important insights into the government's general conception of the aims of refugee determination.

Fourth, the government has stressed that the amendments are not part of an anti-refugee agenda. To support this view, it has referred repeatedly to its program of resettling refugees from overseas, and the projected increase in the numbers of those being resettled. The relative generosity of Canada compared with all other countries has been emphasised.[26] Nevertheless, refugee claimants who have travelled great distance to Canada instead of seeking protection in a country nearer their homeland have also been routinely censured and labelled as 'queue jumpers' on the ground that they should have entered the resettlement process that operates beyond Canada's borders rather than arrive irregularly in Canada.[27] The fact that they have bypassed more proximate countries of protection is cited as evidence that both raises a reasonable suspicion about the plausibility of their claim to be fleeing persecution, and also tends to show they are, in fact, disguised economic migrants. Complicated motivations for migrating are reduced to simplistic accounts based on a set of prejudices and prejudgements about the identity of those involved.

Reaction to the legislation

Both types of designation have sparked strong opposition from refugee lawyers[28] and social organisations that have historically protected the interests of refugees and claimants.[29] The critiques have articulated a number of general themes: that the new system is procedurally unfair to some if not all refugee claimants, that it infringes their constitutional rights, that it grants too much power to the executive, politicising issues that should be decided by non-partisan bodies, and that it imposes severe sanctions and hardships on claimants and refugees solely for reasons of general deterrence and without sufficient regard to mitigating or excusing factors tied to the vulnerability of the individuals themselves. These general points have been bolstered by specific legal arguments that have pinpointed the precise constitutional and legal doctrines that are engaged by the changes and have shown how they apply. In the coming months, we can expect to see numerous cases being brought to the courts that will identify in detail the legal and constitutional objections.

In the interim, however, the government has been quite successful in responding to these objections and has garnered a relatively high level of media and popular support.[30] It has attempted to neutralise the arguments of legal organisations by representing the legal profession as a self-interested special interest group with selfish motivations for promoting the interests of refugee claimants.[31]

The general narrative – that the changes do not reflect a significant change in policy but merely streamline processes and offer less opportunity and incentive for abuse – appears to have gained widespread acceptance. The focus on 'queue jumping' has resonated particularly strongly with recent immigrants who have spent many months if not years negotiating the maze of immigration regulations before being granted permanent resident status. By locating the refugee claimant within a cast of wrongdoers and ne'er-do-wells, the government has confirmed if not increased public scepticism about the need for continued commitment to our practice of providing an independent hearing and protection to those who come to our shores and borders seeking protection. If many of the refugee claimants who arrive on our shores are 'bogus' and almost all of them are queue jumpers,[32] it is unsurprising that support for existing determination processes would wane.

Contrary to government claims, there is good reason to assert that the 2012 amendments have in fact introduced momentous change by reformulating the essential character of Canadian refugee law. As I outline in the next section, in the new paradigm, the rights-based principles that underlay the pre-existing regime have been replaced by other justifications that pay significantly less attention to the interests and experiences of particular claimants.

Determining status and determining rights

Prior to the adoption of the new amendments, the dominant and seemingly uncontroversial account of refugee law identified the rights of refugees as an important and exceptional constraint on governmental power. Within this dominant account, there have been some differences of opinion about the relative importance of and the relationship between domestic refugee law and international law, but these differences have not weakened the generally unified approach. Conceived as an aspect of international human rights law, the refugee's rights are identified as constraining the power of sovereign states to exclude or remove foreign nationals from their territory. A clear example of an articulation of this conception has been provided by Robyn Lui:

> The international protection regime for refugees and uprooted people is a striking example of the tension between human rights as rights of the individual (each of whom is entitled to equal moral consideration) and sovereignty as the rights of states to determine their internal affairs without external non-interference.[33]

From this general perspective, when it acceded to the Refugee Convention in 1969, Canada undertook a variety of obligations, based on its willingness to respect and promote the fundamental rights of refugees. The model of refugee law as rights based can be traced to three factors found in the Convention: the recognition of a specific status for people who have a well-founded fear of persecution, mandatory provisions that impose duties on state parties, and third a strong statement found in its preamble that acknowledged that contracting parties agreed to the terms of the Convention having acknowledged that 'the Charter of the United Nations and the Universal Declaration of Human Rights . . . have affirmed the principle that human beings shall enjoy fundamental rights and freedoms without discrimination' and that ' the United Nations has, on various occasions, manifested its profound concern for refugees and endeavoured to assure refugees the widest possible exercise of these fundamental rights and freedoms'.[34] There has been little doubt that the grant of status and the mandatory duties are regarded as a mode of protecting the fundamental interests of vulnerable people.

Conceived as an aspect of domestic constitutional law, refugee law reveals a different tension while still pitting the individual right against democratic accountability. Christian Joppke has emphasised the importance of this tension:

> As I have tried to demonstrate, conflicts over asylum policy are domestic conflicts over competing principles of liberal nation-states: that is, to be the

state of the people while corresponding to the constitutional mandate to respect human rights.[35]

While governments act primarily on behalf of and in the name of their citizenry, constitutions frequently guarantee rights to non-citizens and thereby set up the tension to which Joppke alludes.

James Hathaway has attempted to tie these two views together by noting the reliance placed on international human rights law by judicial bodies around the world. Courts have shown a willingness to build international human rights law into constitutional analysis:

> [T]he Refugee Convention and its Protocol are conceived here not as accords about immigration, or even migration, but as part and parcel of international human rights law. This view is fully in line with the positions adopted by senior courts which have analyzed the object and the purpose of the Refugee Convention. In perhaps the earliest formulation, the Supreme Court of Canada embraced the view that the essential purpose of the Refugee Convention is to identify persons who no longer enjoy the most basic forms of protection which a state is obliged to provide. In such circumstances refugee law provides surrogate or substitute protection of basic human rights.[36]

Each of these authors whether tracing the refugee's legal rights to international or to domestic sources, promotes a rights-based model that has dominated thinking about refugee law. It has been accepted as common wisdom that a special status within the country of protection coupled with attendant legal rights should vest in those who meet the definition of a refugee, despite their non-membership in the political community, and that the rights in question are rights held against this government. It is unsurprising, then, that the determination hearing has in the past been conceived as a forum in which claimants have been offered the opportunity to show that they have this legal entitlement.

The idea of the hearing as an inquiry into rights has some drawbacks for the claimant. For example, it is taken for granted that as a person who is making the claim against the government the refugee claimant has the burden of showing that they meet the requirements. The hearing has not been conceived as an open-ended inquiry in which the government is required to show the legality of its stance towards the individual. One important consequence of conceiving of refugee law as rights based is that on the occasions where claimants are unable to show that they meet the required definitional elements of refugee status, it is not improper for the government to deny them status and to deny surrogate protection. The suspicion that a person may face persecution in their country of origin but is unable to prove it will be regarded as insufficient ground for demanding that the status be granted. Moreover, the recognition that with further resources and time the claimant may be able to obtain the required proof is equally insufficient. The government meets its obligations to respect the fundamental rights of individuals by providing them with a fair opportunity to obtain proof and present it. Conceived as an inquiry into rights, the determination hearing is dependent on the provision of due process for its legitimacy.

This model of refugee determination has been well entrenched in Canadian law. It was adopted in unequivocal terms by Wilson J. in the seminal Supreme Court of Canada case of *Singh* v. *Minister of Employment and Immigration.*[37] Starting from the premise that refugees are rights-holders, but recognising that the rights in question do not vest in refugee claimants who are still seeking the status, Wilson J. draws the conclusion that the constitution nevertheless guarantees strict procedural rights to claimants, including the right to an oral hearing:

> [I]f the appellants had been found to be Convention refugees as defined in s. 2(1) of the *Immigration Act, 1976* they would have been entitled as a matter of law to the incidents of that status provided for in the Act. Given the potential consequences for the appellants of a denial of that status if they are in fact persons with a 'well-founded fear of persecution', it seems to me unthinkable that the *Charter* would not apply to entitle them to fundamental justice in the adjudication of their status.[38]

The 'unthinkability' of not recognising a constitutional guarantee appears to be based solely on the idea that refugees are legal rights-holders, that the rights in question are of basic importance and that those claiming to be rights-holders must be accorded the procedural right to persuade the government that they do indeed have the entitlements in question. A person claiming to be a rights-holder is in an analogous position to that of a rights-holder who is being denied their rights. Each is entitled to due process. When specifying the boundaries of procedural fairness in this context, Wilson J. focused on the procedural elements that permit the claim to be made effectively. Procedural fairness assumes a constitutional dimension because the refugee hearing is understood as an inquiry into whether the government would be violating the pre-existing right of a refugee to life, liberty and security of the person. Thus, the substantive issue is conceived in deontological terms: to *refoule* this claimant would be a violation of her right if she were indeed a refugee; the procedural guarantees that should be accorded are those that offer the opportunity to the claimant to show that it would be such.

The general outline of this model can be summarised in relatively simple terms: because status is an access point to a variety of important rights, the determination hearing exists to provide each claimant the opportunity to show that she meets the requirements for being recognised as having the status. In order to show adequate concern for the interests at stake, the government must provide a forum in which the issue may be fairly adjudicated. Adequate concern may be shown by placing the onus on claimants to show that they are entitled to a remedy from the government. While less formal, the refugee determination process has in the past borne close similarity to a private law action in which plaintiff seeks, *as a matter of corrective justice* and as a vindication of individual rights, a judicial order requiring the defendant to live up to an undertaking to protect refugees. In Hathaway's words, 'refugee law is a remedial or palliative branch of human rights law'.[39]

It is important to note that a system of designating countries as safe is not per se inconsistent with this model. Well-established in Canadian law is the idea that claimants from different countries will meet different challenges in the hearing room. According to the analysis of the Supreme Court of Canada in *Ward*,[10] there is a particularly heavy onus on the claimant whose country of origin is characterised as a democracy to show that she sought state protection and that it was not forthcoming. The court first noted the heavy onus on all claimants, stating that 'clear and convincing confirmation of a state's inability to protect must be provided'.[41] It then cited *Satiacum*, an earlier judgment of the Federal Court of Appeal which held:

> In the absence of exceptional circumstances established by the claimant, it seems to me that in a Convention refugee hearing, as in an extradition hearing, Canadian tribunals have to assume a fair and independent judicial process in the foreign country. In the case of a nondemocratic State, contrary evidence might be readily forthcoming, but in relation to a democracy like the United States contrary evidence might have to go to the extent of substantially impeaching, for example, the jury selection process in the relevant part of the country, or the independence or fair-mindedness of the judiciary itself.[42]

Ultimately, the court in *Ward* concluded:

> Although this presumption increases the burden on the claimant, it does not render illusory Canada's provision of a haven for refugees. The presumption serves to reinforce the underlying rationale of international protection as a surrogate, coming into play where no alternative remains to the claimant.[43]

It should also be noted that it is not inconsistent with the rights-based model for the minister to draw up a list of countries which attract a higher burden, rather than leave it to the discretion of each adjudicator in each case. There are sound reasons for assuring consistency in decision making and concerns about improper political reasons improperly influencing the minister may be addressed by providing access to judicial review by an independent court.

However, from within this rights-based model, the mode of designation of countries that is found in the new Canadian legislation is problematic for two reasons. First, it is peculiar to consider the percentage of failed claimants who come from a specific country of origin when hearing a particular claim, since the percentage of failed claims has no bearing on the validity of any particular claim. This will be particularly so where the country produces a large number of claimants. Even a success rate of 25 per cent in such circumstances indicates a strong reason to believe that the country is not safe for a large number of people. As noted in the UK decision, *Husan v. Secretary of State*:[44]

> [I]t does not necessarily follow that the number of invalid claims suggests an absence of serious risk of persecution in Bangladesh. It is not difficult to imagine why the number of aspiring economic migrants from Bangladesh . . . all shrouding their claims with illegitimate invocation of the Convention might be unusually high.

If a designated country is defined as one that does not normally produce refugees, then it is irrational to base designation solely on the high percentage of failed claimants. There is no reason to connect the high percentage of failed claimants with safety.

But, second, to allow the standards of procedural fairness to be diluted by a predetermination of the likelihood of success reveals a rejection of the idea that the hearing is remedial in nature. To provide an individual with less opportunity to make her case because she has a more difficult case to make (and is therefore likely to be unsuccessful) undermines the very reason for the hearing. The suggestion that we need to be more punctilious about claims that are likely to succeed indicates a failure to understand that remedial hearings are necessarily individualistic rather than generic in nature. They exist to allow the individual to prove that their particular circumstances warrant a remedy. By way of analogy, consider a situation where the government was authorised to deny access to the courts to individuals bringing an action against the government on the ground that it was of the opinion that the claim was unlikely to succeed.

And so we arrive at the conclusion that the new amendments are based on something other than safety in the country of origin and that the inquiry that will determine a person's status is no longer to be conceived as an inquiry into whether the fundamental rights of an individual are in jeopardy. Which raises the questions: what are the amendments about? And how is the inquiry conceived?

Designation, self-assessment and fraud

The key to understanding the new designation process is that claimants from specific countries have shown themselves to be poor assessors of whether or not their claim is a good one. It is this fact that seems to have sparked the new amendments. It explains the reliance on statistical assessments of the *rate* of unsuccessful claims rather than the actual numbers of successful claimants. One may not be able to conclude that a country with a high failure rate is safe, but one can conclude that, as a general rule of thumb, claimants from that country are relatively poor judges of whether or not they face a well-founded fear of persecution on one of the proscribed grounds compared with claimants from other countries.

There are two reasons why a group's general inability to self-assess may be held to be relevant to refugee decision making.

First, from the generalisation that members of a group are poor self-assessors one may also draw another general conclusion, that among those who are poor self-assessors, some are likely to be fraudulent claimants. From these two generalisations one can move to a third generalisation that individuals from these countries are less likely to be credible witnesses than witnesses from countries where there is a lower rate of failed claims. Since our hearing process is heavily dependent on the testimony of claimants and since they have the onus of proving their claim, it may be thought to be justifiable to provide less scrutiny to these claims and to devote more attention to claims from other countries. Consequently, it may be thought to be justifiable to regard their claim as implicitly less trustworthy and hence less deserving of consideration. Where resources are scarce and the provision of hearings to all claimants is proving too costly, it may be thought to make sense to use these generalisations to reduce the access of those who are likely to be poor self-assessors.

If this is the argument that underlies the recent amendments, then it bodes ill for refugee claimants since it can be extended further. If we accept the logic in the argument, then it is hard to avoid concluding that because more refugee claimants (from any country) are rejected than are accepted, all claimants have shown themselves to be poor self-assessors, which in turn it could lead to the conclusion that access should be reduced for all. Moreover, the argument stands on a faulty premise. We have only been able to adjudge that some countries produce a higher rate of unsuccessful claims because we have granted full individual hearings to each claimant. Should we stop doing that, we would stop obtaining accurate data.

However, there is a second and more basic reason why the government would be willing to take into account the poor ability to self-assess and the possibility of fraud. Based on the view that it is justifiable to introduce a curtailed process because it is not an efficient use of government resources to offer the same facilities and opportunities to claimants from designated countries of origin, the recent amendments indicate that the government conceives the question of access to decision-making procedures as a *distributive* rather than a corrective issue. From this perspective, claimants are regarded as competing with each other for access to this valued benefit and it is justifiable to base the distribution on both a prior assessment of the claimant's need and desert. In this competition, there is no entitlement to win.

Much like a protocol instituted in the emergency room of a hospital that prioritises the treatment of some patients on the basis of their symptoms and demotes other patients to less timely access on the ground that past experience indicates a weaker connection between their symptoms and the need for immedi-ate care, the recent amendments indicate a willingness to tailor the determination process to match a prior assessment of likelihood of success. Such methods aim to ensure that the process is used exclusively by those who require it, although some who require it will be diverted.

The radical implication is that the status determination hearing is no longer conceived as a remedial forum offering an opportunity for the vindication of rights. It is now reshaped as a public investigation into the possibility of persecution.

The complaint is lodged but the government must consider whether it has the resources to investigate and if so how these resources should be expended and divided. The claimant's complaint may be the reason for the investigation but the nature of the investigation will be shaped by a broad range of considerations – including the goal of encouraging claimants to do a better job of self-assessment before making their claim.

Another analogy that reveals the internal logic of this model is that of a police force drawing up priorities about complaints that it should investigate. The fact that a person may have a valid complaint is not reason enough for the police to investigate if its resources are stretched. Although an individual's interests may be in jeopardy she may find that an investigation into her situation will depend on a number of protocols designed to ensure a more efficient use of resources. Refusal to investigate, or to investigate with as high a level of scrutiny, does not indicate that the particular claim is groundless or less worthy. It merely indicates that political and economic reasons are relevant when determining the optimal institutional response.

Under this new model, the government is showing first that it believes that there is a reason to offer protection to people with a well-founded fear of persecution, and second that there is therefore a reason to investigate whether a particular person requires protection. However, it is also demonstrating that it believes that the reason to protect is based on *an aspect of the public interest* rather than an individual right . This could be the case where the government was intent on taking measures to reduce the risk that it would become complicit or be seen to be complicit in future acts of persecution. There are sound political reasons for wishing to take these steps that are wholly unrelated to the interests of the claimant. Where the public interest is driving the investigation, it makes sense to require the person who initiates it to meet some basic criteria of trustworthiness. Where there is good reason to suspect that the claimant is untrustworthy, there is also good reason not to initiate an investigation. Where there is good reason to believe that the initiator is less trustworthy than others, there is also good reason to expend fewer resources on the investigation or to reduce its costs.

Reasoning along lines similar to this may ground the conclusion that safety in the country of origin or the percentage of false claims from a country should serve as reasons for expending fewer resources in the investigation of this matter. It may also ground a decision to offer less time or opportunity to the claimant for the production of evidence. Thus, by altering the character of the hearing from a remedial adjudication to a public inquiry, the government may justify the introduction of a new standard of due process.

By developing and imposing this model the government is able to re-identify refugees as merely one type of migrant. That they meet the definition found in the Refugee Convention may be a reason for selecting them but by itself, this reason is insufficiently powerful to create a duty to do so. It must be weighed against reasons for not investigating particular claims or not investigating them with the highest level of scrutiny.

By this means, we arrive at the conclusion that the status is no longer conceived as an entitlement. The process of status determination is no longer conceived as involving adjudication of rights. It has been restructured as the settlement of what Lon Fuller labelled as 'polycentric' issues, matters that are unsuited to judicial analysis.[15] It is no coincidence that at the same time as it has reshaped the process of status determination, the government has transferred the decision-making authority from quasi-judicial adjudicators to public servants.

As noted earlier, it is not only in the hearing room that the new model for conceiving the relationship between government and refugee is applied. The government will now also profile those foreign nationals who arrive irregularly in groups as presumptively false claimants. The assumed statistical correlation between irregular modes of arrival and the genuineness of claims coupled with the costs associated with coping with multiple claims made simultaneously now serve as reasons for the government to impose restrictions on those individuals who arrive irregularly, again with the aim of deterring others who intend to follow suit. While some restrictions are placed on all Designated Foreign Nationals, others are reserved for those who have been granted a hearing and found to be refugees. Unlike other successful claimants, these refugees are denied a travel document and are barred from applying for permanent residence for five years.[16] These restrictions cannot be fitted easily within the language of the Refugee Convention. For example, Article 28 provides:

> The Contracting States shall issue to refugees lawfully staying in their territory travel documents for the purpose of travel outside their territory, unless compelling reasons of national security or public order otherwise require, and the provisions of the Schedule to this Convention shall apply with respect to such documents.

Likewise, Article 31 provides that:

> The Contracting States shall not impose penalties, on account of their illegal entry or presence, on refugees who, coming directly from a territory where their life or freedom was threatened in the sense of article 1, enter or are present in their territory without authorization, provided they present themselves without delay to the authorities and show good cause for their illegal entry or presence.

The failure of the government to respect these provisions by denying, for reasons of general deterrence, a travel document to DFNs and imposing the penalty of postponing access to permanent residence confirms not only that the government does not consider that refugees have entitlements, but also that it believes that any international obligations undertaken and respected by its predecessors are defeasible and subject to qualification. The obligations of international refugee law according to the new regime will always be shaped by the countervailing need to ensure that the undeserving are not encouraged or able to benefit from laws intended only for the deserving. The new regime will produce different categories of refugee, each with an identity shaped by matters beyond their control and by government policy if not whim.

The impact on social status

The denial of rights-holder status to refugees renders their position both within and outside the hearing room more precarious. Within the hearing room, it allows the claimants' role to be reduced; they are to be the object of the hearing rather than its subject. Outside the hearing room, their status as beneficiary rather than as rights-holder is to be used to reduce their access to social services and may be expected to increase levels of suspicion and resentment.

By profiling refugees and claimants and by publicly encouraging the public to adopt a general image that implies fraud, the government has distinguished itself from previous governments that were punctilious about maintaining a neutral stance between two distinct generic images of refugee claimants – one of which portrays them as heroic figures who have survived extreme hardship in their escape from tyranny, oppression or violence and who have defeated the odds by managing to cross the globe to find a country committed to respecting human freedom and dignity; the other of which portrays them as self-interested fraudsters. Instead, the government has allowed independent decision makers to make a determination about which of these representations was more accurate in each particular case, and permitted the public and the media to select the appropriate generic image based on its understandings of these decisions. However, as noted earlier, the current government has not been reticent to turn its back on the heroic image and to announce its view that the choice between generic images of the refugee claimant is either that of the queue jumper or that of the petty crook who relies on criminal organisations to take advantage of the generosity and benevolence of relatively wealthy social democracies.

One can hypothesise that the fundamental reason underlying this stance has little to do with refugees and more to do with broader governmental aims. Two in particular stand out.

Refugee laws have proved to be a thorn in the flesh for governments aiming to develop international economic markets by allowing for the free movement of business people. The well-established methods of controlling migration and avoiding obligations under the Refugee Convention, imposing visas on foreign nationals and delegating border control functions to transportation companies, have become irritants to governments aiming to develop trading partnerships. The reframing of refugee law has been guided by single-minded pursuit of the economic promises of international trade.[47]

Second, the current government is also intent on developing a strong and cohesive Canadian society and to that end has identified the importance of expressing a vision of social virtue. It has expressed this importance in many contexts, for example when defending its 'tough on crime' agenda and when amending citizenship law by rendering access to citizenship more difficult. The image of the virtuous community that it is pursuing is one that identifies the importance of not being exploited by fraudsters. Willingness to tolerate antisocial activity is identified as a character flaw that can diminish the communal solidarity needed for a society to flourish. Supporting this image is a conception of the rule of law that emphasises the connection between legality and the enforcement of norms rather than a connection between legality and the protection of rights and freedoms.

Ultimately it is this more general vision that is informing the changes to refugee law. In my title to this chapter, I have suggested that the refugee is being re-identified. I have attempted throughout to indicate the primary traits that the government is using to categorise and reclassify refugee claimants. Their failure to self-assess successfully is being presented as imposing an unacceptably costly burden on the community and is being attributed to the worst of motives. At every moment from the time when they decide to depart to the moment when they present themselves for determination they are being defined as undeserving, a characterisation that justifies pro forma processes and stringent deterrents. In addition, it is important to observe how the irregularity of the refugee's situation has come to define their essential identity. The irregularity of their situation is now conceived as inconsistent with the commitment to legality itself. The refugee is becoming illegal.

Notes

1 SC 2010, c 8.
2 SC 2012, c 17.
3 Convention relating to the Status of Refugees, Geneva, 28 July 1951, 1989 UNTS 137, supplemented by the Protocol relating to the Status of Refugees, 31 January 1967, 19 UST 6223, 6257 ('Refugee Convention').
4 The provisions of both Acts and have been folded into the pre-existing statute, the Immigration and Refugee Protection Act SC 2001 c 27 (IRPA) <http://laws-lois.justice.gc.ca/eng/acts/I-2.5> (accessed 9 December 2013).
5 Government of Canada (16 February 2012) 'Backgrounder – Designated Countries of Origin', Citizenship and Immigration Canada <www.cic.gc.ca/english/department/media/backgrounders/2012/2012-02-16i.asp> (accessed 9 December 2013). The ambiguity in the first sentence is clearly unintended. DCOs do respect human rights and offer state protection but do *not* normally produce refugees.
6 See UNHCR Statement on the right to an effective remedy in relation to accelerated asylum procedures <www.unhcr.org/4deccc639.pdf> (accessed 9 December 2013).
7 For claims made at a port of entry this would be 45 days instead of 60 days.
8 The Regulations establish that documentary evidence from all claimants must be submitted ten days before the scheduled hearing.
9 The provisions limiting access to the Refugee Appeal Division of the Immigration and Refugee Board have been incorporated into s. 110 of the IRPA.
10 Thus, claimants from a DCO are denied a work permit while they await determination of their claim. They are also denied the opportunity to make an application for a pre-removal risk assessment for three years after their claim has been rejected. In addition, claimants from a DCO are entitled to reduced medical coverage while they await the determination of their claim. They are entitled to hospital services only if they are required to diagnose, prevent or treat a disease posing a risk to public health or to diagnose or treat a condition of public safety concern (such as HIV or TB). See <www.cic.gc.ca/english/refugees/outside/ifhp-info-sheet.asp> (accessed 9 December 2013). For more detailed information on the negative consequences attached to claimants from a DCO, see generally <www.cic.gc.ca/english/refugees/reform-ppra.asp> and <www.cic.gc.ca/english/resources/manuals/bulletins/2013/ob440G.asp> (accessed 9 December 2013).

11 Government of Canada (16 February 2012), Summary of Changes to Canada's Refugee System in the Protecting Canada's Immigration System Act, Citizenship and Immigration Canada <www.cic.gc.ca/english/department/media/backgrounders/2012/2012-02-16f.asp> (accessed 9 December 2013).

12 The current criteria are found in s. 109.1 of the IRPA.

13 See Stephanie Levitz (14 February 2013) 'Israel, Mexico added to list of "safe countries for refugee claimants"', *Globe and Mail* <www.theglobeandmail.com/news/politics/israel-mexico-added-to-list-of-safe-countries-for-refugee-claimants/article8677347> (accessed 9 December 2013); John Geddes (14 December 2012), 'Kenney assertive on Roma refugees, but critics argue the details', *Maclean's* <www2.macleans.ca/2012/12/14/kenney-assertive-on-roma-refugees-but-critics-argue-the-details> (accessed 9 December 2013).

14 Statistics are available from the Human Rights Research and Education Forum at the University of Ottawa <www.cdp-hrc.uottawa.ca/projects/refugee-forum/projects/documents/REFUGEESTATSCOMPREHENSIVE1999-2011.pdf> (accessed 9 December 2013).

15 See Government of Canada (22 February 2013), 'News release – Canada's new asylum system a success', Citizenship and Immigration Canada <www.cic.gc.ca/english/department/media/releases/2013/2013-3-02-2-22.asp> (accessed 9 December 2013).

16 Government of Canada (30 August 2012) Operational Bulletin 440-D Designated Foreign Nationals – Restrictions on Applications for Permanent Residence, Citizenship and Immigration Canada <www.cic.gc.ca/english/resources/manuals/bulletins/2012/ob440D.asp> (accessed 9 December 2013).

17 See generally Government of Canada (29 June 2012) Overview: Ending the Abuse of Canada's Immigration System by Human Smugglers, Citizenship and Immigration Canada <www.cic.gc.ca/english/department/media/backgrounders/2012/2012-06-29i.asp> (accessed 9 December 2013); see also discussion below.

18 The most recent are on the website of Citizenship and Immigration Canada at <www.cic.gc.ca/english/department/media/backgrounders/2012/index.asp> (accessed 9 December 2013).

19 Whether or not it is appropriate to bundle withdrawn claims and abandoned claims together to indicate fraud, the statistics indicate that the rate of acceptance between 2001 and 2011 varied between 38 and 47 per cent. See IRB Refugee Status Determinations 1998–2011 published by the University of Ottawa's Refugee Forum at <www.cdp-hrc.uottawa.ca/projects/refugee-forum/projects/Statistics.php> (accessed 9 December 2013).

20 See for example Government of Canada (16 February 2012) Speaking notes for the Honorable Jason Kenney, PC, MP Minister of Citizenship, Immigration and Multiculturalism – at a news conference following the tabling of Bill C-31, Protecting Canada's Immigration System Act, Citizenship and Immigration Canada <www.cic.gc.ca/EnGlish/department/media/speeches/2012/2012-02-16.asp> (accessed 9 December 2013).

21 See 'Harper Government takes action against human smuggling' <http://news.gc.ca/web/article-eng.do?nid=710859> (accessed 9 December 2013). It should be noted that the legal provision defining human smuggling has been declared to be unconstitutional on grounds of being overly broad by a judge of the British Columbia Supreme Court. See *R* v. *Appulonappa*, 2013 BCSC 31 (2013) BCJ No. 35. The impact of this decision on the new amendments has yet to be determined.

22 Reference is made to this practice in Steven Chase (21 February 2013) 'New fast-track rules see big drop in refugee asylum claims', *Globe and Mail* <www.theglobeandmail.com/news/politics/new-fast-track-rules-see-big-drop-in-refugee-asylum-claims/article8961268> (accessed 9 December 2013).

23 See above, n. 15. I have resisted providing in this chapter a detailed account of the exact process that is contemplated by the new legislation. The government's own accounts provide a clear analysis.

24 Ibid.

25 See above, n. 6.

26 The projected increase in 2013 to 14,500. However, it should be noted that the resettlement numbers published in March 2013 do not substantiate the government's claims. See Government of Canada (27 February 2013) Preliminary tables – Permanent and temporary residents, 2012, Citizenship and Immigration Canada <www.cic.gc.ca/english/resources/statistics/facts2012-preliminary/01.asp> (accessed 17 March 2013).

27 See Government of Canada (30 March 2010) Speaking notes – remarks by the Honorable Jason Kenney, Citizenship and Immigration Canada <www.cic.gc.ca/english/department/media/speeches/2010/2010-03-30.asp> (accessed 17 March 2013).

28 See for example <www.carl-acaadr.ca/articles/37> (accessed 9 December 2013)

29 See for example Canadian Council for Refugees, Refugee Reform – Bill C-31 changes to the refugee determination system <https://ccrweb.ca/en/refugee-reform> (accessed 9 December 2013).

30 For example, Jeffrey Simpson (23 January 2013) 'Refugee reform: give Kenney's plan a chance to work', *Globe and Mail* <www.theglobeandmail.com/commentary/refugee-reform-give-kenneys-plan-a-chance-to-work/article7623935> (accessed 9 December 2013).

31 Including charges against the judiciary.

32 I am assuming that the government would not identify a *sur place* claimant as a queue jumper.

33 Robyn Lui, 'State Sovereignty and International Refugee Protection', in Trudy Jacobsen, Charles Sampford and Ramesh Thakur (eds), *Re-envisioning Sovereignty: The End of Westphalia?* (Ashgate, 2008), 151.

34 Refugee Convention, above n. 3, Preamble.

35 Christian Joppke, 'Asylum and State Sovereignty' (1997) 30 *Comparative Political Studies* 253.

36 James C. Hathaway, *The Rights of Refugees under International Law* (Cambridge University Press, 2005), 4.

37 *Singh* v. *Minister of Employment and Immigration* (1985)1 SCR 177, (1985) SCJ No. 11.

38 The relevant section of the Charter guarantees the right to life, liberty and security of the person and the right not to be deprived thereof except in accordance with the principles of fundamental justice.

39 Hathaway, above n. 36, 5.

40 *Canada (Attorney General)* v. *Ward* (1993)2 SCR 689 (1993) SCJ No. 74.

41 Ibid., 50.

42 *Minister of Employment and Immigration* v. *Satiacum* (1989) FCJ No. 505, 99 NR 171 (FCA), at 173.

43 Ibid., 51.

44 *Husan* v. *Secretary of State* (2005) EWHC 189 (Admin), 57.

45 Lon L. Fuller, 'The Forms and Limits of Adjudication' (1978) *Harvard Law Review* 353.

46 See Operational Bulletin 440-D, above n. 16.

47 Analysis of the economic implications of imposition of a visa requirement on Mexico has been well documented, see Levitz, above n. 13. For analysis of the connection between the designation of Hungary as a DCO and the free trade talks between Canada and the European Union, see Audrey Macklin, 'A safe country to emulate? Canada and the European refugee' (<http://papers.ssrn.com/sol3/papers.cfm?abstracts_id=2355727>).

4   The Refugee Convention at 60: still fit for purpose?

Protection tools for protection needs[1]

Erika Feller

A recent article in the *Daily Telegraph* declared as its title suggested, that 'The UN Convention on Refugees is not fit for purpose'.[2] That is a sweeping observation in a text which singularly failed to try to define what the purpose of the Refugee Convention actually is.[3] Nevertheless, it is worth unpacking a little the arguments made by the author, given that 2011 marked the sixtieth anniversary of this instrument and it is more than likely that this will attract – as it should – quite some analysis about its strengths and weaknesses. So, has the Convention seen its day?

If you agree with the author of the article, it has. His central thesis is that the 'concept of asylum [is] an outdated and unworkable relic from the mid-20th century'.[4] He supports this, slimly, by pointing to world population growth, proliferation of abusive regimes, greatly enhanced movement possibilities and the incentives to move created by badly functioning asylum systems which reward misuse. He asserts that the problems are compounded by reluctance or inability of, in this case the UK government, to properly distinguish between economic migration and protection-motivated flight and he lays at the feet of the Convention the responsibility for what he calls the people trafficking industry.

In a speech made in November 2010, on the other side of the world, by the opposition party immigration spokesperson in the Australian Parliament, Scott Morrison, in different language, a rather similar posture was taken. He argued that the Convention is increasingly an inadequate instrument for dealing with 'global people movement', which he asserted will become an ever bigger problem, but for other than Convention-related reasons, such as climate change, financial collapse, natural disasters or growing societal inequities.[5] Commenting on the Morrison speech, Australian academic Klaus Neumann[6] noted that 'the absence of other instruments dealing with these more general risks forcing people to move are likely to lead to the Refugee Convention being abused as a surrogate – with claims being confected to attract protection'.[7]

It is important to listen to such concerns, even if they are ill informed (as many will be) because perception can be as important as reality when it comes to understanding and dealing with the problems which today confront international refugee protection.[8]

One hears often that the Convention is an increasingly inadequate response to 'global people movements'. The main message being disseminated is that what we have is insufficient and that there is a need for something more. The UNHCR agrees. But what, and for whom? This will be the focus of what I want now to develop in this chapter.

The background setting

The world for many millions remains very insecure. An estimated 45.2 million people are forcibly displaced worldwide. More than 35.8 million people – 10.5 million refugees and 17.7 million internally displaced persons (IDPs) – were receiving protection or assistance from UNHCR at the end of 2011.[9]

Of course these bald statistics do not tell a nuanced enough story. Refugees can and do go home: witness the 2009 returns to Southern Sudan of more than 330,000 refugees, i.e. around 75 per cent of the UNHCR registered 428,000 refugees in the neighbouring countries at the time the Comprehensive Peace Agreement was signed. When it comes to resettlement, there are now 24 countries offering resettlement places with over 73,000 persons able to benefit from this solution in 2010. And there have been a number of positive initiatives to move refugees away from care and maintenance to self-sufficiency.[10] The naturalisation of over 162,000 long-term refugees in Tanzania particularly stands out. There is a legal instrument for the protection of internally displaced persons in Africa which is a major step forward,[11] and UNHCR has also welcomed the openness with which its overtures on behalf of stateless people are now being received.[12]

Asylum in the industrialised world remains, still, an important durable solution. Sizeable numbers in Europe, North America and Oceania (in 2009, around 150,000 persons) received Convention status or subsidiary protection, with accompanying rights necessary for social inclusion.

This being said, there has been a worrying consistency when it comes to the persistent problems. Insecurity and narrowing protection space are prevalent in many countries, with the deliberate targeting of civilians, to destabilise populations through displacement and terror – including by resorting to brutal sexual violence – as we see for example in the DRC. *Refoulement* incidents of high visibility continue. Refugees are frequently hosted in areas too close to conflicts and in environments which represent diverse threats to their physical safety. Urbanisation of refugee situations is making the delivery of assistance and protection both more complicated and less effective, even if it means, to use a popular phrase, less 'warehousing'. Refugee education is everywhere a challenge, and particularly problematic against the fact that the non-availability of solutions has left millions of refugees (and IDPs) locked in exile situations for years on end.

If nationality might seem like a universal birthright, an estimated 12 million people around the world – probably a much underestimated number – are struggling to get along without it. This means, in practice, a daily struggle for legitimacy, to establish a legal residence to move freely, to find work, to access medical assistance and education for their children.

There are many asylum systems that remain ineffective or unresponsive, with some purposefully in decline, perhaps aimed at serving a deterrent function.

These are the systems which, variously, receive asylum applicants in remote and isolated reception centres; which provide only limited, if any, access to low-quality state legal aid and interpretation services; or which lack procedural guarantees for accelerated procedures or for handling claims from vulnerable groups. Many asylum systems are not 'child friendly', take no account of the special circumstances of child applicants, and legitimate the automatic repatriation of children, without resort to established protection, such as determination in the best interests of the child. Applications based on sexual orientation have been subject also to discriminatory and unproven testing such as phallometry. Detention of asylum seekers continues to create great individual hardship in many countries and research shows that it has no impact as a deterrent.[13] The duration can be overlong, the conditions unjustifiably harsh and the possibilities for legal oversight or review very limited. It has reached the point in some countries where there are actually more due process safeguards regulating detention of criminals than of asylum seekers.

In short, in the sixtieth anniversary year of the 1951 Refugee Convention, physical insecurity, legal insecurity, socio-economic insecurity and environmental insecurity were commonplace. Quite predictably as a result, so too was forced displacement and, with it, protection gaps. This continues to be the case. The Middle East unrest may well just reconfigure global politics, and refugee and asylum situations with it. The power of social media as a tool of protection and game-changer when it comes to refugee and migration situations has enormous potential yet to be realised. This is the context for any analysis of the place of the Convention as a protection tool in today's world.

The frame for the analysis: protection tools for protection needs

There are many ways to approach this analysis. I want to do it by categories of situations, where the persons caught up in them will most likely encounter, at some point, the legislation or the practical arrangements states have put in place to meet their own protection responsibilities. The situations can broadly be broken down as follows:

1   the 'classical' persecution-driven movement where refugees, individually or in small groups, flee state or non-state persecution, including that comprising deliberately targeted acts of violence;
2   the mass-influx situations where large-scale displacement is provoked by danger or violence accompanying conflicts or civil disturbance and which overwhelms receiving state apparatuses;
3   cross-border displacement provoked by natural disasters or human-made calamities, such as nuclear disasters; and
4   mixed flows of persons moving as an integral and often indistinguishable part of an asylum/migration movement.

These situations may not always be so easy to distinguish, one from another. Clearly the applicability and utility of the 1951 Convention will differ markedly, situation by situation. Whether the Convention will be applicable is a legal decision linked closely to the characteristics which give members of each group their differing identities. Whether the Convention is the most useful instrument to resort to, even where it may legally apply, will in part depend upon the protection needs at issue, which may differ among the groups, even if there are also many concerns in common. An analysis of where the Convention should apply and why is a first step to measuring its alleged outdatedness or irrelevance and should provide some indication of what, in addition, may be needed.

The first situation: individual refugees from persecution and targeted violence

When it comes to refugees from persecution, the 1951 Convention remains the foundation of protection obligations owed to them. It is the one truly universal instrument setting out the baseline principles. The Convention tells us who is a refugee. It requires that refugees should not be returned to face persecution, or the threat of persecution (the principle of *non-refoulement*); that protection must be extended to all refugees without discrimination; that persons escaping persecution cannot be expected to leave their country and enter another country in a regular manner, and, accordingly, should not be penalised for having entered into or for being illegally in the country where they seek asylum; that given the very serious consequences the expulsion of refugees may have, such a measure should only be adopted in exceptional circumstances directly impacting on national security or public order; that the problem of refugees is social and humanitarian in nature, and therefore should not become a cause of tension between states; that since the grant of asylum may place unduly heavy burdens on certain countries, a satisfactory solution of the problem of refugees can only be achieved through international cooperation; that cooperation of states with the High Commissioner for Refugees is essential if the effective coordination of measures taken to deal with the problem of refugees is to be ensured. Such prohibitions are not time bound.

The 1951 Convention was drafted to confer a right to protection on persons made otherwise exceptionally vulnerable through being temporarily outside the normal framework of national state protection. Its object and purpose was to give voice and force to rights for refugees, and to responsibilities for their surrogate protection.

In recognition of the importance of these objectives, the Convention is widely adhered to, even if there is still no universal sign-on to it. To date there are 148 states parties to the 1951 Convention and/or its 1967 Protocol. The problem is less the number of accessions and more the will to implement.

Weakened political will to support the Convention has at its root the growing numbers of asylum seekers, exacerbated both by disenchantment with them within civil societies and heightened government concerns about terrorism and transnational crime. Asylum is seen as a costly burden which is not equally distributed; refugees can become a cause of social tensions and a divisive political issue; they can be difficult to extricate from an illegal migration flow in any reliable manner; and when it is all said and done, generosity to them is not understood to be bringing in internationally the political dividends that it used to.

It is, though, not weak political will alone that accounts for the malaise of the Convention today. Part of the problem lies in the Convention text itself which, if the baseline, is also, in many respects a basic statement only.

The scope of the refugee definition in the Convention has long been identified as a limiting factor. In particular, the grounds of persecution stipulated in it leave too much scope for narrow interpretation, making it easier for those so inclined to deny its applicability when it comes to causes not specifically mentioned, such as gender. Partly to promote more modern interpretations, ten years ago we launched a global consultations process on refugee protection. The result was an Agenda for Protection, which has guided the actions of UNHCR, and in many ways those also of states and other protection partners, intergovernmental and non-governmental, for a decade. We have, as a result, guidelines which have helped to modernise the interpretation and application of the Convention regime in important areas, from gender persecution to family reunification, from *non-refoulement* to internal protection, from exclusion to cessation, and others as well. We have serious and implementable commitments from states to address more holistically the protection needs of women and children at risk, refugees with disabilities, or urban refugees. Solutions are more actively embraced and strategically used and we have new tools, from the 10-Point Plan for the asylum–migration nexus, to participatory planning for age, gender and diversity sensitive protection.

What we do not have, however, is any firmer commitment than previously that asylum, for however long, will be made available by receiving states to all refugees who need it. It is particularly important to note that absent from the Convention are provisions which specifically compel access to national procedures and the granting of asylum. Even Article 14 of the Universal Declaration of 1949 went no further than to state that 'Everyone has the right to seek and enjoy asylum from persecution'. The original formulation, i.e. the right 'to be granted asylum' was dropped. Regional instruments have gone further than the international text in this regard, in reverting to the notion of a responsibility to grant. And the European Court of Human Rights recently accepted that the 1951 Convention imposed obligations on states to grant asylum to those who met its protection terms.[14] The Convention, while providing for a whole range of rights enjoyed by refugees, does not impose a legal duty on a state which can be construed to require it to admit any particular refugee on any permanent basis, however. The Convention only establishes the right of seriously at-risk persons to cross international borders to seek safety until the threat in their home country is eradicated. The *non-refoulement* principle prevents – or should prevent – return to persecution, but non-return can be achieved in a number of ways short of durable entry and stay.

Paradoxically, this could be seen as one of the Convention's strengths, even through the optic of states. Convention-based asylum is not a solution in itself;

rather it is a protection mechanism which creates space for solutions to be worked out. It should be reassuring that Convention protection in fact does not automatically equate only and absolutely with permanency and integration. It can lead to permanent stay, just as it can lead to voluntary repatriation, or resettlement at the right time. States have allowed fears and pressures to cloud perceptions here, sometimes leading to an 'either/or', or rather a 'neither/nor', approach to implementing the Convention. Concerns about asylum obligations flowing from Convention adherence need to be accordingly tempered.

In short, when it comes to the persecuted refugees the Convention remains the cornerstone of their protection even if the language of some of its provisions has allowed, unfortunately, for over narrow interpretation. In my assessment, there would be too much to lose in trying to amend the core of the Convention to address this problem. Attention could more constructively turn to better methods of implementing the Convention so that states act affirmatively to ensure every refugee has the right to enjoy asylum somewhere and not act in such a manner that renders the right meaningless.

The second situation: large-scale influxes involving (presumptive) refugees

Armed conflicts continue to displace large numbers of persons. There were reportedly more than 300 armed conflicts in the second half of the twentieth century, involving a proliferation of state and non-state actors, causing around 100 million deaths and countless millions of refugees and displaced persons. At least 300,000 people have been killed in Darfur since the conflict erupted in 2003.[15] In Europe in 2010, around 20 per cent of asylum applicants came from just three countries in conflict: Afghanistan, Iraq and Somalia.[16] The roots of the conflicts vary, with many, albeit not all, stemming from causes (including ethnic and religious divisions) which are refugee-generating according to the 1951 Convention and/or the regional refugee instruments, notably the 1969 OAU Refugee Convention.

While doctrinally the Convention should apply in such contexts, in practice it serves more as an aspirational basis for extending protection than the blueprint for what is needed. It is certainly not a good camp management tool, beyond its non-derogable provisions. What is implementable will be much more a product of exigencies on the ground than the letter of the law. In such situations there is a need to complement the Convention framework with additional approaches better tailored to mass arrivals and the complexities thereof.

The sheer size of the outflow is one such complexity. It can make individualised identification of refugee status and the grant of all the rights envisaged in the Convention purely impractical, at least in the first instance. Another issue is that the daunting task of creating a measure of physical security for refugees, as well as for the humanitarian staff, can in practice become the overriding protection objective, which renders longer-term, if even reachable, other aspects of protection envisaged in the Convention. Prima facie recognition has become, in effect, one tool employed to circumvent some of the obvious difficulties in applying the more individual-oriented and integration-focused provisions of the Convention, beyond its fundamental protections. As an approach, it has its limits, particularly when it comes to ensuring the civilian character of camps or when complicated issues of status come to the fore, like exclusion or cessation. A bridge certainly needs, in my view, to be built between prima facie recognition of refugee status and the Convention regime. The UNHCR is looking at this.

The Convention's absence of burden-sharing provisions is a clear liability when it comes to mass influx. A recently released World Bank 'World Development Report 2011 Background Note' looks at the burdens and opportunities for host states of significant refugee influxes.[17] The report records that the largest percentage of refugees (75.19) is found in countries neighbouring their country of origin, more often than not in fragile or low-income countries, or housed in low-income and fragile border regions, where the economic, social, political and environmental impacts hit hardest.[18] Some of these host states (like Pakistan, Chad, Yemen or Jordan) are struggling not only with refugee influxes, but also with sub-national conflicts of their own. Some also have large IDP populations to contend with (Pakistan, Sudan, Kenya, Chad and Yemen). Often, lack of accountable and responsive governance and rule-of-law structures, particularly at the local level, is also a feature.

In such circumstances, competition between refugees and local citizens for scarce resources such as water, food and housing can become fierce. Similarly the competing demands on education, health and infrastructure services such as water supply, sanitation and transportation and, in some cases, natural resources such as firewood or grazing land, can heighten social tensions to breaking point. This becomes more likely the longer the situation drags on.

These facts are a part of the particular and telling context for refugee protection in large-scale influxes. Burdens and responsibilities are not well shared at all. In spite of the fact that the 1951 Convention is predicated on international solidarity and sharing responsibilities to balance the burdens, the absence of clear parameters for burden-sharing is a serious gap in the Convention architecture. There have been several tentative, but ultimately shelved, attempts to articulate general benchmarks. This does not have to mean new instruments. Practical arrangements which offer some dependability would be a real advance. Certainly the Convention needs buttressing in this regard.

The third situation: drivers of forced displacement other than persecution and violence

There is a high probability that patterns of forced displacement will be increasingly impacted by environmental factors such as population growth, declining resources and inequality of access to them, together also with ecological damage and climate change. Natural disasters are forcing more people into displacement inside and outside their countries. Others will be displaced across borders by a combination of factors which leave them very vulnerable, or exacerbate vulnerabilities to the point where flight becomes more feasible than stay.

The legal implications of displacement driven by forces other than persecution, serious human rights violations and ongoing conflict have not been sufficiently examined. The displaced are likely to have many of the same protection needs as Convention refugees as well as different ones – they may, for example, be in a legal limbo situation, having lost identity or land title documents, or worse they may have lost family members and be single women heading households, or unaccompanied children. Vulnerability to sexual or gender-based violence may be high, including high risks of trafficking of persons.

In spite of such protection needs, the Convention at least as it currently stands, is unlikely to be applicable or applied. Nor should it necessarily have to be. There are instruments other than the Convention which offer greater potential here. As refugee law academic, Guy Goodwin Gill has recently observed:

> If the concept of international protection might once have been perceived as merely another form of consular or diplomatic protection, limited to one closely confined category of border crossers, today its roots are securely locked into an international law framework which is still evolving. This encompasses refugee law, human rights law, aspects of international humanitarian law, and elementary considerations of humanity.[19]

While there is an impressive body of jurisprudence being built up by entities such as the European Court of Human Rights, or the UN Committee Against Torture (CAT), around for example the *non-refoulement* or non-expulsion provisions of the human rights conventions, it is fair to say coverage is still partial. This increasingly interconnected web of international law is both complicated and sometimes contradictory. The challenge remains to weave it into a coherent and complementary body of protections.

It is, however, far from easy to identify the exact unifying threads. At the risk of causing the international law purists some discomfort, I suggest that one that bears looking at in this connection is the principle of asylum. There is a continuing ambiguity in the relationship between Convention refugee status and asylum. They are not one and the same thing. It is true that within the international law framework of the 1951 Convention, asylum has closely accompanied the granting of refugee status, with the content of asylum tending to be most closely attuned to the circumstances and needs of Convention refugees. However, asylum is also one of the responses suitable to situations which do not fit the classical refugee paradigm, and which involve the need for protection of temporary duration. This has been partially recognised, particularly in Europe, through subsidiary protection arrangements, but also through discretionary provisions of various sorts in the immigration laws of a number of countries outside this region.

Big immigration countries like the US, Canada and Australia are in fact at this moment discussing, with their European counterparts, to which 'emergent scenarios immigration systems must be prepared to respond'.[20] They are posing for analysis such questions as: should a government open its borders to people fleeing a country devastated by disaster, natural or otherwise? If so, then how should a state identify which group of individuals requires additional aid or protection? What categories of aid or protection should a state provide? The questions continue, embracing such issues as whether the aid and protection can be provided by a state outside its territory? The overall issue for the concerned states is framed in part as 'defining the limits of what an immigration system can/ should reasonably do in response to crises' or 'scenarios where migration is one aspect of more complicated problems'.[21] A priority from the state perspective is stated to be preserving the integrity of immigration services during crisis response, but with a focus on response, not denial.

I see such a discussion as being warranted and very timely. Seriously at-risk persons fleeing devastation and disaster do not, yet at least, have a generally recognised right to cross international borders to seek safety until the threat in their home country has passed. This despite the right to leave any country.[22] Human rights law may be applicable in some situations, but the fact that such temporary protection has not yet achieved broad international endorsement in legal form – as part of the growing fabric of asylum-based responses to interim needs – is a gap both of law and practice. In our assessment the time has come to work with states to develop an internationally agreed doctrine of temporary protection, which would ensure the availability of interim protection to people in temporary need. The beneficiaries must, in the first instance, be made more precise. They could even include, for example, persons who leave situations which constitute the aftermath, but not the continuation, of refugee-producing situations, where the transitional period is nevertheless still uncertain. For temporary protection to be meaningful in this context, clearer guidance is certainly needed on how and when a temporary protection situation may be declared, what rights it should entail, how to terminate it, and when to conclude that return should or should not be pursued. The indicators of safety have to be made more precise, and the role of voluntariness as an aspect of return in temporary protection situations needs to be better defined. Such guidelines might even take binding form, at some point, through an instrument on temporary protection.[23]

The fourth situation: mixed flows including migrants

Asylum seekers with justified claims often move together with persons who make no claims to refugee protection, or where they do, on grounds which do not substantiate the claim.

Turning to the migrant element first, while economic push factors can be compelling in themselves, by and large (cumulative and persecutory deprivations aside), they were never intended to be addressed through refugee protection mechanisms, and certainly not the 1951 Convention. It seems obvious, but is worth stressing nevertheless, that this is not a failing of the Convention, which cannot be held responsible for states' incapacity to effectively manage irregular migration. The Convention does impact on the sovereign right to regulate borders, but only with a view to introducing a needed exception for a defined category of persons. Its purpose was not broader.

It requires no great leap of the imagination to understand why there are so many irregular migrants in today's world. The 2010 Human Development report contains a wealth of interesting statistical data. It concludes that:

> People around the world have experienced dramatic improvements in some key aspects of their lives. They are healthier, more educated and wealthier and have greater power to select their leaders than at any other time in history. But the pace of progress is highly variable and people in some countries and regions have experienced far slower improvements. Stark inequalities and vulnerabilities remain and are increasing in many places, giving rise to – and reflecting – acute power imbalances.[24]

Events in the Middle East at the moment certainly bear this out.

More specifically, the Report draws attention to some telling facts:

- a significant aggregate progress in health, education and income is qualified by high and persistent inequality, unsustainable production patterns and disempowerment of large groups of people around the world[25]
- an estimated one third of the population in 104 developing countries, or approx 1.75 billion people, experience multi-dimensional poverty[26]
- international, inter-group and interpersonal inequalities remain huge in all dimensions of well being, and income disparities are on the rise[27]

The plight of migrants in humanitarian need can be particularly dire. This can include the so-called 'stranded migrants' of which we have seen so many recently, as a result of the events in Libya – witness the mass exodus of migrant workers from Bangladesh, Egypt, Chad or Ghana for example – and the humanitarian rescue operation. But the turmoil in the region is presenting the international community with quite a mosaic of challenges going beyond returning the stranded migrants. There were at one point close to 5,000 Tunisians on the southern Italian island of Lampedusa, in a one-to-one ratio with the local population.[28] Most said that they had come to look for employment. The 25,000 persons, many of them Tunisians, who are known to have come to or through Italy, and who are now comprising a stream of irregular onward movers into France and beyond, could well lead to partial unravelling of hitherto sacrosanct EU innovations, such as free movement under the Schengen arrangements.

The 1951 Convention is obviously not the answer here. In fact, with the Italian authorities having initially designated many of the new arrivals as asylum seekers, had it continued, this could have served to undermine the integrity of asylum in Italy.

Adam Smith advocated 'the ability to go without shame'.[29] UNHCR has promoted for some time now a more imaginative approach to accessible migration channels as an alternative to unduly stretching international instruments to accommodate short- or medium-term socio-economic stresses. The link between easing the strain on asylum systems and the creation of more accessible temporary migration channels is obvious. Iran has begun to use it to positive effect with Afghan migrant arrivals. Thailand and Malaysia have unmet labour needs which irregular migrants already help to meet and putting this on a more regular footing would reduce the risk of exploitation which currently is quite high. Whatever ideas are explored, innovative thinking is called for which stimulates development of migration opportunities.

Mixed flows by definition include not only regular migrants, but also others who may have compelling protection needs of various sorts, refugee-related or not. Migration as a so-called 'fourth solution' in refugee situations is, incidentally, an approach we are advocating to address some protracted situations of displacement. More generally, and in recognition of the fact that refugees and non-refugees do resort to the same route and means of departure. UNHCR developed and has been actively promoting use of its '10-Point Plan of Action on Refugee Protection and Mixed Migration'. The plan, conceived of as a planning and management tool, has found wide favour globally with governments and intergovernmental and non-governmental entities, and is increasingly resorted to. The goal of the plan, simply put, is to ensure: (a) that different protection needs, if any, are identified and addressed in the way most appropriate to the needs; (b) that those who do not have protection concerns are assisted to return home; and (c) that all people are treated with dignity while appropriate solutions are found.

The plan has found a particular use in mixed flow situations which have regional dimensions, impacting several countries. The South-East Asian region is one area where regional approaches are starting to be more actively explored, including through the colloquially entitled 'Bali Process', led with some resolution by Indonesia and Australia. The countries in the region are now more accepting of the fact that the diversity of national responses to mixed flows has become part of the problem in itself, in that it has distorted the push-and-pull factors influencing the choices of the people moving and has facilitated their exploitation by people smugglers and human traffickers. From UNHCR's particular perspective, this has also meant instability and unpredictability for protection delivery and in the realisation of longer-term solutions for the persons of our concern. Hence the organisation has been prepared to work cooperatively with efforts now under way to complement and embed national and bilateral responses within a regional approach which takes careful cognisance of the 10-Point Plan framework. For example, it is currently looking at how regional protection mechanisms which contribute to capacity building and ensure better burden-sharing for solutions, as well as facilitate returns, might be developed as a complement to national asylum systems. These would relieve some of the pressures or distortions of push-and-pull factors and secondary movement, which is particularly of interest where people-smuggling and human trafficking have compromised the capacity of national systems to fully perform.

Conclusions

I used to argue that there is no real difference between the refugee problem and the asylum problem which would justify some of the distinctions being made in Europe and elsewhere. The argument went that a refugee is a refugee whether she is present as part of a mass influx into a neighbouring country or whether she presents her claim for recognition after irregular entry into a chosen state further afield. It is only double standards that drive a policy which becomes more generous and sensitive to refugee protection needs the further away these needs are able to be addressed, and that to locate the response to refugee influxes in the foreign affairs portfolio and the response to asylum arrivals in the immigration or interior portfolio was at best ingenuous.

Intellectually, this is of course a legitimate way to reason. However, I believe that, increasingly, there is an argument to be made that protecting the persecuted and dealing with asylum dilemmas are tasks which, in some important respects, may have to proceed on common foundations but somewhat different tracks.

At the risk of oversimplifying the analysis, when a problem is genuinely one of refugee protection, protection responsibilities are a given and the challenge is not whether but how to deliver upon them, particularly against the backdrop of large-scale displacement situations and unequal distributions of burdens. The asylum problem is becoming a subset of more nuanced issues within the refugee problem broadly defined. In essence the challenge is to determine to whom protection is owed, with what content, for how long and in what circumstances.[30] This is more complicated than it used to be against the realities of mixed asylum and migration flows, the spectre of environmentally driven displacement on the rise, and with the international environment increasingly unpredictable and insecure.

The conclusion I then reach is that it would be irresponsible not to review the role of the 1951 Convention, to recognise and reaffirm its enduring strengths but also to buttress it when it comes to the 'refugee problem' in all its dimensions, where these are understood to include asylum–migration nexus issues and new drivers of displacement. This is not, at all, to argue against the centrality of the Convention. It is though to suggest it needs to be built upon, even legally.

In a pertinent comment, and in his personal capacity, the former Legal Adviser to the British Foreign Office, Daniel Bethlehem recently observed: 'We the international legal community need to have a clear vision of international society [as well as] the role that the law can and should play in shaping that society in ways that will be most conducive to its peaceful and productive development.'[31] Are we, he asks, 'seeing the world in sufficiently non-parochial terms to allow us to take comfort that we are seeing the challenges sufficiently clearly, or indeed at all'.[32] Any review of the international legal system and its adequacy to meet new challenges should particularly be shaped by, among other considerations: the international environment with all its now shared spaces and global commons; the movement of people and the economic flows as well as the civic and social integration that goes with this; the challenges to human, animal and plant life and health, and to global food security that comes from a growing interdependent world; and the challenges and opportunities of technological and cyber systems.

Close to 33 years ago the General Assembly was invited to reconsider, when the time would be ripe, the reconvening of the Conference on Territorial Asylum. Perhaps the time has arrived.

Notes

1 An earlier version of this chapter was made as a speech to the Chatham House International Law Discussion Group on 24 March 2011.
2 Ed West, 'It's not the Home Office's fault – the UN Convention on Refugees is not fit for purpose', *The Telegraph*, 11 January 2011.
3 Convention relating to the Status of Refugees, Geneva, 28 July 1951, 1989 UNTS 137, supplemented by the Protocol relating to the Status of Refugees, 31 January 1967, 19 UST 6223, 6257 ('1951 Refugee Convention').
4 Above n. 2.
5 Scott Morrison, 'A real solution: an international, regional and domestic approach to asylum policy' (speech to the Lowey Institute, Sydney, 30 November 2010).
6 Klaus Neumann, 'Whatever happened to the right of asylum' (address to the Law and History Conference, Melbourne, 13 December 2010).
7 Morrison, above n. 5.
8 The words 'International Protection' are to be understood as referring to all activities designed to improve the physical security of refugee and guarantee to them the enjoyment of their fundamental rights within a framework where these basic rights are both accessible and respected by the authorities, pending the realization of a durable solution and restoration of national protection.
9 *UNHCR Global Trends 2012* <www.unhcr.org/51bacb0f9.html> (accessed 9 December 2013).
10 United Nations High Commissioner for Refugees, 'UNHCR promotes innovation and self-sufficiency at annual NGO meet' (3 July 2012) <www.unhcr.org/4ff300320.html> (accessed 9 December 2013).
11 African Union for the Protection and Assistance of Internally Displaced Persons in Africa (adopted by the Special Summit of the Union held in Kampala, Uganda, 22 October 2009) ('Kampala Convention') .
12 Seventeen states have acceded to one or both Convention on Statelessness with a total of 26 accessions since the beginning of 2011, 14 to the 1961 Convention on the Reduction of Statelessness and 12 to the 1954 Convention relating to the Status of Stateless Persons. For further information relating to statelessness, see UNHCR website: <www.unhcr.org/pages/49c3646c155.html> (accessed 9 December 2013).
13 Alice Edwards, Back to Basics: *The Right to Liberty and Security of Person and 'Alternatives to Detention' of Refugees, Asylum-Seekers, Stateless Persons and Other Migrants* (PPLA/2011/01. Rev.1) <www.unhcr.org/refworld/docid/4dc935fd2.html> (accessed 9 December 2013); United Nations High Commissioner for Refugees, Global Roundtable on Alternatives to Detention of Asylum-Seekers, Refugees, Migrants and Stateless Persons: Summary Conclusions, July 2011 <www.unhcr.org/refworld/docid/4e315b882.html> (accessed 9 December 2013).
14 Patricia Mallia, 'Case of *MSS* v. *Belgium and Greece*: A Catalyst in the Re-thinking of the Dublin II Regulation' (2011) 30 *Refugee Survey Quarterly* 3,108.
15 American Free Press (AFP), 'Darfur security improving, says UN', AFP (online) 20 January 2011 <www.google.com/hostednews/afp/article/ALeqM5gq98Pe059PiiJ67UaAoJvyag1ptg?docId=CNG.3ea14670ae7810525482e4f34288f079.211> (accessed 9 December 2013).

16 United Nations High Commissioner for Refugees, 'Asylum Levels and Trends in Industrialised Countries 2009' (Division of Programme Support and Management, 23 March 2010) <www.unhcr.org/4ba7341a9.html> (accessed 9 December 2013).

17 Margarita Puerto Gomez and Asger Christensen, 'The Impacts of Refugees on Neighboring Countries: A Development Challenge' (World Development Report 2011 Background Note, World Bank, 29 July 2010).

18 Ibid., 3.

19 Guy Goodwin-Gill, High Commissioner's Dialogue on Protection Challenges, 2 December 2010.

20 See overall the Theme Paper for the 2010 IGC Full Round, Miami, May 2010.

21 Ibid.

22 Universal Declaration of Human Rights 1948, Art. 13(2).

23 See for discussion on possible template for temporary protection UNHCR, Discussion Paper, Roundtable on Temporary Protection, 19–20 July 2012 (International Institute of Humanitarian Law, San Remo, Italy) <www.refworld.org/pdfid/506d8ff02.pdf> (accessed 9 December 2013).

24 United Nations Development Programme, *Human Development Report 2010* (UNDP, 2010), 118.

25 Ibid., 85.

26 Ibid., 86.

27 Ibid.,101.

28 UN News Centre, 'UN calls Italy to ensure better conditions for Tunisian migrants on Italian Island' (22 March 2011) <www.un.org/apps/news/story.asp?NewsID=37849&Cr=tunisia&Cr1=#.Ua6inhp--M8> (accessed 9 December 2013).

29 Adam Smith quoted in Amartya Sen, 'Social Exclusion: Concept, Application, and Scrutiny' (Social Development Papers No. 1, Office of Environment and Social Development, Asian Development Bank, June 2000), 10 <http://housingforall.org/Social_exclusion.pdf> (accessed 9 December 2013).

30 See, e.g., presentation by Alice Edwards, Senior Legal Coordinator and Chief, Protection Policy and Legal Advice Section, Division of International Protection, UNHCR, to the Workshop on Refugees and the Refugee Convention 60 Years On: Protection and Identity, Prato, 2 May 2011, entitled: 'Rethinking the right to asylum and the notion of temporary protection', which examined the legal basis, if any, for derogating from 1951 Convention obligations in mass influx situations.

31 Daniel Bethlehem, 'The end of geography' (Comments on the Keynote Address at the Biennial Conference of the European Society of International Law, Cambridge, 2–4 September 2010).

32 Ibid.

Part II

Refugee identities and protection: historical shifts

5 Shifting conceptions of refugee identity and protection: European and Middle Eastern Approaches

Dallal Stevens

Introduction

No analysis of contemporary refugee protection and identity should take place without consideration of historical perspectives. An understanding of historical (and religious) antecedents is crucial to appreciate fully some of the key questions of this volume: who is a 'refugee'; how that label influences state behaviour towards those seeking asylum; and the broader implications for refugee identity and protection. This chapter has two aims: (a) to provide a foundation for subsequent contributions in this collection and to highlight some of the major concerns with both the Refugee Convention and the framework for international protection in the twenty-first century; and (b) to focus on the Middle East, where the majority of states are not party to the Refugee Convention or Protocol, but which currently hosts millions of displaced people. The discussion opens with a consideration of the Refugee Convention and its Protocol ('the Refugee Convention')[1] in their historical contexts, briefly describing the change from group-based to individual protection, the emergence of a legal identity of the refugee, and the subsequent shifts in conceptualisation of both refugee protection and refugee identity that have occurred in the past 60 years. The importance of the UNHCR in this development is highlighted. The chapter then moves on to the second, and main part, and addresses the historical context of forced migration in the Middle East, before exploring the current problems associated with law, refugee identity and protection in the region.

Identity and protection: the European model

Legal identity of the refugee

While refugee movements and the provision of protection by individual countries has a long history, the twentieth century is the most significant period in terms of interstate cooperation.[2] The flight of so many peoples in the early part of the twentieth century, Greeks, Turks, Armenians and victims of the First World War, together with a rather restrictive approach to immigration, forced the hand of states (loosely termed the 'international community') to support a framework aimed at assisting refugees. The League of Nations, founded in 1919, assumed responsibility for fulfilling the aspiration of an international refugee regime. Then, as now, the make-up of such a regime was of paramount importance. Skran, in her influential book, *Refugees in Interwar Europe*, argues that an international regime 'consists of four major elements: principles, norms, rules, and decision-making procedures'.[3] These are broken down variously to: sovereignty and humanitarianism (principles); asylum, assistance and burden-sharing (norms); rules in the form of international conventions; and the League of Nations as a forum for state decision making.[1] These four elements continue to be relevant today. In relation to the last, the role of agencies was crucial. Not only did the League of Nations deal with the different emerging groups of refugees, but the establishment in 1921 of a 'High Commissioner on behalf of the League (of Nations) in connection with the problems of Russian Refugees in Europe', and the subsequent Nansen International Office, proved to be seminal moments in the history of international refugee policy.

From a legal perspective, one of the notable features in the development of international refugee law is the move from a group-based analysis, in the period prior to the Second World War, to an individualised approach incorporated post-war.[5] The focus on groups is manifested most clearly by the definitions of a 'refugee' in the 1933 and 1938 Conventions.[6] The 1933 Convention applied to 'Russian, Armenian and assimilated refugees', while the 1938 Convention concerned 'refugees coming from Germany'.[7] Under such provisions, the individual was not required to establish his or her claim, since the reasons for flight were largely the basis for defining the group as refugees.[8] This, then, was an early example of the prima facie presumption that individuals within a group were refugees.[9]

Following the Second World War, a more individualised approach to the refugee emerged in the practice of the International Refugee Organisation (IRO) – the UN-created body to oversee the handling of war refugees. Although the IRO's mandate continued to cover certain refugee categories – basically, the pre-war refugees – it also extended to

> any person . . . who is outside his country of nationality or former habitual residence, and who, as a result of events subsequent to the outbreak of the second world war, is unable or unwilling to avail himself of the protection of the Government of his country of nationality or former nationality.[10]

This can be regarded as the first non-group-based definition, or at least a move towards an individualised approach, in the sense that the refugee is not defined by membership of an ethnic group. Jackson argues further that the way in which the IRO functioned under its constitution introduced an aspect of individualisation to the mandate.[11] In order for refugees to become the concern of the IRO, they had to establish that they required the assistance of the Organisation to repatriate or that they expressed 'valid objections' to returning to their countries of nationality of former residence.[12] These individual issues of concern to prevent removal included: persecution for the grounds which were to be adopted in the Refugee Convention,[13] objections of a political nature, compelling family reasons arising from previous persecution, or compelling reasons of infirmity or illness.[14]

The focus on the individual following the Second World War was also reflected by the Preamble to the United Nations Charter 1945 in its emphasis on the 'dignity and worth of the human person', and fully endorsed by the Universal Declaration of Human Rights 1948 (UDHR).[15] It might seem unsurprising, then, that the IRO's hesitant steps towards the individualised character of the refugee were replaced by seemingly confident new phraseology in both the mandate of its successor, the UNHCR, and in the Refugee Convention. Unlike the pre-war instruments, the Convention had no group membership requirement based on nationality,[16] though some do regard the temporal limitation in the original definition as an example of refugee status based on category.[17]

An examination of the records from the Ad Hoc Committee on Statelessness and Related Problems[18] reveal that many state representatives were keen to maintain a definition based on categories rather than a broader, generous approach, favoured by the French expert attending the Committee as being in the spirit of the UDHR.[19] Much of the concern leading up to the final adoption of the refugee definition in the Convention was about the potentially unrestricted nature of a state's future obligations, a disquiet that persists today.[20]

This new, arguably more inclusive legal identity was constrained by an apparently politically constructed definition.[21] Hathaway, for example, argues that 'the two main characteristics of the Convention refugee definition are its strategic conceptualization and its Eurocentric focus'.[22] He refers to the prioritisation of pro-Western political motivations for flight[23] in the definition of a refugee contained in Article 1A(2), which has a seemingly narrow focus on the fear of 'persecution' for civil or political grounds. While intended, in part, to facilitate the admission of dissidents from the USSR, the corollary of this focus was the ostensible exclusion of economic and social rights, resulting in a definition which has been described as adopting 'an incomplete and politically partisan human rights rationale',[24] under which humanitarianism was subjugated to political and economic goals.[25] In so far as the Eurocentric bias is concerned, the *travaux préparatoires* show that, in fact, there was much discussion about non-European refugee issues and, partly to address these, Recommendation E was included in the Final Act of the UN Conference of Plenipotentiaries on the Status of Refugees and Stateless Persons. It urged 'all nations to be guided by [the Convention] in granting . . . to persons in their territory as refugees and who would not be covered by the terms of the Convention, the treatment for which it provides'. It was hoped further that the Convention would have 'value as an example exceeding its contractual scope'.[26]

Recommendation E was aimed at encouraging states to accept refugees who were not covered by the Convention on account of the 1951 dateline or the European geographical limitation; it was not intended to apply to those who did not meet the criterion of well-founded fear of persecution 'but who might nevertheless somehow find themselves in a "refugee-like" situation'.[27] In addition, Article 1B of the Convention enabled states with a more 'universalist' approach to declare the Convention to apply to 'events occurring in Europe *or elsewhere*' (emphasis added). Of course, the adoption of the 1967 Protocol, with its lifting of the temporal and geographic limitations, together with the UNHCR's activities, has encouraged a more inclusive, global definition of the refugee with broader applicability.[28]

The individualised approach to refugee status is undoubtedly a key component of post-1951 legal identity;[29] in the main, the refugee was to be assessed on his or her own merits, not as part of a wider ethnic group.[30] However, it is important to note that during drafting of the Convention, the participants considered that the definition would apply to situations of mass/group flight, and neither war or civil war were treated differently.[31] This approach to groups is demonstrated more obviously in the Statute of the UNHCR, in which it is stated that: 'The work of the High Commissioner ... shall relate, as a rule, to groups and categories of refugees'.[32] Since the Statute also includes a definition of the refugee that is basically the same as that in the Convention, some regard the coexistence of an individualistic definition alongside a mandate that appears group-oriented as an 'apparent contradiction'.[33] Others suggest that the refugee definition applies to mass flight situations if the criteria are met and that 'refugee status might be accorded on a group basis to prima facie refugees, as well as on the basis of individual case review'.[34] It is certainly the case that, to deal with group situations, prima facie group determination has been implemented, usually with the involvement of the UNHCR, and was, according to Jackson, applied regularly when an individual examination of the reasons for departure was not practicable in view of the numbers involved.[35] Recently, Albert has argued that prima facie refugee status determination is not reserved for large-scale arrivals.[36] A further contentious issue has been whether prima facie determination warrants a lower level of protection. The current consensus is that it is a unique procedure giving rise to a unique legal status, and to which certain rights attach.[37] The actual content of these rights is perhaps questionable, though during the Global Consultations in 2001, the Roundtable on International Cooperation to Protect Masses in Flight reported that 'there was a strongly held view that refugees recognised on a *prima facie* basis are entitled to the same rights as refugees recognised under an individual refugees status determination scheme'.[38]

The discussion in this collection shows that legal identity of the refugee has not remained static; rather, it has evolved, and continues to evolve, as a direct consequence of the movement of peoples across borders, whether individually or en masse, and of the changing way in which such movement is perceived by host states. As explained in this chapter, while the UNHCR has, unsurprisingly, enlarged its protective capacity, many states have sought to limit their duty to protect through a variety of policies and mechanisms, including a narrow legal interpretation of who is a 'refugee'. As will be shown in the context of the Middle East, the state–UNHCR relationship has given rise to confusing as well as conflicting identities with uncertainty surrounding how the refugee is being defined – individual, prima facie, state/UNHCR recognised, or beneficiary of temporary protection – with resulting consequences for 'protection'.

Protection

While protection for the 'refugee' is the ultimate objective of the international refugee law regime, as with all the terms included in the Convention, the concept of protection itself was left undefined by the instrument. Grahl-Madsen, writing in 1965, offered the following thoughts on protection:

> The word 'protection' denotes measures of some kind or other taken by a subject of international law in order to safeguard or promote the integrity, rights, or interests of an individual. Protection may take many shapes. We may distinguish between internal protection ('the protection of the Law') and external protection (diplomatic or consular protection etc). Moreover, protection may be active or passive.

While 'lack of protection' was a reason to grant refugee status to pre-Second World War refugees,[39] persecution and lack of protection were not overtly linked in this period.[40] In accordance with the understanding of the time, a refugee 'lacked protection', meaning she or he lacked 'consular and diplomatic protection' – that is, the protection to be given by a state to its subjects or citizens.[11] Grahl-Madsen argues that

> as a person is a refugee because there is something basically wrong with the political relationship between him and the government of his home country, we should not obscure this basic 'ailment' by overemphasising symptoms of the ailment, such as lack of protection, which, like so many other symptoms, are ambivalent.[12]

Indeed, he goes further, claiming that 'the use of the term "unprotected person" also gives rise to certain terminological dangers', and is unprecise'.[13] In his view, the only precise way of describing a refugee is as 'a person who is not being given the protection which a State normally may give its nationals'.[14] Furthermore, defining refugees as 'unprotected persons' takes no account of the modern trend towards alternatives to state protection such as international protection offered by the UNHCR, United Nations Relief and Works Agency (UNRWA) or non-governmental organisations (NGOs).[15]

Contemporary refugee law can be seen to still require this negative approach to protection – that is, there is a need for a *lack* of protection, or to use current terminology, a *failure* of state (of nationality) protection before a finding of persecution and a consequent determination of refugee status. Following Hathaway's definition of persecution as 'the sustained or systemic violation of basic human rights demonstrative of the failure of state protection'[16] and its acceptance by leading courts around the world,[17] establishing whether the home state is able to provide protection – often interpreted as a functioning criminal and judicial system[48] – is a key feature of the refugee's identity (as the object of surrogate protection).[49]

But protection is not simply about its lack or failure. It can also be regarded as a positive obligation of the country of asylum. Indeed, the Convention itself sets out the responsibilities owed by the hosting state towards the refugee, which, while not expressed in the language of protection, as such, are implied as part of the protective function.[50] In addition, the UNHCR Statute introduces a notion of 'international protection' to be provided by the Office, and, as discussed above, its mandate is extensive, extending to both individuals and groups/categories of refugees.[51] A list of activities expected to assist in the provision of 'protection' are set out in Paragraph 8,[52] but these shed little light on the fundamental nature of protection.[53] The UNHCR has over the years furnished Notes on Protection that seek to explain its approach to protection, and the statements by the Director of International Protection (formerly Assistant High Commissioner for Protection) provide further useful elaboration.[54] Arguably, though, while the term 'protection' is widely employed in discussing asylum and refugee issues, there is a lack of a clear or consistent meaning.[55] Often, it is an overarching term to describe simply what is happening on the ground. Protection will vary, depending on the state involved, whether it has entered reservations to the Convention, and whether and to what extent it is fulfilling its legal obligations. As will be evident from the discussion on the Middle East, where the UNHCR is fundamental to the provision of protection, the context will again matter. The space in which the UNHCR is functioning – camps or urban settings – the time-scale – emergency or protracted situation, and the relationship with the host state as well as other NGOs will all play a part in determining the nature of the available protection.

That said, there is perhaps one legal point on which there is almost universal agreement. This relates to the principle of *non-refoulement*, which can be regarded as central to any meaningful notion of protection. The agreement of states – even if only as a result of customary practice[56] – to refrain from returning an asylum seeker to the frontiers of a territory where his or her life or freedom would be threatened ensures that *non-refoulement* is foundational to protection.[57] The reference to *non-refoulement* in the Refugee Convention was not the first time that the concept had appeared in a refugee instrument: Article 3(2) of the 1933 Convention had also incorporated a prohibition against *refoulement*; however, 1951 was the first time that states were prevented from entering a reservation against the Article.[58]

The Refugee Convention clearly provides a legal identity for the refugee. For an individual to be determined to be a 'refugee' in law, she or he must meet the stringent criteria of Article 1A(2). As several chapters in this book reveal, due to decades of somewhat restrictive interpretation of the criteria for refugee status by governments, case officers and the courts, the numbers of people judged to meet the peculiar requirements of the definition are very low, considering the millions of displaced people in the world. This has implications not only for refugee identity itself but also for the meaning of protection. Paradoxically, at the same time as there has been a retrenchment in individual refugee status grants under the Refugee Convention in many states, a willingness over the years to maintain open borders in mass influx situations has resulted in greater protection for large groups of people in certain regions of the world; the Middle East, to which we next turn, is one such region.

Identity and protection: the Middle Eastern model

The chapter now examines how the identity and protection of refugees are understood in the Middle East, with a particular focus on the countries of the Levant. To appreciate the current approach to these issues, it is essential to place them in context. A brief analysis of the history of displacement and forced migration in the region is therefore undertaken before proceeding to consider refugee identity, and the different approaches adopted by a number of countries. The chapter concludes with an examination of some of the implications for protection that arise from the complex and conflicting identities within the region.

The historical context

At the outset, it is important to recognise that the term 'Middle East' is, in fact, somewhat contentious, due to its apparent British origins,[59] and to the fact that the area defined as the Middle East is open to debate. The traditional definition includes Egypt to the west, the Arab peninsula, the countries of the Levant,[60] Israel, Turkey, Cyprus, and Iran to the east, while the Greater Middle East incorporates Mauritania and Arab-speaking North African states, as well as Afghanistan and Pakistan. Some commentators exclude Cyprus, preferring an Islamic linkage between states in the region. For the purposes of this discussion, when addressing historical migrations, the definition of the Middle East encompasses the territory controlled by the Ottoman Empire at the peak of its power and prior to twentieth-century state construction; the modern-day analysis focuses largely on those countries of the Levant that have experienced particularly high levels of refugee arrivals in the past 60 years, namely Syria, Jordan and Lebanon.

The history of the Middle East, however defined, is one of conflict, enormous upheaval and mass movement of peoples, and a basic understanding of the historical roots of displacement is crucial when exploring centuries of forced migration in the region. Events in the nineteenth century are particularly relevant. In her study on the subject, *Displacement and Dispossession in the Modern Middle East*,[61] Dawn Chatty provides an illuminating account of the causes and extent of displacement in the Ottoman Empire from the mid-nineteenth century onwards.[62] While the (contentious) history of Armenian massacres in the late nineteenth century and early twentieth century is well known, in which it is claimed that between 1.5 to 2 million people were uprooted,[63] and anywhere between 600,000 to 1.2 million died,[64] widespread ethnic or religious cleansing or the so-called 'unmixing of peoples'[65] undertaken in the same period is less familiar. Yet, here too, in the eighteenth and nineteenth centuries, we find numerous accounts of the forced migration of hundreds of thousands of people.[66] Many of those driven to make the long marches in search of safety died of disease or starvation. It is claimed that 27 per cent of the Muslim population of Ottoman Europe were forced to move as a result of the Balkan Wars,[67] while 500,000 perished on the route from the Caucasus to Anatolia. And this is only a snapshot of the many migrations and re-migrations that occurred in the region over a relatively short period of history.

How were these migration movements handled? At the time, pre-League of Nations, the international political community was unwilling to address these crises in a coordinated manner, though international aid did reach the territory. Rather, as expected at the time, the host state was often left to fend for itself. As a result of the severe deprivation of those reaching Ottoman territory, the 'potential instability permeating the makeshift refugee camps',[68] as well as the localised nature of assistance and resettlement, the Ottoman government sought new ways to deal with the influx on a centralised basis.[69] One such intervention was the promulgation of the Refugee Code (*Muhacirin Kanunnamesi*) in 1857 which stipulated that immigrants with little capital were provided with plots of land and exempted from taxes and conscription for six years, if they settled in Rumelia, and for 12 years, if they settled in Anatolia.[70] They also had to agree to cultivate the land, not to sell it or leave for 20 years, and to become subjects of the Sultan.[71] Some were free to practise their religion, and permitted to build churches.[72] This new tolerance and offer of support led to an increase in arrivals, especially once persecution of Muslims started in earnest following the Crimean War. As a consequence, the Ottoman government established a special Refugee Commission in 1860 to process the applications for land and settlement.[73] In 1877, on resumption of the flows of peoples from the Balkans and the Caucasus, a new Commission had to be established,[74] followed by another in 1893.[75] While the Refugee Commission was concerned with settlement issues, a second body – the Charity Commission – was set up to collect and distribute aid, provide healthcare, and find employment for both Muslims and Christians reaching Istanbul.[76] The Sultan's view was that such charity and hospitality were a religious obligation: since those arriving were, in the main, 'destitute and in need of charity and mercy and had taken refuge here because of the enemy's aggression on their lands, it was essential for the entire population of Istanbul to fulfil their [Islamic] obligations of hospitality and protection as already evident in the willingness of everybody to aid the immigrants'.[77]

Though the Sultan's opinion was clear, the increasing numbers of arrivals, and consequent pressures on the Commission, resulted in the late 1880s in the inevitable debate on what to do about the unrelenting rise in immigration. Some preferred Muslims from the Caucasus and Balkans to remain where they were; others perceived a military advantage in encouraging Muslims to Ottoman lands and into the army, thereby enhancing Ottoman power against the European enemy. A further argument was forwarded, based on Islamic principles, 'that any Muslim who did not want to live under non-Muslim rule should be allowed to immigrate and settle on Muslim lands and be accepted and cared for'.[78] In the end, it was decided that Muslims who desired to leave their countries and settle in Ottoman territory should be welcomed. While this might be seen as highly altruistic behaviour on the part of the Ottoman government, based on moral or religious principle, Kemal Karpat suggests that the chief reason that the government encouraged inward migration was 'the fear that the Muslims under foreign rule might be conscripted into the army and forced to fight against their Muslim brethren (as already done by Russia)'.[79] Migration policy eventually became instrumental in supporting the government's Islamist agenda.[80]

A number of important points emerge from this brief overview: forced migration in the Middle East is of long-standing, involving huge numbers of people of different races and religions moving across vast spaces. The region has substantial experience in handling large-scale movements of people, and the Ottoman Empire sought to integrate and support new arrivals through a centralised policy and specially established body, a development that might be described as a nascent refugee/immigration regime. Generous migration policies were, in the early stages, underpinned by the Islamic principles of asylum and hospitality and despite the Islamic principle of asylum, refugee/migration policy became somewhat politicised and a tool of government policy. It is clear that the often brutal causes of the inward migration to the Ottoman lands helped to foster an emergent Muslim identity, which superseded any identity as 'refugee'. The extent to which this changed in the twentieth century is now considered.

Refugee identity in the Arab world

With such a history, one might have expected the Middle Eastern states of the reconstituted Ottoman Empire to have been enthusiastic proponents of an international law of asylum and refuge. This has not been the case. Surprisingly few Arab states are party to the 1951 Refugee Convention, and, those that have acceded are in Africa, with the exception of Yemen, Turkey[81] and Israel. Why is this? Various explanations have been proffered. It has been suggested that the Refugee Convention ignored the traditions, laws and values relating to asylum and forced migration in other parts of the world and very few Muslim states participated in the drafting.[82] Yet, it is the case that representatives from Egypt, Iraq, Turkey and Iran were present at the Conference of Plenipotentiaries and participated in discussions; Israel, too, was represented. Others have stressed that, at the time of drafting, Arab states were concerned about how Palestinian refugees were to be dealt with under the Convention and feared that they 'would become submerged and . . . relegated to a position of minor importance',[83] weakening their 'separate and special status'.[84] It is often argued that Arab States were anxious to ensure that Palestinian refugees were not subjected to the prevailing norm – resettlement – but would be guaranteed repatriation and compensation as specified in international law and in line with the refugees' own wishes.[85] Even when the desired Article 1D was included in the Convention, Arab States did not accede, except those states, such as Egypt and Yemen, in which UNRWA was not operating.[86]

It is perhaps unsurprising, then, that so many Muslim states have resisted signing the Refugee Convention or Protocol because of their ongoing frustration with the international community for the failure to implement numerous UN General Assembly resolutions on the right of return for Palestinian refugees.[87] Alongside the unresolved issue of finding a durable solution for Palestinians, recent studies point to a number of reasons for the continuing refusal to sign: national opposition to refugee integration; concern about resources and implications for the host population; inaccurate information on the economic and social burden of refugees on the host state; national security fears; and uncertainty about the obligations that come with the Convention or Protocol.[88] It has also been maintained that there is 'deep-seated ambivalence in the region towards refugees and their international rights',[89] which is rather harsh in view of the numbers of refugees admitted to the states' territories, particularly in recent years.

Although unwilling to commit to the Refugee Convention, many Arab states have ratified the major international human rights instruments.[90] And, constitutionally, they appear deeply committed to the principles of international human rights law, as in the case of the Lebanese Constitution.[91] Furthermore, under the auspices of either the Arab League or the Organisation of the Islamic Conference, Arab and Islamic states have, over the years, made their own provision for asylum seekers and refugees, for example: Article 9 of the 1981 Universal Islamic Declaration on Human Rights;[92] Article 12 of the 1990 Cairo Declaration on Human Rights in Islam;[93] the 1992 Cairo Declaration on Protection of Refugees and Displaced Peoples;[94] the 1994 Arab Convention on Regulating Status of Refugees in the Arab Countries;[95] and the 2003 Resolution on the Problem of Refugees in the Muslim World.[96] But even these have failed to have much impact, with limited ratifications where required, and a general apathy towards implementation. Well-meaning though these initiatives might be, lack of realisation begs the question: why draft and sign such instruments in the first place?

The record on national law is similar to that on international law. Few Middle Eastern countries have formal domestic refugee legislation or asylum processes in place.[97] Both signatory and non-signatory states are often reliant on the UNHCR to conduct registration, documentation and refugee status determination (RSD), and to provide assistance as well as seek durable solutions.[98] As Kagan has rightly noted, the burden on the UNHCR is immense, with serious implications for protection.[99] Even where a state is committed to international refugee law, there might be an inclination to enter a number of reservations to the Convention and Protocol, watering down their impact.[100] For example, past calls in Jordan by human rights researchers for accession to the Convention/Protocol have suggested the possibility of reservations.[101] Though recognising the controversial nature of such a proposal, the researchers felt that it was 'a necessary evil' and included it 'for purely pragmatic ends, in order to deny the government its argument against signing based on national interest'.[102] Israel, which is party to the Convention, has yet to incorporate it into national law and to introduce formal refugee legislation.

It relies instead on secondary legislation in the form of regulations.[103] That said, national statutes are not all devoid of any reference to asylum or refugees. Both the 1952 Jordanian Constitution and the 1973 Syrian Constitution, for example, contain provisions barring extradition of political refugees,[104] though the term 'political refugees' is not defined, while the Lebanese Constitution of 1926 (as amended) asserts Lebanon's commitment to the international Covenants and to the UDHR and promises to uphold their principles in all areas and without exception – thereby committing itself to Article 14, UDHR and the right to seek asylum.[105]

Nonetheless, the tendency of Arab states is to rely on immigration laws to monitor entry and exit of all, and to include reference to refugees within such legislation. Thus, in Jordan, Law No. 24 of 1973 on Residence and Foreigners' Affairs states vaguely that the Law does not apply to 'Persons exempted by the Minister on account of special consideration connected with international and humanitarian courtesy or of the right to political asylum or yet in application of the principle of reciprocity'.[106] But, in reality, little reference is made to Law No. 24 in relation to asylum. Rather, those seeking a safe haven are admitted, usually temporarily. Like Jordan, Syria has no asylum law and relies on immigration law to control entry.[107] Though the same approach is employed in Lebanon, with an immigration law of its own – Law Regulating the Entry and Stay of Foreigners in Lebanon and their Exit from the Country (Law of Entry and Exit) – the legislation does include specific measures relating to asylum, six Articles in fact.[108] Thus, Article 26 states that 'Every foreigner who is persecuted or sentenced for a political crime outside Lebanon, or whose life or liberty is threatened on account of political activity, may apply for asylum in Lebanon.'[109] The Law also provides for *non-refoulement* of a former political refugee.[110] Unusually in the region, a process for making asylum decisions is outlined in the Law: the authority to grant asylum rests with a committee composed of the Minister of Interior, the Directors of the Ministries of Justice, Foreign Affairs and General Security. Their decision is final and cannot be appealed, even in the case of abuse of power.[111] Political asylum by this method has, however, only been granted once,[112] and the provisions on asylum are in reality redundant. Lebanon, like Jordan, Syria and Egypt, has adopted alternative practices, discussed below.

Conflicting and complex identities

It is evident that refugee identity in the Middle East is complex. First, the association of 'refugee' with Palestinian is strong in Arab countries and has a bearing on the states' approach to displacement, particularly in the Levant. A number of countries/territories in the region have hosted displaced Palestinians since 1948: Syria, Jordan, Lebanon, Egypt, Iraq, the Gulf States, the West Bank and the Gaza Strip.[113] The experience of Palestinians in the different states is varied – from the offer of citizenship to all refugees and their descendants in Jordan to considerable marginalisation in Lebanon.[114] But the impact for all, including states, has been significant and has undoubtedly affected the perception of both 'refugee' identity in the region and the role of the United Nations in assisting host states. As indicated, the protracted Palestinian issue is often cited as a reason for continued refusal to sign the Refugee Convention/Protocol. However, this excuse might now be wearing a little thin, particularly in a country like Jordan where most Palestinians have Jordanian citizenship, and are therefore excluded under Article 1(C) of the Refugee Convention (as well as by Article 1D). Palestinians, therefore, assume multiple identities – they are, *inter alia*, Arab, Palestinian, Muslim, Christian, refugee and sometimes citizen.

Despite the uncertainty surrounding domestic or international asylum and refugee law in many countries in the Middle East, non-Palestinian asylum seekers and refugees have not been turned away at the borders. There are two main reasons for this: law and religion. As discussed above, notwithstanding the association of 'refugee' with Palestinian, a number of countries do make provision for 'political refugees' in their constitutions or national laws on the treatment of foreigners.[115] They may have memoranda of understanding signed with the UNHCR, which will apply the refugee definition of the Convention if assigned responsibility for refugee status determination.[116] A fascinating example is provided by the Iraqis who fled the first and second Gulf Wars in 1991 and 2003 and were processed in Jordan under visa and residency laws; once admitted, they were subjected to different treatment – they were often granted entry on temporary visas only and care was taken by politicians and by the press alike to distinguish them from Palestinians by referring to them as 'guests'. This despite many registering with the UNHCR, and being considered 'asylum seekers' until individual refugee status determination was conducted by the Office.[117] Interestingly, certainly in the early days of the migration, Iraqis preferred to be seen as guests, since they too associated the 'refugee' nomenclature with a particular form of refugeehood – that of Palestinian hardship and victimhood. So, non-Palestinians have been labelled 'Arab brethren' or 'guests' in preference to 'refugee', and such labelling is not imposed by the state alone, but can be embraced willingly by the exile. Indeed, a number of Iraqis, for example, favoured such terms as *muhajirin* (emigrants), *manfiyin* (the forgotten) or *mughtarabin* (the alienated/exiles) as more representative of their personal histories than the semantically charged word 'refugee'.[118]

The idea of the refugee as guest has deep-seated cultural and religious roots. According to Arafat Madi Shoukri, there are in Islam three terms that are similar to refugee: *mustajīr* (which applies to Muslims and non-Muslims), *muhājir* (which refers to Muslims alone) and *musta'min* ('a loose term that includes all the foreigners who enter the Islamic state looking for protection, whether they are refugees or not, without specifying the reason for their visit'),[119] though it is suggested that *musta'min* is the closest to the legal term 'refugee'.[120] Muslims are expected to take care of the *musta'min* and protect him until he reaches a place of safety; similar to the concept of *non-refoulement*, this implies that he should not be returned to a country or place where his safety would be jeopardised.[121] Some scholars promote the view that the Islamic tradition of offering protection to refugees is wider than the Refugee Convention, for, unlike the Convention, there are no established grounds for seeking refuge; it is for the Islamic state to determine who should be admitted as a refugee.[122] Understanding the Islamic tradition of asylum is an important first step towards appreciating the behaviour of Arab states towards contemporary refugees; states clearly feel an obligation to admit those seeking sanctuary, or *aman*, and to offer temporary protection at the very least. Yet, it is also evident that the underlying religious duty can conflict with the perceived political, economic, social or legal duty.

The power of labelling and the meaning attributed to refugee identity is exemplified by recent events in the Middle East. Often the perception by the UNHCR of who is a refugee comes into conflict with that of the state. For example, in Jordan, the UNHCR's attempts following the second Gulf War to introduce a temporary protection regime for Iraqi 'refugees' ran into difficulties. Jordan claimed that any temporary protection to which it had agreed in its 2003 Letter of Understanding with the UNHCR had very limited application and withdrew it in 2005.[123] Jordan also rejected any application of a prima facie refugee status, arguing that the UNHCR should adhere strictly to the Memorandum of Understanding (MOU).[124] It is understood that the government was concerned that prima facie status, rather than its rather meaningless 'guest status', carried with it an implicit right to protection (that is, a right to remain), even if only temporary. The grant of citizenship to millions of Palestinians has certainly cast a long shadow over Jordanian politics. By contrast, the Syrian government did consent in 2003 to a temporary protection regime, and accepted prima facie status, but, like Jordan, it does not accord any special treatment to asylum seekers/refugees, other than some acceptance of an obligation not to detain or deport.[125]

Recent events in Syria, with the movement of over 2.1 million Syrians across the border to neighbouring countries,[126] appeared to have led to a shift away from the semantic arguments that surrounded the case of the Iraqis. The term 'refugees' seems to have been adopted widely by the press and governments of a number of Arab countries. But this is not universal. Terminology is still highly charged in the region. For example, the non-governmental organisation ALEF – Act for Human Rights, based in Lebanon, recently reported that there was disagreement in the country about the correct expression to be used in relation to Syrians, the outcome being that 'displaced' was preferable to 'refugees', since it was suggestive of a less permanent status.[127] Jordan, too, which, as discussed, insisted upon a guest identity for its Iraqi asylum seekers/refugees, has alternated between 'refugees' and 'guests'. Although 'refugees' is the widely utilised term, there have been occasional lapses: an anonymous official stated to the *Jordan Times* in November 2011 that 'the government does not consider Syrians residing in the Kingdom as refugees, but rather guests who left their country temporarily because of the current unrest there'.[128] Interestingly, once Syrians started to cross the border into Turkey at the end of 2011, Turkish officials also insisted that they were 'guests' and not 'refugees'. Turkey has implemented a temporary protection regime for the Syrian refugees, revealing once more the regional tendency to align refugee status with permanent protection or residence.[129]

Israel, like Turkey, is party to the Refugee Convention. It is the least reliant on the UNHCR of the Middle Eastern countries, being the first to have assumed responsibility for refugee determination. Nonetheless, it, too, has adopted a nuanced approach to who is an asylum seeker or refugee. Faced in the recent past with increased migration from Africa, the Israeli government has implemented a policy according to which Eritreans and Sudanese are not permitted to apply for asylum; instead, they are granted a type of temporary protection based on their nationality.[130] Israel's attitude to asylum, perhaps more than any other country in the region, is heavily influenced by political and security concerns, which has resulted in the introduction of a number of contentious and at times shocking policies: 'hot returns' of asylum seekers/refugees across the Sinai border to Egypt; the building of an enormous fence along the border between Israel and Egypt to keep out would-be entrants; and the construction of large 'open' detention centres in remote desert areas near the Egyptian border to house African asylum seekers. In contrast to neighbouring countries, the Israeli judiciary and legislature are increasingly engaged in battles over the legality of many of these policy initiatives, which ultimately revolve around the question of who is a refugee.[131] So, even in a country founded by refugees, and which is party to the Refugee Convention, refugee identity has become a political construct and is based on notions of the 'good' refugee and the 'bad'.

Protection in the Middle East

Reference has already been made to Islam's concept of asylum. For most countries in the region, Islam is an important link between the past and present, especially with regard to protection; until relatively recently, though, this has been insufficiently acknowledged.[132] The significance of the pre-Islamic traditions of hospitality and sanctuary should not be underestimated, particularly among nomadic Arabs, where guests were welcome and should be granted protection if sought. Generosity and hospitality were fundamental characteristics of the desert inhabitants and they are still regarded as potent values among Arabs.[133] Likewise, it is asserted that protection and asylum were an important aspect of the 'moral ideal' of the desert Arabs.[134] Such concepts found their way into the Islamic doctrines of *hijra* (migration),[135] *ijarah* (asylum), *aman* (safety), *malja* (refuge) and *jiwar* (protection).[136] The Qur'an requires that refugees and migrants be welcomed and treated well, and should not be refused admission, rejected at the borders, or sent back to the country of origin.[137] Arab scholars contend that Islam was in fact first to adopt principles of *non-refoulement* and non-extradition of those who have committed political offences.[138] The obligation to grant asylum applies to Muslims and non-Muslims alike, to rich and to poor. It is non-discriminating. In Islam, both the state and the individual can grant asylum. Furthermore, according to Islam, the fact of an asylum seeker placing him or herself under the protection of Islam is sufficient to warrant a grant of asylum.[139] This can be seen as similar to the more generous draft Article 12 of the UDHR, which provided that: 'Everyone has a right to seek and be granted asylum, in other countries, from persecution.'

The Qur'anic principle of asylum is not only a religious tenet but has been legalised through shariah law and was, for some, possibly 'the most generous legal right to asylum',[140] certainly in the first century.

With the roots of the concept of asylum owing much to the notion of hospitality, as understood historically by the Arabs, and incorporated within Islam, the Middle East provides a useful basis for examining the substantive concept of protection. However, as is now very evident, there appears to be a problem in contemporary Middle East as to the true nature of asylum, safe haven or protection. While the states are willing to open their borders to allow entry for those in need – as advocated by Islamic principles – the hospitality offered contrasts with that of nomadic Arabs (which came close to the Derridian notion of absolute hospitality: namely, an unconditional hospitality that permits guests or seekers of sanctuary to treat one's home as theirs and provides for all their needs).[141] A divide appears to have occurred between territorial protection and protection of the person (in the sense of maintenance of human dignity and self-worth) in the Middle East. And international human rights law has failed to fill the gap. By resisting signing the Refugee Convention, and/or depending heavily upon the UNHCR, Arab states have arguably elevated territorial sovereignty over the needs of the individual in contradiction to the largely generous protection provided under the Ottoman Empire.

This is not to suggest that no protection is provided by the state, but support has emerged slowly and has often been piecemeal. Some of the key components of protection, such as food, shelter, security, health, education and employment, are not systematically provided, or are delivered on a piecemeal basis, and often over time. Further, they are frequently seen as 'needs' rather than 'rights'. In the majority of these countries, the UNHCR has had to adjust to government demands as to what it finds acceptable or not, and work within a loose non-legal interpretation of protection. The most striking aspect of protection delivery in the Levant, as demonstrated by the Iraqi and Syrian refugee crises, is the extent to which the UNHCR and civil society assume responsibility for addressing the needs of the refugees.[142] The move away from what might be termed 'holistic protection' of Islam and traditional Arab hospitality owes much to the twentieth century history of the region, the influence of the UK, France and the US, and the dependence on international humanitarian assistance.

The 'shift in responsibility' that has occurred from state to UN or NGOs, which has been addressed by Crisp and Slaughter,[143] and, more recently by Kagan,[144] is seen as problematic. Of course, the UNHCR is caught in a difficult position of negotiating with states, registering asylum seekers, carrying out RSD, addressing protection needs of asylum seekers/refugees, liaising with partner (I)NGOs, seeking resettlement, and seeking expansion of what has now become known as 'protection space'.[145] The more recent resort to use of camps for Syrians has added a further dimension to the provision of 'protection'.

Protection concerns in the Middle East do not simply revolve around the needs of the displaced. There are more serious issues at stake as well: detention and deportation. Though it would appear that some of the main hosting countries – such as Jordan and, in the past, Syria – have relatively good records on detention and deportation, the approach of others, such as Lebanon, Israel and Egypt towards refugees is worrying. In the recent past, for example, Lebanon accommodated fewer refugees that its neighbours, but, even so, its somewhat hostile attitude towards refugees meant that they could be at risk. For example, a report in 2011 by the Lebanese Centre for Human Rights, *Asylum Seekers and Refugees in Lebanon*, highlighted what they termed were 'major violations committed against asylum seekers and refugees in Lebanon'.[146] One example was detention of refugees; since the Lebanese authorities do not recognise the status of asylum seekers and refugees, they were often treated as illegal entrants or overstayers and sentenced to one to three months' imprisonment and occasionally fined as well.[147] Some have been held for much longer and have then been removed – even where recognised by the UNHCR as a refugee.[148] The Syrian crisis has altered the landscape significantly. At the time of writing, Lebanon is hosting 880,000 refugees from Syria, including about 50,000 Palestinian refugees from Syria (PRS).[149] Syrians thus comprise more than 20 per cent of the Lebanese population. There is some credible evidence of refusal of entry of PRS, and of detention of Syrians, although deportations, which were more usual in 2011, have now ceased in the main.[150] Israel, too, with its creation of 'detention space' and past use of forced returns, is adopting an aggressive attitude towards certain asylum seekers, while Egypt is said to have turned on Syrian refugees since the removal of President Mohammed Morsi in July 2013, many being accused of supporting the Muslim Brotherhood. Human Rights Watch reports that 1,500 have been detained, with Palestinians being especially at risk, and suggestions that the authorities are coercing refugees to leave the country.[151]

The protection umbrella has to achieve much. The challenge is to develop a meaningful concept of protection that places human flourishing at its heart and shares responsibility for the individual in a clear, systematic and fair way. The creation of 'protection space' may meet short-term objectives, but it does not necessarily address or resolve fundamental issues about the nature, provision and cost of – and responsibility for – enduring protection in the Middle East, even where accession to the Refugee Convention has occurred.

Conclusions

The Middle East is a fascinating region in relation to refugee identity and protection, particularly when considered in light of the original aims of the Refugee Convention. A number of refugee protection models operate in the region – the main three being represented by Israel, Egypt and Jordan. Israel is party to the Refugee Convention and has implemented regulations and legislation to handle the flow of asylum seekers. In this sense, it is the most advanced of the countries in the region in terms of asylum processing, and the UNHCR's role tends to be advisory in the main. Egypt, while also being party to the Convention, is heavily reliant upon the UNHCR to conduct refugee status determination,[152] and civil society and charities are required to provide care and assistance to fill the protection gap. Egypt's relationship with its refugees is somewhat volatile, compounded by the present political situation, whether they be Africans or Syrians. Jordan, by contrast, is not party to the Convention and is dependent on the UNHCR for refugee status determination and practical advice and assistance through an MOU. It hosts millions of Palestinians in camps and as Jordanian citizens. NGOS, charities and the UNHCR are largely responsible for the provision of basic care and assistance, and, in the case of Syrian refugees, the administration of recently established camps.

Each of these models reveals the uncertainty surrounding refugee identity in the region. The term 'refugee' carries an apparent intrinsic power suggestive of enduring residence in the host state and, perhaps, an entitlement to basic rights such as employment, housing, health and education. As such, it is a term that has tended to be avoided by states – preferred alternatives including 'guest', 'displaced', beneficiaries of temporary or subsidiary protection, while external bodies such as the UNHCR,[153] NGOs and non-Middle Eastern countries have labelled those crossing borders en masse as 'refugees' (whether prima facie or group refugees). Prima facie refugee status is subject to reassessment if individual refugee status determination is conducted and the Refugee Convention criteria are not met. A 'refugee' as part of large-scale cross-border migration may subsequently be redefined as a 'non-refugee'. The variety of identities is matched with variety in protection provision. UNHCR's latest reflections on international protection for those fleeing Syria are illuminating in this regard:

> Persons having fled Syria who cross international waters in search of international protection should be allowed to disembark at a place of safety, meaning a place which is physically safe, where basic needs can be met, and where they are safe from *refoulement*. UNHCR appeals to all States to ensure Syrian civilians are protected from *refoulement* and afforded international protection, the form of which may vary depending on the processing and reception capacity of countries receiving them, while guaranteeing respect for basic human rights.[154]

Thus, there is no single 'refugee' identity; nor is there a single meaning to 'protection'. Not only is the attempt in 1951 to define the refugee as an individual with well-founded fear of persecution proving unwanted, impractical and unrealistic in the face of mass displacement, but the distinction between state and non-state parties, in terms of protection provision, is increasingly difficult to pinpoint. It is time to acknowledge openly that the highly stratified protection framework that now pertains globally no longer meets the interests and needs of the refugee. The international community should urgently revisit the rationale for the creation of an international refugee law framework: 'that the problem of refugees is international in scope and nature and that its final solution can only be provided by the voluntary repatriation of the refugees or their assimilation within new national communities'.[155] Key to fulfilling this objective is recognising the right of the refugee to be a refugee.

Notes

1 Convention relating to the Status of Refugees, Geneva, 28 July 1951, 1989 UNTS 137, supplemented by the Protocol relating to the Status of Refugees, 31 January 1967, 19 UST 6223, 6257 ('Refugee Convention').
2 See for example, Claudena Skran, *Refugees in Inter-War* Europe (Clarendon Press, 1998); Tommie Sjöberg, *The Powers and the Persecuted* (Lund University Press, 1991), ch.1; Aristide Zolberg, Astri Suhrke and Sergio Aguayo (eds), *Escape from Violence* (Oxford University Press, 1989), ch. 1; Michael R. Marrus, *The Unwanted* (Temple University Press, 2002), chs 2–3; Dallal Stevens, *UK Asylum Law and Policy* (Sweet & Maxwell, 2004), ch. 4.
3 Skran, above n. 2, 66.
4 Ibid., 66–74.
5 See also Chapter 6 in this volume; Hathaway refers to three perspectives between 1920 and 1950: the juridical (membership of a particular group deprived of government protection), the social (casualties of social or political occurrences), and the individualistic (individuals in search of escaped from injustice or incompatibility with her home state) (James C. Hathaway, *The Law of Refugee Status* (Butterworths, 1991), 2–6).
6 Prior to the Conventions, a number of Conferences were convened in the 1920s to deal with the refugee question, which led to the Arrangement with Regard to the issue of Certificates of Identity to Russian Refugees, signed at Geneva 5 July, 1922 LNTS 13 No. 355, 237–42; Arrangement of 12 May 1926 relating to the Issue of Identity Certificates to Russian and Armenian Refugees, Supplementing and amending the previous Arrangements dated 5 July 1922, and 31 May 1924, LNTS 89 No. 2004, 47–52; Arrangement concerning the Extension to other Categories of Refugees of certain Measures taken in favour of Russian and Armenian Refugees, LNTS 89 No. 2006, 63–7.
7 Convention relating to the International Status of Refugees, 28 October 1933, LNTS 159 No. 3663, Art. 1; Convention concerning the Status of Refugees coming from Germany, 10 February 1938, LNTS 92 No. 4461, 59.
8 Ivor C. Jackson, *The Refugee Concept in Group Situations* (Kluwer Law International, 1999), 1.
9 Ibid. See below for further discussion of prima facie status.
10 Constitution on the International Refugee Organization, 15 December 1946, 18 *UNTS* 3, Annex 1, Section A, para. 1.
11 Jackson, above n. 8, 2.
12 Above n. 10, para. 1.
13 With the exception of 'membership of a particular social group'.
14 Above n. 10, para. 1(a).
15 United Nations General Assembly, Resolution 217 A(III), adopted 10 December 1948.
16 See also Chapter 6 in this volume, pp. 100–1.
17 Art. 1A(2): 'For the purposes of the present Convention, the term "refugee" shall apply to any person who [a]s a result of events occurring before 1 January 1951 and owing to well-founded fear of being persecuted for reasons of race, religion, nationality, membership of a particular social group or political opinion, is outside his country of his nationality and is unable or, owing to such fear, is unwilling to avail himself of the protection of that country.'
18 Established in 1949 by the Economic and Social Council and tasked with, *inter alia*, considering options for a revised refugee convention relating to refugees and stateless persons. See also Ad Hoc Committee on Statelessness and Related Problems, Status of Refugees and Stateless Persons – Memorandum by the Secretary General, Statelessness Conference, 2 January 1950 <www.unhcr.org/3ae68c280.html> (accessed 14 January 2014).
19 Ad Hoc Committee on Statelessness and Related Problems, First Session: Summary Record of the Third Meeting Held at Lake Success, New York, 17 January 1950,

E/AC.32/SR.3, para. 25 <www.refworld.org/docid/40aa193f4.html> (accessed 14 January 2014).

20 Terje Einarsen, 'Drafting History of the 1951 Convention and the 1967 Protocol', in Andreas Zimmermann (ed.), *The 1951 Convention Relating to the Status of Refugees and Its 1967 Protocol* (Oxford University Press, 2011), 60–1.

21 See for further discussion James C. Hathaway, 'A Reconsideration of the Underlying Premise of Refugee Law' (1990) *Harvard International Law Review* 31, 129–83.

22 Hathaway, above n. 5, 6.

23 Ibid.

24 Ibid., 7–8.

25 Hathaway, above n. 5.

26 *Travaux préparatoires*, 25 July 1951 <www.refworld.org/docid/40a8a7394.html> (accessed 14 January 2014); see also Chapter 14 in this volume.

27 Jackson, above n. 8, 75.

28 Protocol relating to the Status of Refugees, 606 UNTS 8791, entered into force 4 October 1967.

29 While the majority of commentators refer to the 'individualistic' nature of the Convention definition, there are some, such as Jean-François Durieux, who argue that such a reading of the Convention is incorrect, if not dangerous, and that it is clear from the definition's wording that it is intended to protect those fearing persecution because of membership of a group ('The Many Faces of "prima facie": Group-Based Evidence in Refugee Status Determination' (2008) 25 *Refuge* 151–63, 153).

30 It is clear from the *travaux préparatoires* that a group-based approach was not excluded from refugee status; the important issue is whether persecution is directed at a whole group.

31 Einarsen, above n. 20, 67.

32 Statute of the Office of the UN High Commissioner for Refugees, UNGA Res. 428(v), adopted 14 December 1950, para. 2.

33 Guy Goodwin-Gill and Jane McAdam, *The Refugee in International Law* (Oxford University Press, 2007), 23; this point is also discussed in Chapter 1 of this volume, 8.

34 Einarsen, above n. 20, 67.

35 Jackson, above n. 8, 471.

36 Matthew Albert, 'Governance and Prima Facie Refugee Status Determination: Clarifying the Boundaries of Temporary Protection, Group Determination and Mass Influx' (2010) 29 *International Refugee Law Journal* 61–91, 66, 71.

37 Ibid.

38 Ministerial Meeting of States Parties to the 1951 Convention and/or its 1967 Protocol relating to the Status of Refugees, 'Chairperson's Report on Roundtable 2, "International Cooperation to Protect Masses in Flight" (inter alia mass influx, burden and responsibility sharing, security and additional instruments)', 13 December 2001 <www.unhcr.org/3c1f1aab4.html> (accessed 28 January 2014).

39 For example, the Arrangement of 12 May 1926 relating to the Issue of Identity Certificates to Russian and Armenian Refugees defines Russian and Armenian refugees as follows: 'Russian: Any person of Russian origin *who does not enjoy or who no longer enjoys the protection of the Government* of the Union of Socialist Soviet Republics and who has not acquired another nationality' (emphasis added). 'Armenian: Any person of Armenian origin formerly a subject of the Ottoman Empire *who does not enjoy or who no longer enjoys the protection of the Government* of the Turkish Republic and who has not acquired another nationality' (emphasis added).

40 The 1938 Convention excluded for the first time 'Persons who leave . . . for reasons of purely personal convenience', thereby incorporating the notion that there needed to be a forced aspect to migration for inclusion as a refugee under the Convention (Art. 2). See also Chapter 6 in this volume.

41   See for discussion of this point Atle Grahl-Madsen, *The Status of Refugees in International Law*, Vol. I (AW Sijthoff-Leiden, 1972), 95–7. Grahl-Madsen states: 'It may be an accurate observation that most refugees are, indeed, without the protection of the country of their nationality (if they have a nationality), but it seems that little may be won – and much may be lost – if we place so much emphasis on this aspect of the situation of refugees that we consider the lack of protection as one of the essential facts which characterize refugeehood, or as one of the criteria . . . of a "general definition" of the concept of "refugee"' (ibid., 100); see Chapter 6 in this volume, for discussion of the current view.

42   Ibid., 101.

43   Ibid., 98–9.

44   Ibid.; see Chapter 6 in this volume, which discusses Shacknove's influential article 'Who Is a Refugee?' (1985) 95 *Ethics* 274, in which Shacknove focuses on the significance of the bond between state and citizen.

45   See Chapter 6 in this volume, for a detailed analysis of the concept of 'surrogate protection' and how asylum seekers are now expected to establish that the state or even non-state actors are unable or unwilling to provide protection.

46   See Hathaway, above n. 5, 105 and alternatively, 112: 'persecution is most appropriately defined as the sustained or systemic failure of state protection in relation to one of the core entitlements which have been recognised by the international community'.

47   See for example *Shah v. Islam* [1999] UKHL 20, *per* Lord Hoffmann citing the *Gender Guidelines for the Determination of Asylum Claims in the UK* (published by the Refugee Women's Legal Group in July 1988) ('Persecution = Serious Harm + The Failure of State Protection').

48   See *Horvath v. Secretary of State for the Home Department* [2000] UKHL 37.

49   See Chapter 6 in this volume.

50   See in particular Articles 3, 4, 12, 13, 15, 17, 21–4, 26, 32, 33.

51   Above n. 32.

52   Para. 8:

> The High Commissioner shall provide for the protection of refugees falling under the competence of his Office by:
>
> (a)   Promoting the conclusion and ratification of international conventions for the protection of refugees, supervising their application and proposing amendments thereto;
>
> (b)   Promoting through special agreements with Governments the execution of any measures calculated to improve the situation of refugees and to reduce the number requiring protection;
>
> (c)   Assisting governmental and private efforts to promote voluntary repatriation or assimilation within new national communities;
>
> (d)   Promoting the admission of refugees, not excluding those in the most destitute categories, to the territories of States;
>
> (e)   Endeavouring to obtain permission for refugees to transfer their assets and especially those necessary for their resettlement;
>
> (f)   Obtaining from Governments information concerning the number and conditions of refugees in their territories and the laws and regulations concerning them;
>
> (g)   Keeping in close touch with the Governments and inter-governmental organizations concerned;
>
> (h)   Establishing contact in such manner as he may think best with private organizations dealing with refugee questions;
>
> (i)   Facilitating the co-ordination of the efforts of private organizations concerned with the welfare of refugees.

53 For further discussion of this and other issues surrounding the nature of protection, see Dallal Stevens, 'What Do We Mean by Protection?' (2013) *International Journal of Minority & Group Rights* – Critical Issues in Refugee Law, 20: 233–62.

54 See for example, Statement by Volker Türk, Director of International Protection to the 64th Session of the Executive Committee of the High Commissioner's Programme, 3 October 2013.

55 Above n. 53.

56 Not all ascribe to the view that *non-refoulement* is a principle of customary international law. See, for example, James C. Hathaway, *The Rights of Refugees under International Law* (Cambridge University Press, 2005).

57 Art. 33(1).

58 According to Grahl-Madsen, Contracting Parties were under a misapprehension about the obligation owed under a principle of *non-refoulement* due to the inaccurate English translation of *refouler* to mean to refuse entry (above n. 41, 98–9); this may have resulted in the hard line adopted by countries such as the UK.

59 The first usage of Middle East is generally ascribed to an article by Alfred Thayer Mahan: 'The Persian Gulf and International Relations' (September 1902) *National Review* 40, 39, but it appears that, in fact, General Gordon coined the term two-and-a-half years earlier in Thomas E. Gordon (March 1900) 47 'The Problems of the Middle East', *The Nineteenth Century*, 413–24, though he did not define the area – see Clayton R. Koppes, 'Captain Mahan, General Gordon, and the Origins of the Term Middle East' (1976) *Middle Eastern Studies* 12(1): 95–8, 96.

60 The area of the Levant generally comprises Lebanon, Syria, Jordan, Palestinian territories, Israel, and sometimes Cyprus.

61 (Cambridge University Press, 2010).

62 For further discussion, see Justin McCarthy, *Death and Exile: The Ethnic Cleansing of Ottoman Muslims, 1821–1922* (Darwin Press, 1995); Justin McCarthy, *The Ottoman Peoples and the End of Empire* (Arnold, 2001); Kemal Karpat, 'The Transformation of the Ottoman State, 1789–1908' (1972) *International Journal of Middle East Studies* 243–81; James Meyer, 'Immigration, Return, and the Politics of Citizenship: Russian Muslims in the Ottoman Empire', 1860–1914 (2007) 39 *International Journal of Middle East Studies* 15–32.

63 Mathew J. Gibney and Randall Hansen (eds), *Immigration and Asylum: From 1900 to the Present*, Vol. I (ABC CLIO, 2005), 13.

64 Chatty, *Displacement*, above n. 61, 83.

65 It is widely suggested that Lord Curzon first used the term the unmixing of peoples when describing population exchanges, some voluntary, the majority compulsory, in the construction of nation states following the break-up of empire (Rogers Brubaker, 'Aftermaths of Empire and the Unmixing of Peoples: Historical and Comparative Perspectives' (1995) 18 *Ethnic and Racial Studies* 189–218, 192; Marrus, above n. 2, 41.

66 In the 1780s, it is estimated that about 300,000 Tatars left the Crimea for the Ottoman Empire, and then again, as a result of the Crimean war of 1854–6, 300,000 Tatars fled (McCarthy, *Death and Exile*, above n. 62, 14–17); following Russian expansionism in the nineteenth century, around 2 million Circassians, Abazas and Abkhazi fled the Caucasus for the Ottoman lands (Chatty, above n. 61, 96); 1–1.5 million, mainly Muslims, escaped the Balkans in the course of the various Balkan wars (ibid.); and approximately 1.2 million Turks were forced out from Aegean coastal and inland areas by the Greek occupation in 1919 (McCarthy, *Ottoman Peoples*, above n. 62, 135).

67 McCarthy, above n. 62, 92.

68 Meyer, above n. 62, 28.

69 Chatty, above n. 61, 97.

70 S. Shaw and E. K. Shaw, *Ottoman Empire and Modern Turkey, Vol. II: Reform, Revolution and Republic* (Cambridge University Press, 1977), 115.

71 Ibid.

72 Ibid.

73 Ibid.

74 Kemal Karpat, *Studies on Ottoman Social and Political History: Selected Articles and Essays* (Brill, 2002), 660.

75 Ibid., 663.

76 Ibid., 661.

77 BA, İrade, Dahiliye, 61326, 17 Rejep 1294 (28 July 1877), cited in Karpat, above n. 74, 661.

78 Karpat, above n. 74, 661.

79 Ibid., 663.

80 Ibid., 665.

81 Turkey is one of the few countries in the world to maintain the geographical limit of the Refugee Convention and therefore only considers people coming from Europe as refugees. However, it passed a Law on Foreigners and International Protection (Law No. 6458) on 4 April 2013 which has no restriction on country of origin and has a broad definition of 'international protection'.

82 Khadija Elmadmad, 'An Arab Convention on Forced Migration: Desirability and Possibilities' (1991) 3 *International Journal of Refugee Law* 461–81, 473.

83 As stated by one of the Saudi Arabian Representatives in the drafting meetings: UN GAOR, 3d Comm. (III), UNGA Plenary Meetings, 3rd Session, 5th Session, 328th meeting, paras 52 and 55, UN Doc. A/C.3/SR.328.

84 Lex Takkenberg, *The Status of Palestinian Refugees in International Law* (Clarendon Press, 1998), 66.

85 Susan Akram, 'Palestinian Refugees and Their Legal Status: Rights, Politics and Implications for a Just Solution' (2002) 31 *Journal of Palestine Studies* 36–52, 40.

86 Other Muslim states which are also signatories are Algeria, Tunisia, Djibouti, Morocco, Somalia, Sudan.

87 Kirsten Zaat, 'The Protection of Forced Migrants in Islamic Law' (UNHCR, New Issues in Refugee Research, Research Paper No. 146, 2007).

88 See for example Leila Hilal and Shahira Samy, *Asylum and Migration on the Mashrek – Asylum and Migration Country Fact Sheet: Syria* (Euro-Mediterranean Human Rights Network, 2008), 3.

89 Ibid., 65.

90 For example, the Convention against Torture and Other Cruel, Inhuman or Degrading Treatment or Punishment, 1465 UNTS 85, 113 (adopted 10 December 1984); International Covenant on Civil and Political Rights, 999 UNTS 171 (adopted 16 December 1966), International Covenant on Economic, Social and Cultural Rights, 993 UNTS 3 (adopted 16 December 1966). For a list of ratifications, see <www.unhchr.ch/tbs/doc.nsf/Statusfrset?OpenFrameSet> (accessed 12 January 2014).

91 See below.

92 21 Dhul Qaidah 1401, 19 September 1981: 'Every persecuted or tyrannized person shall have the right to seek refuge and asylum. This right shall be guaranteed for each human being, regardless of race, religion, colour or gender.'

93 Organization of the Islamic Conference (OIC), 5 August 1990: 'Every man shall have the right, within the framework of the Shariah, to free movement and to select his place of residence whether within or outside his country and if persecuted, is entitled to seek asylum in another country. The country of refuge shall be obliged to provide protection to the asylum-seeker until his safety has been attained, unless asylum is motivated by committing an act regarded by the Shariah as a crime.'

94 19 November 1992.

95 League of Arab States, 1994.

96 No. 15/10-P (IS), Adopted by the Tenth Session of the Islamic Summit Conference Putrajaya, Malaysia, 16–17 October 2003.

97 There are exceptions, such as Sudan and Morocco, which have enacted domestic refugee law and created internal bodies to handle refugee claims and/or appeals.
98 In accordance with agreements between the UNHCR and the specific country: in the case of Egypt, the 1954 Framework Agreement between UNHCR and the Government of Egypt; in the case of Jordan, the Memorandum of Understanding between the Government of Jordan and the UNHCR, 5 April 1998; and for Lebanon, the Memorandum of Understanding between the Directorate of the General Security (Republic of Lebanon) and the regional Office of the UN High Commissioner for Refugees, Concerning the processing of cases of asylum-seekers applying for refugee status with the UNHVR Office, 9 September 2003. (Note that the Lebanese MOU is being renegotiated with the UNHCR.)
99 Michael Kagan, 'The Beleaguered Gatekeeper: Protection Challenges Posed by UNHCR Refugee Status Determination' (2006) 18 *International Journal of Refugee Law* 1–29.
100 Egypt is such an example and has entered reservations in respect of Article 12 (1), Articles 20 and 22 (1), and Articles 23 and 24.
101 Interview with author, on file.
102 Khair Smadi, 'Towards Adopting a Legal System for Asylum in Jordan' (January 2011) *Fahamu Refugee Legal Aid Newsletter* 11 <www.pambazuka.org/images/articles/510/FRLANJanuary2011.pdf> (accessed 24 January 2014).
103 Ministry of Interior, Population Immigration and Border Authority, Procedure for Handling Political Asylum Seekers in Israel, entered into force 2 January 2011. <http://piba.gov.il/Regulations/Procedure%20for%20Handling%20Political%20 Asylum%20Seekers%20in%20Israel-en.pdf> (accessed 12 January 2014).
104 Article 21 (Jordan): 'Political refugees shall not be extradited on account of their beliefs or for their defence of liberty'; Article 34 (Syria): 'Political refugees shall not be extradited on account of their political principles or for their defence of liberty.'
105 Preamble, para. b: 'Lebanon . . . abides by its covenants and by the Universal Declaration of Human Rights. The Government shall embody these principles in all fields and areas without exception.'
106 Article 29(h).
107 Legislative Decree No. 29 of 15 January 1970 – The Entry and Exit of Aliens to and from the Syrian Arab Republic and their Residence therein; Ministry of Interior Decision No. 1350 of 15 August 1948 (regulation governing entry, exit and residence of non-Syrian Arab nationals).
108 *Bulletin de législation libanaise (Journal Officiel)*, No. 28-1962, 10 July 1962.
109 'Tout étranger faisant l'objet d'une poursuite ou d'une condamnation de la part d'une autorité non libanaise pour cause d'un crime politique, ou dont la vie ou la liberté est menacée, également pour des causes politiques, peut demander le droit d'asile politique au Liban.' Available at <www.unhcr.org/refworld/docid/3ae6b4f30. html> (accessed 24 January 2014).
110 Article 31: 'En cas d'expulsion d'un ancien réfugié politique, celui-ci ne pourra être conduit sur le territoire d'un pays où sa vie ou sa liberté est menacée.'
111 Article 27.
112 'Legality *vs* Legitimacy: Detention of Refugees and Asylum Seekers in Lebanon' (Beirut: Frontiers Association, 2006), 15; Lebanese Centre for Human Rights, *Asylum Seekers and Refugees: Languishing in Injustice* (2011), 6.
113 The two main flows of Palestinians took place in 1948 and 1967.
114 See Michael Dumper, 'Palestinian Refugees', in Gil Loescher, James Milner, Edward Newman and Gary Troeller (eds), *Protracted Refugee Situations – Political, Human Rights and Security Implications* (United Nations University Press, 2008), ch. 10. Michael Dumper has written extensively on Palestinian refugees, see also *The Future for Palestinian Refugees: Towards Equity and Peace* (Lynne Rienner, 2007); Michael Dumper (ed.), *Palestinian Refugee Repatriation: Global Perspectives* (Routledge, 2006).

115 For example, Jordan and Lebanon.
116 The UNHCR has signed Memoranda of Understanding with Lebanon and Jordan permitting it to register asylum seekers and conduct refugee status determination. See Memorandum of Understanding signed between the Government of the Hashemite Kingdom of Jordan and the Office of the United High Commissioner for Refugees, 5 April 1998; Letter of Understanding signed between the Government of the Hashemite Kingdom of Jordan and the Office of the United High Commissioner for Refugees, 15 April 2003; Memorandum of Understanding between the Directorate of the General Security and the United Nations High Commissioner for Refugees concerning the processing of asylum seekers applying for refugee status, 9 September 2003.
117 See below. The position was complicated since there were attempts by the UNHCR to introduce a temporary protection regime as well as refer to Iraqis from central and southern Iraq as '*prima facie* refugees'. This was justified (a) on the targeted and extreme violence, as well as lack of law, order and security (generalised violence), in those areas amounting to persecution; and (b) on the size of the migration making individual RSD unrealistic (Andrew Harper, 'Iraq's Refugees: Ignored and Unwanted' (2008) 90 *International Review of the Red Cross* 169–90, 175–6). For an in-depth analysis, see Dallal Stevens, 'Legal Status, Labelling and Protection: The Case of Iraqi "Refugees" in Jordan (2013) 25 *International Journal of Refugee Law* 1–38.
118 Stevens, above n. 117, 19.
119 Arafat Madi Shoukri, *Refugee Status in Islam* (IB Tauris, 2011), 83.
120 Ibid., 93.
121 Madi Shoukri, above n. 119, 83, 108–14.
122 Ibid., 95.
123 UNHCR, *Country Operations Plan 2008–09, Hashemite Kingdom of Jordan* <www.unhcr. org/49cb98a42.html> 2 (accessed 24 January 2014).
124 See above n. 117.
125 Although this has occurred in all countries under consideration.
126 At December 2013, 2,148,571 refugees had been registered or were awaiting registration: HumanCareSyria, *Statistic Report December 2013* <www.humancaresyria. org/images/uploads/documents/Syria-StatisticalReport-December2013.pdf>; the UNHCR estimates that by the end of 2014, there will be 4.1 million refugees (*2014 Syria Regional Response Plan – Strategic Overview*) <www.unhcr.org/syriarrp6/docs/Syria-rrp6-full-report.pdf> (both accessed 24 January 2014).
127 ALEF/IKV Pax Christi, *Two Years on: Syrian Refugees in Lebanon*, September 2013, 14.
128 Hani Hazaimeh, 'Syrian army defectors came as individuals to Jordan', *Jordan Times*, 25 November 2011.
129 A useful resource on the legal position of refugees from Syria is provided by Reliefweb, 'Legal status of individuals fleeing Syria', June 2013 <http://reliefweb.int/sites/ reliefweb.int/files/resources/legal_status_of_individuals_fleeing_syria.pdf> (accessed 16 January 2014).
130 See for further discussion of the situation in Israel, Dallal Stevens, 'Between East and West – the Case of Israel', in Hélène Lambert, Jane McAdam and Maryellen Fullerton (eds), *The Global Reach of European Refugee Law* (Cambridge University Press, 2013), ch. 5.
131 On 10 December 2013, the Knesset passed an amendment to the Prevention of Infiltration Law 1952, as amended in 2012, which had been declared unconstitutional by the Supreme Court in September 2013 for its power to detain 'infiltrators' for up to three years (*Adam and others* v. *The Knesset and others* (7146/12); *Doe and others* v. *Ministry of Interior and others* (1192/13); *Tahangas and others* v. *Ministry of Interior* (1247/13), 7146/12, 1192/13, 1247/13, 16 September 2013 <www.refworld.org/docid/524e7ab54.html> (accessed 20 January 2014)). The court held that a three-year detention violated

the right to liberty enshrined in the Basic Law: Human Dignity and Liberty. The new legislation permits detention for up to 12 months.

132 Contributions include Ghassan Arnaout's seminal text in 1987, *Asylum in the Arab-Islamic Tradition* (UNHCR/Institute of Humanitarian Law, 1987); Elmadmad, above n. 82; Kirsten Zaat, 'The Protection of Forced Migrants in Islamic Law' (UNHCR, New Issues in Refugee Research, Research Paper No. 146, 2007); the 2008 *Refugee Survey Quarterly*'s report and papers of a conference on Asylum and Islam; Ahmed Abou-El-Wafa, *The Right to Asylum, between Islamic Shariah and International Law* (UNHCR, 2009); Arafat Madi Shoukri, *Refugee Status in Islam* (IB Tauris, 2011).

133 Arnaout, above n. 132, 13; Elmadmad, above n. 82, 467.

134 Arnaout, above n. 132, 15.

135 *Hijra* is associated with the Prophet Mohammed's flight from Mecca to Medina in 622 AD.

136 See Abou-El-Wafa, above n. 132.

137 Ibid., 46.

138 Arnaout, above n. 132, 21.

139 Elmadmad, above n. 82, 470.

140 Eduardo Arboleda and Ian Hoy, 'The Convention Refugee Definition in the West: Disharmony of Interpretation and Application' (1993) 5 *International Journal of Refugee Law* 69.

141 Jacques Derrida, *Of Hospitality*, trans. Rachel Bowlby (Stanford University Press, 2000).

142 *2014 Syria Regional Response Plan*, above n. 126; Stevens, above n. 117; ALEF/IKV Pax Christi, *Two Years On: Syrian Refugees in Lebanon*, September 2013.

143 Amy Slaughter and Jeff Crisp, 'A Surrogate State? The Role of the UNHCR in Protracted Refugee Situations', in Gil Loescher, James Milner, Edward Newman and Gary Troeller (eds), *Protracted Refugee Situations* (United Nations University Press, 2008), 123–40.

144 Michael Kagan, 'We Live in a Country of UNHCR': The UN surrogate state and refugee policy in the Middle East (UNHCR, New Issues in Refugee Research, Research Paper No. 201, February 2011).

145 See Chapter 13 in this volume, which criticises the notion of 'protection space', as relevant to South-East Asia as well as the Middle East.

146 Lebanese Centre for Human Rights, above n. 112, 13.

147 Ibid., 15.

148 See examples given in the report by the Lebanese Centre for Human Rights, above n. 112.

149 *2014 Syria Regional Response Plan – Lebanon Response Plan Overview*, above n. 126.

150 ALEF/IKV Pax Christi, above n. 127, 20, 21, 29.

151 Human Rights Watch, 'Egypt: Syria refugees detained, coerced to return' <www.hrw.org/news/2013/11/10/egypt-syria-refugees-detained-coerced-return> (accessed 20 January 2014); UNHCR, 'Egypt: UNHCR concerned over detention of Syrian refugees amid anti-Syrian sentiment', 26 July 2013 <www.unhcr.org/51f242c59.html> (accessed 20 January 2014).

152 Under the 1954 MOU.

153 In its latest guidance, the UNHCR states that the 'UNHCR characterizes the flight of civilians from Syria as a refugee movement ' (International Protection Considerations with regard to people fleeing the Syrian Arab Republic, Update II, 22 October 2013, para. 11).

154 Ibid.

155 UNGA Resolution 319(IV) 3 December 1949.

6   Refugees as objects of surrogate protection: shifting identities

*Susan Kneebone**

Introduction

> In pith and substance, refugee law is not immigration law . . . but rather a system
> for the surrogate or substitute protection of human rights.[1]

In this chapter, I examine the refugee as the object of surrogate protection.
I explain how this seemingly simple construction is laden with ambiguities, and
how use of this concept in interpretation of the Refugee Convention definition
has shifted the refugee's identity from a position whereby, as per the refugee
definition in the 1951 Refugee Convention,[2] a refugee is 'a person who' 'is *unable*,
or owing' to fear of persecution, is '*unwilling* to avail himself' of the protection of
the country of his nationality, to one whose entitlement to protection depends on
the ability and willingness of the *state* (or its agents, or non-state actors) to provide
protection.[3] This shift in focus has implications: first, for the meaning of 'refugee
protection' and hence identity; second, for the practical burden and standard of
proof in refugee law.

The opening quote by Hathaway alludes to three identities of the refugee: the
refugee as the subject of state migration law, the refugee as protected in
international law, and the refugee as a person owed humanitarian protection.
These can be described as the political, legal and 'cosmopolitan'[4] refugee identities.

The 'political' refugee is identified and defined by national policy and laws,
usually as an object of restrictive state migration law, as Maria O'Sullivan
illustrates in her chapter in this book.[5] The refugee is 'securitised' as an irregular
or 'illegal' migrant, often as a 'smuggled person' or participant in criminal
activity. Paradoxically, the refugee may also be 'demonised' for difference[6] in a
host country, on the basis of the very grounds that comprise the Refugee
Convention definition, namely race and nationality, religion, political opinion and
social group.

The 'legal' identity of the refugee arises from international law. When
Hathaway refers to 'surrogate or substitute protection', he identifies the refugee,
as a person who is entitled to state protection. The effect of the Convention is
explained by Hathaway in his argument that: 'Refugee status is a categorical
designation that reflects a unique ethical and consequential legal entitlement to

make claims on the international community.'[7] As Jane McAdam has pointed out, although the human rights of asylum seekers and refugees are covered by other international instruments, 'no comparable status arises from recognition of an individual's protection needs under a human rights instrument'.[8] According to Haddad, these legal scholars make a 'statist'[9] construction of the refugee. That is, they reflect the status-granting function of the state and highlight the central theme of this book, namely the role of law and policy in making and unmaking the refugee category.

Hathaway's statement also identifies the 'cosmopolitan' refugee as the subject of human rights protection, or of 'humanity'. The relationship between the Refugee Convention and human rights is an interesting and contested issue.[10] For example, the EU Qualification Directive 2011/95[11] recognises the status-granting function of Member States (Preamble Recital Clauses 21, 23), which are required to respect the human rights of refugees (and others) under the Charter of Fundamental Rights of the European Union[12] (Preamble Recital Clause 16) as well as those of the 1951 Refugee Convention (Preamble Recital Clause 4). The 'cosmopolitan' identity exposes the conundrum of 'personhood' versus refugee status, and the issue of the 'right to have rights' as Hannah Arendt stated so famously. As Alison Kesby[13] has argued, such rights are hollow without the ability to act on them, to enforce them.

In practice these three refugee identities, the political, legal and cosmopolitan, are in continual tension. For example, for political reasons, the Australian government refuses to exercise its status-granting role for some categories of refugees, even though they qualify for protection in international law.[14] This illustrates the contested role of the state both as the agent of protection and the guardian of state sovereignty.[15] Further, statist notions of refugee law, and of 'refugee identities' are challenged by the presence and prevalence of non-state actors, both as agents of persecution and of protection.[16] As the EU Qualification Directive 2011/95, Article 6 recognises, non-state actors can be actors of persecution if there is a lack of protection as defined in Article 7. This Article also recognises non-state actors as 'actors of protection'.

In this chapter, I describe first the shifting focus of the refugee definition in the development of refugee law, to explain how the notion of protection (and hence identity) has shifted from a collective international approach to a focus on the individual and the need for 'surrogate' protection. I then explain the practical effect of the 'surrogate protection' approach, which developed in Canadian jurisprudence and transmuted through 'transnational judicial conversation' into the EU Qualification Directive 2011/95. Article 7.1(b) of the directive defines actors of protection as the state or 'parties or organisations, including international organisations, controlling the State or a substantial part of the territory of the State'. Article 7.2 of the directive defines protection as 'reasonable steps' taken to prevent persecution by *inter alia* the operation of 'an effective legal system for the detection, prosecution and punishment' of acts of persecution. Through use of 'surrogate protection', this transnational judicial conversation has added an extra requirement to the refugee definition.

Evolution of refugee protection and the state: where does surrogate protection fit?

Underlying the notion of surrogate protection are the contested role of the state, emerging concepts of state membership and conflicting approaches to protection in refugee law.[17] According to Hathaway, international law has a role in refugee law 'only when the state will not or cannot comply with its classical duty to defend the interests of its citizenry'.[18] But, in practice, access to protection is dependent on state discretion; there is no international refugee status. Surrogate protection is described by some as 'internal' protection, in recognition of the need for protection from the failures of the home state.[19] However, historically surrogate protection fitted more typically with a notion of external or diplomatic protection which can be linked to protection of 'nationals', as is explained below.

In this section, I trace the evolution of the refugee definition in international law in the pre-Second World War period, and compare it with developments post 1951. The purpose of this is to show how the notion of internal surrogate protection–refugee identity has evolved.

Evolution of refugee identity through the definition

The refugee 'problem' as we know is not new. Movements of religious minorities were one of the first examples of refugee movements in the 'modern' world; the Protestant French Huguenots who were forced to leave Catholic France after the Edict of Nantes in 1685 are one notable example.[20] The French Revolution of 1789 led to a wave of political exiles or refugees to England and the new world.[21] Haddad explains refugees as:

> an inevitable if unintended consequence of the nation-state system; they are the result of erecting boundaries, attempting to assign all individuals to a territory within such boundaries, and then failing to ensure universal representation and protection.[22]

She comes to the conclusion that 'the idea of refugee protection is tied up with statist definitions . . . that all individuals must fit into the state–citizen–territory trinity'.[23] This is important to understanding the modern idea of 'surrogate protection'.

Under the 1951 Convention definition, the refugee is defined by reference to 'nationality' (rather than citizenship) as one of the grounds of persecution, and lack of protection of a country of nationality is a precondition to refugee status. Further, the need for protection as 'effective nationality' is implicit in other provisions of the Convention definition such as Articles 1C and 1E.[24] Importantly, the refugee test enshrined in the Convention concentrates upon the individualised fear of a person of being persecuted in 'the country of his nationality'.[25]

The idea of protection as 'effective nationality' reflects the historical evolution of approaches to refugee protection, which began in the inter-war period between the two World Wars. A brief glance at the predecessors of the 1951 Convention in the 1920–35 period shows that the focus was on lack of protection of a country of nationality.[26] The treaties defined a refugee as a person who no longer enjoyed the protection of their government and had not acquired another nationality. The first refugee accords addressed the influx of Russian and Armenian refugees. Hathaway describes this as the 'juridical' approach as the purpose of conferring refugee status was to facilitate their international movement. For this purpose certificates of identity were issued. This response recognised the importance of filling the gap between the loss of protection of the country of nationality upon flight and acquisition of a new nationality in another country. It was a truly *inter*-national[27] response. In this period, the international community (which was then basically European) came together to identify those in need of protection by reference to ethnic origin and /or territory or category[28] rather than individualised fear. For example, the 1933 Convention Relating to the International Status of Refugees[29] based refugee status on lack of protection and effective nationality.[30]

In this period, nationality was the link between a state and its members. External or diplomatic protection was owed to nationals outside the state, and this legal status was relevant to relations between states.[31] Some argue that this is the basis of surrogate refugee protection.[32] Later, the International Covenant on Civil and Political Rights (ICCPR) based a host state's responsibility to another's 'national' on the concept of jurisdiction. Consistent with this historical perspective, Hathaway has described refugee protection as 'a response to the disfranchisement from the usual benefits of nationality'.[33] Nationality, however, is 'a territorial and legally constructed' concept[34] whose practical effect is marginally different from the concept of citizenship, which developed in common law jurisdictions post-Second World War.[35]

In the subsequent period, 1935–9 a 'social group' or category approach to refugee protection dominated.[36] Refugees, mostly those fleeing Nazi persecution, were defined as the victims of particular social or political events but they were also required to show loss of de jure or de facto nationality as in the previous period. These agreements encompassed groups of people in contrast to the individualistic definition of the 1951 Convention. It is important to note that it was a collective international response that focused upon protection of groups and categories. Such a collective international response to refugee protection would not be seen again until the formulation of the Comprehensive Plan of Action for Indo-Chinese Refugees (CPA)[37] in the 1970s and 1980s (see below).

At the end of the Second World War, first the UNRRA (United Nations Refugee Relief Association) and then the International Refugee Organization (IRO) were established to organise mass repatriation and resettlement, the latter as a temporary intergovernmental UN agency to regularise the status of refugees stranded after the war. IRO moved away from a categories approach to focus on individuals. On 1 January 1951 the UNHCR was established, with a mandate for both groups and individuals.[38]

The Refugee Convention definition of a refugee emphasises grounds for protection, which by and large arise from the person's civil or political status. It is sometimes said therefore, that it presupposes a public duty on the part of the state to protect the individual (private) applicant. Shacknove, for example, suggests that it contains an implicit assumption that the normal basis of society is the bond of trust and loyalty between the state and its citizens.[39] In his view, the refugee definition presupposes that the bond of allegiance of a citizen with the sovereign country of origin, the persecuting state, has been severed. This concept of refugee protection underlies the seminal decision on non-state actor (gender) persecution in *Islam v. Secretary of State for the Home Department; R v. Immigration Appeal Tribunal, ex parte Shah*[40] (*Islam and Shah*): Persecution = Serious Harm + The Failure of State Protection.

The emphasis in the post-Second World War period on an asylum seeker's civil or political status fitted with identifying refugees as objects of surrogate protection from a European ideological perspective,[41] which implicitly attributed responsibility to the country of origin. However, the emergence of refugee crises in the 1960s in other regions of the world, and new and expanded definitions of the refugee in regional documents, identified refugees more broadly as victims of forced migration. For example, the 1969 Organization of African Unity Convention Governing the Specific Aspects of Refugee Problems in Africa (OAU Convention)[42] contained two important provisions, which identified the refugee as an externally displaced person or asylum seeker. Article I(2) of the 1969 OAU Convention identifies a refugee broadly as:

> every person, who owing to external aggression, occupation, foreign domination or events seriously disturbing public order in either part or the whole of his country of origin or nationality, is compelled to leave his place of habitual residence in order to seek refuge in another place outside his country of origin or nationality.

The OAU Convention envisaged regional solutions for regional refugee problems. Article II(2) states that the grant of asylum is 'a peaceful and humanitarian act'. Similar definitions were inserted in other regional instruments in the 1960s and 1980s. For example, the Asian–African Legal Consultative Organization (AALCO) in 1966 formulated an instrument for the protection of refugee rights, known as the Bangkok Principles,[43] which were reaffirmed in 2001 (Final Text of the AALCO's 1966 Bangkok Principles on the Status and Treatment of Refugees).[44] The 1984 Cartagena Declaration on Refugees adopted at a Colloquium held at Cartagena, Colombia in November 1984[45] was another specific regional response to massive displacements of refugees.[46]

Up to this point, it seemed that the focus of international refugee protection and identity was squarely upon 'exilic' solutions rather than 'source-control' measures.[47] However, in the 1970s and 1980s, as international migration increased and became a permanent global feature, the responses of industrialised states concerned with their security shifted to a containment or 'source-control' focus.[48] As Mertus describes this period, states talked less about their human rights abuses and more about their rights.[49] Moreover, large-scale displacement was evidence that the causes of 'refugeehood' were changing from international to internal conflict.[50]

In this context, there were two notable developments, first, the united international response under the CPA in the 1970s and 1980s,[51] and, second, the development of principles of collective international responsibility for internally displaced persons (IDPs) in the 1990s. I turn to describe each of these briefly as important examples of how refugee identity was constructed by the international community.

The key precepts of the CPA were the responsibility of the international community to resettle Indo-Chinese refugees after the cessation of hostilities in the region, sustained by protection in countries of first asylum in the region and orderly departure from the country of origin. The legacy of the CPA is a topic of debate,[52] although it is clear that this was an international response to an issue which impacted hugely upon the region, by which refugees were constructed as the objects of humanitarian protection. It also focused on controlling movement at source; exilic solutions were at the discretion of receiving states.

Parallel to these refugee crises, the issue of internal displacement alerted the international community to the 'privileged' position of 'external' refugees in international law.[53] However, the response to IDP issues was markedly different in one sense, but similar in another. It led to the creation of a hierarchy of principles, which recognise the role of the international community to provide 'humanitarian' protection upon failure of a state to protect its citizens.[54] The idea of 'responsibility to protect', which is a central concept of the IDP Guiding Principles, became one of collective international responsibility to intervene internally in the failed state. In a sense, this is the reverse of the practical effect of the surrogacy principle, which emphasises the responsibility of the home state rather than that of the international community.

This discussion highlights the shift in the focus of international refugee protection and identity, from collective 'external' protection of displaced nationals to individual 'surrogate' substitute status for exiled citizens. It also exposes the paradox of surrogate protection, that receiving states are needed to substitute for home states. Governments have tended to assume that their surrogate protection obligations under the Refugee Convention equate to a grant of full nationality or citizenship, and consequently seek to avoid them.[55] Shacknove stresses that the refugee is an object of international assistance, that 'refugeehood' is unrelated to migration.[56] He refers to the need for 'international restitution' and assistance.[57] But in practice the notion of surrogate protection has been used to minimise the obligations of receiving states, particularly where non-state actors are the agents of persecution, and often when there is a group identity for those individuals fleeing persecution. This has occurred through interpretation of the Refugee Convention definition.

Non-state actors and interpretation of the refugee definition

In his 1991 book *The Law of Refugee Status*, Hathaway explained that surrogate protection means that 'persecution' is concerned with determining whether there have been human rights abuses, and *additionally*, requires 'scrutiny of the state's ability and willingness effectively to respond to that risk'.[58] This is the key point about surrogate protection: it potentially adds a requirement to the words of the Refugee Convention definition.

In practical terms, the effect of the 'internal' surrogate protection approach is to shift the focus from the reasonableness of the refugee's fear to the reasonableness of the acts of protection. These two criteria are linked as I will show:

> [B]y directing attention to 'reasonable measures', it has led adjudicators to resolve the issue by reference to a State's notional willingness to combat [persecution] rather than by examining its present ability to do so.[59]

Or, put differently, under a surrogate protection approach, application of the Refugee Convention definition risks becoming focused upon state accountability or complicity in the persecution, rather than upon the refugee applicant's 'well-founded fear of persecution' or the simple need for protection as a consequence of failure of state protection.

Surrogate protection is often raised where non-state actors as actors of persecution are involved. In refugee law, the role of non-state actors as actors of persecution has led to two approaches to interpretation of the refugee definition that can be identified respectively as 'accountability' and 'protection'.[60] The 'protection' approach concentrates on the objective reasonableness of the (well-founded) 'fear'. This is arguably consistent with the interpretation of the refugee definition requirement of 'being persecuted', which refers to the reasons for the applicant's fear, not to the act of persecution. As Rodger Haines said in *Refugee Appeal No. 74665/03*:

> The language draws attention to the fact of exposure to harm, rather than to the act of inflicting harm. The focus is on the reasons for the claimant's *predicament* rather than on the mindset of the persecutor.[61]

'Being persecuted' argued the New Zealand Refugee Status Appeal Authority (NZRSAA) 'is the sustained or systemic violation of basic human rights demonstrative of a failure of state protection'.[62] This is a direct quote from Hathaway[63] and echoes the well-known formula from *Islam and Shah* referred to above.

Surrogate protection is most often associated with 'accountability' or 'attribution' in refugee law. It focuses upon the complicity of the home state in the persecution. It emphasises the need for a nexus between the acts of persecution and the state.[64] This is consistent with the notion that the state of origin is at fault[65] and bears responsibility for the conditions which create the need for refugee status. It constructs the fleeing asylum seeker or refugee as the continuing responsibility of the home state, rather than as a person entitled to international protection. The attribution approach has been rejected on the basis that refugee law is not concerned with 'State culpability'[66] or vicarious liability.[67] Rather, it is generally agreed that refugee law is based upon the responsibilities of contracting states to provide protection under international law, not on the obligations of failed states. Importantly, as explained below, in New Zealand (NZ) the accountability approach has been rejected.

In the Australian decision *Minister for Immigration & Multicultural Affairs* v. *Respondents S152*,[68] the majority of the High Court, without choosing between these approaches, adopted a test which requires a state 'to take *reasonable measures* to protect the lives and safety of its citizens . . . [which] would include an appropriate criminal law and the provision of a reasonably effective and impartial police force and justice system'. Article 7.2 of the Qualification Directive mirrors this test when it says that protection will be provided when 'reasonable steps' are taken (as set out above) to prevent persecution, and the applicant has 'access to such protection'.

In commenting on Article 7.2, the UNHCR expressed its concern that:

> Determining the availability of protection requires an assessment of the effectiveness, accessibility and adequacy of available protection in the individual case. Possible guarantors of such protection or the existence of a legal system in a given country may be elements of this examination. However, *the assessment to be made is whether the applicant's fear of persecution continues to be well-founded, regardless of the steps taken to prevent persecution or serious harm.*[69]

That is a succinct summary of the problem faced by refugees. In some jurisdictions, the focus of refugee status determination has shifted from the well-founded fear of the applicant to the 'notional willingness' of the state of origin to combat the particular problem. This is potentially an 'accountability' or 'attribution' approach that implies state 'culpability' in refugee law.

As the joint judgment in the High Court in *Respondents S152* explained, 'surrogate protection' can mean one of three approaches and identities for an asylum seeker, namely:

> It may be relevant to whether the fear is well-founded; and to whether the conduct giving rise to the fear is persecution; and to whether a person such as the respondent in this case is unable, or, owing to fear of persecution, is unwilling, to avail himself of the protection of his home state.[70]

This is an important statement as it shows the potential confusion which can flow from the 'surrogate protection' concept. In the next section, I explain how this position evolved and examine what it tells us about the nature of 'transnational judicial conversations' in refugee law.

The transnational judicial conversation on non-state actors

The view that a transnational judicial conversation is taking place in international refugee law, particularly among the common law and Commonwealth countries, has been encouraged by Hathaway.[71] The implication is that this is a positive development that can lead to 'common judicial understandings, principles and norms concerning refugee matters'.[72] However, my observation is that such conversation can lead to a lowering of standards or demonstrate the lack of consensus among states. Moreover, while the international 'conversation' takes place mainly at the judicial level, it also takes place internally at other levels of government.[73] As I explain, the nature of that conversation in refugee law is complex, as it involves translation of judicial decisions into policy directions, which then feed back into decisions at the administrative and judicial levels, before travelling and transmuting across jurisdictions.

In this section, I trace the conversation which led to Article 7 of the EU Qualification Directive to demonstrate how the idea of surrogate protection spread. I summarise how the conversation began with a Canadian decision, which was then translated into policy for use by the Canadian Immigration Review Board (IRB). According to contemporary analyses of Canadian decisions, this surrogate protection approach is now entrenched in Canadian jurisprudence, albeit without providing a 'comprehensive and comprehensible test'.[74] I explain how the same conversation has led to different standards of protection in the United Kingdom (UK) and Australia. By contrast, this surrogate protection approach has been rejected in New Zealand.

By way of background, it is important to understand the significance of the standard of proof for refugee status determination (RSD),[75] which is to determine whether there is a 'well-founded' objective prospective fear. While there is general agreement that a 'balance of probabilities' standard, or anything approaching it, is clearly inappropriate in refugee determinations where the life and liberty of the applicant are at stake, the test is variously expressed in different jurisdictions. In Australia and New Zealand the standard has been described as a 'real chance' test,[76] in the UK it is described as a 'reasonable degree of likelihood' or a 'real risk' and in the USA and Canada as a 'reasonable possibility' test. Moreover, the burden of proof is to be shared between decision maker and applicant, and a benefit of doubt principle is to apply where the applicant's account 'appears credible'.[77] Further, in relation to the objective 'well-founded' fear, the UNHCR Handbook states that the 'authorities that are called upon to determine refugee status are not required to pass judgment on conditions in the applicant's country of origin', albeit recognising that such conditions are relevant to assessing credibility.[78] But, as I will explain, Canadian decision makers are basing decisions on such assessments and requiring a standard of proof as high as a 'balance of probabilities' standard from applicants.

Canada (Attorney-General) v. *Ward and the surrogacy argument*

The trail begins with the seminal 1993 decision of the Supreme Court of Canada in *Canada (Attorney-General)* v. *Ward*.[79] The applicant in that case had deserted from a politico-military group in Northern Ireland for reasons of conscience and sought refuge in Canada. He was a citizen of both Ireland and the UK but claimed that neither state could offer him protection. He claimed that as a former member of that group he was at risk of persecution from the Irish Republican Army (IRA) in both states. The case turned upon the meaning of 'social group' and whether the applicant had satisfied the burden of proof. On the latter issue, the argument that came before the Supreme Court of Canada was whether the applicant had to establish that the states were complicit in the persecution by non-state actors. The court said that state complicity was not a necessary element of the refugee definition; that inability to protect was enough.

The argument on this point turned upon interpretation of the Refugee Convention definition and the nature of the link between 'persecution' and lack of state protection in the definition. The Refugee Board had said that the words in the definition 'is unable, or owing to such fear, is unwilling to avail himself of the protection of that country' were 'inextricably' linked to the state's inability to offer effective protection. That is, the Board appeared to focus on the level of protection that would be provided. The Supreme Court's reasoning pulled back from that approach and clearly put the focus on the well-founded fear.[80]

In the Supreme Court, La Forest J. accepted the Board's interpretation of the refugee definition and located the relevance of the unable/unwilling words in Article 1A(2) within the well-founded fear requirement, as part of an objective test of persecution. At the outset of his analysis of the issues, La Forest J. referred to the Hathaway view of the international refugee protection scheme as 'surrogate or substitute protection' 'activated upon failure of state protection'.[81] But the reasoning that follows clearly sits within the well-founded fear requirement. The judge said that the test for determining whether there was fear of persecution was one of objective reasonableness, citing Goodwin-Gill[82] who in the first edition of his book said:

> Fear of persecution and lack of protection are themselves interrelated elements. The persecuted clearly do not enjoy the protection of their country of origin, while evidence of the lack of protection on either the internal or external level may create a presumption as to the *likelihood* of persecution and to the *well-foundedness* of any fear.[83]

La Forest J. continued:

> Having established that the claimant has a fear, the Board is, in my view, entitled to presume that persecution will be *likely*, and the fear *well-founded*, if there is an absence of state protection.[84]

It is important to note that in this statement it is made clear that it is for the Board to make a presumption about persecution, only once the *claimant* has established a fear. This is simply another way of restating the well-founded fear test. However, the conversation that I am relating shows that in translation of this judgment into subsequent practice and decisions, this has elided into a rebuttable presumption of state protection, which the applicant has to disprove. That is, the refugee's role in RSD has been reversed, in a similar manner to that which Galloway describes in current-day Canada.[85]

This was not what La Forest J. intended, as she said that ineffective state protection is encompassed within both the concept 'unable' *and* 'unwilling'.[86] She accepted the UNHCR's argument on this point – and their endorsement of the Board's position that 'the absence of protection may create a sufficient evidentiary basis for a presumption of a well-founded fear by the claimant'.[87] As Zambelli explains, *Ward* has come to mean that, 'a fear of harm is presumptively well-founded if it is established that the state cannot protect the person against that harm'.[88] In my view, this arises from how *Ward* was subsequently interpreted and applied at the IRB level.

In the 1999 version of the IRB's policy guidelines,[89] the effect of *Ward* is summarised in chapter 6 under the heading 'Protection'. It refers explicitly to the concept of surrogate protection (see 6.1.1). It is important to note that this discussion of 'Protection' does not relate to any particular part of the refugee definition, unlike other chapters of the guidelines.[90] There is no reference to surrogate protection in the Refugee Convention.

At 6.4 of Chapter 6 it is stated that a presumption 'at play in refugee law' is that:

(b) absent a complete breakdown of state apparatus, states are presumed to be capable of protecting their citizens.

At 6.5 it is stated that the 'claimant must approach his or her state for protection, if state protection might *reasonably* be forthcoming' (emphasis added). At 6.6 it is said that:

The claimant has the burden of rebutting the presumption of state protection. In order to establish the reasonableness of failing to approach the state, the claimant must present 'clear and convincing proof' of the state's inability to protect.

This clearly adds an extra layer to interpretation of the Refugee Convention definition.

As Zambelli and Macklin have shown,[91] Canadian decision makers assume there is a state accountability requirement in Canadian law. Zambelli has examined a number of decisions which illustrate that the 'presumption of ability to protect' has defeated many claims at the IRB level that did not meet the standard of 'clear and convincing proof'. As she explains, this requirement 'morphed over the years into a positive duty on refugee claimants to have "tested" the adequacy of domestic protection'[92] before seeking refugee status.

The year 2008 was a watershed. After a number of decisions such as *Mosilhy v. Canada (Minister of Citizenship and Immigration)*,[93] in which it was said that *Ward* stood for the proposition that 'unless the government apparatus has broken down completely, it should be assumed that a government is capable of protecting a claimant',[94] an attempt was made to pull back on the application of the presumption as it came close to a 'balance of probabilities' standard. In 2008, in *Carrillo* v. *Canada (Minister of Citizenship and Immigration)*,[95] G. Letourneau JA said that La Forest J. in *Ward* was referring to the quality of evidence not to a special or higher standard of proof of state protection.[96] But the *Carrillo* phase was short-lived. In *Flores* v. *Canada*,[97] which involved a Mexican woman who claimed refugee status on the basis of her husband's violence towards her and her subsequent partners, two interpretative approaches were developed. The first was a test of 'adequate' rather than 'effective' protection in the state of origin.[98] This test was subsequently applied in a number of cases where refugee status was refused.[99]

The second interpretative approach was that:

> When the state is a democratic society, such as Mexico, albeit one facing significant challenges with corruption and criminality, the quality of the evidence necessary to rebut the presumption will be higher.[100]

This higher burden of proof was enshrined in administrative policy. On 8 May 2008, the Deputy Chairperson of the Refugee Protection Division issued a Notice of Identification of Persuasive Decision,[101] namely TA6-07453,[102] in relation to applications from Mexico. In this case, the claimant alleged that he was targeted by a criminal gang that wanted to involve him in drug dealings. The Board found that adequate state protection was available. In a passage from the decision which is based on older authority,[103] it was said:

> When the state in question is a democratic state, the claimant must do more than simply show that he or she went to see some member of the police force and that his or her efforts were unsuccessful. The burden of proof that rests on the claimant is, in a way, directly proportional to the level of the democracy of the state in question: the more democratic the state's institutions, the more the claimant must have done to exhaust all courses of action open to him or her.[104]

It was confirmed that:

> The claimant, living in a democratic country, is obliged to attempt to seek protection from the state agencies of the country of his nationality first, prior to seeking international protection.[105]

The presumption has been applied in a number of cases concerning claimants from Mexico, which has become the largest source of refugee claims in Canada in recent years. In many decisions the courts have overturned decisions of the Board on the basis that there was insufficient analysis of state protection.[106] By contrast, in *Mari Cruz Hernandez Fuentes* v. *Canada (Minister of Citizenship and*

Immigration),[107] the applicant who made a claim for protection on behalf of her minor daughter from Mexico was not successful. She claimed that her daughter would be the target of sexual abuse and exploitation by the same male relative who had targeted her. The Board held that the applicant had not provided 'clear and convincing evidence' to rebut the presumption of the state's ability to protect her and her daughter. Justice Pinard said:

> The law is now settled that local failures to provide effective policing do not amount to a lack of state protection, and that an applicant may seek redress and protection from protection agencies other than police.[108]

In some cases such as *Oscar Leonard Perez Mendoza* v. *Canada (Minister of Citizenship and Immigration)*,[109] the decision makers have described the standard of proof of lack of state protection as requiring evidence that is:

> relevant, reliable, and convincing to satisfy the trier of fact on a *balance of probabilities* that the state protection was inadequate (*Carillo*).[110]

In *Samuel* v. *Canada (Minister for Citizenship and Immigration)*,[111] it was specifically stated that the 'onus to rebut the presumption of state protection remains at all times on the refugee claimant'.[112] These decisions suggest that a standard of proof that is higher than is appropriate is applied in refugee status determinations in Canada when state protection is in issue.

The surrogate protection approach in Canada has led the courts away from an assessment of the well-founded fear[113] to focus on 'state protection' in the country of origin, even when as Zambelli points out, the police or military are the direct perpetrators of the harm.[114] This discussion demonstrates that it is easy to lose sight of the purpose of refugee protection and the refugee definition. USA authorities suggest that a standard as high as the Canadian applies.[115] The Canadian case study illustrates how a focus on 'surrogate protection' can distort the meaning of 'protection' in interpreting the Refugee Convention.

The reach of *Ward*: the UK, Australia and New Zealand

The UK and 'cosmopolitan' refugees

In the UK, the key decision dating from 2001 is *Horvath* v. *Secretary of State*,[116] in which the lead judgment of Lord Hope refers expressly to the Hathaway 'surrogate protection' approach and the decision of the Supreme Court of Canada in *Ward*. In that case, the applicant was a Roma citizen of Slovakia who claimed that he feared persecution by 'skinheads' against whom the Slovak police failed to provide adequate protection. The Immigration Appeal Tribunal found as a matter of evidence that there was an increasing level of police protection of Roma in Slovakia, and that the behaviour that the applicant feared could not be said to amount to persecution. The Court of Appeal upheld the decision, holding that persecution by non-state actors required both serious harm and failure of state protection.[117] This decision was confirmed by the House of Lords, with Lord Lloyd dissenting.

Lord Hope formulated the issue in the House of Lords as follows:

> does the word 'persecution' denote merely sufficiently severe ill-treatment, or does it denote sufficiently severe ill-treatment against which the state fails to afford protection?[118]

He answered the last part of that question affirmatively by relying upon the Hathaway concept of 'surrogacy', which he said was the central principle for interpreting the Refugee Convention and *Ward*.[119] By contrast, Lord Lloyd who dissented said that the absence of state protection was not relevant to the meaning of 'persecution' but was relevant to the objective test of a 'well-founded fear' of persecution.[120] He was critical of the use of a concept of 'surrogate protection' to define 'persecution' and he also expressly relied upon *Ward* to support his conclusion. This decision demonstrated that a focus on 'surrogate protection' could lead to different emphases in interpreting the Refugee Convention definition.[121] Subsequent developments showed that it was a short step from focusing upon 'persecution' to state complicity.

Horvath has been widely applied and cited in the UK, notably in the 2005 decision in *R v. Secretary of State for the Home Department, ex parte Bagdanavicius*.[122] The latter is accepted as authority for the proposition that there must be 'sufficient but not total protection' from the home state.[123] The standard, as expressed in the instrument implementing the Qualification Directive into national law,[124] is similar to the words of the directive, requiring: 'reasonable steps to prevent the persecution . . . by operating an effective legal system'. However some UK jurisprudence stresses the availability of protection in individual cases.[125]

In later cases, through another avenue of EU law, the standard of protection has come to focus on the individual's human rights and *access* to state protection. This occurred through the decision in *Osman v. United Kingdom*,[126] which was not a case about a refugee but about the sufficiency of state protection in human rights law. *Osman* considered the issue in the context of the prohibition on inhuman and degrading treatment in Article 3 of the European Convention on Human Rights (ECHR).[127] This standard has been adopted in asylum cases and has cross-fertilised into refugee law. As expressed in *SA (Pakistan) v. Secretary of State for the Home Department*:[128]

> under either head [asylum claims or Article 3 claims] a judge must address not only the matter of whether there is a general sufficiency of protection in a country *but also* the question of whether the appellant's particular circumstances are such that he or she *would receive* adequate protection.[129]

In *Gardi v. Secretary of State for the Home Department*,[130] Keene LJ stated that while it is not necessary to eliminate all risk, what is required is a 'practical standard' taking proper account of the duty owed by a state to its nationals. Thus, it seems that the UK approach focuses on an objective assessment of the individual's protection needs and human rights without requiring the very high standard of proof that Canadian law imposes.

While UK jurisprudence is constrained by the ECHR standard, in Australia there is no restraining force. The approach is both pragmatic and confused.

Australia: shifting protection

As mentioned above, the decision in *Respondents S152,* which is the leading decision in Australia, is authority for the proposition that 'surrogate protection' can mean one of three approaches and identities for an asylum seeker. Further, the High Court relied upon the decision of the House of Lords in *Horvath* as authority for that view. The joint judgment of Gleeson CJ, Hayne and Heydon JJ in *Respondents S152* relied upon *Ward* for the proposition that a person's unwillingness to seek protection is related to fear of persecution. They said that he must justify not merely assert unwillingness.[131] According to the RRT (Refugee Review Tribunal) Guide to Refugee Law in Australia, Chapter 8 entitled 'State Protection':

> The joint judgment in *S152/2003* shows that the existence of the appropriate level of state protection leads to the conclusion that there is not a justifiable unwillingness to seek the protection of the country of nationality, even if the fear of harm remains well-founded.[132]

The subsequent application of *Respondents S152* illustrates these three shifting 'surrogate protection' identities: a focus on the reasonableness of the refugee's fear; a focus on the reasonableness of the acts of protection; and proof of state protection as an extra requirement to the refugee definition.

An analysis of jurisprudence reveals confusion over which approach *Respondents S152* sanctioned. In *A99 of 2003* v. *Minister for Immigration*,[133] Mansfield J. said it meant that 'the willingness and ability of the state to protect its citizens is relevant to whether an individual has a well-founded fear of persecution'.[134] Thus, he stated: 'The appropriate level of state protection need not lead to the finding that the fear of harm is not well-founded, or that there is no real chance of the feared harm occurring.'[135] By contrast in *MZRAJ* v. *Minister for Immigration*,[136] Heerey J. said that a finding that the state did not condone the violence was necessarily a finding that the state was willing to provide protection.[137]

The RRT Guide to Refugee Law suggests that the relationship between 'protection' and 'persecution' is a matter of divided opinion in the High Court,[138] but opines that in situations of non-state actors:

> the prevailing view in Australia is that where the required level of internal protection is available, the claim to refugee status cannot succeed because, among other things, the conduct in question will not be 'persecution'.[139]

Another contentious issue in Australian jurisprudence is the relevance of international standards in assessing whether there is a reasonable level of protection in the home state. *Osman*'s case was referred to with apparent approval by the joint judgment in *Respondents S152*.[140] While some decision makers initially applied an international standards test with the reasonable level of protection test (see below),[141] in *MZRAJ* v. *Minister for Immigration*,[142] Heerey J. said that *Respondents S152* did not require proof of failure to meet international standards.[143]

In practice, the test is whether there is a reasonable level of protection. In *SZBBP* v. *Minister for Immigration*[144] the Full Court said that the issue is whether 'the Tribunal is satisfied that the person fearing harms will not receive State protection, not that he will receive it'.[145] In that case it was noted that the RRT's role is to assess whether the protection in Egypt against abuse and harm by Muslims against Coptic Christians was 'effective and adequate'.[146] A similar test was applied in subsequent cases.[147] Notably this is a different standard from the Canadian test of 'adequate' rather than 'effective' protection in the state of origin.

In some decisions, courts have overturned decisions of the tribunal where there is evidence of failure of analysis of individual factors.[148] In *AZAAR* v. *Minister for Immigration and Citizenship and another*,[149] the applicant was a citizen of Vanuatu who claimed she was the object of significant domestic violence at the hands of her husband. She claimed that she was not provided, and would not be provided, with effective state protection due to systemic discrimination against women resulting from cultural norms and practices. Finn J. rejected the RRT's findings that the applicant was obliged to have personally sought state protection to prove an absence of adequate state protection, and held that when determining whether adequate state protection exists it is necessary to determine the practical reality, not just examine the legal mechanisms available. He said:

> If the tribunal was suggesting that actually seeking the protection of the authorities was a prerequisite for a finding of absence of adequate state protection, then it clearly was in error. If cultural norms, practices or widely held assumptions in a particular society engender a reasonable apprehension that such an approach would only exaggerate a victim's predicament, I can see no conceivable reason why the law would require a victim to expose herself to likely future harm to substantiate that she was being persecuted for convention purposes.[150]

Notably, this is similar to the NZ approach which links surrogate protection to the well-founded fear. This decision was disapproved by the Full Court in *Minister for Immigration* v. *SZONJI*[151] on similar facts. In that case, the court said the correct inquiry was not into the adequacy or otherwise of the protection afforded to women who were victims of domestic violence in Fiji but, in contradistinction, into the motives of the state and whether 'the failure by Fiji to protect such victims was itself a manifestation of a persecutory policy directed towards them'.[152] The court found no error in the RRT's assessment of state protection, and its conclusion that Fiji had taken reasonable measures to get rid of domestic violence, including criminalising it, and having a police force and judicial system to enforce the law.

As the RRT Guide to Refugee Law in Australia summarises, although in Australia there is no *legal* presumption of state protection, an asylum seeker bears the practical burden of establishing that protection is lacking. It cites *Ward as* authority for the proposition that 'in the absence of a state admission as to its inability to protect its nationals, clear and convincing evidence of a state's inability to protect must be provided'.[153] It suggests that *Respondents S152* is consistent with that proposition.[154]

The New Zealand 'predicament' approach

New Zealand decision makers[155] identify the issue of surrogate protection and persecution by non-state actors within the objective part of the well-founded fear test. Although the *Ward* decision is applied in NZ to determine whether a person is 'being persecuted', NZ has rejected the 'persecution' approach taken in *Horvath*'s case.

In *Refugee Appeal No. 76044*,[156] R. P. G. Haines Chairperson and B. Dingle Member said that the issue is 'whether the protection available from the state will reduce the risk of serious harm to below the level of well-foundedness, or, as it is understood in New Zealand, to below the level of a real chance of serious harm'. They explained:

> This is a more exacting standard than that which is applied in the United Kingdom subsequent to *Horvath* . . . but has the distinct advantage of securing compliance with the non-refoulement obligation in art 33 of the Convention (Refugee Appeal No. 74665/03. at para [54]).[157]

Thus, while accepting the idea of surrogate protection, the NZ jurisprudence focuses on the risks to the claimant. Although the decision makers recognise a presumption of state protection, it is applied as an evidential rule only.[158]

Conclusion

The refugee can be identified through political, legal and cosmopolitan constructs. In this chapter, I have argued that by identifying asylum seekers and refugees in law as objects of surrogate protection, the interpretation of the Refugee Convention definition in some jurisdictions has moved far from its legal 'protective' purpose. As I have shown, the focus of interpretation of the definition under a surrogate protection approach in Canada has shifted from the refugee applicant's 'well-founded fear of persecution' to an assessment of state accountability or complicity in the persecution. In this transmutation, the courts have raised the burden of proof on a refugee applicant to an inappropriate standard.

The notion of surrogate protection, which is not as such part of the Refugee Convention definition, has three potential meanings as explained in *Respondents S152*. In Canada the courts have chosen to turn it into an additional requirement which treats the refugee as a suspect person. There is a real risk of this approach travelling into other jurisdictions, including individual EU Member States, although the EU does have the constraining ECHR human rights protection as in the UK. Rather than seeing a coherent transnational judicial conversation on these issues, there is, as Colin Harvey articulates, 'an international and transnational dialogue about refugee law within which alternative sources of authority are contested and resolved in localized contexts'.[159]

The discussion in this chapter questions the idea that a transnational judicial conversation leading to 'common judicial understandings' is taking place in international refugee law. This is because of differences in approach between jurisdictions about the correct interpretative approach to the Refugee Convention definition when non-state actors of persecution and protection are present. However, this context is important as it challenges the traditional notion of international law as consensus among contracting states[160] and the idea that states are the main actors in international law. This points us to thinking anew about the nature of contemporary international law and refugee law and in turn about the identity of key actors.[161] It challenges us to think about how the Refugee Convention definition should be interpreted.

As I have shown, the notion of surrogate protection exemplifies the shifting strands of refugee protection and identity in refugee law. In particular, it reveals the ability of the international community to avoid responsibility to significant groups of asylum seekers. It is therefore timely to reflect on how the law and legal interpretation has altered the identity of refugees through use of the surrogate protection notion, to return to the words of the Refugee Convention definition, and to remind contracting states of their international obligations.

Notes

*My thanks to Lisa Harrison for invaluable assistance in collecting material for this chapter and to Reyvi Marinas for editorial assistance.

1 James C. Hathaway, *The Rights of Refugees Under International Law* (Cambridge University Press, 2005), 5.
2 Convention relating to the Status of Refugees, Geneva, 28 July 1951, 1989 UNTS 137, supplemented by the Protocol relating to the Status of Refugees, 31 January 1967, 19 UST 6223, 6257 ('1951 Refugee Convention').
3 The 1951 Refugee Convention Art. 1A(2) defines a refugee as: 'any person who . . . owing to a well-founded fear of being persecuted for reasons of race, religion, nationality, membership of a particular social group or political opinion, is outside the country of his nationality and is unable or unwilling to avail himself of the protection of that country'.
4 Emma Haddad, *The Refugee in International Society: Between Sovereigns* (Cambridge University Press, 2008), 85.
5 Chapter 7.

6 Daniel J. Steinbock, 'The Refugee Definition as Law: Issues of Interpretation', in Frances Nicholson and Patrick Twomey (eds), *Refugee Rights and Realities: Evolving International Concepts and Regimes* (Cambridge University Press, 1999), 21–3.

7 James C. Hathaway, 'Forced Migration Studies: Could We Agree Just to "Date"?' (2007) 20 *Journal of Refugee Studies* 349, 352. Note that some refer to this as subsidiary protection.

8 Jane McAdam, 'The Refugee Convention as a Rights Blueprint for Persons in Need of International Protection', in Jane McAdam (ed.), *Moving on: Forced Migration and Human Rights* (Hart, 2008), 267.

9 Haddad, above n. 4, 47, 88.

10 Colin Harvey, 'Is Humanity Enough? Refugees, Asylum Seekers and the Rights Regime', in Satvinder Juss and Colin Harvey (eds), *Contemporary Issues in International Refugee Law* (Edward Elgar, 2013), ch. 3.

11 EC Qualification Directive, Directive 2011/95/EU of the European Parliament and of the Council of 13 December 2011 on standards for the qualification of third-country nationals or stateless persons as beneficiaries of international protection, for a uniform status for refugees or for persons eligible for subsidiary protection, and for the content of the protection granted (recast), OJ 2011 No. L337/9 ('2011 Qualification Directive').

12 Charter of Fundamental Rights of the European Union: OJ 2000 No. C364/01 ('EU Charter on Fundamental Rights').

13 Alison Kesby, *The Right to Have Rights: Citizenship, Humanity and International Law* (Oxford University Press, 2012).

14 Chapter 7 in this volume.

15 Julie Mertus, 'The State and the Post-Cold War Refugee Regime: New Models, New Questions' (1998) 10 *International Journal of Refugee Law* 321.

16 Maria O'Sullivan, 'Acting the Part: Can Non-State Entities Provide Protection under International Refugee Law?' (2012) 24 *International Journal of Refugee Law* 85.

17 Dallal Stevens, 'What Do We Mean by Protection?' (2013) 20 *International Journal on Minority and Group Rights* 233.

18 James C. Hathaway, *The Law of Refugee Status* (Butterworths, 1991), 125.

19 E.g. Andrew Shacknove, 'Who Is a Refugee?' (1985) 95 *Ethics* 274; Walter Kalin, 'Non-State Agents of Persecution and the Inability of the State to Protect' (2001) 15 *Georgetown Immigration Law Journal* 415, 427. As Dallal Stevens shows in Chapter 5 in this volume, the focus of protection shifted from the *need* for protection to internal home state *failure* of protection. This 'internal protection' is distinguished from the concept of internal flight alternative or protection, which is another interpretative approach that has developed in refugee law.

20 Haddad, above n. 4, 51–2.

21 Ibid., 53; Laura Barnett, 'Global Governance and the Evolution of the International Refugee Regime' (2002) 14 *International Journal of Refugee Law* 238, 239.

22 Haddad, above n. 4, 60.

23 Ibid., 88.

24 Susan Kneebone and Maria O'Sullivan, 'Commentary on Art 1C of the Refugee Convention', in Andreas Zimmerman (ed.), *The 1951 Convention Relating to the Status of Refugees and its 1967 Protocol: A Commentary* (Oxford University Press, 2011).

25 Susan Kneebone, 'Strangers at the Gate: Refugees, Citizenship and Nationality' (2004) 10 *Australian Journal of Human Rights* 33.

26 James C. Hathaway, 'The Evolution of Refugee Status in International Law: 1920–1950' (1984) 33 *International and Comparative Law Quarterly* 348, 350–61.

27 Daniel Warner, 'The Refugee State and State Protection', in Nicholson and Twomey (eds), above n. 6, 258 emphasises this point.

28 Barnett, above n. 21, 242.

29 28 October 1933, League of Nations, Treaty Series Vol. CLIX No. 3663.

30 Barnett, above n. 21, 242.

31 Kesby, above n. 13, 41.

32 Antonio Fortin, 'The Meaning of "Protection" in the Refugee Definition' (2001) 12 *International Journal of Refugee Law* 548; cf. Niraj Nathwani, 'The Purpose of Asylum' (2001) 12 *International Journal of Refugee Law* 354.

33 Hathaway, above n. 18, 124.

34 Kalin, above n. 19, argues that this is the defining characteristic of refugee protection.

35 Kesby, above n. 13, 38.

36 Hathaway, above n. 26, 361–70; see Chapter 5 in this volume.

37 International Conference on Indo-Chinese Refugees, Geneva, 13–14 June 1989; Declaration and Comprehensive Plan of Action, UN Doc A/CONF.148/2, 13 June 1989.

38 Susan Kneebone, 'Refugees and Displaced Persons: The Refugee Definition and "Humanitarian" Protection', in Sarah Joseph and Adam McBeth (eds), *Research Handbook on International Human Rights Law* (Edward Elgar, 2010), ch. 9; see Chapter 5 in this volume.

39 Shacknove, above n. 19.

40 [1999] 2 AC 629, at [635].

41 See Chapter 5 in this volume.

42 Entered into force on 20 June 1974.

43 Principles Concerning Treatment of Refugees as adopted by the Asian–African Legal Consultative Committee at its Eighth Session, Bangkok, August, 1966; reproduced in Eberhard Jahn, 'The Work of Asian–African Legal Consultative Committee on the Legal Status of Refugees' 1967 Max-Planck-Institut <www.zaoerv.de/27_1967/27_19 67_1_2_b_122_138.pdf> (accessed 10 December 2013).

44 Report of the 40th Session of the Asian–African Legal Consultative Organization, Fifth General Meeting, New Delhi, 24 June 2001 <www.aalco.int/report40thsession/ Fifth%20General%20Meeting%202001.pdf> (accessed 10 December 2013); Report of the 40th Session of the Asian–African Legal Consultative Organization, Seventh General Meeting <www.aalco.int/report40thsession/Seventh%20General%20Meeting% 202001.pdf> (accessed 10 December 2013).

45 OAS/Ser.L/V/II.66, doc.10, rev.1, 190–3.

46 Susan Kneebone and Felicity Rawlings-Sanaei (eds), *New Regionalism and Asylum Seekers: Challenges Ahead* (Berghahn, 2007), 5–8.

47 T. Alexander Aleinikoff, 'State Centred Refugee Law: From Resettlement to Containment' (1992) 14 *Michigan Journal of International Law* 120, 121.

48 Mertus, above n. 15.

49 Ibid., 328.

50 Ibid.

51 See Kneebone and Rawlings-Sanaei, above n. 46, 11–16.

52 Ibid.

53 David Turton, 'Who Is a forced migrant?', in Chris de Wet (ed.), *Development-Induced Displacement: Problems, Policies and People* (Berghahn, 2006), ch. 2.

54 Report of the Representative of the Secretary-General, Mr Francis M. Deng, submitted pursuant to Commission resolution 1997/39, Addendum, Guiding Principles on Internal Displacement, E/CN.4/1998/53/Add.2 (11 February 1998).

55 James C. Hathaway and R. Alexander Neve, 'Making International Refugee Law Relevant Again: A Proposal for Collectivised and Solution-Oriented Protection' (1997) 10 *Harvard Human Rights Journal* 115.

56 Shacknove, above n. 19, 283.

57 Ibid., 284.

58 Hathaway, above n. 18, 125.

59　Anna Dorevitch and Michelle Foster, 'Obstacles on the Road to Protection: Assessing the Treatment of Sex-Trafficking Victims under Australia's Migration and Refugee Law' (2008) 9 *Melbourne Journal of International Law* 1.

60　Susan Kneebone, 'Moving beyond the State: Refugees, Accountability and Protection', in Susan Kneebone (ed.), *The Refugees Convention 50 Years on: Globalisation and International Law* (Ashgate, 2003), ch. 11.

61　[2005] NZAR 60, at para. 36 (emphasis in original).

62　Ibid.

63　Hathaway, above n. 18, 105.

64　In *Horvath* v. *Secretary of State* [2001] 1 AC 489 a majority of the House of Lords interpreted the meaning of 'persecution' in the case of non-state agents as requiring evidence of the failure of the 'home' state to provide protection. This is also sometimes referred to as the internal protection approach, in contrast to the external protection approach (which is linked to the older concept of diplomatic protection). See n. 19 above.

65　Aleinikoff, above n. 47.

66　*Minister for Immigration & Multicultural Affairs* v. *Respondents S152* (2004) 222 CLR 1 (*Respondents S152*), *per* McHugh J. In that case McHugh J. interpreted the 'protection' approach as focused on a state duty to protect and rejected it. See also: Volker Turk, 'Non-State Agents of Persecution', in Vincent Chetail and Vera Gowlland-Debbas (eds), *Switzerland and the International Protection of Refugees* (Kluwer Law International, 2002), 95–110; Jennifer Moore, 'Whither the Accountability Theory: Second-Class Status for Third-Party Refugees as a Threat to International Refugee Protection' (2001) 13 *International Journal of Refugee Law* 32.

67　By contrast, general human rights literature on non-state agents is concerned with attributing liability or responsibility to non-state actors by stretching principles of international law state responsibility. See Philip Alston (ed.), *Non-State Actors and Human Rights* (Oxford University Press 2005); O'Sullivan, above n. 16.

68　(2004) 222 CLR 1.

69　UNHCR Annotated Comments on the EC Council Directive 2004/83/EC of 29 April 2004 on minimum standards for the qualification and status of third country nationals or stateless persons as refugees or as persons who otherwise need international protection and the content of the protection granted, OJ 2004 No. L304/12, 18 (emphasis added).

70　(2004) 222 CLR 1, [21].

71　Hathaway, above n. 1, 1–2.

72　Hélène Lambert, 'Transnational Law, Judges and Refugees in the European Union', in Guy S. Goodwin-Gill and Hélène Lambert (eds), *The Limits of Transnational Law: Refugee Law, Policy Harmonization and Judicial Dialogue in the European Union* (Cambridge University Press, 2010), 2.

73　Jane McAdam, 'Migrating laws? The "Plagiaristic Dialogue" between Europe and Australia', in Hélène Lambert *et al.* (eds), *The Global Reach of European Refugee Law* (Cambridge University Press, 2013), ch. 2.

74　Pia Zambelli, 'Problematic Trends in the Analysis of State Protection and Article 1F(a) Exclusion in Canadian Refugee Law' (2011) 23 *International Journal of Refugee Law* 252, 266; Audrey Macklin, 'A Safe Country to Emulate? Canada and the European Refugee', in Lambert *et al.* (eds), above n. 73, ch. 4; Udara Jayasinghe and Sasha Baglay, 'Protecting Victims of Human Rights within a "Non-Refoulement" Framework: Is Complementary Protection an Effective Alternative in Canada and Australia?' (2011) 23 *International Journal of Refugee Law* 489.

75　As *per* UNHCR, *Handbook on Procedures and Criteria for Determining Refugee Status under the 1951 Convention and the 1967 Protocol Relating to the Status of Refugees*, HCR/IP/4/Rev.1, 1979, re-edited, Geneva, January 1992 ('UNHCR Handbook') [195]–[205]. See Brian

Gorlick, 'Common Burdens and Standards: Legal Elements in Assessing Claims to Refugee Status' (2003) 15 *International Journal of Refugee Law* 357.

76 *Chan Yee Kin* v. *Minister for Immigration* (1989) 169 CLR 379.

77 UNHCR Handbook [196].

78 Ibid., [42].

79 [1993] 2 SCR 689.

80 Cf. Zambelli, above n. 74, 257.

81 [1993] 2 SCR 689 at 709, citing Hathaway, above n. 18, 135.

82 Guy S. Goodwin-Gill, *The Refugee in International Law* (Clarendon Press, 1983), 38. Note that Zambelli, above n. 74, 257, attributes the presumptive approach which subsequently developed to this statement.

83 [1993] 2 SCR 689, at 722 (emphasis added by La Forest J.).

84 Ibid., 722, emphasis in original.

85 Chapter 3 in this volume.

86 [1993] 2 SCR 689 at 719.

87 Ibid., at 711.

88 Zambelli, above n. 74, 258.

89 Legal Services, Immigration and Refugee Board, Interpretation of the Convention Refugee Definition in the Case Law: Key Points (1999) (copy on file with the author).

90 Chapter 3 deals with the meaning of persecution, chapter 4 with the grounds and chapter 5 with the meaning of 'well-founded fear'.

91 Above n. 74.

92 Zambelli, above n. 74, 262.

93 2007 FC 1302.

94 Ibid., [35], *per* EP Blanchard J.

95 2008 FCA 94.

96 Ibid., [26]. The *Carrillo* reasoning was applied in *Lozada* v. *Canada (Minister of Citizenship and Immigration)* 2008 FC 397 (applicant did not succeed in persuading the court that state protection did not exist in Mexico); *Erdogu* v. *Canada (Minister of Citizenship and Immigration)* 2008 FC 407, Turkish woman at risk of honour killings – the court relied on a report from Amnesty International to confirm her claim and to rebut the presumption of state protection.

97 2008 FC 723.

98 Jayasinghe and Baglay, above n. 74.

99 E.g. *Samuel* v. *Canada (Minister for Citizenship and Immigration)* 2008 FC 762; *Espinoza* v. *Canada (Minister for Citizenship and Immigration)* [2009] FCJ No. 918; *Cosgun* v. *Canada (Minister for Citizenship and Immigration)* [2010] FCJ No. 458; *JNJ* v. *Canada (Minister for Citizenship and Immigration)* [2010] FCJ No. 1361.

100 *Flores* v. *Canada* 2008 FC 723, [10]. This test was articulated in *Canada (Minister for Citizenship and Immigration)* v. *Kadenko* (1996) 143 DLR (4th), 532.

101 <www.irb-cisr.gc.ca/Eng/BoaCom/references/pol/persuas/Pages/TA607453Ide Des.aspx> (accessed 17 December 2013).

102 <www.irb-cisr.gc.ca/Eng/BoaCom/references/pol/persuas/Pages/TA607453Ide Des.aspx> (accessed 17 December 2013).

103 *Canada (Minister for Citizenship and Immigration)* v. *Kadenko* (1996) 143 DLR (4th) 532.

104 Above n. 102.

105 Ibid.

106 E.g. *Hurtado-Martinez* v. *Canada (Minister of Citizenship and Immigration)* 2008 FC 630 (21 May 2008) following *Avila* v. *Canada (Minister of Citizenship and Immigration)* 2006 FC 359; *Alejadrina Dayna Gallo Farias* v. *(Minister of Citizenship and Immigration)* 2008 FC 1035 (16 September 2008); *Oscar Leonard Perez Mendoza* v. *Canada (Minister of Citizenship and Immigration)* 2010 FC 119.

107 2010 FC 457 (29 April 2010).

108 Ibid., [13]. See also *Baku* v. *Canada (Minister of Citizenship and Immigration)* 2010 FC 1163; *Garcia* v. *Canada (Minister of Citizenship and Immigration)* 2011 FC 1368.

109 2010 FC 119, emphasis added.

110 Ibid., [33] (emphasis added); see also *Cosgun* v. *Canada (Minister for Citizenship and Immigration)* [2010] FCJ No. 458

111 2008 FC 762.

112 Ibid., *per* M. E. Lagace DJ [10].

113 Cf. *RAFA* v. *Canada (Minister for Citizenship and Immigration)* [2011] FCJ No. 217.

114 Above n. 74, 264.

115 *Neivi Demaris Guillen-Hernandez; Keni Yamileth Guillen-Hernandez; Ana Sinia Guillen-Hernandez, Petitioners* v. *Eric H. Holder, Jr., Attorney General of the United States, Respondent* No. 09–1279 United States Court of Appeals for the Eighth Circuit, *592 F.3d 883; 2010 US App. Lexis 1508*, 20 October 2009, submitted 25 January 2010, filed. The applicant was required to show that the government 'condoned it or at least demonstrated a complete helplessness to protect the victims' in order to succeed in a claim for refugee status. A number of US authorities were cited to support this proposition.

116 [2001] 1 AC 489.

117 [2000] INLR 15.

118 Ibid., 494. Note three separate questions were posed, but the House of Lords found it unnecessary to answer the other two.

119 Ibid., 495.

120 On that basis, Lord Lloyd found that the applicant did not satisfy the refugee test.

121 The judgments are discussed in full in Kneebone, above n. 60, 289–92.

122 [2005] UKHL 38 (26 May 2005). In the following decisions applications for refugee status were refused: *IM (Sufficiency of protection) Malawi* [2007] UKAIT 0071 (30 July 2007); *Y K M* v. *Secretary of State for the Home Department* [2007] ScotCS CSIH 55 (22 June 2007); *Butt* v. *Secretary of State for the Home Department* [2006] ScotCS CSOH 59 (05 April 2006); *ZQ and the Secretary of State for Home Department (serving soldier) Iraq* [2009] UKAIT 00048.

123 *R (on the application of Djakija)* v. *Secretary of State for the Home Department* [2005] EWHC 1394 (Admin); *R (on the application of P)* v. *Secretary of State for the Home Department* [2008] EWHC 2447 (Admin).

124 The Refugee or Person in Need of International Protection (Qualification) Regulations 2006 (No. 2525).

125 E.g. *Svazas* v. *Secretary of State for the Home Department* [2002] EWCA Civ 74; [2002] WLR 1891.

126 (1998) 29 EHRR 245. Note there was no reference to *Ward* in *Bagdanavicius*.

127 Convention for the Protection of Human Rights and Fundamental Freedoms 1950, ETS No. 005 ('ECHR'). Notably ECHR Art. 3 has become the protective mechanism in refugee cases as discussed in Chapter 7 in this volume; e.g. *MSS* v. *Belgium and Greece* (European Court of Human Rights, Grand Chamber, Application No. 30696/09, 21 January 2011).

128 [2011] UKUT 30 (IAC).

129 Ibid., [6]. See also *MN (South Africa)* v. *Secretary of State for the Home Department* [2011] CSOH 121.

130 [2002] EWCA Civ 750.

131 Ibid., [19], *per* Gleeson CJ, Hayne and Heydon JJ.

132 MRT-RRT, *A Guide to Refugee Law in Australia* (Legal Services RRT 2013), 8–6 <www.mrt-rrt.gov.au/Conduct-of-reviews/Guide-to-refugee-law.aspx>.

133 (2004) 83 ALD 529. Note that the title of the minister changes frequently e.g. sometimes the office is titled 'Minister for Immigration and Multicultural and Indigenous Affairs', or 'Minister for Immigration and Citizenship'. For the sake of simplicity this is abbreviated as 'Minister for Immigration' in the references.

134 Ibid., [35].
135 Ibid., [38].
136 [2004] FCA 1261.
137 Ibid., [17].
138 Above n. 132, 8–6. Here the Guide is referring to jurisprudence on the issue of converting 'private' harm into 'public' wrongs. See discussion of *Islam and Shah* above.
139 MRT-RRT, *A Guide to Refugee Law in Australia* above n. 132, 8–7; e.g. *SZBBP* v. *Minister for Immigration* [2005] FCAFC 167.
140 Ibid., [27] and [28].
141 *SHKB* v. *Minister for Immigration* [2004] FCA 545; *SZLWB* v. *Minister for Immigration* [2009] FCA 1067 (Besanko J.).
142 [2004] FCA 1261.
143 Ibid., [26].
144 [2005] FCAFC 167.
145 Ibid., [30].
146 Ibid., [14].
147 *NAWN* v. *Minister for Immigration* [2005] FCA 328; *SZDWR* v. *Minister for Immigration* [2006] FCAFC 36.
148 E.g. *Applicant A99 of 2003* v. *Minister for Immigration and Others* [2004] FCA 773; *SZAIX Appellant* v. *Minister for Immigration* [2006] FCA 3 – Chinese Christian woman in Indonesia claimed fear that she would be raped again should she return to Indonesia, either by the man who raped her on both occasions, or by Muslim men; *AZAAR* v. *Minister for Immigration* 2009 [FCA] 912.
149 2009 [FCA] 912.
150 Ibid., [25].
151 (2011) 278 ALR 608.
152 Ibid., [25].
153 MRT-RRT, *A Guide to Refugee Law in Australia*, above n. 132, 8–14.
154 Ibid.
155 Both at the level of the Refugee Status Appeals Authority (RSAA) and the courts there seems to be coherence.
156 [2008] NZAR 719.
157 Ibid., at [63].
158 Refugee Appeals Nos 72558/01 and 72559/01 (19 November 2002).
159 Above n. 10, 70.
160 E.g. *Minister for Immigration* v. *Ibrahim* (2000) 204 CLR 1, at 34 [107], *per* Gummow J.
161 David Armstrong, Theo Farrell and Hélène Lambert, *International Law and International Relations* (Cambridge University Press, 2007).

7 Identifying asylum seekers as potential refugees: transfers and 'acquired rights' under the Refugee Convention

Maria O'Sullivan

Introduction

The construction of refugee identity (and resulting refugee *status*) is a complex matter which is influenced by social, political and legal elements. Under international law, the *legal* identity of refugees is determined by the 1951 Convention relating to the Status of Refugees ('the Refugee Convention')[1] which defines a refugee as a person who is outside their country of nationality and who cannot return to that country due to a well-founded fear of persecution for a Convention reason.[2] However, the way in which persons can turn their *international* identity as a refugee into a *domestic* status as a refugee is complicated by *non-entrée* measures directed at preventing access to asylum. Although a refugee has an identity and status at international law, his or her ability to obtain protection is dependent on being recognised as a refugee with a status under the particular national jurisdiction in which the refugee is situated.[3] Thus, the conferring of refugee status and its associated rights depends on the willingness of the state to accept an asylum seeker[4] into its territory to grant them access to the relevant refugee determination procedure.

In this context, the legal determination of a person as a refugee is shaped by the political and social identity of asylum seekers and refugees in relevant asylum host states. One influential element in this context is the categorisation of asylum seekers in some states as 'illegals' or 'irregular migrants'.[5] In Australia this discourse has proved to be particularly potent, with politicians and the media labelling asylum seekers arriving by boat as 'queue jumpers'. That is, persons are portrayed as subverting the law by not utilising the accepted Australian migration pathways for refugees such as resettlement.[6]

Such labels are particularly influential in the identification and treatment of *asylum seekers* (as opposed to those *granted refugee status*), as they often lead to policies of containment and denial of access to asylum. The designation of asylum seekers as 'illegals' is problematic as asylum seekers are associated with criminal activities and viewed by states as not having any status under either international or national law. As the London-based NGO, the Information Centre about Asylum and Refugees (ICAR),[7] has pointed out:

> the problem with asylum seekers' identity is that they do not belong to any group: they have to flee their home country, which makes them 'outsiders' of that group whilst they also do not belong to the society of the country where they seek protection.[8]

An interesting aspect about this 'outsider' discourse is that asylum seekers tend to be categorised as a group, rather than a collection of individuals. This is important as asylum seekers will have different circumstances and claims for refugee status that must be assessed *individually* against Article 1A(2) of the Refugee Convention. In this way the political and social identity given to asylum seekers in the domestic sphere which 'groups' individuals as one, contradicts their individual status and rights under international law.

As we shall see in this chapter, domestic refugee law strongly reflects national political imperatives, as illustrated vividly by the *non-entrée* measures utilised in Australia. Under Australian law, asylum seekers who arrive by boat (without a visa) are designated as 'offshore entry persons'[9] and 'unauthorised maritime arrivals'.[10] Such persons are liable to be transferred from Australian territory to the Pacific Island states of Nauru and Papua New Guinea (PNG), where they are detained and their claims are processed under the so-called 'Pacific Solution'.[11] The Australian refugee system is unique in that it subjects asylum seekers to differential treatment depending on their mode and date of arrival.[12] Refugees are identified within a strongly defined political and legal framework of deterrence, border security and the criminalisation of people-smuggling. Thus, those who arrive by boat are seen as threats to national security and are disadvantaged and penalised under law.

Although boat arrivals are penalised in this way, recent jurisprudence of the Australian courts indicates that the law can also play an important role in constraining government action by recognising the legal identity and associated rights of asylum seekers under the Refugee Convention. This is illustrated by the Australian High Court decision in *Plaintiff M70/2011* v. *Minister for Immigration and Citizenship* ('Plaintiff M70'),[13] where the court utilised the idea that asylum seekers are persons with acquired rights under the Refugee Convention (together with administrative law principles) to constrain the transfer of asylum seekers to Malaysia under the proposed 'Malaysian Solution'.[14] By referring to the rights of asylum seekers under the Refugee Convention in declaring that arrangement to be unlawful, the court highlighted the importance of those 'acquired rights', the status of the right to seek asylum and the essential identity of the asylum seeker. This is important because states have tended to focus on the *non-refoulement* principle under Article 33 of the Refugee Convention as the sole constraint on transfers, rather than on the other rights set out in the Convention.

The identity of asylum seekers as holders of acquired rights under the Refugee Convention can therefore be a useful tool for constraining the practice of states in transferring asylum seekers to so-called 'safe countries' under bilateral or regional arrangements. In Europe, transfers between states are governed by the Dublin Convention.[15] Although there is a developing jurisprudence on the Dublin Convention and related refugee issues from the Court of Justice of the European Union (CJEU),[16] the protection of the rights of transferees has been primarily defined as a human rights issue which is litigated under the provisions of the European Convention on Human Rights (ECHR).[17] In the latter jurisdiction the question addressed has tended to be whether the person transferred will face a real risk of inhuman or degrading treatment.[18] In contrast, the Australasian region does *not* have a regional human rights treaty or court. Further, although Australia is a party to the main international human rights instruments, it does not have a national bill of rights. Instead, statutory interpretation and administrative law principles can be utilised in order to interpret migration legislation in line with the Refugee Convention and thereby to constrain unlawful government action. This illustrates the broader point made in this book about the power of the law and its institutions as instruments for making and unmaking the refugee category – particularly the role of courts in providing judicial protection of rights.

The 'acquired rights approach' analysed in this chapter illustrates that 'protection' under the 1951 Refugee Convention is not limited to simply protection against persecution, but also the associated rights and benefits that refugees (and in some instances, asylum seekers) are entitled to receive under the Convention. It reflects the declaratory nature of refugee status determinations[19] and the identity of asylum seekers as aspirant or presumptive refugees.

Against this background, in this chapter I explain how asylum seekers are identified as potential or presumptive refugees or holders of 'acquired rights' under the Refugee Convention. I also explain how this conflicts with the way that asylum seekers are identified in current regional transfer arrangements in the Asia-Pacific region. The second part of this chapter will examine the identity of asylum seekers and refugees as 'rights-holders' under the Refugee Convention. In third section I discuss the identity of asylum seekers as potential refugees and how this interacts with the rights of asylum seekers. The fourth section brings together these two principles, to analyse the way in which Australian law reflects asylum seeker identity and status. In the concluding section, some reference will also be made to the EU regional system by way of comparison, before coming to some conclusions about how 'acquired rights' define the legal identity of asylum seekers.

Acquired rights under Articles 2–34 of the Refugee Convention

Acquired rights and refugees

When a person is recognised as a refugee by an asylum host state under national procedures, the state is obliged to grant them certain rights under Articles 2–34 of the Refugee Convention. In addition to the primary obligation of *non-refoulement* under Article 33, these rights include freedom of religion and association, access to courts, wage-earning employment, welfare, housing, public education, public relief, labour legislation and social security (these are referred to as refugees' 'acquired rights').[20] A refugee is therefore given an identity and status under international law as a *rights-holder*. The acquired rights in the Convention also recognise the need for refugees to have a level of personal security, dignity and stability. This is important as increasingly these values are being put aside due to the labelling of asylum seekers as a threat to national security.[21] Further, some states such as Australia utilise temporary protection visas for refugees which carry fewer rights than those given permanent status.[22]

Under the Refugee Convention, acquired rights accrue to the refugee according to the level of attachment he or she has to the host state. Some apply to those refugees present in the territory of the state,[23] some to those 'lawfully in their territory'[24] and some to those 'lawfully staying' in the territory of the state.[25] Others are not conditioned on presence within or lawful residence in territory, but refer simply to 'refugees', that is, to persons who meet the requirements of the Refugee Convention definition.[26]

Thus, as noted in the Introduction to this book, protection under the Refugee Convention is provided according to the intensity of the new bond created with the country of asylum, and according to the laws of that country.[27] These levels of attachment reflect the increasing acceptance of the refugee into the asylum host state. Thus, the acquired rights in the Refugee Convention are linked to the strength of the bond between the refugee and the asylum host state and the content of those rights increases as the refugee is accepted into his or her new society. This graduated level of rights based on attachment and integration therefore focuses on social and political membership in the state, rather than simply on the broader human rights of the refugee as a person.

This raises the question: within this 'membership' and 'attachment' framework, what rights apply to those refugees who are not yet 'lawfully present' in the territory of an asylum host state, but who may be otherwise subject to that state's jurisdiction? This question is particularly relevant in transfer situations as in some cases asylum seekers may not be able to reach the territory of an asylum state (for instance, where they are interdicted and transferred to a third 'safe' country). If such asylum seekers are labelled under domestic law as 'unlawful non-citizens' or 'offshore entry persons' and excluded from the normal protections of the laws of that state what rights do they have? And what is the relevance of domestic migration status to international law in this context?

This raises one of the grey areas in relation to acquired rights: *all* the rights set out in Articles 2–34 of the Convention are stated to apply to 'refugees'. But at what point does an asylum seeker, who may be a 'refugee' under international law, but has not yet been recognised as such under a state's domestic law, become entitled to these acquired rights? In this situation, the asylum seeker may identify him or herself as a refugee and under international law may be a refugee, but because they are not permitted to lodge an asylum claim with the first state, they cannot be given domestic recognition of that status/identity. This links to the themes discussed elsewhere in this book: the implications of the practice of many states in sheltering refugees within their territory, but not necessarily conferring them with refugee status. It also illustrates the link between refugee identity and protection.

Acquired rights and asylum seekers

A number of academic commentators have argued that asylum seekers should be entitled to some acquired rights under the Refugee Convention irrespective of status under domestic law. One of the chief proponents of this view is James Hathaway, as set out in his influential text, *The Rights of Refugees under International Law*.[28] Hathaway recognises that 'the rights set by the Refugee Convention are those only of genuine Convention refugees, not of every person who seeks recognition of refugee status'.[29] However, he notes that:

> because it is one's de facto circumstances, not the official validation of those circumstances, that gives rise to Convention refugee status, genuine refugees may be fundamentally disadvantaged by the withholding of rights pending status assessment. They are rights holders under international law, but are pre-cluded from exercising their legal rights during the often protracted domestic processes by which their entitlement to protection is verified by officials.[30]

Hathaway continues:

> This dilemma can only be resolved by granting any person who claims to be a Convention refugee the *provisional benefit of those rights which are not predicated on regularisation of status*, in line with the Convention's own attachment requirements.[31]

Hathaway makes a distinction between asylum seekers who are within the 'jurisdiction' of a state and those within the 'territory' of a state.[32] He notes that while most rights in the Refugee Convention are made available to refugees once a refugee is either present, lawfully present or lawfully residing in an asylum state, there are a number of 'core' rights under the Refugee Convention that do not depend on the refugee being within the asylum state territory or having a 'lawful presence'. These include: the right to non-discrimination (Article 3); movable and immovable property (Article 13); access to courts (Article 16); access to rationing (Article 20); education (Article 22); fiscal charges (Article 29); *non-refoulement* (Article 33); and naturalisation in the asylum state (Article 34).[33] Hathaway argues that this set of 'core' or acquired rights applies to states which exercise 'de facto' jurisdiction over refugees not physically present in their territory.[34] As transfer to a safe third country may result in divestiture of Convention rights, he states that:

> it seems reasonable to insist that, at a minimum, a country be deemed a 'safe third country' only if it will respect in practice *whatever Convention rights the refugee has already acquired by virtue of having come under the jurisdiction or entered the*

territory of a state party to the Refugee Convention, as well as any other international legal rights thereby acquired; and further that there be a judicial or comparable mechanism in place to enable the refugee to insist upon real accountability by the host state to implement those rights.[35]

Other academic writers have also argued that the obligations of a transferring state under the Convention extend beyond Article 33. For instance, Michelle Foster, in a 2007 paper, 'Protection Elsewhere', notes that:

> a good faith application of Convention obligations requires that, in order to transfer a refugee to another state in accordance with the Refugee Convention, a state is under an obligation to ensure that the refugee will enjoy the rights to which she is entitled under the Convention scheme. This includes all Convention rights to which she is entitled at the time of transfer. In addition, 'he or she must also acquire in the receiving state such additional rights as are mandated by the requirements of the Convention'.[36]

Foster agrees that some of the acquired rights in the Convention apply to persons 'even if state agencies have not yet determined that the applicant satisfies the refugee definition, since it is well-established that recognition of refugee status is declaratory only'.[37]

Similarly, Stephen Legomsky, a US scholar, emphasises that a state which transfers an asylum seeker to a third state may be liable for any violations carried out in that third state under a 'complicity principle'.[38] That is

> no country may return a refugee or asylum seeker to a third country knowing that the third country will do *anything* to that person that the sending country would not have been permitted to do itself.[39]

Legomsky states that this is not limited to Article 33 of the Refugee Convention, but also extends to the associated rights flowing from refugee status under the Refugee Convention, such as non-discrimination, free movement, legal status and documentation, family life, subsistence, education, healthcare and employment.[40]

Now I turn to discuss how these acquired rights relate to the identity of 'asylum seekers'. That is, what is the legal identity of a person in the period *prior* to the determination of that person as a refugee under national law and what *rights* do such persons have?

The identity of an asylum seeker under international law: a person seeking asylum and a potential refugee

As recognised in the Introduction to this book, persons fleeing their homelands and intending to apply for refugee status do in fact hold a legal identity and status as an 'asylum seeker'.[41] This arises from the principle, generally accepted by states, that refugee status is *declaratory* in nature.[42] That is, an applicant becomes a refugee upon fleeing his or her country for a Convention reason, and later domestic recognition of refugee status by a host state simply *declares* that person to be a refugee. In this respect, the domestic grant of refugee status by an asylum state is merely acknowledging an existing refugee status under international law.

The asylum seeker as a potential refugee

Identifying and reflecting the status of asylum seekers as potential refugees, who are therefore entitled to certain rights under the Refugee Convention poses a dilemma, as the Convention does not contain a specific right to seek asylum. Such a right is set out in Article 14 of the Universal Declaration of Human Rights (UDHR)[13] which provides that '[e]veryone has the right to seek and to enjoy asylum from persecution in other countries'.[14] This instrument gives the asylum seeker a clear 'human rights identity'. Asylum seekers are also entitled to internationally recognised human rights such as freedom of movement and freedom from torture or degrading treatment or punishment, as set out in the International Covenant on Civil and Political Rights (ICCPR)[15] and regional instruments such as the ECHR.[16]

It is often noted by states that the 1951 Refugee Convention does not explicitly set out a right to seek asylum or refer to 'asylum seekers'. But neither does Article 1A(2) require a refugee to be 'formally recognised' as such in order to be protected by the provisions of the Convention. Indeed, refugee status under the Convention is widely recognised as being declaratory in nature,[17] as is explained in the UNHCR Handbook. It states:

> A person is a refugee within the meaning of the 1951 Convention as soon as he fulfils the criteria contained in the definition. This would necessarily occur prior to the time at which his refugee status is formally determined. Recognition of his refugee status does not therefore make him a refugee but declares him to be one. He does not become a refugee because of recognition, but is recognized because he is a refugee.[18]

This has also been affirmed by a number of conclusions of UNHCR Executive Committee ('Ex Com'). For instance, in Ex Com Conclusion 6, the Executive Committee reaffirmed the 'fundamental importance' of the observance of the non-refoulement principle to persons 'irrespective of whether or not they have been formally recognised as refugees'.[19] In the European Union, the 2011 Qualification Directive also states that '[t]he recognition of refugee status is a declaratory act'.[50]

Thus, UNHCR and some scholars have recognised that asylum seekers can be viewed as potential refugees, until their status is determined. The UNHCR Note on Protection recognises that:

> Every refugee, is initially, an asylum-seeker; therefore, to protect refugees, asylum-seekers must be treated on the assumption that they may be refugees

until their status has been determined. Otherwise, the principle of non-refoulement would not provide effective protection for refugees, because applicants might be rejected at borders or otherwise returned to persecution on the grounds that their claim had not been established.[51]

As Vedsted-Hansen points out:

> asylum applicants enjoy *presumptive refugee status*. Thus, the declaratory nature of the recognition of refugee status implies that an asylum seeker has the same rights as a refugee unless and until his or her non-refugee status has been established.[52]

A small number of court decisions have also recognised asylum seekers as aspirant refugees. For instance, Justice Jowitt in the 1993 decision of the UK High Court in *R v Secretary of State for the Home Department, ex parte Jahangeer*,[53] held that:

> In my view though, the term 'refugee' is not used with the same meaning wherever it appears in the Convention. It is used, I think, in some cases to refer to an *aspirant refugee whose status has not yet been determined* and who may, or may not, be shown on investigation to be a refugee; and in other cases to someone who is already established to be a refugee. There may be uses of the term applying to both the aspiring and the recognised refugee.[54]

Justice Jowitt referred, in particular, to Article 16(1) of the Refugee Convention as illustrative of this. Article 16(1) provides that '[a] refugee shall have free access to the courts of law on the territory of all Contracting States'.[55] Justice Jowitt found that

> the use of the word 'refugee' there is apt to include the aspirant, for were that not so, if in fact it had to be established that he did fall within the definition of 'refugee' in article 1, he might find that he could have no right of audience before the court because the means of establishing his status would not be available to him so that he could not have access to the courts of this country on judicial review.[56]

Similarly, Justice Jowitt held that Article 31, which prohibits contracting states imposing penalties on refugees in certain circumstances,[57] also applied to 'the aspirant refugee whose status as a refugee has still to be determined by the immigration authorities of the country to which he has come'.[58] In this case, Justice Jowett ultimately rejected the applicant's arguments against transfer under the Dublin Convention on the basis that Article 32 (the central provision at issue in the litigation) applies to the refugee whose status has already been established.[59] Article 32(1) states that 'Contracting States shall not expel a refugee *lawfully in their territory* save on grounds of national security or public order'.[60] Although this was interpreted as applying only to refugees lawfully in territory under *domestic* laws, the remarks of Justice Jowitt in relation to Article 31 are nevertheless important for their recognition of the identity of asylum seekers as aspirant refugees who may have an entitlement to certain rights under the Refugee Convention.

In the slightly later UK case of *R v. Uxbridge Magistrates Court, ex parte Adimi*, Justice Brown also recognised that Article 31 of the Refugee Convention applies to 'presumptive refugees'. Justice Brown observed:

> That Article 31 extends not merely to those ultimately accorded refugee status but also to those claiming asylum in good faith (presumptive refugees) is not in doubt. Nor is it disputed that Article 31's protection can apply equally to those using false documents as to those (characteristically the refugees of earlier times) who enter a country clandestinely.[61]

Article 31 has also been interpreted by academics and some judges as applying to presumptive refugees.[62]

However, apart from these examples, recognition of the rights of asylum seekers has generally been limited to the *non-refoulement* principle under Article 33 of the Refugee Convention. The *non-refoulement* principle under Article 33 is undoubtedly one of the principal provisions in the Convention and is considered by many commentators to have the status of customary international law.[63] However, it is reflective of state sovereignty interests and therefore fails to explicitly grant any right of access to state territory for the purpose of claiming asylum. As Aleinikoff notes:

> Recognizing the fundamental international law norm that states have complete control over the entrance of aliens into their territory, the Convention carefully fails to establish any duty upon states to admit refugees. Its central protection is the guarantee of *non-refoulement* – the right of refugees not to be returned to a country in which they would suffer persecution.[64]

The protective possibilities of other parts of the Refugee Convention therefore require closer inspection. In this context, the recognition by the Australian High Court of the relevance of acquired rights to protect asylum seekers in certain situations, beyond mere reliance on Article 33, is a significant example of how such refugees may be identified in law.

Australia: unlawful non-citizens and offshore processing

The identity of asylum seekers and refugees in Australia is very much shaped by the unique structure of Australian migration policy. Australian refugee law and policy is made up of two systems: a resettlement programme for those asylum seekers who apply *outside* of Australia, and a policy of deterrence for arrivals who enter Australian waters without a visa, that is, those that arrive by boat. This two-tiered system prioritises the selection of refugees from overseas as part of a managed, 'orderly' resettlement programme and penalises those who flee their countries of origin and come to Australian shores to apply for asylum.[65]

This differentiated regime is reflected in the widespread public perception in Australian society that there is a resettlement 'queue' which onshore applicants are seeking to evade and that those arriving by boat take places away from 'genuine' refugees in overseas camps. There is also growing public concern and political debate as to how to deter asylum seekers from making what is often a dangerous journey by boat from Indonesia to Australia.[66] This deterrence theme, together with the criminalisation of people-smuggling, has contributed to a punitive approach to those asylum seekers who arrive by boat.[67]

How is this reflected in the identity and status of asylum seekers in transfer situations and the rights they are given?

Reflections of the 'queue jumper' label in the Australian Migration Act

The Migration Act deals with a vast array of immigration issues and is focused on control of arrivals. This influences the way in which Australian courts interpret both domestic legislation and the Refugee Convention. The Migration Act establishes a clear demarcation between 'lawful' and 'unlawful' non-citizens which is dependent on the holding of a valid visa.[68] In this regard, section 4 of the Migration Act gives primacy to the visa system as the only source of lawfulness of stay in Australia. Section 4(2) provides:

> To advance its object, this Act provides for visas permitting non-citizens to enter or remain in Australia and the Parliament intends that this Act be the only source of the right of non-citizens to so enter or remain.[69]

Due to the controls operated in international airports in the region, those arriving by aeroplane generally hold a valid visa and are able to claim asylum. It is those arriving by boat on unauthorised voyages ('boat people') who do not hold such visas and who are therefore delineated as 'unlawful non-citizens' under the Migration Act – thereby obscuring their identity as asylum seekers. Under the Australian 'offshore processing' regime, asylum seekers who arrive by boat are classified as 'offshore entry persons' and are unable to apply for a protection visa under Australian migration legislation, unless the Minister for Immigration exercises his or her discretion to permit this.[70]

Refugees are further identified as being outside the normal Australian migration system by the 'excision' of Australian territory. In 2001, all outlying territories belonging to Australia were 'excised' from the Australian migration zone. This had the effect that asylum seekers intercepted and held on these territories (e.g. Christmas Island) were not permitted to lodge a protection visa application under mainstream Australian law,[71] but were processed separately.[72] More recently, in May 2013, the Migration Act was again amended to excise the Australian mainland from the Australian migration zone. Following this amendment, all those who arrive by boat, including those who actually land on Australia's shores, are now barred from lodging a valid application for a visa.[73] Thus, Australian law assigns separate identities to different asylum seekers depending on their mode of arrival and excludes and penalises those that are compelled to come to Australia by boat to seek protection.

This is where the acquired rights approach becomes significant, as it can be argued that the responsibility of Australia towards asylum seekers under international law continues to operate, notwithstanding any attempt to exclude territory from Australia's domestic migration zone. Australia can still be held to be responsible under international law or treatment of persons outside the excised territory due to the exercise of 'jurisdiction' and 'control' over them.[74]

I now turn to examine the way in which the 1951 Refugee Convention and the rights of asylum seekers and refugees have been interpreted by Australian courts, before then moving to examine the issues arising from current transfer arrangements.

The identity of asylum seekers as rights-holders: the Australian High Court

The High Court of Australia has, historically, taken a restrictive, literal interpretation of the Migration Act in relation to the rights of asylum seekers and refugees. In the controversial decision of the High Court in 2002, *Al Kateb* v. *Godwin*, the court upheld the constitutionality of provisions of the Migration Act which mandate detention of asylums seekers, even if that detention is indefinite.[75] In contrast, the position of UNHCR is that mandatory detention of asylum seekers is contrary to international law.[76] Further, in the leading High Court case on cessation of refugee status, *Minister for Immigration* v. *QAAH*, the court held that Australian domestic law is determinative of the legal questions relating to cessation. The court held that 'it is the law of Australia which prevails in case of any conflict between it and the Convention. It is the law of Australia which must first be identified'[77] and that despite the ways in which 'the Convention may be used in construing the Act, it is the words of the Act which govern'.[78] As Susan Kneebone has noted:

> As the very manner of incorporation of the Refugees Convention under the Migration Act demonstrates, in Australia the rights of refugee are seen by the executive as an aspect of immigration control, rather than of implementation of international treaty obligations. It is therefore unsurprising that the judiciary sometimes overlook the human rights dimensions of the claims of these 'non-citizens'.[79]

However, recent decisions of the High Court dealing with 'offshore processing' of refugee claims seem to indicate a change of approach to the interpretation of the Refugee Convention. In the 2010 decision of the court in *Plaintiff M61/2010E*,[80] the court described the Migration Act as:

> an elaborated and interconnected set of statutory provisions directed to the purpose of responding to the international obligations which Australia has undertaken in the Refugees Convention and the Refugees Protocol.[81]

This case was important as the High Court held that outsourced 'independent' reviewers utilised to process asylum applications from those detained on Christmas Island[82] were in fact obliged to afford procedural fairness to applicants.[83] It also held that such decision makers were 'bound to act according to law by applying relevant provisions of the Migration Act and decided cases'.[84] This case is interesting in terms of refugee identity because it underlined the importance of the Migration Act and Refugee Convention to 'offshore persons' – thereby recognising to some extent the international status of asylum seekers. As Susan Kneebone has noted:

> In its reasons, the High Court made it clear that the Australian government could not contract out of its obligations under the Refugee Convention by establishing a separate offshore process.[85]

Further, in 2011, the court delivered a landmark judgment on the legality of an offshore processing arrangement in *Plaintiff M70*.[86] In this case, the court had been called upon to consider the lawfulness of an 'arrangement' made between Australia and Malaysia, under which up to 800 asylum seekers who arrived by sea in Australia were to be transferred to Malaysia for assessment of their claims to be refugees (the so-called 'Malaysian Solution').[87] In that decision, the High Court of Australia underlined the importance of the acquired rights under Articles 2–34 of the Refugee Convention in the transfer of asylum seekers to third countries.[88]

The litigation centred on Section 198A of the Migration Act which, at that time, permitted the transfer of asylum seekers to a third country if certain criteria were satisfied. These criteria included protective provisions which mirror those recognised in refugee and human rights law, such as access to protection, a refugee status determination procedure and basic human rights standards.[89] In a majority decision (6:1), the High Court held that the Malaysian Arrangement did not meet the criteria in section 198A of the Migration Act and the Australian government was therefore prevented from implementing the arrangement. The court held that the declaration made under section 198A in relation to Malaysia was invalid, and stated that the criteria stipulated in that provision of the Act:

> must be understood as referring to access and protections of the kinds that Australia undertook to provide by signing the Refugees Convention and the

Refugees Protocol. In that sense the criteria stated in s 198A(3)(a)(i) to (iii) are to be understood as a reflex of Australia's obligations.[90]

Importantly, the court recognised that the prohibition against *refoulement* in Article 33 was not the only important provision in the Refugee Convention, but that the other rights set out in Articles 2–34 were also of significance. The majority of the High Court in *Plaintiff M70* therefore held that:

> Australia, as a party to the Refugees Convention and the Refugees Protocol, is bound to accord to 'persons who are given refugee status' the rights there identified. Those rights include, but are by no means limited to, rights relating to education, the practice of religion, employment, housing and access to the courts.[91]

As noted earlier in this chapter, these rights are important as they are intended to provide personal security, human dignity and a level of security to refugees.

Although this statement related to Section 198A which deals with transfers, rather than section 36 of the Migration Act which deals with recognition of refugee status, the decision is indicative of a move by the High Court to extend Australia's Refugee Convention obligations under the Migration Act from its narrow focus on Article 1 of that Convention. As Tamara Wood and Jane McAdam note:

> The decision also demonstrates that, despite Australia's dualist legal system, it does contain mechanisms for the limited recognition and application of international law, in particular through common law principles of statutory interpretation which provide that a statute is to be interpreted so far as is possible in conformity with Australia's international obligations and other established rules of international law.[92]

Thus, the decision of the High Court of Australia in *Plaintiff M70* underscores the importance of acquired rights and indicates a shift in approach by the High Court to a more liberal, purposive interpretation of the Migration Act and an improved level of adherence to the Refugee Convention. Indeed, in a recent 2013 case on the definition of a 'particularly serious crime' under Australian domestic law, the High Court again emphasised that the 'protection obligations' referred to in section 36(2)(a) of the Migration Act are not limited to the *non-refoulement* obligation in Article 33(1) of the Refugee Convention.[93] This is important to refugee identity because it recognises that there is a point at which an asylum seeker's act in seeking asylum in a state creates a link to the Refugee Convention and thereby enlivens state responsibility under that Convention. Further, *non-refoulement* is only part of the protection framework for refugees: it is a negative obligation (state must not return an asylum seeker to harm), which must necessarily be supplemented by the positive obligations set out elsewhere in the Refugee Convention.

Developments since Plaintiff M70

Unsurprisingly, the Australian government was disappointed by the High Court decision in *Plaintiff M70* which identified asylum seekers as rights-holders under the Refugee Convention. As part of its response to the judgment, in late June 2012, the government commissioned an 'Expert Panel' to review Australia's refugee policy.[94] In addition to disapproval of the High Court's stance on the Malaysian Solution, the report was also prompted by a number of fatalities of asylum seekers at sea, and an extended and highly publicised parliamentary debate about the direction of Australia's refugee policy.[95]

There have been many attempts at formulating 'solutions' to increasing refugee flows to Australia since the failure of the Malaysian arrangement. One theme underlying all of these policies has been the designation of boat arrivals as 'irregular' or 'unauthorised' arrivals who are subverting the 'proper' migration channels.

Under the Labor government led by Prime Ministers Rudd and Gillard (2007–13), a 'no advantage principle' was introduced into Australian law. Under this, boat arrivals who arrived between 13 August 2012 and 19 July 2013, and who were recognised as refugees were only to be given a protection visa after such time as they would have been given a resettlement place within the Asia-Pacific region. The underlying principle was that those who arrive 'unlawfully' would obtain no advantage over those who arrived via 'regular Australian migration pathways' such as Australia's resettlement programme.[96] As a recent parliamentary committee on human rights noted, the 'no advantage' principle as implemented by the Australian government focuses on the date and mode of an asylum seeker's arrival in Australia rather than their *status* as a person seeking asylum under the 1951 Refugee Convention (and, I argue, their status as a *potential refugee*).[97]

The Labor government also reinstigated the use of 'offshore processing' of asylum seeker claims via a second (and more restrictive) version of the so-called 'Pacific Solution'. This was underpinned by a suite of legislative measures passed to overturn the findings of the High Court decision in *Plaintiff M70*. The government repealed section 198A of the Migration Act – the provision which had been so central to the High Court of Australia's findings and which identified asylum seekers as 'rights-bearers'. This provision was replaced with different criteria under a new provision (s. 198AB),[98] which make the minister's view of the 'national interest' the paramount criteria for designation of a regional processing country. In deciding this, the minister must have regard to assurances by the third country that it will assess persons under Article 1A(2) and will not return persons in contravention of the *non-refoulement* principle in Article 33. However, it contains no explicit requirements as to the level of protection to be provided in that third country and omits any recognition of the acquired rights of asylum seekers and refugees under the Refugee Convention.

Section 198AB of the Migration Act is important as it has been utilised by the Australian government to declare and utilise PNG and Nauru as 'regional processing centres'.[99] Significantly, in making these declarations, the Minister for Immigration placed great emphasis on discouraging boat arrivals:

> I think that it is in the national interest to take action that is directed to discouraging irregular and dangerous maritime voyages to Australia and thereby to reducing the risk of loss of life at sea . . . I think that designating Nauru to be a regional processing country may act as a circuit breaker in relation to the recent surge in the number of irregular and dangerous maritime voyages to Australia.[100]

The minister also referred to the need to give priority to resettlement refugees, and to promote regional cooperation on 'irregular migration'.[101] Problematically, the Memorandum of Understanding between Australia and Papua New Guinea defines the term 'irregular migration' as 'the phenomenon of people moving without proper authorisation to a country *including for the purpose of seeking asylum*'.[102] This illustrates the legal implications of labelling asylum seekers as 'irregular' and the continuing linkages made in Australian law between asylum seekers, border security and the criminalisation of people-smuggling.

Moreover, the minister prioritised domestic law over Australia's international obligations. In designating Nauru as a 'regional processing country', the Minister for Immigration explicitly stated that:

> even if the designation of Nauru to be a regional processing country is inconsistent with Australia's international obligations, I nevertheless think that it is in the national interest to designate Nauru to be a regional processing country.[103]

Thus, the changes instituted by the Australian government to counteract the High Court decision in *Plaintiff M70* reflect how asylum seekers are identified within a border security framework in Australian political discourse and law. They also demonstrate the elevation of domestic political imperatives over international law. This trend appears likely to worsen over the next years, as the policy of the current coalition government (which has held power since September 2013) is to establish a 'regional deterrent framework' – thus explicitly emphasising deterrence rather than protection. As part of this, it has established a military-led border protection programme (led by a three-star military commander).[104] These measures underscore how the refugee is 'securitised' in Australian law and policy.

Implications: acquired rights, transfers and South-East Asian regional cooperation

In addition to the bilateral arrangements Australia has in place with Nauru and PNG, Australia is also attempting to establish a wider regional framework between countries in South-East Asia, particularly the major asylum host states of Malaysia and Indonesia. Some groundwork for this has been done via creation of the 'Regional Cooperation Framework' agreed at the Bali Process in 2011.[105] However, the Bali Process is focused on border security and prevention of people-smuggling and thus the cooperation framework reflects that focus.

The attempt by Australia to forge cooperation in the South-East Asian region increases the importance of recognising refugee-specific rights in transfer situations within the region. This is because, unlike the EU, there is no harmonisation of refugee law, procedure or reception standards in the Asian region. Most states in the region are not parties to the Refugee Convention[106] and some of those that are parties (e.g. PNG) have made reservations to important acquired rights, such as the right to education.[107] Moreover, unlike the European region, there is no regional human rights instrument such as the ECHR, or a supervisory body such as the European Court of Human Rights which provides human rights protection to asylum seekers. Some countries in South-East Asia are signatories to the key international human rights instruments,[108] but many are not.[109] In order to illustrate these differences, I now turn to examine the human rights identity of asylum seekers in Europe.

Asylum seeker rights in transfer situations: Europe

The identity of the asylum seeker within the EU regional system provides an interesting comparator to that of the Asia-Pacific. Although asylum seekers are liable to be transferred between EU Member States, this is done so on the basis of the responsibility of the first EU country in which the asylum seeker arrived.[110] In the EU, the legal identity of asylum seekers is shaped by the Dublin Convention and the associated harmonised asylum directives under the Common European Asylum System (CEAS).[111] These mechanisms are aimed at preventing 'secondary movement' of asylum seekers between EU Member States.[112] The rationale for the Dublin Convention transfer regime is that asylum seekers are expected to seek protection in the first safe country entered and any secondary movement will be for non-asylum purposes (that is, economic in nature).[113] Within the EU, any secondary movement is therefore identified as 'non-refugee' in nature. European law and policy does not apply different standards according to the mode of arrival of asylum seekers as adopted by Australia.

The rights to which asylum seekers are entitled within the EU context is also shaped *additionally* by the regional human rights framework within Europe. This includes the Charter of Fundamental Rights of the European Union ('EU Charter of Fundamental Rights')[114] and the ECHR,[115] underpinned by the jurisprudence of the European Court of Human Rights. In this environment, the European asylum seeker tends to asserts rights as a *human being* and a holder of *human* rights, rather than relying on a special status as a potential refugee.

Indeed, some commentators have noted that in some ways the ECHR is more effective than the Refugee Convention in protecting asylum seekers in Europe.[116] For instance, Magdalena Forowicz has noted that:

> in the particular context of refugee rights, it is often more beneficial to rely on the ECHR than on the 1951 Refugee Convention: the ECHR framework provides a more effective enforcement mechanism, and also often grants greater protection to the applicant than the 1951 Refugee Convention.[117]

The human rights identity of asylum seekers in Europe

The EU Charter of Fundamental Rights sets out some important provisions which asylum seekers can utilise.[118] Importantly, Article 18 sets out a 'right to asylum'[119] and Article 19(2) imposes a *non-refoulement* obligation upon Member States.[120] However, it is the ECHR, particularly Article 3 and its prohibition on torture and other ill-treatment, which has (to date at least) been the main protective provision for asylum seekers facing transfer within Europe and to third countries outside the region. A long line of case law of the European Court of Human Rights has established that the expulsion of an asylum seeker by a contracting state may give rise to breach of Article 3 where:

> substantial grounds have been shown for believing that the person concerned faces a real risk of being subjected to torture or inhuman or degrading treatment or punishment in the receiving country. In such circumstances, Article 3 implies an obligation not to expel the individual to that country.[121]

The strength of Article 3 as a protective provision for asylum seekers is illustrated by the findings of the European Court of Human Rights in *MSS* v. *Belgium and Greece*.[122] In this case, the applicant asylum seeker was subjected to a Dublin Convention transfer from Belgium to Greece where he alleged he was detained and subjected to ill-treatment.[123] The European Court of Human Rights (Grand Chamber) held that Greece had breached Article 3 of the ECHR in its treatment of the applicant and that Belgium had breached Article 3 by transferring the applicant to Greece. On the facts, the Court found that the applicant's conditions of detention and living conditions in Greece were degrading[124] and that the general situation in Greece in relation to the treatment of asylum seekers was known to the Belgian authorities prior to the transfer of the applicant.[125] In making its ruling, the Court attached 'considerable importance to the applicant's status as an asylum seeker' and 'a member of a particularly underprivileged and vulnerable population group in need of special protection'.[126] The Court found that the applicant had been 'the victim of humiliating treatment showing a lack of respect for his dignity'.[127] The Court held Belgium was also liable because the transfer of asylum seeker to another EU country leaves 'the responsibility of the transferring State intact'.[128]

The ruling is interesting in terms of the identity and status given to asylum seekers. The Court recognised that certain economic, social and cultural deprivations (such as destitution and homelessness) may, if sufficiently serious, lead to a violation of Article 3 of the ECHR. That is a significant development in jurisprudence affecting asylum seekers and refugees. The Court emphasised the status of asylum seekers as vulnerable persons in society, and its findings were very much influenced by this. This view therefore recognises the unique identity of an asylum seeker as a person who has fled persecution and is without the protection of a state. The framework is also one which recognises asylum seekers as bearers of human rights and the need to uphold the human dignity of such persons. This contrasts with the approach taken by the Australian High Court in *Plaintiff M70*,[129] which linked the transfer requirements to the specific acquired rights of asylum seekers under the Refugee Convention.[130] This latter approach is of interest as it links protection to refugee identity: it interprets protection as going beyond the prohibition of *refoulement* and recognises the framework of graduated rights depending on attachment set out in the Refugee Convention. Recognising that the rights of asylum seekers go beyond *non-refoulement* is important in reflecting the identity of asylum seekers as potential refugees and holders of positive rights.

Which approach is preferable and more fully reflects the identity and status of asylum seekers under law, will now be discussed, as will the role of law in making and unmaking the refugee category.

Analysis and conclusions

The acquired rights framework recognised in the landmark decision of the High Court of Australia in *Plaintiff M70*, is a valuable endorsement of the identity of asylum seekers as persons who acquire rights under the Refugee Convention, that must be respected by the receiving state, particularly in situations of transfer. This approach suggests that the criterion for transfer of asylum seekers from one country to another should take account of refugee rights beyond mere adherence to Article 33. In this sense, 'protection' under the 1951 Refugee Convention is not limited to simply protection against persecution, but extends also to the associated rights and benefits that refugees are entitled to receive under the Convention. It therefore accurately reflects the declaratory nature of refugee status and the identity of asylum seekers as aspirant or presumptive refugees. This also illustrates the broader point made in this book about the power of the law and its institutions as instruments for making and unmaking the refugee category, and the potential role of courts in providing judicial protection of the rights of refugees.[131]

The Refugee Convention defines refugees as being entitled to certain accrued rights and states as being obliged under treaty law to give refugees those rights. The acquired rights framework is therefore beneficial in that it identifies refugees as holders of unique rights under the Refugee Convention's incremental framework of attachment. More broadly, it recognises that refugees require a secure status and dignified existence – as holders of acquired rights such as those relating to education, freedom of religion, work and social security rights which provide personal security to refugees. As discussed in this chapter, presumptive refugees (asylum seekers) are also entitled to some of these rights.

Such a framework may be a useful protector of rights in relation to transfers to 'safe' third countries. As discussed in this chapter, Australia is currently attempting to forge a 'regional protection framework' within the South-East Asian region. Much work has been done in establishing such a regional system in the EU. However, the underlying rights structure and legal identity of asylum seekers and refugees are different in each region. In the EU, the transfer of asylum seekers between Member States is supported by harmonised refugee laws and procedures. All EU Member States have signed regional asylum directives which set out minimum standards on refugee law, procedures and living conditions. The EU region has a level of uniformity in human rights standards due to the existence of binding treaties such as the EU Charter on Fundamental Rights and the European Convention on Human Rights. This infrastructure is supported by strong regional oversight mechanisms such as the European Court of Justice and European Court of Human Rights. Importantly, although the common standards on refugee law are linked to the Refugee Convention, a live issue remains as to the relationship between the Convention and EU measures for human rights protection.

In contrast, no such regional mechanisms yet exist in the Asia-Pacific region. The Bali Process has operated since 2002, but this is primarily an anti-people-smuggling initiative rather than an agenda for refugee protection.[132] Within Australia, the priority given in government policy and community debate to the resettlement 'queue' has led to labelling of boat arrivals as 'unlawful non-citizens' and 'offshore entry persons'. As a result of these labels, these asylum seekers are externalised and excluded from the usual protections of Australian law.

These differences reflect the comparison between asylum seekers as bearers of human rights and/or as presumptive refugees and whether human rights protections such as those provided by Article 3 of the ECHR in Europe are stronger protectors of rights than the acquired rights framework under the Refugee Convention. This is important because the influence of strong ECHR jurisprudence on Article 3 has led to the prominence of regional human rights in litigation and this has, to some extent, overshadowed the Refugee Convention in Europe.

It is clear that the protections afforded by human rights law, such as the ECHR, are valuable for asylum seekers subject to transfer under the Dublin Convention and other deportation cases involving asylum seekers.[133] However, this should not eclipse the identity of asylum seekers as potential refugees with rights under the Refugee Convention. The application of certain of the Refugee Convention's acquired rights to asylum seekers can be a powerful protector, particularly in a country such as Australia which does *not* have a federal bill of rights and in South-East Asia which has no regional human rights treaty or supranational court.

Further, there are a number of limitations to the European human rights regime provided via the ECHR. First, it is binding only upon members of the Council of Europe. Second, Article 3, which is the main provision utilised in relation to asylum seekers, requires a high threshold of evidence of destitution or other treatment. In cases where destitution and other ill-treatment cannot be proven, but there are other concerns such as whether the third state will offer elementary education to children or employment rights, then the acquired rights framework under the Refugee Convention may be more appropriate.[134]

More broadly, the analysis of refugee identity provided in this chapter links into the related issue of the relationship between human rights, and the Refugee Convention. Although James Hathaway posits refugee law within the broader framework of international human rights law, he does underline the need to 'affirm the importance of refugee-specific rights'.[135] Colin Harvey also points to the trend towards development of legal standards which address personhood, rather than membership and national status.[136] He states that this trend means that 'what really matters is not a "constructed status" but the fact of humanity itself'.[137] He notes that international refugee law 'continues to make a plain statement: a defined status matters, and this includes individual membership of a legally constructed group'.[138]

Utilisation of the acquired rights approach could therefore be criticised on the grounds that it is a state-centred framework which assumes eventual belonging and membership in a state. While this may be so, refugee status does identify a person with very specific needs. Refugees are not only fleeing violations of human rights, but they are also unable to obtain the protection of their own state from those violations. The acquired rights regime in the Refugee Convention therefore reflects the special position of refugees vis-à-vis the state system.

This chapter concludes that, at least in some domestic jurisdictions, refugee-specific rights may be a necessary protector of asylum seekers in regional transfer regimes where there is no regional human rights infrastructure in place to otherwise regulate such transfers. The acquired rights of asylum seekers and refugees under the Refugee Convention also reflect their important status as not simply human beings, but persons who lack the protection of their own state and who therefore may be able to claim the protection of another. Further, the above analysis demonstrates that by recognising the unique identity and status of asylum seekers as potential refugees, the judicial arm of an asylum host state can redefine an asylum seeker as a holder of certain 'acquired' rights under the Convention, rather than simply a 'burden' to be shared as part of a regional response to refugee flows.

Notes

1 Convention relating to the Status of Refugees, Geneva, 28 July 1951, 1989 UNTS 137, supplemented by the Protocol relating to the Status of Refugees, 31 January 1967, 19 UST 6223, 6257 ('1951 Refugee Convention').

2 1951 Refugee Convention, Art. 1A(2) states that the term 'refugee' shall apply to any person who 'owing to well-founded fear of being persecuted for reasons of race, religion, nationality, membership of a particular social group or political opinion, is outside the country of his nationality and is unable or, owing to such fear, is unwilling to avail himself of the protection of that country'.

3 This can pose significant problems for the way in which certain asylum host states interpret national law as against the terms of the 1951 Refugee Convention. For instance, in a number of cases, the High Court of Australia has held that Australian domestic law, rather than the Refugee Convention, is determinative of legal questions about refugee law – see discussion below at footnotes 75–7.

4 An 'asylum seeker' is a person seeking asylum from persecution who has yet to be recognised as a refugee as defined in Art. 1A(2) of the 1951 Refugee Convention.

5 See Matthew J. Gibney, *The Ethics and Politics of Asylum: Liberal Democracy and the Response to Refugees* (Cambridge University Press, 2004), 245–46; Maria O'Sullivan, 'The Intersection between the International, the Regional and the Domestic: Seeking Asylum in the United Kingdom', in Susan Kneebone (ed.), *Refugees, Asylum Seekers and the Rule of Law: Comparative Perspectives* (Cambridge University Press, 2009); Council of Europe Parliamentary Assembly, Committee on Migration, Refugees and Population, 'The image of asylum-seekers, migrants and refugees in the media', Doc. 11011, 10 July 2006.

6 There are many examples of use of these terms in Australian political and media discourse, one example is Peter Alford, 'Jumping asylum queue pays off', *The Australian*, 24 December 2010. These misconceptions of asylum seekers in Australian discourse are discussed in Katharine Gelber, 'A Fair Queue? Australian Public Discourse on Refugees and Immigration' (2003) 27 *Journal of Australian Studies* 23–30; Janet Philips, 'Asylum Seekers and Refugees – What Are the Facts', Commonwealth Parliamentary Library, 11 February 2013.

7 The Information Centre about Asylum and Refugees (ICAR) is an independent academic and research organisation based in the UK, <www.icar.org.uk/2078/about-us/about-icar.html>.

8 ICAR, Asylum Seekers and Media Briefing, <www.icar.org.uk/Asylum_Seekers_and_Media_Briefing_ICAR.pdf>.

9 Migration Act 1958 (Cth), s. 46A(1): 'An application for a visa is not a valid application if it is made by an offshore entry person who: (a) is in Australia; and (b) is an unlawful non-citizen'.

10 Migration Act 1958 (Cth), s. 5AA defines an 'unauthorised maritime arrival' as a person who enters Australia by sea at an excised offshore place, or any other place, and becomes an unlawful non-citizen as a result.

11 P. Billings, 'Irregular maritime migration and the Pacific Solution Mark II: back to the future for refugee law and policy in Australia?' (2013) 29(2) *International Journal on Minority and Group Rights*, 279–305.

12 Due to constant changes of policy by the Labor government, the treatment of asylum seekers varied widely depending on their date of arrival. Parliamentary Joint Committee on Human Rights examination of legislation in accordance with the Human Rights (Parliamentary Scrutiny) Act 2011 Migration Legislation Amendment (Regional Processing and other Measures) Act 2012 and related legislation, Ninth Report of 2013, Commonwealth of Australia, June 2013, 82 [2.191].

13 *Plaintiff M70/Plaintiff M106* [2011] HCA 32 (*'Plaintiff M70'*).

14 Arrangement between the Government of Australia and the Government of Malaysia on Transfer and Resettlement (25 July 2011) ('Malaysia Arrangement').

15 The Dublin Convention first came into force on 1 September 1997 for the first 12 signatories (which included the UK). A revised version now applies between most Member States: Regulation (EU) No. 604/2013 of the European Parliament and of the Council of 26 June 2013 establishing the criteria and mechanisms for determining the Member State responsible for examining an application for international protection lodged in one of the Member States by a third-country national or a stateless person ('Dublin Convention').

16 See e.g. *Federal Republic of Germany* v. *Kaveh Puid (Reference for a preliminary ruling from the Hessischer Verwaltungsgerichtshof (Germany)*, Case C-4/11, European Union: Court of Justice of the European Union, 5 January 2011; CJEU: Opinion of Advocate General Jääskinen, C-4/11 Puid, 18 April 2013.

17 Convention for the Protection of Human Rights and Fundamental Freedoms 1950, ETS No. 005 ('ECHR').

18 See ECHR, Art. 3. While there has been some important jurisprudence on other articles of the ECHR (e.g. Art. 8 – right to a family life and Art. 13 – right to a remedy), the primary focus of litigation has been on Art. 3.

19 See UNHCR, *Handbook on Procedures and Criteria for Determining Refugee Status under the 1951 Convention and the 1967 Protocol Relating to the Status of Refugees*, HCR/IP/4/Rev.1, 1979, re-edited, Geneva, January 1992 ('UNHCR Handbook'), [28].

20 1951 Refugee Convention, above n. 1, Arts 2–34.

21 As Alice Edwards points out: 'Whether they are viewed as victims of security deficits or as potential threats to national or international security, security is a defining element in the refugee protection landscape' ('Symposium: Territory without Boundaries: Immigration beyond Territory: Human Security and the Rights of Refugees:

Transcending Territorial and Disciplinary Borders' (2009) 30 *Michigan Journal of International Law* 763, 774); see also Chapter 8 in this volume.

22 See Maria O'Sullivan, 'Withdrawing Protection under Article 1C(5) of the 1951 Convention: Lessons from Australia' (2008) 20(4) *International Journal of Refugee Law* 586, 593–5. Australia stopped the use of Temporary Protection Visas in 2008, but the current government is currently attempting to reintroduce them.

23 1951 Refugee Convention, above n. 1, Art. 4 on freedom of religion applies to refugees 'within' the territory of the contracting state. See also Art. 27: 'The Contracting States shall issue identity papers to any refugee in their territory who does not possess a valid travel document.'

24 1951 Refugee Convention, above n. 1, Art. 18 – self-employment; Art. 26 – freedom of movement. James Hathaway states that a refugee is 'lawfully present' in a territory if 'admitted to a state party's territory for a fixed period of time, even if only for a few hours'. Such presence is lawful as long as it is 'officially sanctioned' (*The Rights of Refugees under International Law* (Cambridge University Press, 2005), 174). It is recognised by some commentators and some national courts that once a refugee applies for refugee status, they are considered to be lawfully present, even if they were not pre-authorised to enter the country (ibid., 175). Hathaway seems to conclude that 'where persons seeking recognition of refugee status meet the requirements of Art. 31 – that is, they "present themselves without delay to the authorities and show good cause for their illegal entry or presence" – their presence must be deemed lawful' (ibid., 178).

25 See e.g. Art. 17, which provides that: 'The Contracting State shall accord to refugees *lawfully staying in their territory* the most favourable treatment accorded to nationals of a foreign country in the same circumstances, as regards the right to engage in wage-earning employment' (emphasis added). See also Art. 19 – liberal professions; Art. 21 – housing; Art. 23 – public relief; Art. 24 – labour legislation and social security. As Alice Edwards notes: 'The meaning of "lawfully in", like the standard of "lawfully staying" applied in Arts. 17 and 19, is not clear on its face. At a minimum, it requires "legal" presence, rather than mere physical presence' ('Article 18 1951 Convention', in Andreas Zimmerman (ed.), *The 1951 Convention Relating to the Status of Refugees and Its 1967 Protocol: A Commentary* (Oxford University Press, 2011), 976). Edwards also states that the right 'as it is articulated in Art. 17' and 'read literally' 'does not appear to extend to asylum seekers or others only temporarily admitted or in transit' (ibid., 965).

26 E.g. Art. 3 – non-discrimination; Art. 13 – movable and immovable property; Art. 16 – access to courts; Art. 20 – rationing; Art. 29 – fiscal charges; Art. 33 – *non-refoulement*; Art. 34 – naturalisation.

27 See the Introduction to this volume.

28 Hathaway, above n. 24.

29 Ibid., 158.

30 Ibid., 158–9 (citations omitted).

31 Ibid., 159 (emphasis added).

32 It is widely recognised under international law that states can exercise 'jurisdiction' extra-territorially (ibid., 166–9).

33 Ibid., 160. I note that this catalogue of rights is slightly different to that recognised by the High Court of Australia in *Plaintiff M70*. In that decision, the court referred to Arts. 3, 4, 16, 17(1), 22(1) and 26. But they did not specify Art. 13 (movable and immovable property), 20 (rationing) or 29 (fiscal charges) as Hathaway does in his 2005 text. This may be because these were viewed by the High Court as less important in practice in contemporary refugee protection.

34 Ibid., 160–1.

35 Ibid., 332–3 (footnotes omitted, emphasis added).

36 Michelle Foster, 'Protection Elsewhere: The Legal Implications of Requiring Refugees to Seek Protection in Another State' (2007) 28 *Michigan Journal of International Law* 223, 270.

37 Ibid., 267.
38 Stephen Legomsky, 'Secondary Refugee Movements and the Return of Asylum Seekers to Third Countries: The Meaning of Effective Protection' (2003) 15 *International Journal of Refugee Law* 567.
39 Ibid., 620 (emphasis in original).
40 Ibid., 634: 'The same complicity principle that prohibits destination countries from sending asylum seekers to third countries that will violate their *non-refoulement* rights under Article 33 should, with equal logic, prohibit destination countries from sending asylum seekers *to third countries that will violate any of these other Convention rights*' (emphasis added).
41 See the Introduction to this volume.
42 See UNHCR Handbook [28]; Guy Goodwin-Gill and Jane McAdam, *The Refugee in International Law* (Oxford University Press, 2007), 51, 244; and EC Qualification Directive, Directive 2011/95/EU of the European Parliament and of the Council of 13 December 2011 on standards for the qualification of third-country nationals or stateless persons as beneficiaries of international protection, for a uniform status for refugees or for persons eligible for subsidiary protection, and for the content of the protection granted (recast), OJ 2011 No. L337/9 ('2011 Qualification Directive'), Preamble Recital Clause (21).
43 UNGA Res. 217A (III), 10 December 1948.
44 However, the UDHR is generally regarded as a non-binding inurement.
45 International Covenant on Civil and Political Rights 999 UNTS 171.
46 ECHR, above n. 17.
47 UNHCR Handbook, above n. 19, [28].
48 Ibid.
49 UNHCR, Ex Com Conclusion No. 6 (XXVIII) of 1977, 12 October 1977. See also UNHCR Ex Com Conclusion 82 of 1997 (XLVIII) where it reaffirmed the fundamental importance of the principle of *non-refoulement* which applies to refugees 'whether or not they have been formally granted refugee status'.
50 2011 Qualification Directive, above n. 42, Preamble Recital Clause (21).
51 UNHCR, Note on International Protection, 31 August 1993, A/AC.96/815, [11].
52 Jan Vedsted-Hansen, 'Non-admission policies and the right to protection: refugees' choice versus states' exclusion?', in Frances Nicholson and Patrick Twomey (eds), *Refugee Rights and Realities: Evolving International Concepts and Regimes* (Cambridge University Press, 1999), 275 (emphasis in original).
53 *R* v. *Secretary of State for the Home Department, ex parte Jahangeer and others* [1993] Imm AR 564, United Kingdom: High Court (England and Wales) 11 June 1993 <www.refworld.org/docid/3ae6b65e2c.html> ('*Jahangeer*').
54 *Jahangeer* (emphasis added) (no pagination in judgment).
55 1951 Refugee Convention, above n. 1, Art. 16(1).
56 *Jahangeer*, above n. 53.
57 1951 Refugee Convention, above n. 1, Art. 31(1): 'The Contracting States shall not impose penalties, on account of their illegal entry or presence, on refugees who, coming directly from a territory where their life or freedom was threatened in the sense of Article 1, enter or are present in their territory without authorisation, provided they present themselves without delay to the authorities and show good cause for their illegal entry or presence.'
58 *Jahangeer*, above n. 53.
59 Ibid.
60 1951 Refugee Convention, above n. 1, Art. 32 (emphasis added).
61 *R* v. *Uxbridge Magistrates Court and another, ex parte Adimi* [1999] EWHC Admin 765, UK: High Court (England and Wales) <www.refworld.org/docid/3ae6b6b41c.html>.
62 See e.g. Guy Goodwin-Gill, 'Article 31 of the 1951 Convention relating to the Status of Refugees: Non-Penalization, Detention and Protection', in Erika Feller, Volker Türk

and Frances Nicholson (eds), *Refugee Protection in International Law: UNHCR's Global Consultations on International* Protection (Cambridge University Press, 2003), 193; Justice Collins, 'The Courts and Detention – the United Kingdom Experience', IARLJ Conference 2002, 313 <www.upf.pf/IMG/pdf/12_Collins.pdf>; Hathaway, above n. 24, 389.

63 See e.g. Eli Lauterpacht and Daniel Bethlehem, 'The Scope and Content of the Principle of Non-Refoulement', in Erika Feller *et al.* (eds), *Refugee Protection in International Law*, 78, 149; Goodwin-Gill and McAdam, above n. 42, 248.

64 T. Alexander Aleinikoff, 'State Centred Refugee Law: From Resettlement to Containment' (1992–3) 14 *Michigan Journal of International Law* 120, 124.

65 See discussion of this issue in Susan Kneebone, 'The Australian Story: Asylum Seekers outside the Law', in Susan Kneebone (ed.), *Refugees, Asylum Seekers and the Rule of Law: Comparative Perspectives* (Cambridge University Press, 2009), 171, 174. This is reflected in the 'no advantage' principle espoused by the Expert Panel on Asylum Seekers (Australia) *The Report of the Expert Panel on Asylum Seekers*, 13 August 2012, 38–40, 64–5 <http://expertpanelonasylumseekers.dpmc.gov.au/report> ('Expert Panel Report').

66 See Expert Panel Report, 56–7.

67 Deterring People Smuggling Act 2011 (Cth). The Act in its draft (Bill) form is discussed in Commonwealth Parliament, Legal and Constitutional Affairs Legislation Committee, 'Deterring People Smuggling Bill 2011' Commonwealth of Australia, November 2011.

68 Section 14 of the Migration Act 1958 (Cth) defines an 'unlawful non-citizen' as a person in the migration zone who is not a lawful non-citizen. Section 13(1) defines a lawful non-citizen as a 'non-citizen in the migration zone who holds a visa'.

69 Migration Act 1958 (Cth), s. 4(2).

70 Ibid., s. 46A.

71 Ibid., s. 46. Section 46A(1) provides: 'An application for a visa is not a valid application if it is made by an offshore entry person who: (a) is in Australia; and (b) is an unlawful non-citizen.' This restriction can be lifted by a decision of the Minister for Immigration.

72 Under the Australian mainland legal system, asylum claims are assessed by the Department of Immigration and negative decisions may be appealed to a merits review body called the Refugee Review Tribunal and then onto a full judicial review process made up of the Federal Magistrates Court, Federal Court and the High Court of Australia. Both the merits and judicial review system in Australia is very strong. The Refugee Review Tribunal is made up of decision makers who are independent of the Department and is a well-regarded institution in Australia and internationally.

73 Migration Amendment (Unauthorised Maritime Arrivals and Other Measures) Act 2013 (Cth).

74 As Hathaway notes, some refugees are subject to a state's jurisdiction, in the sense of being under its control or authority (above n. 24, 156).

75 *Al-Kateb* v. *Godwin* [2004] HCA 37 (High Court of Australia). The High Court by a majority held that sections 189, 196 and 198 of the Migration Act authorised and required the detention of an unlawful non-citizen even if his removal from Australia was not reasonably practicable in the foreseeable future.

76 See UNHCR, Guidelines on the Applicable Criteria and Standards relating to the Detention of Asylum-Seekers and Alternatives to Detention, 2012, 16 <www.unhcr.org/505b10ee9.html>.

77 *Minister for Immigration and Multicultural Affairs* v. *QAAH of 2004* [2006] HCA 53, [33].

78 Ibid., [34].

79 Susan Kneebone, 'What We *Have* Done with the Refugees Convention: The Australian Way' (2005) 22 *Law in Context* 83, 112.

80 *Plaintiff M61/2010E* v. *The Commonwealth* (2010) 243 CLR 319 ('*Plaintiff M61*').

81 Ibid., [27]. Cited in *Plaintiff M70*, above n. 13, [90] (*per* Gummow, Hayne, Crennan, Bell JJ) and in *Plaintiff M47-2012* v. *Director General of Security* [2012] HCA 46 at [12] (*per* French CJ).

82　This is part of Australian territory, but not part of the mainland Australian migration system.

83　*Plaintiff M61*, above n. 80, [8].

84　Ibid.

85　Susan Kneebone, 'Outing Offshore Processing: The High Court of Australia Defines the Role of the Refugee Convention' (2012) 26 *Immigration, Asylum and Nationality Law* 156, 159.

86　*Plaintiff M70*, above n. 13. This case is discussed in several recent articles, including: Kneebone (ibid.); Michelle Foster, 'The Implications of the Failed "Malaysia Solution": The Australian High Court and Refugee Responsibility Sharing at International Law' (2012) 13 *Melbourne Journal of International Law* 1; Tamara Wood and Jane McAdam, 'Australian Asylum Policy all at Sea: An analysis of *Plaintiff M70/2011* v. *Minister for Immigration and Citizenship* and the Australia–Malaysia Arrangement' (2012) 61 *International and Comparative Law Quarterly* 274.

87　Malaysia Arrangement, above n. 14.

88　*Plaintiff M70*, above n. 13, [119]. In considering the obligation of Australia to ensure the protection of asylum seekers transferred to Malaysia, the court examined Arts 3, 4, 16(1), 17(1), 22(1) and 26 of the Refugee Convention (see *Plaintiff M70*, above n. 13, [117]).

89　Section 198A(1), as it was then drafted, provided that: 'An officer may take an offshore entry person from Australia to a country in respect of which a declaration is in force under subsection (3).' Section 198A(3) then provides that: 'The Minister may: (a) declare in writing that a specified country: (i) provides access, for persons seeking asylum, to effective procedures for assessing their need for protection; and (ii) provides protection for persons seeking asylum, pending determination of their refugee status; and (iii) provides protection to persons who are given refugee status, pending their voluntary repatriation to their country of origin or resettlement in another country; and (iv) meets relevant human rights standards in providing that protection; and (b) in writing, revoke a declaration made under paragraph (a).'

90　*Plaintiff M70*, above n. 13, [119] (*per* Gummow, Hayne, Crennan, Bell JJ). Justice Kiefel, also of the majority, also stated that the court's construction of s. 198A(3)(a) 'most closely accords with the fulfilment of Australia's Convention obligations and it is to be preferred to one which does not' (at [246]).

91　Ibid., [119].

92　Wood and McAdam, above n. 86, 288.

93　*SZOQQ* v. *Minister for Immigration and Citizenship* [2013] HCA 12, [14–17], [31] <www.refworld.org/docid/519bc6374.html>.

94　Expert Panel Report, above n. 65. The panel consisted of Air Chief Marshal Angus Houston (retired), Mr Paris Aristotle, Director of the Victorian Foundation for Survivors of Torture Inc. and Professor Michael L'Estrange, Director, National Security College.

95　Alison Rourke, 'Australian vessels rescue refugees: rescue ships save more than 120 Afghan asylum seekers after a second boat in a week capsizes off Indonesia', *Guardian*, 27 June 2012 <www.guardian.co.uk/world/2012/jun/27/australian-indonesian-vessels-rescue-refugees>.

96　Expert Panel report, above n. 65, 47–9. Note that the use of third countries in this context is different from the processing and detention use of Christmas Island, an excised Australian territory: see discussion of the Christmas Island processing regime in Kneebone, above n. 79, 157–60.

97　This has been recognised in a recent parliamentary report on human rights which concludes, *inter alia*, that the 'no advantage' test has 'resulted in a confusing array of measures focused not so much on the status of the person as their mode and date of arrival in Australia' (Parliamentary Joint Committee, above n. 12 [2.191]).

98 Migration Act 1958 (Cth) (as amended in 2012). Subsections 198AB(1) and (2) provide that the minister may designate that a country is a regional processing country and that the only condition for the exercise of the power is that the minister thinks that is in 'the national interest'. Subsection 198AB(3) does provide that in doing so the minister must have regard to the risk of *non-refoulement* and the existence of refugee determination procedures in the third country. However, the provisions lack the much stronger protective provisions contained in the previous s. 198A.

99 In September 2012, the then Minister for Immigration, Mr Chris Bowen designated Nauru as a 'regional processing country'. The designations of Nauru and of Papua New Guinea as a 'regional processing country' came into effect on 12 September 2012 and 10 October 2012 respectively, having been approved by both Houses of Parliament. These arrangements are underpinned by Memoranda of Understanding (MOU) between Australia and the countries concerned: see e.g. Chris Bowen MP Minister for Immigration press release, 'Australia signs Memorandum of Understanding with Nauru', 29 August 2012 <www.minister.immi.gov.au/media/cb/2012/cb189579.htm>.

100 Instrument of Designation of the Republic of Nauru as a Regional Processing Country under Subsection 198AB(1) of the Migration Act 1958, [20–1] ('Nauru Designation Instrument').

101 Ibid., [3]–[4]: 'I consider designating Nauru to be a regional processing country will promote the maintenance of a fair and orderly Refugee and Humanitarian Program that retains the confidence of the Australian people; I consider designating Nauru to be a regional processing country will promote regional co-operation in relation to irregular migration and address people smuggling and its undesirable consequences.'

102 Memorandum of Understanding between the Government of the Independent State of Papua New Guinea and the Government of Australia, Relating to the Transfer to and Assessment of Persons in Papua New Guinea, and Related Issues, September 2012 (emphasis added).

103 Nauru Designation Instrument, above n. 100, [36].

104 Coalition Government, 'Operation Sovereign Borders Policy', July 2013, 7–10.

105 The Bali Process on People Smuggling, Trafficking in Persons and Related Transnational Crime ('Bali Process'), see <www.baliprocess.net>.

106 E.g. Indonesia and Malaysia are not a party to the 1951 Refugee Convention.

107 UNHCR, 'Reservations and declarations to the 1951 Refugee Convention', 1 March 2006: Papua New Guinea (another country in the region) also has reservations with respect to Arts 17 (1), 21, 22 (1), 26, 31, 32 and 34 of the Convention under which it states that it 'does not accept the obligations stipulated in these articles'. I note that PNG has agreed to remove these reservations in relation to those asylum seekers transferred from Australia. However, this has yet to be formally carried out.

108 Thailand, Indonesia and Timor-Leste (East Timor) are parties to the Convention against Torture, the ICCPR and ICESCR. Vietnam is a party to the ICCPR and ICESCR, but not the Convention against Torture (see <http://treaties.un.org/Home.aspx?lang=en>).

109 Singapore, Malaysia and Fiji have neither signed nor ratified the Convention against Torture, the ICCPR or the ICESCR (see <http://treaties.un.org/Home.aspx?lang=en>).

110 Contrast Chapter 7 in this volume where it is argued that this is based on the responsibility of third-country states, which is 'inflicted' on the asylum seeker.

111 EU Council Document 14292/1/04 Rev. 1, 8 December 2004, s. 1.3.

112 See e.g. Recital (13) of the 2011 EC Qualification Directive, above n. 42: 'The approximation of rules on the recognition and content of refugee and subsidiary protection status should help to limit the secondary movement of applicants for

international protection between Member States, where such movement is purely caused by differences in legal frameworks.'

113 Goodwin-Gill and McAdam, above n. 42, 391; Hélène Lambert, 'Safe Third Country in the European Union: An Evolving Concept in International Law and Implications for the UK' (2012) 26(4) *Journal of Immigration, Asylum and Nationality Law* 318, 318.

114 Charter of Fundamental Rights of the European Union: OJ 2000 No. C364/01 ('EU Charter on Fundamental Rights').

115 ECHR, above n. 17.

116 See e.g. Michelle Foster, 'Book Review: Asylum and the European Convention on Human Rights' (2009) 21(3) *International Journal of Refugee Law* 645, 645; Magdalena Forowicz, *The Reception of Law in the European Court on Human Rights* (Oxford University Press, 2010), 281.

117 Forowicz, above n. 116, 281.

118 EU Charter on Fundamental Rights, above n. 114.

119 Ibid., Art. 18: 'The right to asylum shall be guaranteed with due respect for the rules of the Geneva Convention of 28 July 1951 and the Protocol of 31 January 1967 relating to the status of refugees and in accordance with the Treaty establishing the European Community.'

120 Ibid., Art. 19(2).

121 *MSS* v. *Belgium and Greece* (European Court of Human Rights, Grand Chamber, Application No. 30696/09, 21 January 2011, [365]) referring to previous case law such as *Soering* v. *UK*, judgment of 7 July 1989, Series A No. 161, [90–1]; *Vilvarajah and others* v. *UK*, judgment of 30 October 1991, Series A No. 125, [103].

122 *MSS* v. *Greece*, above n. 121.

123 According to the applicant's evidence, he was locked up in a small space with 20 other detainees, access to the toilets was restricted, detainees were not allowed out into the open air, were given very little to eat and had to sleep on dirty mattresses or on the bare floor. When released, he was homeless and had no means of subsistence (summary of evidence, *MSS* v. *Greece*, above n. 121, [34]–[37]).

124 Ibid., [366].

125 Ibid., [352].

126 Ibid., [251].

127 Ibid., [263].

128 Ibid., [342].

129 *Plaintiff M70*, above n. 13.

130 This was partly due to the way in which the relevant section of the Migration Act 1958 (Cth) (s. 198A) was framed and the judicial review function of the court.

131 See Introduction to this volume.

132 Susan Kneebone, 'The Bali Process and Global Refugee Policy in the Asia Pacific Region' (2014) (forthcoming).

133 See e.g. *Chahal* v. *UK* (1996) 23 EHRR 413.

134 See e.g. Hathaway, who states that 'the Refugee Convention's guarantee of access to elementary education is more comprehensive than the cognate right under Art. 13(2) (a) of the Covenant on Economic, Social and Cultural Rights. Under the Covenant, some flexibility in achieving free elementary education for all is available, at least to poorer states, as rights under that treaty need only be implemented progressively, albeit without discrimination' (above n. 24, 599–600 (citations omitted)).

135 Ibid., 13.

136 Colin Harvey, 'Is Humanity Enough? Refugees, Asylum Seekers and the Rights Regime', in Satvinder Juss and Colin Harvey (eds), *Contemporary Issues in International Refugee Law* (Edward Elgar, 2013), ch. 3.

137 Ibid., 68.

138 Ibid., 76.

Part III

Law, power and refugee identity: macro and state perspectives

8 Conflicting identities and securitisation in refugee law: lessons from the EU

*Elspeth Guild**

Introduction

The European Union (EU) formally commenced its project to create a Common European Asylum Policy (CEAS) in 1999 when changes to the EU treaties gave the EU institutions the power and objective to do so, mindful that the CEAS must be consistent with the UN Convention relating to the Status of Refugees 1951 together with its 1967 Protocol (the '1951 Refugee Convention')[1] and the EU Member States' other international obligations to those in need of international protection.[2] The first phase of the CEAS was completed in 2005 with the adoption of all the mandated measures to provide for the common system. In 2008 the EU institutions began the second phase of the CEAS which involved the revision of all of the instruments adopted in the first phase in light of the objective of making the system truly common rather than one of minimum standards. The operation of the first phase instruments revealed numerous structural weaknesses, the most problematic of which has been that outcomes for people from the same country of origin seeking international protection in different EU states vary dramatically. For instance, according to the UNHCR Yearbook 2011 protection rates for Syrian nationals in the EU vary from 83.1 per cent in Austria to 2.7 per cent in Greece and 3.4 per cent in Cyprus.[3] In this chapter, I ask why the CEAS does not appear to be resulting in protection to people from the same countries of origin across the EU and whether the structural defects have been addressed in the second phase.

Refugee protection has long been an issue of great moral and legal importance among the countries in Europe. European states sent representatives to participate in the drafting of the 1951 Refugee Convention and were among the first signatories. They have also been strong supporters of the UN Agency established as guardian of the Refugee Convention – the United Nations High Commission for Refugees (UNHCR) and participate as members of the UNHCR's Executive Committee. However, these same states, when adopting legislation on refugee protection in EU[4] appear Janus faced. On the one hand, statements of commitment to refugee protection are plentiful, on the other, mechanisms are adopted which aim to exclude the refugee even from being heard. In this chapter I will examine this contradiction using the concept of governmentality as developed by Michel

Foucault.[5] Deploying the three techniques of governmentality which Foucault developed most fully – sovereignty, discipline and biopolitics, I seek to dissect the asylum protection system the EU is developing and to make visible the underlying structure of authority and power. While some academics place great emphasis on the development of a 'risk society',[6] my project is not that. It is an investigation of the articulation between discipline and biopolitics in relation to law which demonstrates how the 'refugee' is constructed in law.

Background

Before 1999, asylum was an issue for the Member States and the role of the EU was no more than to provide a space within which discussion could take place and to reach political agreement. As the numbers of persons seeking protection as refugees in Europe began to rise from about the mid-1980s to the mid-1990s and when the political significance of refugee protection in Western European states as flight from Communism lost its meaning after 1989,[7] the enthusiasm of European states to provide refugee protection came under strain. Increasingly, people seeking refugee protection in Europe were stigmatised as 'bogus' and were the object of suspicion regarding their motives.[8] The fact that asylum claims dropped in number by more than half in Europe between 1995 and 2013 is a fact that is rarely mentioned in the debate.[9]

As the image of the deserving refugee became detached from that of the 'bogus' asylum seeker (that is someone who is seeking international protection but in respect of whom the state authorities have yet to make a decision regarding the claim), and the latter became the object of increasing odium, some European states which are members of the European Union (Member States) began to discuss asylum policy among themselves. These discussions began around 1985 but were only formalised in 1993 within the EU framework. It was not until 1999 that the EU was given powers to develop the CEAS. Elsewhere I have examined how and why refugees became excluded from EU rules on movement of persons which date from 1957.[10] Instead, refugees were increasingly marginalised into their own separate universe in EU law.

The first five-year programme for the development of an asylum system, the Tampere Conclusions 1999, called for two phases to the development of the CEAS – a first ten-year period within which the adoption of minimum standards would take place and a second beginning in 2008 moving to one common system. A second multiannual programme in 2004 (The Hague Programme) prodded the institutions to complete the first round of asylum legislation, and the third multiannual programme adopted in Stockholm in December 2009 called for the completion of a truly common CEAS. In the meantime the European Commission proposed a series of changes to the existing legislation to achieve a common set of standards in 2008.[11] All of the second phase measures were adopted in June 2013. What has happened to refugee protection under the system – how can we understand the nature of refugee protection in light of the EU's engagement in the field?

Through use of Foucault's concept of governmentality, this chapter widens our understanding of the mechanisms of governance at work in the CEAS while at the same time avoiding what can be a somewhat simplistic argument about the denial of humanity to asylum seekers in the EU. The latter rather sterile approach not only fails to provide insights into the processes at work and the power structures in transformation but more critically, it is blind to the complexity of sovereignty which is at the centre of the changes. While my approach opens many questions and new avenues of research, nonetheless, it permits a more complete understanding of mechanisms which are at work and which push the changes which we are observing. My focus in this chapter is how and with what consequences the EU moves into the field of asylum and what structural changes take place either as a result of or in tandem with this shift of power. My objective is not to plot a cause-and-effect relationship but rather to understand what has happened to refugees over this ten-year period.

My contention is that the CEAS is in fact creating a system which not only changes the meaning of sovereignty but which changes the way in which governance takes place in respect of the individual. Much has been written about the moving of sovereign powers between the EU institutions and the Member States.[12] My focus in this chapter, however, is to escape that debate characterised by a rather Aristotelian hierarchy of authority[13] and instead to look at how the EU measures change the nature of power relations among state authorities and individual asylum seekers. To carry out this examination, Michel Foucault's concept of governmentality is particularly apt.[14] What are the mechanisms of governmentality which the CEAS enables, blocks or transforms and which regulate the lives of individuals seeking international protection in the EU? It is important to bear in mind that governance and governmentality are not the same thing. I am interested in the governmentality of the governance of the EU. Governance encompasses the formal structures within which authority is exercised. Governmentality, on the other hand, examines the conditions under which authority is constituted and dissipated.

Foucault and governmentality

In the critical social sciences beyond law, the work of Michel Foucault has been applied to the question of detention of foreigners and the situation of asylum seekers.[15] I will not repeat this work, some of which I have criticised elsewhere for an inability to take into account the transformation of how power is exercised in Europe.[16] Here I want to examine the EU's engagement with asylum seekers in order to understand better the mechanism of power and how it operates between the EU and the Member States played out on the lives of asylum seekers and refugees. Foucault suggests three different ways of thinking about power as a relationship among people.[17] The first is sovereignty. Unlike the usual meaning of sovereignty as relations among states and state structures, Foucault focuses on the sovereign as the individual/entity with the power of life and death over others in a relationship where the sovereign does not need, or enter into, any other relationship of power with the individual.[18] Law provides the mechanism to determine life and death according to Foucault. The sovereign form of power, or as Foucault seems to indicate in his later work, 'governmentality', is that of *raison d'état*, or police state (*Polizeistaat*) transformed and restructured by discipline and biopolitics when the notion of people and law are placed at the heart of the decision making about death and punishment.[19]

The second form of exercise of power or governmentality[20] which Foucault uses is that of discipline. Here the individual is differentiated from all other living bodies on which power can be inscribed and the individual which is also the site of resistance.[21] Power is exercised through the differentiation of the individual through discipline which is the flipside of individualisation. Through mechanisms of discipline: prisons, schools, insane asylums etc, individuals are conducted[22] towards conformity through a set of rules. The modalities of discipline include self-discipline and responsibility. Discipline is thus a productive form of power according to Foucault's approach.[23] There are techniques which generate obedience and resistance which are necessary in relation to forms of authority which are more complex.[24]

The third form is biopolitics which depends centrally on the creation of knowledge through the categorisation of life.[25] The collection of statistics about beings creates the possibility of allocating attributes such as normal/abnormal, human/animal and so on to groups and individuals as they are tested against a norm created through the amassing of information. Instead of conceiving discipline as a relationship to a body, power is conceived as being transmitted through the creation of norms according to their relationship with 'risk'.[26] Life is managed through the establishment of norms based on the collection of amounts of information and their synthesis into common characteristics which can then be applied to the individual.[27] Foucault distinguishes between 'normalisation' which is the result of statistically determined averages, and 'normation' which is the way we determine what is 'normal' as opposed to 'abnormal'.[28]

None of the three forms of power operates in a vacuum. Aspects of all three different modalities of the exercise of power may be in operation at the same time. Altogether they constitute the means of governmentality – the way in which authority is constructed and deployed. Foucault's world is populated by apparent contradictions and overlaps among the ways in which power relations are constructed and managed. Law as a form of governance works equally satisfactorily in all three different modes (sovereignty, discipline and biopolitics) through the attributes of the rule of law, which include human rights norms.[29]

An important aspect of Foucault's reasoning is the distinction between the pastoral form of power, where the analogy of the shepherd and the flock is used, and utilitarian exercise of power. Under the pastoral form of power, the shepherd has a duty to find the lost lamb even if this places at risk the flock. This pastoral power is contrasted to utilitarian and predatory exercise of power where in the name of the good of the people, anyone or any group can be sacrificed.[30] The originality of Foucault's approach is not least in its ability to escape from what was becoming an increasingly sterile debate among political philosophers about the nature of the state and state relations.[31] By focusing on the practices of power, Foucault opens a whole series of new perspectives on how power works. However, Foucault takes for granted the relationship of the sovereign to space – the sovereign exercises power over a space or territory within which he/it has control including the 'last word'.[32] Whether this *form of power* can be seen as the right to kill or not (the first form), to determine transgression and decide on punishment (the second form) or to choose which categories of information will be collected and what meaning they will have vis-à-vis the management of life (the third form), they do not permit a further layer of interaction and mediation between the sovereign and the supranational where the last word is the outcome of other mechanisms of power relations.[33]

To take a simple example from the EU, in 2011 there was a discussion raging about the treatment of Afghan and Iraqis asylum seekers in different Member States of the EU. UNHCR criticised heavily the CEAS because outcomes for Iraqis are so inconsistent among Member States (for Afghans this means a zero recognition rate in Greece and 75 per cent in Finland in 2009).[34] The European Commission responded to these criticisms indicating that the CEAS is still under construction and as the system begins to work better these differences should disappear.[35] The result is that in this scenario of a supranational entity, applying a Foucauldian analysis, the national administrators who are applying the CEAS become the people at the cutting edge of being disciplined. They are the ones who must do better to render the system coherent (that is, to reduce differences among recognition rates for asylum seekers from the same countries) rather than respond to the indications given by their national administrations (that is, the sovereigns) on how countries of origin (or applications) should be assessed.

I will now look at two different aspects of the CEAS through the lens of the overlapping power mechanisms formulated by Foucault.

First, I examine how asylum seekers are rendered visible and invisible as rights-holders through EU law; here the key is the Procedures Directive[36] which describes which asylum applications must be determined and which can excluded – some asylum seekers cease to be an undifferentiated part of a flow of persons and become individuals with rights, claims and a story to tell. Others remain part of a group subject to life and death decisions but not individualisation. Mechanism after mechanism is described which permits the administrator to avoid listening to the story of the asylum seeker. Safe country of origin, safe third country, presumptions of manifestly unfounded applications, assessments of countries of origin – all these mechanisms are designed to release the national administrator from the duty to treat the individual as an individual. Instead, the individual becomes part of a category about which a variety of information is collected and then applied to prevent the individual from being able to differentiate him or herself from the category. This differentiation of the asylum seeker into an individual with rights corresponds best to Foucault's second category of discipline. The individual must fulfil the criteria to be a refugee or suffer the fate of the rejected asylum seeker – expulsion. When the EU took the opportunity to revise the Directive, all of these mechanisms were retained, without exception.

The second issue I examine is how does the CEAS operate as a system of biopolitics? This is the management of life through statistics and assessment of risk. This is the murkiest of Foucault's categories which he developed least in his work but which has been the subject of substantial discussion and analysis since.

The right to seek asylum: the right to have a claim determined

Foucault's notion of governmentality rests on three connected mechanisms. First there is the mechanism of discipline – the construction of authority through the establishment of rules and hence of a claim to discipline and punish the offender – an act carried out *inter alia* on the body.[37] Foucault uses Bentham's concept of a panopticon to exemplify this mechanism of governmentality.[38] The authority in a prison is expressed through the possibility of the guards in the guardhouse at any time to see any prisoner. The structure of Bentham's prison permits the guard to look into the cell and see the prisoner and thus to know at any given moment whether the prisoner is obeying the rules. The capacity to punish is enhanced through the capacity to keep the individual under surveillance. While the guards may not watch each prisoner all the time, the prisoner does not know when he or she is under surveillance and when he or she is not. This results in asymmetry of knowledge which brings a differential in the power relation. The prisoners cannot see the guards so have no knowledge of whether their actions which conform to or break the rules are under surveillance and thus may result in punishment, but the opposite is true for the guards. Indeed, this is an example of power operating by itself (the power operates whether or not the guards are watching) – not as something possessed by individuals.[39]

Two aspects of the panopticon are important. First, the guards are able to exercise much greater control as they are able to see prisoners whenever they wish to ensure that the rules are observed and are able to punish more quickly offenders. Second, the prisoner who knows that there is this capacity of surveillance knows that punishment for offending against the rules does not depend on the prisoner being aware of whether the guards are watching or not. In order to avoid punishment the prisoners are drawn to exercise auto-discipline – they do not undertake acts against the rules as they fear punishment.[40] The third step for Foucault in the explanation of how governmentality works is responsibility. The authorities acknowledge the freedom of the individual to act but warn the individual of the consequences of any particular act.[41] The example which Löwenheim provides is that of foreign ministries in liberal democracies which publish warnings to their citizens regarding various countries, advising them not to go to those countries because of a variety of risks, spelled out in the notifications.[42] On the one hand, the authority reinforces the individual's perception of freedom by accepting that the individual can travel to any country he or she wishes to visit. On the other hand, the authorities create a responsibility on the individual related to risk, danger and bodily harm (which finally, according to some of the steps Foucault takes towards biopolitics, the individual has learned is the greatest ill to be avoided) – if the individual insists on going to a dangerous country he or she takes the risk of the consequences. This then has important consequences for the state's responsibility of protection for its citizens abroad.

So, discipline, as the political technology of the body, includes directly disciplining individuals, auto-discipline and responsibility.[43] As Dean points out: 'Foucault himself puts this argument for the interdependence of citizenship rights and disciplinary power in a more general form: the "Enlightenment" which discovered the liberties, also invented the disciplines.'[44] The question now is how does this approach provide clarity to the CEAS – does Foucault illuminate the structure of the CEAS and the construction of authority in respect of the asylum seeker?

The surveillance of the EU external border by the Member States and coordinated by Frontex,[45] echoes Foucault's use of Bentham's panopticon, but only in part. As Bigo has suggested,[46] the EU external border is more of a 'banopticon', invisible or very light for the so-called *bona fide* traveller but a block to the asylum seeker and the person suspected of seeking to enter the EU irregularly. Among the fundamental problems of this approach in the EU is determining who is likely to be an irregular migrant, who an asylum seeker and who is a bona fide traveller (thereby creating these population categories). People coming from the same countries may fall into all three categories.

Contrary to the idea of clear-cut categories (such as Weberian ideal types),[47] those of sovereignty, discipline and biopolitics are intertwined in time. The suggestion that each period of time is dominated by one category only would entail the disappearance of sovereignty, law and discipline in a risk management society governed by biopolitics only. This is obviously not the case. It is important to show that discipline is embedded into biopolitics of population and reframed in order to supplement this biopolitics. The EU, however, has taken a risk-oriented approach – if there is a risk of irregular migration then further exclusionary procedures apply (visa requirements, in-depth interviews at consulates abroad before travel, immigration liaison officers at some airports to provide advice to airlines about whom to refuse boarding access, reinforced border patrols at land and sea borders, etc). The creation of the category of foreigner who is risky, who should be under surveillance is established. The group is based on heterogeneous characteristics – profiled according to different countries of nationality, social and economic classes (though the poor are generally assumed to be a risk), and genders. The measures are adopted to keep under surveillance and outside the EU this collection of people who are transformed into a population though they share no common characteristics other than those which are allocated to them by the EU border surveillance system.[48]

Having established the subject population (which does not, for instance include US nationals who do not require visas, in respect of whom no immigration liaison officers are posted at US airports, who are assumed not to be poor) the next step is to establish surveillance. This is the illusion of a panopticon, the EU immigration guards can see every EU external border simultaneously though they may not be looking at any given moment. But it is actually more of a banopticon where the majority of travellers are unaware of the possibility of being under surveillance. Where individuals are perceived to be irregularly crossing or seeking to cross a border then they are the subject of discipline. The EU's external border surveillance system, Eurosur is designed to do exactly this.[19] The proposal sets out a road map for setting up a 'system of systems' interconnecting and rationalising border surveillance systems at the national level, improving the performance of surveillance as a tool and creating a common monitoring and information-sharing environment for the EU maritime domain. The objective is to focus on the EU's southern and eastern maritime borders and achieve full awareness for border guards of the situation at the external borders.

If the (wrong) individuals manage to cross the border into the EU then they may be detained and should be expelled.[50] If they are perceived to be trying to arrive at the EU external border, Frontex operations aim to prevent their arrival and to send them back whence they came. If they are obstinate and continue their journey, they are at high risk of drowning in the Atlantic en route to the Canary Islands, in the Mediterranean en route to the Italian, Maltese, Greek or Spanish coasts.[51] Alternatively, they may be killed by the border guards of neighbouring states outside the EU (which are the major beneficiaries of EU border surveillance funds) such as Libya, Tunisia or elsewhere[52] or left to die.[53] Thus, there is the establishment of authority through a system of surveillance and punishment of a population designated by the authority itself in accordance with rules it has unilaterally determined. What is new in this constellation is the way in which the power is cut free from the state. Instead of Member State actions, these are European initiatives and measures, an EU agency which is at the centre of the project of surveillance and punishment. The punishment is presented as a form of risk rather than direct punishment. Frontex officials and state border guards consistently deny that they are in any way complicit in the drowning of persons in the Atlantic or Mediterranean or the killing of individuals by border guards in third countries when those individuals are seeking to enter the EU.[54] Nonetheless, the numbers of persons who lose their lives in this way raises serious questions. If the EU agency is so successful at surveillance of the external border surely it is capable of ensuring that people do not die there?[55]

Assuming that the population is a homogeneous one, as the EU seeks to do, then the fact of punishment through death, detention and expulsion ought to create self-discipline of each individual coming within the group of people on the move, not only the one who has been the subject of the measure. The deterrence effect should result in the 'conduct of the conduct' in other words the capacity to structure the choices of others.[56] The individuals should learn not to behave in this way – that is, to try to gain access to the EU as this will create a high risk of death, detention or expulsion. The problem is that this is not a homogeneous population.[57] People who move are a highly diverse group who travel for such a wide variety of reasons that it is virtually impossible to classify them all. The third of Foucault's mechanisms of governmentality – responsibility – is embedded in the second, auto-discipline in the case of EU approaches to irregular migration. The pervasive argument is that these persons ought to know that they are putting themselves at risk. If they do not know, then this is the fault of another image which has taken shape in the hands of the EU – the trafficker and smuggler of human beings. This is the evil exploiter of human misery who hides the risk from the irregular migrant and charges high fees for doing so.[58] However, the intermediary between the authority and the offender is only a secondary target, the main target is the foreigner.

The asylum seeker creates a series of tensions within the system by belonging to a class entitled to international protection. At great cost to logical argument, even common sense, the EU and the Member States resist strenuously all suggestions that the right to protection to which the refugee is entitled from them in international law includes a right to arrive at the border of the territory.[59] Instead, the EU and the Member States cling relentlessly to the idea that only the lucky or devious refugee who has managed to escape all the obstacles (legitimate, according to the EU and its Member States) which have been placed to prevent him or her from ever getting near an EU border, and has arrived in the state is entitled to protection (if, of course, he or she can present an argument which the state accepts as entitling him or her to protection). UNHCR continues to argue that the foreigner who claims asylum from the authorities of a state is entitled to a consideration of that claim. This is the principle contained in the Dublin III Regulation and the Qualification Directive.[60] Thus the foreigner is part of a population which is being actively persuaded (by a Frontex operation for instance) not to enter the territorial waters of an EU Member State, nonetheless if the individual is seeking international protection he or she should be entitled to the benefits of the Qualification and Procedures Directives. This is a very inconvenient position for the EU border surveillance system. If accepted, it cuts a huge hole in the centre of the design – the population which has been constructed as the object of the governmentality project cannot be treated as a single population because of the so-called mixed flows problem (that is, flows of both potentially irregular migrants and refugees together).

When the individual arrives in the EU, as so many still do notwithstanding,[61] he or she faces a series of disciplining measures in the search for protection. Asylum seekers start as individuals, foreigners who arrive at the border of a territory. If they have not read the Geneva Convention and the EU Procedures Directive (a common failing among them as a group) they do not know that they are obliged to seek asylum from an official as soon as they arrive at the territory. But if they delay in making their asylum application they may not obtain a full procedure. Article 31(8)(b) and (f) (formerly Article 23(4)(i) and (j)) of the Procedures Directive states that Member States may prioritise or accelerate (which means a truncated procedure) any application which is considered unfounded because 'the applicant has failed without reasonable cause to make his/her application earlier, having had the opportunity to do so or the applicant is making an application merely in order to delay or frustrate the enforcement of an earlier or imminent decision which would result in his/her removal'. The state authorities decide whether an individual comes within one of these categories. However, if the asylum seeker has read the Procedures Directive he or she might baulk at making an application for asylum at the border after reading Article 43 (formerly Article 35) which permits Member States to maintain border procedures which do not fulfil the procedural requirements of 'normal' applications, in particular they may be denied a judicial remedy.

The problem of complex identities

Once asylum seekers are on the territory and have made an asylum application they are within the Eurodac system and so under surveillance in a very obvious way. But just to make sure that the asylum seeker does not seek to hide his or her 'true' identity, Article 31(8)(c) (formerly Article 23(4)(d)) of the Procedures Directive allows Member States to truncate the investigation of the claim to international protection because 'the applicant has misled the authorities by presenting false information or documents or by withholding relevant information or documents with respect to his/her identity and/or nationality that could have had a negative impact on the [protection] decision'. State authorities will not tolerate complex identities. Asylum seekers are not like other people: they are obliged to inform the state about all aspects of their existence. Article 13(2) (formerly Article 11(2)) of the Procedures Directive sets out among the obligations on the asylum seeker to the state:

- A requirement to report to the competent authorities or to appear before them in person either without delay or at a specified time (specified by the state authorities);
- A requirement to hand over to the authorities documents in their possession relevant to the examination of the application, such as passports;
- A requirement to inform the competent authorities of their current place of residence or address and of any changes thereof as soon as possible. Member States may provide that the applicant shall have to accept any communication at the most recent place of residence or address which he/she indicated;
- A requirement to submit to searches by the competent authorities both of the person and of any items which the asylum seeker has with him/her;
- A requirement to submit to photographs;
- A requirement to submit to recording of oral statements (though the authorities must advise the asylum seeker that a recording is being made).

Asylum seekers are defined out of rights such as privacy, the obligation on the state that it has reasonable suspicion of the commission of a crime before interfering with the liberty of the person or imposing penalties. The state has claimed the right to carry out searches on asylum seekers bodies and property without the obligation to justify why or to have reasons for such searches. However, this EU framed exclusionary move may be countered by another supranational legal framework (European Convention on Human Rights) which at the same time prohibits it.[62] The struggle is one between the capture of individuals into a population as a category and the supranational human rights legal system which entitles the individual to escape.

In order to move from being asylum seekers to refugees, individuals need to engage with the Member States' administrations and to persuade them of the validity of their claims. While individuals have lives and stories full of contradictions, incoherence and detail, the claim to international protection must be accompanied by a single coherent, consistent story without deviations or messy edges which proves that the individual fulfils the definition of a refugee – a well-founded fear of persecution on the basis of race, religion, nationality, membership of a particular social group or political opinion. The punishment for failing to present a clear, consistent and coherent story comes in a number of forms. First, a messy claim will not get a full procedure. Article 31(8)(e) (formerly 23(4)(g)) Procedures Directive states that a Member State can prioritise or accelerate (that is, limit procedural rights) where:

> the applicant has made clearly inconsistent and contradictory, clearly false or obviously improbable representations which contradict sufficiently verified country-of-origin information, thus making his or her claim clearly unconvincing in relation to whether he or she qualifies as a beneficiary of international protection.

This will assist towards the claim being rejected outright. In this case the individual will probably become a person irregularly present on the territory and subject to detention and expulsion. Alternatively, the state authorities may decide that although the refugee claim is not made out the individual needs international protection and so under the Qualification Directive[63] is entitled to subsidiary protection.

In the first case the punishment is immediately evident – reduced procedural guarantees for the asylum claim. In the second the punishment is no protection, the threat of detention and the menace of expulsion. These punishments are normally accompanied by notification that the individual is illegally present (i.e. use of the criminal law directly),[64] a prohibition on working and the denial of all social benefits and housing. Once refused asylum, the individual can no longer claim material support under the Reception Conditions Directive.[65] The individual is thus further punished by destitution. In the second case, the punishment is more subtle. While the individual gets a status, those who are given subsidiary protection rather than refugee status have many fewer entitlements. They may be granted lower social benefits and limited healthcare. They get reduced access to family reunification. Articles 9–12 of the Family Reunification Directive 2003/86[66] which provide for family reunion for refugees under conditions which are more favourable than those applying to other third-country nationals. However, Article 3(c) excludes from its scope persons with subsidiary protection. Thus access to family reunification for anyone with a status less than full refugee is left to the vagaries of national law. Persons with subsidiary protection have residence documents of shorter duration than those which must be accorded to refugees. They are punished for their failure to provide a sufficiently coherent story by being allocated a less favourable residence status. However, in most Member

States the majority of persons who are given subsidiary protection come from the same countries as those who receive refugee status as the UNHCR statistics have shown since 1999 and continue to show up to the present.

Once again, the asylum seeker ought to know that he or she is required to provide a clear and consistent statement. Indeed, in many Member States information pamphlets are given to asylum seekers warning them of the necessity to provide a clear and concise statement which corresponds to the refugee definition in the Qualification Directive. Thus states seek to make the individual responsible for his or her fate. If the individual persists in being unable to provide such a clear and coherent statement then the risk of a lower status or refusal is on him or her.

Responsibility for acts of third countries

Further, the asylum seeker is also made responsible for the acts of third states through a transmission of duties of third countries onto the figure of the asylum seeker. For instance, if the asylum seeker is trying to enter the state or has entered the state 'illegally' from a country which ought to be safe, then the Member State where the application is made has no obligation to examine the application at all. There can be no procedure at all within which the asylum seeker can make his or her claim for international protection (Article 39 (formerly Article 36) Procedures Directive). The directive then goes on to set out how these countries which ought to be safe are to be determined – European safe third countries as they are designated. The characteristics of the European safe third country which have the consequence of denying the asylum seeker an opportunity to have his or her claim to protection heard in an EU Member State are:

- the country has ratified and observes the Refugee Convention;
- it has in place an asylum procedure proscribed by law; and
- it has ratified the European Convention on Human Rights (ECHR) and observes its provisions including standards relating to effective remedies.

According to EU's statistical agency, Eurostat, in both 2010 and 2011 Russian nationals were the second largest group of persons seeking asylum in the EU (after Afghans).[67] A case can be made that the Russian Federation fulfils the three criteria to be a European safe third country: it has ratified and observes the Refugee Convention, it has an asylum procedure in place, it is a party to the ECHR and appears regularly before the Court. If one examines UNHCR statistics for 2011,[68] protection rates in EU countries for asylum seekers from the Russian Federation vary from 53.2 per cent in Finland to 4.3 per cent in the Netherlands.

State authorities' capacity to punish the asylum seeker and the practices of punishment are not always coextensive. However, the key point here is that it is the asylum seeker who, by reason of having travelled through the Russian Federation and having arrived at the border of an EU state or entered 'illegally', is made responsible for the Russian Federation's treatment of asylum seekers. He or she could be returned to the Russian Federation without any examination of his or her asylum claim in the EU as the Russian Federation can be classified, according to the EU's criteria as a safe third country. The fact that Russia is an important country of origin of refugees and beneficiaries of subsidiary protection in the EU does not affect the EU's capacity to classify that state as safe for asylum seekers from other countries. The asylum seeker's alleged choice of travelling through Russia to get to the EU results in the asylum seeker bearing the consequences of the EU's assumption that the Russian Federation is a safe place for the asylum seeker to seek protection. If the asylum seeker does not want to be sent to the Russian Federation to seek international protection, he or she should not travel through it on his or her way to the EU![69]

The Procedures Directive adds a number of finesses to the discipline, auto-discipline and responsibility of asylum seekers. The directive includes punishments in the form of procedural presumptions against the individual which apply in various circumstances. As outlined above these apply to the individual who failed to apply for asylum immediately or as soon as possible after arrival in the territory of a Member State may be punished by being given few procedural guarantees. Similarly, the individual who has trouble providing a story which fulfils the strict legal definition of a refugee is punished by a presumption that his or her claim is manifestly ill-founded because the state authorities consider that it is not plausible or there are internal inconsistencies. These procedural punishments lead towards rejection of the protection claim – the greatest punishment for failing to persuade the authorities of the need for international protection. Similarly, a careless, unwitting or unavoidable travel choice may result in the asylum seeker getting no consideration of his or her protection claim in the EU.

To give the system of punishments against the asylum seeker greater coherence and impact, many Member States have increased the expulsion of persons to whom they have refused asylum. These persons are designated as 'failed asylum seekers'. The use of the term 'failed' evokes fault of the individual that he or she has not succeeded in obtaining international protection just as students who fail their exams did not study sufficiently or were inadequate. The individual is responsible for his or her fate, the authorities warned him or her of the risk of a poor application but he or she persisted in pursuing, inadequately, the claim.[70] Foucault's template for analysis of governmentality through discipline provides a most revealing picture of the CEAS.

The CEAS as an instrument of biopolitics

In this final section, I will examine the most complex of Foucault's categories – that of biopolitics – and how it assists us to understand the system of governmentality which is at work in the CEAS. In his own work, Foucault opened a number of windows of research regarding biopolitics which lead in rather different directions. He was less than clear about what the term means.[71] The separation of life into zôê – the force of life itself not limited to humans, and bios – life as lived by humans alone has been developed by Agamben[72] in particular in relation to foreigners and detention centres. His contention is that in Europe there is a trend to deny the bios of the foreigner. Butler[73] follows quite a different approach to biopolitics which Foucault opened, that relating to the learned and thus ultimately political nature of even those responses which we considered to be our most intimate. Butler develops, in particular, Foucault's interest in the example of gender and sex.

For the purposes of this section, I will focus on another aspect of Foucault's concept of biopolitics which is that related to the management of life itself.[71] How does the CEAS reduce the individual to a population which is managed, not least through statistical information which is then applied to the individual and has the consequence of preventing the individual from escaping through his or her claim to differentiation? At the heart of the CEAS is the endless search for the mechanism to differentiate the deserving asylum seeker from the one who must become the failed asylum seeker. A quicker, surer system for reaching decisions on individual cases is the holy grail – in particular a system which does not require too much expenditure of state resources in personnel, training, etc. Indeed, if there is a safe way to decide cases which is collective and thus avoids the need for officials to spend time looking at individual stories and trying to decide whether they are true or false, this is what many Member States would like most of all from the CEAS. On the other hand, UNHCR endlessly reminds the Member States and the EU institutions of their duty under the Refugee Convention to consider each asylum claim and to make sure that no one who has sought international protection is rejected if the consequence would be that he or she would be sent back to persecution.[75] The problem is how to reconcile these two objectives, satisfy UNHCR and fulfil the state's obligations in international law and decide cases rapidly and with a minimum expenditure of resources.

The Procedures Directive provides a tool in the form of a number of concepts which allow state authorities to divide individuals into groups and deal with them collectively, rather than as individuals. These are:

* the European safe third country (discussed above);
* the first country of asylum;
* the [general] safe third country; and
* the safe country of origin.

The key is to create a category according to a set of rules which are not subject to change by the individual, then to ensure that the individual classified as belonging to the category has little or no chance of escaping it. The justification for the class is based on statistical information used to construct the group. The individual once classified as belonging to it, is not allowed to differentiate him or herself from it. I have described the European safe third-country principle above. In this case, Member States can simply dispense with a procedure altogether where the asylum seeker has passed through a European safe third country en route to the Member State. These people simply do not exist for the Member State as a category in respect of which the authorities are obliged to consider a protection claim at all, the individual is fully and successfully subsumed into a group which does not enjoy a right to protection in the Member State under the Refugee Convention (Article 39 (Formerly Article 36) Procedures Directive).

Similarly, the concept of first country of asylum creates a category of persons in respect of whom any application for asylum can be dismissed without consideration as inadmissible (Article 33 (formerly Article 25) Procedures Directive). Like the European safe third-country concept, the category is constructed not in relation to the individual characteristics of the asylum seeker and his or her claim, but by virtue of the state authorities' assessment of a third country (that is, not the country from which the asylum seeker fears persecution). This class of persons contains every asylum seeker who can be sent to a country which fulfils, in the opinion of the decision maker, one of two characteristics (Article 35 (formerly Article 26) Procedures Directive):

- The country has recognised the asylum seeker as a refugee (and that status is still available to the individual); or
- The person otherwise enjoys sufficient protection in that country, including benefiting from the principle of non-refoulement.

The unifying feature of the two branches of the concept is that state officials are entitled to believe and rely upon assurances from other countries regarding what their officials will or will not do in respect of the asylum seeker and thereby avoid considering the claim of the asylum seeker him or herself. There is no obligation on Member States even to listen to an account of the individual's claim regarding persecution so long as the authorities of another state confirm that they will permit the individual back into their state and not *refoule* him or her to a state where there is a real risk that he or she will suffer persecution.

The (general) safe third-country concept creates yet another category of asylum seekers, *sui generis* among themselves, as the only characteristic which they share is the way in which they have been designated by the Member State where they seek asylum as persons whose claims are inadmissible. The consequence of being designated as an asylum seeker with a safe third-country option is that the protection claim can, once again, be treated as inadmissible (Article 33(2)(c) (formerly Article 25(2)(c)) Procedures Directive). As above in respect of first safe country of asylum, this means that the state authorities are not required even to receive, let alone read or struggle with, the account of the individual's persecution. The elements of the safe third-country concept, like those of the safe first country concept, depend on the confidence of the state authorities regarding the practices of another state's authorities. The individual has no control over that assessment as it has nothing to do with the individual characteristics of the asylum seeker. It becomes a matter between states. The Member State where the asylum seeker has sought protection can consider the application inadmissible if there is another state which fulfils the Member State officials' assessment that it is a first country of asylum.[76]

- The state will not threaten the life of liberty of the asylum seeker on account of his or her race, religion, nationality, membership of a particular social group or political opinion;
- There is no serious risk of harm in that country;
- The state will not refoule the individual to a country where there is a substantial risk he or she will suffer persecution;
- The state will not send the individual to a country where there is a substantial risk that he or she will suffer torture, inhuman or degrading treatment;
- The possibility exists to request refugee status and, if found to be a refugee, to receive protection in accordance with the Refugee Convention.[77]

Instead of the individual's claim of persecution being the subject of careful scrutiny, it is the assessment by the Member State authorities of the adequacy of the third-country's asylum system which becomes the focus of attention. Article 38(2) (formerly Article 27(2)) Procedures Directive permits state authorities to have national legislation regarding the safe third-country concept (formerly it was a requirement to have such legislation). The rules must include some connection between the asylum seeker and the third country which makes it reasonable to send the person there, though there is no need for the individual ever to have set foot in the third country, and there are no examples provided of what kind of connection might be adequate. The matter is left to the imagination of the Member State authorities and their legislators. The methodology by which the Member State authorities determine safe third countries must fulfil one of two requirements: either it includes a case-by-case consideration of the safety of the country for the particular asylum seeker or it includes a national designation of countries considered to be generally safe. In the first limb of the provision there is a vestigal and displaced asylum determination procedure which instead of considering whether the asylum seeker would be persecuted by the state which he or she claims intends to persecute him or her, it requires an examination whether the individual will be persecuted by quite another state with which the individual may have only the most tenuous ties (Article 37(2) (formerly Article 27(2)(b)) Procedures Directive). The second limb removes the asylum seeker from the equation – the only relevant consideration is whether some state through which the individual passed on his or her way to the EU state has been designated by the national authorities as safe.

Nonetheless, the Member State must have rules which allow the asylum seeker to challenge the safe third-country allocation on the basis that he or she would be subject to torture, inhuman or degrading treatment in that country (Article 38(2) (c) (formerly Article 27(2)(c) Procedures Directive). One has a sense that here, at least, the individual can escape the oppression of the category into which he or she has been pushed. However, on examination, one sees that in fact, this escape valve is the direct and unavoidable application of Article 3 ECHR. Council of

Europe states, whether they are EU Member States or not, are under a general duty not to return someone to a country where there is a substantial risk that he or she would suffer torture, inhuman or degrading treatment or punishment. The European Court of Human Rights (ECtHR) has held that this obligation must be carried out on the basis of an individual consideration of the circumstances of each person.[78] Effectively, what the Procedures Directive does here is acknowledge that it is subservient to international rule of law at least as regards the ECHR. As the ECHR has its own court which interprets the meaning of the ECHR, the EU is obliged to acknowledge the primacy of that interpretation of the ECHR rights, rather than one which some Member States might prefer. Indeed, Article 6 Treaty on European Union (TEU) acknowledges the duty of the EU (including its Member States when within the scope of EU law) to respect the ECHR. Further it calls for the EU to accede to the ECHR.

This is the most important difference between the way in which the ECHR operates as a restraint on the EU legislator through its independent judicial supervisory body and the way the Refugee Convention operates. In respect of the latter the EU legislator can and does make endless references to the supremacy of the Refugee Convention and its obedience to international rule of law and then goes on to interpret the Refugee Convention as it wishes whether or not that coincides with the interpretation which the Member States themselves agreed in the context of the UNHCR Executive Committee.[79] The TEU now also calls for the EU to accede to the Refugee Convention.

The final concept which I will consider here is that of safe country of origin. This is a category which designates the individual by reference to his or her country of origin. It is the classification of people as not refugees because they are nationals of a specific state. As such it is the most controversial as it denies the very essence of the refugee, the individual who claims a well-founded fear of persecution from his or her country of origin. The concept is one which obliterates Refugee Convention protection on the basis of where an individual comes from. It is inherently contradictory to the Refugee Convention as it undermines the universality of the right to protection. Instead of all people being eligible for protection from persecution only people from some countries are, not those from other states. For this reason the category of asylum seekers who can be denied a consideration of their claims on this ground is more fluid than the other categories. As in respect of the category of European safe third countries, the construction of the group originally required a decision by the Council. For the same reasons as in respect of the European safe third-country category, this list was never established under the previous directive. In the recast directive, Article 36 merely permits Member States to establish a list of safe countries of origin. This means that variations among the Member States regarding which countries are safe countries of origin cannot be questioned under the directive.[80] The logic of the provision means that where an individual comes from a country which has been designated a safe country of origin his or her application can be considered as unfounded (Article 31(8)(b) (formerly Article 23(4)(c)(i)) Procedures Directive). Article 32 (formerly Article 28) of the directive requires that the individual must not be a refugee in accordance with the Qualification Directive, but the same provision allows Member States to treat the application as manifestly unfounded under national law. So while under the directive the Member State authorities are not permitted to avoid a consideration of refugee status, they are allowed to apply national law to treat the application as manifestly unfounded. This is not only contradictory but smacks of dubious good faith.

The search for the collective designation of the individual in order to avoid the consideration of the individual application which is apparent in the CEAS corresponds to one of the meanings of biopolitics which Foucault suggested. The state's control over life and death, as asylum is a matter of life or death, is incorporated into a statistically or collectively based approach to the management of population. The management of risk takes place through the sealing of the individual into a category which is determined according to a collective assessment of the seriousness of the risk. Every effort is made to ensure that the individual does not escape that category as every exception is costly in terms of state resources. The cost of life or death for the individual is subsumed into the state's collective risk assessment strategy which is privileged. The EU becomes an instrument through which there is a generalisation of the mechanism of population management through risk assessment. This fulfils two important objectives, it provides interstate solidarity for the system against complaints by UNHCR, other international organisations, non-governmental organisations and others that the system is inconsistent with the Member States' obligations under the Refugee Convention; second, it provides reinforcement against internal dissent within EU states against the application of mechanisms of biopolitics against the most vulnerable individuals in the community – asylum seekers.

Conclusions

In this chapter I have examined the three techniques of governmentality which Foucault develops – sovereignty, discipline and biopolitics in the context of the EU's CEAS. Using Foucault's framework to understand the logic of power and authority, the underpinnings of the CEAS become visible. I examine the management of the EU's external border and the categorisation of asylum seekers by reference to the external border through discipline as a technology of governmentality. The existence of refugees as a group of persons entitled to cross borders to seek international protection fits uneasily with the EU's development of a common external border control designed to admit and exclude third-country nationals on the basis of criteria incompatible with refugee protection. The logic of discipline, auto-discipline and responsibilisation of the asylum seeker provides a way to escape the conundrum. If the drowning of the individual in the Mediterranean is the fault of the asylum seeker him or herself for engaging in risky behaviour against the discipline of the EU, criticism is deflected from the EU institutions. Instead, it is the asylum seeker who is failing to respond properly to the discipline and punishment of governmentality.

In the final section I turn to biopolitics as a means of governmentality in the CEAS. The management of life itself (to adopt Rose's terminology) through the creation of categories supported by statistics becomes a particularly powerful tool in the CEAS. The creation of categories of asylum seekers whose claims to protection never need to be heard because they belong to groups excluded from consideration is a cornerstone of the CEAS. The categories are defined on the basis of the Member States assessment of third countries and countries of origin. The asylum seeker is excluded from influencing the assessment in any substantive manner. The life of the individual asylum seeker is managed through the state's categorisation of his or her state of origin or some state through which he or she passed en route, supported by statistics about the incidence of human rights violations there. The individual's capacity to escape the category and to be entitled to differentiation is denied or impaired irreparably. The individual is subsumed, possibly fatally, into a category deemed safe for expulsion.

The CEAS reveals the three techniques of governmentality at work simultaneously. The analytical framework of governmentality indicates some deep flaws in the CEAS as a system which claims to provide international protection to those who need it.

Notes

1 Convention relating to the Status of Refugees, Geneva, 28 July 1951, 1989 UNTS 137, supplemented by the Protocol relating to the Status of Refugees, 31 January 1967, 19 UST 6223, 6257 ('1951 Refugee Convention'). In this chapter to use the language of the Council Directive 2011/95/EU of 13 December 2013 on minimum standards for the qualification and status of third-country nationals or stateless persons as refugees or as persons who otherwise need international protection and the content of the protection granted, OJ L 337, 20/12/2011, 9 (Qualification Directive 2013) the 1951 Refugee Convention is referred to as 'the Geneva Convention'.

2 For instance, under the Convention Against Torture and Other Cruel, Inhuman or Degrading Treatment or Punishment, 10 December 1984, United Nations, Treaty Series, Vol. 1465, 85 (entry into force 26 June 1987).

3 UNHCR, *Statistical Yearbook 2011*, table 12 <www.unhcr.org/51628f589.html>.

4 All references to the EU take into account the changes brought about in December 2009 by the entry into force of the Lisbon Treaty which creates two treaties – the Treaty on European Union (TEU) and the Treaty on the Functioning of the European Union (TFEU).

5 Michel Foucault, *Security, Territory, Population: Lectures at the Collège de France 1977–1978* (Palgrave Macmillan, 2009), 110; see also Michel Foucault, 'Governmentality', in Graham Burchell, Collin Gordon and Peter Miller (eds), *The Foucault Effect: Studies in Governmentality* (University of Chicago Press, 1991),102–3.

6 This term is coined by the German sociologist Ulrich Beck. He defines 'risk' as a 'systematic way of dealing with hazards and insecurities induced and introduced by modernisation itself' (*Risk Society: Towards a New Modernity* (Sage Publications, 1992), 21).

7 In particular the fall of the Berlin Wall is the signifier of the end of the Soviet Union-style Communist regimes in Europe.

8 Daniéle Joly (ed.), *Global Changes in Asylum Regimes* (Palgrave Macmillan, 2002); Patricia Tuitt, *False Images: Law's Construction of the Refugee* (Pluto, 1996).

9 UNHCR, *Asylum Levels and Trends in Industrialized Countries 2009* (UNHCR, 23 March 2010); and its predecessors since 2000.

10 Elspeth Guild, 'The Europeanisation of Europe's Asylum Policy' (2006) 18 *International Journal of Refugee Law* 630.

11 European Commission, *Policy Plan on Asylum: An Integrated Approach to Protection Across the EU*, 17 June 2008, COM(2008) 360 <http://eurlex.europa.eu/LexUriServ/Lex UriServ.do?uri=COM:2008:0360:FIN:EN:PDF>.

12 James A. Caporaso, 'Regional Integration Theory: Understanding Our Past and Anticipating Our Future', in Wayne Sandholtz and Alec Stone Sweet (eds), *European Integration and Supranational Governance* (Oxford University Press, 1998); Andrew Moravcsik, 'Preferences and Power in the European Community: A Liberal Inter-governmentalist Approach'(1993) 31 *Journal of Common Market Studies* 473; Christian Joerges, 'Deliberative Political Processes Revisited: What Have We Learned about the Legitimacy of Supranational Decision Making' (2006) 44(4) *Journal of Common Market Studies* 779.

13 R. B. J. Walker, *Inside/Outside: International Relations as International Theory* (Cambridge University Press, 1993).

14 Michel Foucault, *Discipline and Punish: The Birth of the Prison* (Vintage, 1977); Michel Foucault, *Society Must Be Defended: Lectures at the Collège de France 1975–76* (Palgrave Macmillan, 2003); Michel Foucault, *The Birth of Biopolitics: Lectures at the Collège de France 1978–1979* (Palgrave Macmillan, 2008).

15 Michael Dillon and Andrew Neal (eds), *Foucault on Politics, Security and War* (Palgrave Macmillan, 2008); Thomas Spijkerboer, *Gender and Refugee Status* (Ashgate, 2000).

16 Elspeth Guild, 'Exceptionalism and Transnationalism: UK Judicial Control of the Detention of Foreign "International terrorists"' (2003) 28 *Alternatives: Global, Local, Political* 491.

17 Barry Hindess, 'Government and Discipline' (2008) 2 *International Political* Sociology 268.

18 Frédéric Gros, *États de violence: Essai sur la fin de la guerre* (Gallimard, 2006).

19 Foucault, *Discipline and Punish*, above n. 14.

20 See Mitchell Dean's explanation in *Critical and Effective Histories: Foucault's Methods and Historical Sociology* (Routledge, 1994): 'It is germane – in light of the possible totalizing reading of the "carceral" apparently authorised by the final part of *Discipline and Punish* (1977) – that here the power of government attains pre-eminence over other forms such as not only sovereignty but also, rather intriguingly, discipline' (176).

21 Didier Bigo, 'Security: A Field Left Fallow', in Michael Dillon and Andrew Neal (eds), *Foucault on Politics, Security and War* (Palgrave Macmillan, 2008), 93–114.

22 Nikolas Rose and Peter Miller, *Governing the Present: Administering Economic, Social and Personal Life* (Polity, 2008). In their introduction, they develop Foucault's notion of governmentality as 'conduct of conduct'.

23 Mitchell Dean, *Governmentality* (Sage, 2009).

24 Foucault, *Society Must Be Defended*, above n. 14.

25 Although discipline is also related to the creation of knowledge as a form of power, as Bonditti points out, this makes discipline and biopolitics different from sovereignty (Philippe Bonditti, 'Biométrie et maîtrise des flux: vers une "géo-technopolis du *vivant-en-mobilité*"?' (2005) 58 *Cultures & Conflits*) <http://conflits.revues.org/1825>.

26 The idea of 'risk' in a Foucauldian sense can be understood in the context of the rise of new techniques and practices of power connected to the crisis of the 'welfare state'. The main idea of 'risk' is summarised by François Ewald: 'The expression "taking risks", used to characterise the spirit of enterprise, derives from the application of this type of calculus to economic and financial affairs' ('Insurance and Risk', in Burchell *et al.*, above n. 5, 199). See also Robert Castel, 'From Dangerousness to Risk' (ibid., 281–98). One such example of risk management is insurance technique (Ewald, ibid., 197); another example is surveillance against illness, abnormality and deviant behaviour (see Castel, ibid., 288).

27 Foucault, *Birth of Biopolitics*, above n. 14.

28 Charles Ruelle, 'Population, milieu et normes: Note sur l'enracinement biologique de la biopolitique de Foucault' (2005) 22 *Labyrinthe* 27, 36.
29 Mariana Valverde, 'Law versus History: Foucault's Genealogy of Modern Sovereignty', in Michael Dillon and Andrew Neal (eds), *Foucault on Politics, Security and War* (Palgrave Macmillan, 2008), 135–50. Human rights norms here take their normal meaning of international and supranational human rights treaties.
30 Andrew Neal, 'Goodbye War on Terror? Foucault and Butler on Discourses of Law, War and Exceptionalism', ibid., 43–64.
31 R. B. J. Walker, *After the Globe/Before the World* (Routledge, 2009).
32 The phrase 'last word' was used by Foucault in the context of eighteenth-century execution and public spectacle, where the process of punishment is seen as a discourse and the very moment of execution becomes that moment when the accused can speak his/her 'last words'. Foucault used the phrase 'last words of a condemned man' (Foucault, *Birth of the Prison*, above n. 14, 66).
33 See Colin Gordon, 'Governmental Rationality: An Introduction', in Burchell *et al.*, above n. 5, 3.
34 UNHCR, *2009: Global Trends* <www.unhcr.org/4c11f0be9.html>.
35 European Commission, above n. 11.
36 Council of the European Union, Council Directive 2005/85//EC of 1 December 2005 on minimum standards on procedures in Member States for granting and withdrawing refugee status, OJ L326, 13 <http://eurlex.europa.eu/LexUriServ/LexUriServ.do?uri=OJ:L:2005:326:0013:0034:EN:PDF>. This directive has been revised and the revised version, Council Directive 2013/32/EU of the European Parliament and of the Council of 26 June 2013 on common procedures for granting and withdrawing international protection (recast), OJ L160/60 <http://eurlex.europa.eu/LexUriServ/LexUriServ.do?uri=OJ:L:2013:180:0060:0095:EN:PDF>. This must be transposed by the Member States at the latest by 22 July 2015. Denmark, Ireland and the UK do not participate in this directive.
37 Foucault, *Discipline and Punish*, above n. 14, 222.
38 Ibid., 200.
39 Dean, above n. 23.
40 Didier Bigo, 'Security: A Field Left Fallow', in Dillon and Neal (eds), above n. 29, 93–114.
41 Foucault, *Birth of Biopolitics*, above n. 14.
42 Oded Löwenheim, 'The Responsibility to Responsibilize: Foreign Offices and the Issuing of Travel Warnings' (2007) 1 *International Political Sociology* 203.
43 Foucault uses the phrase 'political technology of the body' to analyse how 'the body is also directly involved in the political field', that is 'the political economy of the body' and how 'the body becomes a useful force only if it is both a productive body and a subjected body' ('The Body of the Condemned', in *Discipline and Punish*, above n. 14, 24–26).
44 Dean, above n. 23, 222–3.
45 The EU's external border agency: Regulation 2007/2004 establishing External Borders Agency (OJ 2004 No. L349/1).
46 Didier Bigo, 'The Birth of Ban-Opticon: Detention of Foreigners in (Il)liberal Regimes' (paper presented at the annual meeting of the International Studies Association, Hilton Hawaiian Village, Honolulu, Hawaii, 1–5 March 2005).
47 There are six major principles in the Weberian ideal type of bureaucracy, which are: (1) a formal structure; (2) managed by rules; (3) functional organisation; (4) a focused mission; (5) all relationships are impersonal; and (6) employment based upon qualifications (Max Weber, *Economy and Society* (University of California Press, 1978)).
48 For a collection of essays which develop this subject, see Bernard Ryan and Valsamis Mitsilegas (eds), *Extraterritorial Immigration Control: Legal Challenges* (Martinus Nijhoff, 2010) <http://nijhoffonline.nl/book?id=nij9789004172333_nij9789004172333_i-441>.

49 European Commission, Examining the Creation of a European Border Surveillance System, 13 February 2008, COM(2008) 68 final <http://eurlex.europa.eu/Lex UriServ/LexUriServ.do?uri=COM:2008:0068:FIN:EN:PDF>.

50 Council Directive 2008/115/EC of the European Parliament and of the Council of 16 December 2008 on common grounds and procedures in Members States for returning illegally staying third-country nationals, OJ L348/98 (referred to as the 'Returns Directive') – deadline for transposition: 24 December 2010 <http://eurlex.europa.eu/LexUriServ/LexUriServ.do?uri=OJ:L:2008:348:0098:010 7:EN:pdf>.

51 No Borders is an NGO which keeps statistics of migrants who die seeking to enter the EU. Since December 2002 they have received information of 3,893 deaths <www. noborder.org/dead.php>.

52 Human Rights Watch, *Pushed Back, Pushed around: Italy's Forced Return of Boat Migrants and Asylum Seekers and Libya's Mistreatment of Migrants and Asylum Seekers* (HRW, 21 September 2009) <www.hrw.org/sites/default/files/reports/italy0909webwcover_0.pdf>.

53 Tineke Strik, 'Lives Lost in the Mediterranean Sea: Who Is Responsible' (Report from the Committee on Migration, Refugees and Displaced Persons, Doc. 12895, 5 April 2012) <http://assembly.coe.int/ASP/Doc/XrefViewPDF.asp?FileID=18095>.

54 Jorrit J. Rijpma, *Frontex: Successful Blame Shifting of the Member States?* (ARI) Real Instituto Elcano, Madrid, Spain, 13 April 2010 <www.realinstitutoelcano.org/wps/wcm/conn ect/391e6a00421a96f98d66ef8b6be8b54b/ARI69–2010_Rijpma_Frontex_ Memeber_State_European_Union.pdf?MOD=AJPERES&CACHEID=391e6a0042 1a96f98d66ef8b6be8b54b>.

55 The NGO, Fortress Europe, maintains a site with information about the deaths <http://fortresseurope.blogspot.com/2006/02/immigrants-dead-at-frontiers-of-europe_16.html>.

56 Rose and Miller, above n. 22.

57 An academic who has used Foucault's notion of conduct of conduct in relation to the treatment of asylum seekers and refugees is Jennifer Hyndman – for an overview, see 'Introduction: The Feminist Politics of Refugee Migration' (2010) 17(4) *Gender, Place and Culture* 453–9.

58 Rey Koslowski and David Kyle (eds), *Global Human Smuggling: Comparative Perspectives* (John Hopkins University Press, 2001).

59 A good example from the UK can be found in the judgment *R* v. *Secretary of State, ex parte European Roma Rights Centre* [2004] UKHL 55.Violeta Moreno-Lax, 'Must EU Borders Have Doors for Refugees? On the Compatibility of Schengen Visas and Carriers' Sanctions with EU Member States' Obligations to Provide International Protection to Refugees' (2008) 10(3) *European Journal of Migration and Law* 315–64; see also Chapter 5 in this volume on the issue of 'surrogate protection'.

60 See Council Regulation (EC) No. 604/2013 of 26 June 2013 establishing the criteria and mechanisms for determining the Member State responsible for examining an asylum application lodged in one of the Member States by a third-country national (known as 'Dublin III'), OJ L 180, 29/06/2013, 31; see also Qualification Directive 2011, above n. 1.

61 According to UNHCR, in 2005 the EU 27 states entertained 240,950 asylum applications; in 2006 the number was 201,000; in 2007 it was 223,670, the next year 239,150 and in 2009 it reached 246,210 (UNHCR, above n. 9). The population of the EU 27 is over 500 million.

62 Of course asylum seekers can claim the benefit of Article 8 ECHR which the ECtHR interpreted as incompatible with police stop-and-search powers which are not based on reasonable suspicion of criminal activity (*Gillan & Quinton* v. *UK* ECtHR 28 June 2010 Application No. 4158/05). However, the fear of being refused asylum acts as a disciplining technique which means asylum seekers very rarely complain about human

rights abuses other than in relation to the substance of their claims at least during the procedure.

63 Council Directive 2011/95/EU of the European Parliament and of the Council of 13 December 2011 on standards for the qualification of third-country nationals or stateless persons as beneficiaries of international protection, for a uniform status for refugees or for persons eligible for subsidiary protection, and for the content of the protection granted (recast), 20 December 2011, OJ L 337 <http://eur-lex.europa.eu/LexUriServ/LexUriServ.do?uri=OJ:L:2011:337:0009:0026:EN:PDF>.

64 Council of Europe: Commissioner for Human Rights, 'It Is Wrong to Criminalize Migration', 28 September 2008 <www.refworld.org/docid/48e34d8a2.html>.

65 Directive 2013/33 of 26 June 2013 laying down standards for the reception of applicants for international protection, OJ L 180, 29/06/2013, 96.

66 Council of the European Union, Council Directive 2003/86/EC of 22 September 2003 on the Right to Family Reunification, 3 October 2003, OJ L 251, 3: transposition deadline 3 October 2005 <http://eur-lex.europa.eu/LexUriServ/LexUriServ.do?uri=OJ:L:2003:251:0012:0018:en:PDF>.

67 Eurostat, *Asylum Statistics* (data from August 2012) <http://epp.eurostat.ec.europa.eu/statistics_explained/index.php/Asylum_statistics>.

68 UNHCR, above n. 3.

69 The Commission's proposal for a recast of the Procedures Directive published in 2009 recommended the abolition of the category of European safe third countries, but this did not find favour with the Council which could only agree to adopt the recast proposal with the reintroduction of the category: see European Commission, Proposal for a Directive of the European Parliament and of the Council on minimum standards on procedures in Member States for granting and withdrawing international protection (Recast) 21 October 2009 COM(2009) 554 final <http://eur-lex.europa.eu/LexUriServ/LexUriServ.do?uri=COM:2009:0554:FIN:EN:PDF>.

70 For instance, the UK statistics' use in the title 'removals of failed applicants'. The numbers of so-called failed asylum seekers removed from the UK varied from 6,800 in 2003 to 3,035 in 2007 (Home Office Statistics, *Asylum Statistics United Kingdom 2007*, 21 August 2008) <http://webarchive.nationalarchives.gov.uk/20110218135832/rds.homeoffice.gov.uk/rds/pdfs08/hosb1108.pdf>.

71 Foucault, *Birth of Biopolitics*, above n. 14; see also Graham Burchell 'Liberal Government and Techniques of the Self', in Andrew Barry, Thomas Osborne and Nikolas Rose (eds), *Foucault and Political Reason: Liberalism, Neo-Liberalism and Rationalities of Government* (University of Chicago Press, 1996), 44.

72 See Giorgio Agamben, *Homo Sacer: Sovereign Power and Bare Life* (Stanford University Press, 1998).

73 Judith Butler, *Gender Trouble: Feminism and the Subversion of Identity* (Routledge, 1999).

74 An important discussion also needs to take place on the identity of the target population as regards the management of life – is it the population of asylum seekers or the EU population which must be protected from asylum seekers?

75 See, for instance, Judith Kumin, Remarks to the Cross-Dimensional Corfu Meeting, Organization for Security and Co-operation in Europe (OSCE), Vienna, 28 May 2010 <www.unhcr.org/4c03cf106.html>.

76 Article 33(2) (c) (formerly Article 25(2)(c)) Procedures Directive. See above n. 35.

77 As set out in Article 38 Procedures Directive. See above n. 36.

78 *Salah Sheekh* v. *Netherlands* ECtHR 11 January 2007, Application No. 1948/04.

79 For a good example, see UNHCR on the Procedures Directive: Cathryn Costello, *The European Asylum Procedures Directive in Legal Contest* (UNHCR Research Paper 134, November 2006) <www.refworld.org/pdfid/4ff14e932.pdf>.

80 COM(2009) 554, above n. 69.

9 Survival migration: conflicting refugee identities in Africa

Alexander Betts

Introduction

Drawing upon research that I have published elsewhere on 'survival migration',[1] this chapter engages directly with this book's central themes within the African context. First, by developing the concept of survival migration, it examines a conflict between the dominant legal–institutional category of the 'refugee' as defined by the 1951 Convention relating to the Status of Refugees ('the 1951 Convention') and the contemporary reality of cross-border displacement.[2] Second, it suggests that this gap between legal–institutional identity and empirical reality is in some cases filled by adaptation of the refugee regime at the national and local level. Far from being static or global, 'who is a refugee' is defined by the encounter of international law with a national and local political context. Drawing upon six case studies from sub-Saharan Africa, it explains why the refugee identity sometimes stretches to incorporate people at the margins of the formal legal definition and at other times it fails to adapt, leading to desperate people being rounded up, detained and deported.

In the early 1950s, at the inception of the modern refugee regime in the European context, the main reasons for a need for substitute protection were based mainly around individualised persecution. In Africa and Latin America, this has been supplemented by the recognition that generalised violence and public disorder may also necessitate substitute protection. However, increasingly, the reasons why sanctuary is needed have changed. The legal institutional 'refugee' identity created for a particular context no longer fits the reality of contemporary cross-border displacement. Today, the combination of generalised violence, environmental disaster, food insecurity and state fragility frequently interact in ways that create a need for protection. Significant numbers of people cross international borders because of serious human rights deprivations rather than because of individualised persecution by their own governments.[3] Many are excluded from access to international protection.

In Africa, where the 1969 Organization of African Unity Refugee Convention in theory protects people fleeing 'serious disturbances to public order . . . in whole or in part of the country', this supplementary framework is extremely inconsistently applied and leaves gaps.[4] The mass exodus of people from Zimbabwe between

2000 and 2010, for example, with some 2 million entering South Africa alone, represents the most visible recent case of people with an obvious need for international protection, but who have generally been seen as in a 'neither/nor' position of not being refugees but not being voluntary, economic migrants.[5] However, this type of situation is not unique. In Syria, Iraq, Afghanistan, North Korea, and Myanmar, for example, a significant number of people have fled to neighbouring countries not because of a well-founded fear of individualised persecution, but more often because of serious socio-economic rights deprivations related to the underlying political situation.

In the context of climate change and discussion of 'environmental displacement', there has been an increasing recognition that new sources of external displacement will require the existing refugee regime to be supplemented in some way to ensure adequate international protection. Most so-called slow-onset 'environmental displacement', however, is not mono-causal but is generally based on the complex interaction of the environment with other factors – notably livelihoods and state fragility – and it is this broader context in which there is an institutional gap.[6]

Yet, despite emerging recognition of the new drivers of external displacement, states and international institutions generally continue to see the world largely in terms of the economic migrant–refugee dichotomy. These remain the dominant identities of state practice. UNHCR has begun to talk of 'people on the move' and to have a debate about how to protect vulnerable irregular migrants and people externally displaced for reasons that fall outside the scope of the existing refugee regime.[7] However, states and the international community are struggling to develop a coherent response to the new drivers of external displacement.

The concept of 'survival migration' – which can be defined as 'persons outside their country of origin because of an existential threat to which they have no access to a domestic remedy or resolution' – is intended to reflect the underlying purpose of the refugee regime: to highlight the circumstances under which substitute protection is required, but on a less ethically and legally arbitrary basis than the current refugee regime.[8] It offers an alternative framing that better reflects the identity of vulnerable people crossing borders in the twenty-first century. In theory, survival migrants have rights under international human rights law, which may, in some cases, amount to a right not to be returned to their country of origin. However, in practice, there is no clear or consistent institutional framework for ensuring these rights for those survival migrants who fall outside the scope of the 1951 Convention.

As a means to examine the broader question of how the new drivers of forced migration challenge the existing international protection regime – and what, if any, reforms are needed to address gaps in protection for survival migrants – the chapter starts with an analysis of the status quo. Based on fieldwork, it asks what, in practice, currently exists in order to protect survival migrants who fall outside the scope of the 1951 Convention. It empirically examines national and international institutional responses to non-refugee survival migration within the context of sub-Saharan Africa.

An exploration of this question has significant policy and advocacy implications because it contributes to identifying gaps in the existing institutional and normative framework addressing forced migration. However, it is also driven by a specific intellectual puzzle. The refugee regime was created for a specific era and for specific circumstances. However, subsequently, new drivers of forced migration – environmental disaster, state fragility and food insecurity – have emerged. This begs the question: under what conditions do the existing global 'old institutions' of the refugee regime stretch at the level of implementation to meet the 'new challenges' at the national level that were not originally envisaged by the creators of the regime?

This idea of 'regime stretching' is important because it highlights how international regimes – as norms, rules, principles and decision-making procedures governing a particular issue-area – are not fixed and static entities that exist in abstraction in Geneva or New York – as international relations tends to see them – but rather they are dynamic and adaptive, and vary in their local and national manifestations.[9] In other words, it highlights how the practice of 'who is a refugee' is not defined in abstraction by law alone but instead by its interaction with local and national politics. In some cases the norms (in this case international refugee law) and the organisation (in this case UNHCR) of a formal regime may stretch to address unforeseen circumstances; in other cases they may not. The question is: when and why does this happen, and what does this mean in practical terms for whether (and if so how) the refugee regime needs to be reformed?

In order to explain variation in the extent to which the existing refugee regime has 'stretched' to meet a set of circumstances unforeseen at the time of its creation, the chapter employs a particular methodology. Based on primary research, including fieldwork,[10] it examines national and international institutional responses to three populations of survival migrants in six host countries. It looks at responses to Zimbabweans in South Africa, Zimbabweans in Botswana, Somalis in Kenya, Somalis in Yemen, Congolese in Tanzania and Congolese in Angola. The cases were chosen for their variation in regime stretching: two represent cases of 'stretching', two of 'breakdown' and two of an ad hoc 'muddle through'. In order to explain this variation, the chapter draws upon a qualitative approach, based mainly around interviews (with policy makers, international organisations, NGOs, migrants and refugees).

The chapter divides into four parts. First, it outlines the concept of 'survival migration', and the reasons why a new concept is needed. Second, looking at the sub-Saharan African context, it empirically examines variation in national and international institutional responses to survival migration that falls outside the dominant interpretation of who is a refugee under the 1951 Convention. Third, it offers an explanation for this variation in institutional response, arguing that in the absence of clear international norms on survival migration, interests have determined whether and how far the refugee regime has stretched to address emerging forms of survival migration. Finally, the chapter concludes by highlighting what the analysis means for policy and practice and for academic understanding of how old institutions adapt to new emerging challenges.

The concept of survival migration

So, to begin with, what does this chapter mean by survival migration? States generally tend to view people who cross international borders as either being 1951 Convention refugees or voluntary economic migrants.[11] The idea that people fall between the gaps of this dichotomy is not new, and a range of labels have already been adopted in academic and policy circles to capture this gap: 'externally-displaced people',[12] 'people in distress',[13] 'distress migration'[14] and 'vulnerable irregular migrants'[15] have all been used to capture this; while others have argued that the concept of a 'refugee' simply needs to be interpreted in a more expansive and inclusive way than is currently the case.[16] Despite the different labels to describe people who cross borders in broadly difficult situations that may require some form of protection or assistance, there continues to be a lack of consensus on how to specifically conceptualise those people who cross international borders who have a human rights-based entitlement not to be forcibly returned to their country of origin, even on a temporary basis.

Yet there is a growing recognition that there are a range of new drivers of forced displacement, which mean that people may be outside of their country of origin but fall outside of the refugee/voluntary–economic migrant dichotomy. The high-profile debates on the impact of climate change on migration and displacement have drawn attention to the potential gap in the existing institutional framework for such people. In some cases people displaced outside of their country of origin but who fall outside the framework of the 1951 Convention may need very immediate humanitarian support before returning home; in others they may not be returnable and have an entitlement to temporary or more permanent forms of protection.

States have been gradually trying to fill some of these gaps. But they have been doing so in very particular rather than overarching ways. In practice, the refugee regime has adapted in some geographical contexts to better fit today's circumstances. Sources of 'complementary protection' have emerged to address the grey area between these extremes of 'voluntary, economic migrant' and 'refugee'.[17] The two main examples are regional normative frameworks and international human rights law treaties. Both, however, have enormous limitations – in terms of geographical scope, normative coverage and implementation.

First, at the regional level, the 1969 Organization of African Unity (OAU) Convention incorporates people fleeing 'external aggression, occupation, foreign domination or events seriously disturbing public order'.[18] The 1984 Cartagena Declaration for Latin America incorporates people 'fleeing generalized violence, foreign aggression, internal conflicts, massive violation of human rights or other circumstances which have seriously disturbed public order'.[19] The 2004 European Union Asylum Qualification Directive provides subsidiary protection to people fleeing 'serious harm', which consists of: (a) death penalty or execution; or (b) torture or inhuman or degrading treatment or punishment of an applicant in the country of origin; or (c) serious and individual threat to a civilian's life or person by reason of indiscriminate violence in situations of international or internal armed conflict.[20] However, these three supplementary conventions have major limitations, even beyond their confined geographical scope. The African and Latin American conventions are not consistently used in practice. The coverage for the potentially broader 'events seriously disturbing public order' has limited development in jurisprudence, and UNHCR remains reluctant to use it as a basis for recognition.[21] Meanwhile, the Europe Union directive mainly serves to ensure that people who would otherwise be refugees but are 'excludable' on technicalities are not forcibly returned, rather than to expand the availability of protection to a significantly broader category of people.

Second, aspects of international human rights law have been applied to address the protection needs of non-refugees who may fall outside of the 1951 Convention but may be non-returnable to their country of origin. A range of jurisprudence has emerged, drawing notably upon the European Convention on Human Rights (ECHR), the American Convention on Human Rights (ACHR) and the Convention against Torture (CAT). The most high-profile cases have found that those who are not covered by international refugee law may nevertheless be entitled to international protection if they face, for example, the prospect of torture, cruel, inhuman and degrading treatment upon their return.

However, despite its potential, complementary protection derived from international human rights law remains limited in its scope and application. First, its jurisprudence has been limited to the right to life and to situations in which people will face torture or inhuman and degrading treatment upon return. Second, its application remains regional; most jurisprudence has emerged in the ECHR and ACHR regions, having almost no application to the African context, for example. Third, its application to economic and social rights has been limited and so this jurisprudence tends to exclude economic and environmental causes of flight.[22] While complementary protection fills some of the gaps for survival migration – and indicates recognition of the gaps by states – it represents an inadequate response to the scale of the problem.

Consequently, significant numbers of people fleeing a combination of environmental disaster, livelihood failure and state fragility have limited recourse to international protection. The concept of 'survival migration' can be used to capture this, and to highlight the conditions under which a person cannot get access to a fundamental set of rights in his or her country of origin and so (as a last resort) needs to seek those rights in another country.[23] It can be fully defined as: 'persons who are outside their country of origin because of an existential threat for which they have no access to a domestic remedy or resolution'.

This definition has three elements, which can be explained in turn. First, people are 'outside their country of origin'. This is important because it implies that the people have access to the international community and the international community has access to them.[24] Second, they face 'an existential threat'. This need not literally be reduced to the right to life, but includes the core elements of dignity. One way in which it could be grounded is in the concept of 'basic rights' developed by Henry Shue and applied to the refugee context by Andrew Shacknove.[25] A 'basic right' can be defined as a right without which no other right can be enjoyed. There are three kinds of basic rights: (a) basic liberty; (b) basic security; (c) basic subsistence. At the moment, the refugee definition focuses on basic security and to some extent basic liberty but excludes basic subsistence.[26] Defining an existential threat is obviously complex, but no more so than for the same kind of bureaucratic and judicial decision making required in refugee status determination. Third, 'access to a domestic remedy or resolution' implies the inability to find a solution within the domestic courts or through an internal flight alternative, making cross-border migration the only viable source of protection.[27]

To add conceptual clarity, Figure 9.1 highlights the conceptual relationship of survival migration to refugees and international migration. For analytical clarity, refugees are survival migrants; but not all survival migrants are refugees; survival migrants are international migrants; but not all international migrants are survival migrants.[28]

Sources of survival migration are likely to proliferate in the context of climate change and the transmission of the global economic meltdown, for example. Very few universally accepted sources of subsidiary protection exist to address the needs of people fleeing for reasons other than political persecution. However, this in turn begs the question of what current national and international institutional responses to non-refugee survival migration look like.

National and international institutional response

The chapter now turns to the empirical case studies of national and international institutional responses to non-refugee survival migration in sub-Saharan Africa. The research covers three populations in six host countries: Zimbabweans in South Africa and Botswana; Somalis in Kenya and Yemen; Congolese in Tanzania

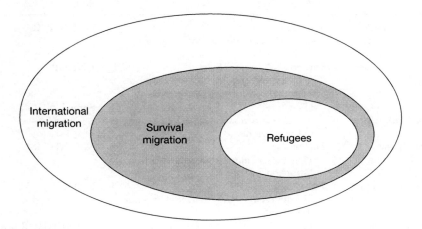

Figure 9.1 Conceptual relationship of survival migration to refugees and international migration

and Angola.[29] Although the cases are all slightly different, they are comparable in the only aspect that matters for the purposes of this analysis: they all involve a national and international response to survival migrants who are outside their country of origin for reasons that fall outside the dominant interpretation of the 1951 Convention. The focus on sub-Saharan Africa means that the findings cannot be generalised but nevertheless offer a useful and important starting point for exploring responses to survival migration. Table 9.1 offers a summary of the case studies. In each case there has been variation in the national and international institutional response to non-refugee survival migration.

Each national response is summarised under a head. Angola's response can be characterised as 'violation' with systematic human rights abuses perpetrated against migrants. Tanzania's response can be characterised as 'paradox' – it has become a de facto protector of long-stay survival migrants, but has refused to protect new arrivals. South Africa's response has been 'ad hoc' – there has been an absence of formal status and lack of economic and social rights. Botswana's response can be characterised as a 'dichotomy', dividing people into migrants or refugees. Kenya's response can be characterised as 'prima facie', with all survival migrants recognised on the face of it but receiving limited rights. Yemen's response can be characterised as 'triage', shifting from prima facie recognition to increasingly exclusionary practices.

The international response has also varied. In Kenya and Tanzania, UNHCR has covered the gaps. In Angola and Botswana, on the other hand, UNHCR has been largely absent from protecting non-refugee survival migrants, and protection has relied upon 'hidden protection actors' with provincial networks such as the church, MSF or the national Red Cross. In South Africa and Yemen, the

Table 9.1 Protection of non-refugee survival migrants

Case	National response	International response
DRC–Angola	Violation – systematic and state-led violation of migrant rights	No UNHCR
DRC–Tanzania	Paradox – de facto protection of long-stay survival migrants/exclusion of new arrivals	UNHCR
Zimbabwe–South Africa	Ad hoc – absence of formal status/lack of economic and social rights	Some UNHCR
Zimbabwe–Botswana	Dichotomy – refugees/voluntary–economic migrants distinction	No UNHCR
Somalia–Kenya	Prima facie – recognition alongside refugees but limited rights to all	UNHCR
Somalia–Yemen	Triage – shift from prima facie towards growing exclusion	Some UNHCR

international response has been somewhere in between, based on an ad hoc muddle-through, with UNHCR offering some – but incomplete – protection to survival migrants who fall outside the dominant interpretation of the 1951 Convention.

Zimbabweans in South Africa

The response to Zimbabweans in South Africa can be characterised as ad hoc.[30] Between 2000 and 2010, large numbers of Zimbabweans fled the country in search of sanctuary. The majority fled to South Africa. It is difficult to estimate the precise number but the NGO network CORMSA claims it could be anywhere between 1 and 9 million,[31] while South Africa's Department of Home Affairs (DHA) agrees that there are likely to have been up to 2 million Zimbabweans in the country.[32]

The modern history of Zimbabwe is highly politicised and there is no single, objective historical account. However, it is clear that, in the words of one South African NGO employee, 'most are escaping the economic consequences of the political situation' rather than political persecution per se.[33] Following the Lancaster House Agreement between the UK and ZANU in 1980, an agreement was reached to defer land reform, provided the UK government continued to provide development assistance. The agreement came to an end with the election of the Labour government in 1997. This triggered a wave of land invasions, leading to international sanctions, capital flight and ultimately hyperinflation. Alongside this, declining productivity and drought contributed to famine. Consequently, by the mid 2000s, there were very few viable livelihood strategies available for those without access to foreign exchange.[34]

In accordance with the country's refugee policy, all Zimbabweans have been given asylum seeker permits pending refugee status determination (RSD). However, given the predominantly economic causes of flight only the approximately 10 per cent of people persecuted because of political links to the opposition MDC were granted refugee status.[35] The rest were liable to be rounded up by police, detained and deported. For most of the period of the exodus, there were practically no alternative viable immigration channels beyond the asylum system for Zimbabweans. A number of reforms were proposed in April 2009, notably a temporary immigration exemption status for Zimbabweans, which led to a moratorium on deportations of Zimbabweans between May 2009 and January 2011.

In addition to a lack of clear status, Zimbabweans have had limited access to material assistance – either sites of reception in the border region or in the urban areas to which many have moved. For example, at the border town of Musina, only an ad hoc coalition of NGOs and international organisations has provided limited protection. Until February 2009, the so-called 'showgrounds' in Musina were a de facto 'camp' with squalid, insecure and violent conditions, and with almost no national or international presence. There they received very limited protection from the government, international organisations or NGOs. In

February 2009, the DHA cleared the 'showgrounds' and instead all Zimbabweans were required to move onwards to urban areas to obtain asylum seeker permits from one of the country's six Refugee Reception Offices in order to obtain a six-month asylum seeker permit. After that, Musina became a transit town in which the only available assistance was on small plots of land provided by the church. The only assistance they received came from an ad hoc coalition of NGOs and international organisations.

Meanwhile, in urban areas, many Zimbabweans were not welcome in the townships since the May 2008 xenophobic violence[36] and were instead forced to live in crime and drug-ridden areas such as Windsor and Hillsborough or, to take sanctuary in the very visible Central Methodist Church, which in March 2009 housed 3,400 Zimbabweans, including 107 unaccompanied minors, in appalling and unsanitary conditions.[37] The only significant sources of material support have consequently come from the church, the South African Red Cross, and NGOs such as MSF and Lawyers for Human Rights (LHR).

UNHCR's role has been nominal, overseeing the asylum system, but remaining on the fringes of debates about how to address those Zimbabweans who fall outside of the 1951 Convention framework.[38] The possibility of applying the broader refugee definition contained in the OAU Refugee Convention and covering events which 'seriously disturb or disrupt public disorder' in his/her country was discussed (Polzer 2008). Indeed South Africa's Refugee Act incorporates both the 1951 and OAU conventions. However, both UNHCR and the government resisted this on the grounds that this clause within the OAU Convention 'lacks doctrinal clarity' (Crisp and Kiragu 2010).

Zimbabweans in Botswana

The response to Zimbabweans in Botswana has been based on a stark 'dichotomy'. In 2009 there were an estimated 40–100,000 Zimbabweans in Botswana, of which only around 900 were recognised as refugees. The legal framework is in many ways more rigid than that of South Africa. Asylum seekers are required to remain in detention in Francistown during their RSD process. If they receive recognition, they are entitled to live in the refugee camp in Dukwe from where they can apply for a work permit if and when they find work. However, the majority of Zimbabweans remained outside the asylum system, facing detention and deportation. According to the NGO Ditshwanelo, round-ups are generally sporadic, and immigration officials will often tolerate the presence of Zimbabweans for long periods of time knowing that deportation is only likely to lead to migrants coming back to Botswana. However, occasional round-ups do take place in large trucks. No NGO or independent agency has the capacity or access to oversee this process.[39] Beyond the asylum system, there is very little additional legal provision that relates to the situation of people who fall outside of the refugee/voluntary–economic migrant dichotomy.[40]

This dichotomous legal framework in turn changes the nature of the international response to undocumented migrants. Unlike South Africa, where the distribution of asylum seeker permits to all arrivals gives UNHCR a mandate to at least engage with the question of undocumented Zimbabweans as asylum seekers, no such 'nexus' exists in the context of Botswana. This has made the international response to the exodus even less developed than that in South Africa.[11] As the Deputy Representative of UNICEF said, 'When people become refugees, a number of things kick in automatically. But for these undocumented, perhaps economic migrants, it is not clear that we have any clear policies, structures or guidelines.'[12] All of the UN agencies in Botswana have effectively been prevented from working with undocumented Zimbabweans who are outside of the refugee framework.

Given this, the Zimbabweans in the country have been living in both rural and urban areas, with a significant proportion based in the 'Little Harare' area of Gaborone. They have mainly had to survive through their own networks. However, many have faced significant degrees of exploitation. According to a recent report published by the African Migration Studies Programme at Witwatersrand University, many face exploitation in domestic or agricultural, prostitution and lack of access to basic services.[13] Healthcare services –including anti-retrovirals (ARVs) – have been unavailable to undocumented migrants. Furthermore, the absence of material assistance means that there are no programmes for undocumented children.[14] There are no reliable figures for the numbers of UAMs (unaccompanied minors) and children among the Zimbabwean populations. However, extrapolating from the proportion of Zimbabwean refugees who are aged under 15 would suggest that, based on the most conservative estimate of 40,000 undocumented Zimbabweans, there would be around 3,000 undocumented Zimbabwean children, who have no access to protection or services such as education or healthcare.[15]

Congolese in Angola

There is a long history of livelihoods migration from the DRC to Angola. However, with the collapse of diamond mines in the southern provinces of Bandundu and Western Kasai, the numbers crossing the border in search of livelihoods appears to have increased over the past decade. Many people who would previously have dug informally for diamonds in the southern provinces of the DRC are now forced to cross into the Lunda Norte region of Angola either to do the same or to find alternative sources of income. In the words of one member of MSF staff in Kinshasa, 'They have nothing. It's a survival strategy; they earn less than an average of 10 dollars a month. The motive is hope and despair.'[16]

The response of the Angolan government has been brutal. According to OCHA, at least 300,000 Congolese have been forcibly deported from the Lunda Norte region of Angola to the DRC in six main waves between 2003 and 2009. The first wave took place in December 2003 with around 20,000 expulsions being recorded in Bandundu and Western Kasai; the second wave (so-called 'Operation Brillante', linked to the Angolan elections) led to a recorded 80,000 expulsions to Bandundu and Western Kasai; in the third wave in September and October 2006

OCHA was only able to record 230 expulsions, but acknowledges that this was because it was 'late on the scene'; the fourth wave in February 2007 involved around 6,000; the fifth wave in July 2007 led to around 33,000 being recorded in Western and Eastern Kasai and Katanga in the context of provincial elections in Lunda Norte; while the sixth wave ('Operation Crisis') led to around 160,000 recorded expulsions to Western Kasai, Bandundu and Bas-Congo.[47]

The waves have frequently been linked to the provincial and national elections and to Angolan concern about the historical relationship between ethnic Congolese and the role of the National Union for the Total Independence of Angola (UNITA) in the Angolan civil war. There has been little documentation of these expulsions by academics, the media or international organisations. However, in 2007 MSF recorded 100 testimonies from women at its mobile clinics who had been deported. These testimonies highlighted systematic and state-sponsored rape, torture and unsterile body cavity searches of those expelled, conducted by people who appeared to be acting as agents of the state.[48]

As one of the few organisations to document the expulsions in detail, MSF has highlighted a pattern to the expulsions. Most of the women were victims of sexual violence, and many others were suffering from dehydration, malnutrition, sleep deprivation, malaria, HIV-related diseases. However, one of the big protection challenges for MSF was that often the waves were small and difficult to monitor, and people dispersed back to their villages in the DRC very rapidly.[49]

The institutional response to the protection needs of these migrants has been extremely limited. On the Angolan side, NGOs like Human Rights Watch have been denied access to the sites of detention and deportation. Meanwhile, there has been limited interest from the government in Kinshasa except in 2009 when Angola expelled Congolese from Cabinda to Bas-Congo and here the concern related not to human rights per se, but to a wider personal squabble between Eduardo do Santos and Joseph Kabila in the context of Kabila's rapprochement with Paul Kagame of Rwanda.[50] The only real sources of protection in the border regions have come from what might be referred to as 'networked actors' such as the church, MSF and the Red Cross which have been able to act through local contacts to offer basic assistance. More formal, UN-based, interagency missions have mainly focused on recording numbers and the main international organisations have been largely uninterested in playing a more active protection role. UNHCR has argued that the issue falls outside of its mandate.[51] OCHA has argued that it is not a priority compared to other challenges in the DRC.[52] The International Organization for Migration (IOM) has tried but failed to obtain the funding to get involved.[53]

Congolese in Tanzania

The fourth case study relates to Congolese from South Kivu in the Kigoma region of Tanzania. The majority of Congolese in Tanzania are in the Nyarugusu refugee camp and have been in the DRC since the mass influxes of 1996 and 1998. The national and international response to survival migration represents something of a paradox. On the one hand, it is now widely recognised by the government and UNHCR that there is limited generalised violence or persecution in South Kivu. Consequently, the government has suspended new RSD for the Congolese and it has sought to bring to an end its status as a refugee-hosting country. On the other hand, there is a general acknowledgement that conditions in South Kivu – in terms of livelihoods and social services – are too poor to actively promote return. Hence, there is a situation in which, in the absence of the cessation clause, Tanzania and UNHCR are de facto protecting non-refugee survival migrants.

On the one hand, there is an increasing recognition that people who leave South Kivu are not in need of international protection. While the government initially provided prima facie recognition in the late 1990s, it shifted to individualised RSD. In the words of one representative of the Department of Refugee Affairs, 'we reject them if they have socio-economic reasons; any other aside from persecution'.[54] In theory then, RSD takes place through interviews coordinated by an 'ad hoc committee'. However, as of September 2009, the Regional Commissioner's Office in Kigoma has effectively suspended the work of the ad hoc committee and no new RSDs were taking place.[55] Furthermore, UNHCR openly acknowledged that the main problems in South Kivu no longer relate to conflict or generalise violence but rather to the lack of infrastructure and social service provision.[56]

On the other hand, however, both the government and UNHCR have fallen short of implementing the cessation clause and insisting upon the return of the Congolese. In contrast to the Burundians, for whom 'promoted return' is taking place, UNHCR and the government are only engaging in 'facilitated return' for the Congolese from South Kivu through offering support items and 'go and see' opportunities, allowing them the choice to return or to remain. Yet, ultimately UNHCR concedes: 'The reasons why they left may not exist anymore but the general situation – for example, in health and education – and the constant fear makes me agree that those that stay, have to stay.'[57] In that sense, UNHCR and the government of Tanzania are de facto protecting long-stay non-refugee survival migrants but, paradoxically, declining to offer protection on the same terms to new arrivals.

Somalis in Kenya

Following the collapse of the Siad Barre regime in Somalia in 1991, civil war led to the mass exodus of refugees from South/Central Somalia into Kenya.[58] Kenya, informally after 1991, and through its legislation since 2006, recognised all Somalis as a group on a prima facie basis, without making them go through individualised RSD. In 2006 when it adopted its Refugee Act, Kenya became the only country in Africa with legislation that allows for prima facie recognition on the basis of the OAU Convention refugee definition.[59]

In contrast to the other cases, this means that non-refugee survival migrants from South/Central Somalia have been de facto protected by Kenya. Prima facie recognition has meant that all Somali survival migrants – irrespective of the cause of their flight – have received the same standards of international protection. Even people from Somalia who may not be directly affected by individualised persecution or generalised conflict are still recognised as refugees. Implicitly, this means that those affected by, say the economic or environmental consequences of the political situation – rather than by political persecution or conflict per se – nevertheless get access to protection.

The challenge in the case of Kenya, however, has been that although the refugee definition has been inclusive, the standards of protection available to all Somalis have been extremely minimal. The majority of refugees have been confined within the insecure, arid and inhumane Dadaab camps close to the Somali border, where there were around 270,000 people at the end of 2009. Despite massive overcrowding, the Kenyan government has refused to allow Dadaab to grow.[60] Nevertheless, unlike the other cases, UNHCR and other international actors have been in a position to provide material assistance within the camps. Meanwhile, a minority have lived as urban refugees in the Eastleigh estate of Nairobi, where international protection and assistance have remained more limited, but at least available on a more or less inclusive basis.

What is interesting about the Kenyan case for the purpose of this chapter is that it highlights the only one of the case studies in which the OAU Convention has been used to address the gap between 1951 Convention refugees and survival migrants, and provide a more inclusive framework. Yet, it simultaneously highlights how inclusivity may have diluted the standards of protection available to all or, at least, is not necessarily synonymous with effective protection.

Somalis in Yemen

In the case of Yemen, an increasingly restrictionist asylum policy has been adopted. As in Kenya, the government previously recognised all Somalis on a prima facie basis. However, with an increasing focus on mixed migration across the Gulf of Aden, there has been a recent shift towards a less tolerance set of policies, with a view to detaining and deporting non-refugees. In that sense, the approach of Yemen has been a gradual shift towards a process of triage.

Yemen serves as a country of transit for Somalis wanting to go to Saudi Arabia and the Persian Gulf States. Although Yemen lacks national refugee legislation, it has a high-level National Committee for Refugees Affairs (NACRA) and the working-level National Sub-Committee for Refugee Affairs (NASCRA) as government bodies that deal with refugees. Migrants who arrive in Yemen by sea can go to Mafyaa and Ahwar reception centres, to access temporary shelter and assistance. There, all Somalis are given travel passes valid for 10 days to enable asylum seekers to go to Sana'a to apply for asylum. There, Somalis can register with UNHCR and all are recognised as prima facie refugees by Yemeni authorities under their group recognition policy provided that they register with UNHCR. Of the 150,000 Somali refugees, only 14,000 Somali refugees live in the Al Kharaz camp, and the remainder lives in urban areas in Sana'a and around the Basateen district in Aden, where they receive very limited material assistance.[61]

However, in addition to those Somalis recognised as refugees, the Ministry of Foreign Affairs estimates that there may be up to an additional 550,000 Somalis in the country. In the context of increasing political concern relating to the start of the civil conflict, Somalis have been detained on the grounds of their involvement with Al Qaida or Al Shabaab. The authorities have subsequently developed an increasingly restrictionist approach towards Somalis. There has been a growing debate on introducing RSD for Somalis – as is currently the case for all other nationalities such as Ethiopian asylum seekers. Furthermore, on 18 January 2010 the Yemeni authorities issued a two-month deadline for unregistered Somalis to register with UNHCR, stating that Somalis who have not registered with UNHCR will be deported. In conclusion, then, the case offers a contrast to the Kenyan response in so far as it represents a gradual shift away from an inclusive approach towards one that increasingly imposes significant restrictions on Somalis.

Explaining variation in responses

The important analytical question, then, is: how can we explain this variation in institutional response – especially at the international level? In order to explain variation in response, I use the concept of 'regime stretching'. Within international relations, a 'regime' can be defined as the norms, rules, principles and decision-making procedures around which actor expectations converge in a given issue-area. The idea that actor expectations and behaviour can converge or diverge around the benchmark of a regime has largely been neglected by scholars of international institutions who have viewed regimes as fixed. In practice, though, few old regimes die and regime creation is rare. What happens is that existing regimes adapt or break down when faced with new sets of circumstances. The idea of 'stretching' can be operationalised around the two core elements of a 'regime': (a) norms and (b) the international organisation – in this case international refugee law and UNHCR. More formally, regime stretching might be defined as the *degree to which the scope of a regime at the national or local level takes on tasks that deviate from those prescribed at the global level*. Such stretching may be regime consistent (taking on tasks that are complementary to the underlying purpose of the regime) or regime inconsistent (contradicting the underlying purpose of the regime).

Figure 9.2 illustrates the spectrum of 'regime stretching'. Towards the right, in Kenya and Tanzania, the refugee regime has stretched to address non-refugee survival migration. In the middle, there has been an intermediate response characterised by 'muddle through' in Yemen and South Africa. Meanwhile, in the case of Botswana and Angola, there has been no stretching and a protection vacuum has resulted.

The obvious null hypothesis to explain this variation would be that the conditions in the country of origin explain the variation. However, this is clearly

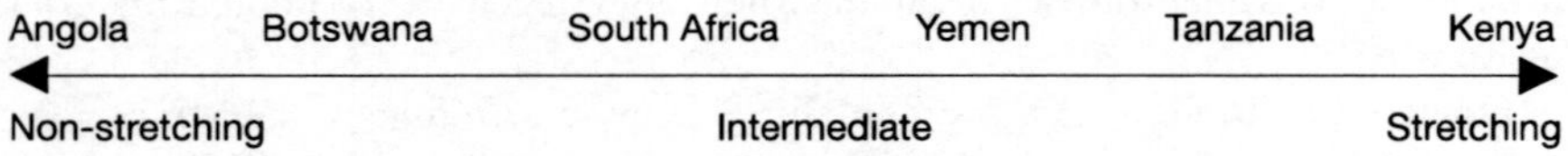

Angola   Botswana   South Africa   Yemen   Tanzania   Kenya

◄───►

Non-stretching   Intermediate   Stretching

Figure 9.2 Dependent variable: spectrum of institutional responses to survival migration

not a sufficient explanation, given the way in which host countries with the same populations appear at different points on the spectrum. The empirical analysis of the six cases tells us something about the nature of the refugee regime. In some cases, it adapts to new challenges and in other cases it does not. In other words, the refugee regime in Botswana is not the same as the refugee regime in South Africa. The same international regime can adapt in very different ways to particular national challenges, even in the absence of any formal renegotiation of the international regime. This begs the broader question of – how and why – does an international regime adapt to new challenges in one way in a particular national context, and a different way in another international context? To understand this, a basic conceptual framework is needed.

How regimes adapt at implementation

The concept of a regime is often defined by its 'consensus definition' of 'principles, norms, rules and decision-making procedures around which actor expectations converge in a given issue-area'.[62] More simply, a regime can be understood to have two core elements: norms and international organisations (which can both be subsumed under the notion of 'international institutions').[63] Within each of these two areas, adaptation and change may take place. Even in the absence of creating a new regime or formally renegotiating norms or international organisations, change and adaptation can and do take place. Regime adaptation – in terms of both norms and international organisations – can be understood to take place at three levels: (a) international bargaining; (b) institutionalisation; and (c) implementation.[64]

At the first level of *international bargaining*, norms may be changed through interstate (re)negotiation, and international organisations may be changed through statute (re)negotiation. For example, norms are sometimes adapted through 'additional protocols' to a treaty, while international organisations may be formally changed through the UN General Assembly choosing to authorise the change in an international organisation's mandate. This level of change is widely recognised within liberal institutionalist literature, which implies that when states'

Table 9.2 Regime adaptation model

	Norms	*International organisation*
International bargaining	Treaty negotiation	Statute negotiation
Institutionalisation	Legislation	Mandate interpretation
Implementation	Policy	Practice

demand for international regimes changes (for example, because of a change in preferences, power or the nature of the problem), they will formally renegotiate the bargain on which the regime is based.[65]

At the second level of *institutionalisation*, norms may adapt in the way in which they are disseminated internationally, and, in particular, in how they are signed, ratified and adopted within national legislation.[66] For example, if states change their ratification of a regime, or whether or not the regime is incorporated within national legislation, this will represent an adaptation of the regime. This type of change if widely recognised within constructivist literature on institutionalisa-tion.[67] International organisations may adapt in terms of the way in which their mandates are institutionalised (and interpreted) by the international organisation. Meanwhile, many organisations' interpretation of their own mandates may change at the global level even in the absence of a formal General Assembly mandate. This type of change within literature on principal–agent theory as applied to international organisations.[68]

At the third level of *implementation*, in relation to norms, the introduction of a norm's precepts into formal legal or policy mechanisms at the national level in order to routinise compliance (i.e. 'policy') may vary between different national contexts.[69] For example, even where two countries have the same degree of institutionalisation of an international norm, one may observe very different outcomes because of a state's willingness or ability to implement norms. In relation to international organisations, the way in which the organisation's national representation interprets its mandate (i.e. 'practice') may vary between different national contexts. For example, a national representation in one country may act differently from the same organisation in a different country. In contrast to the other two levels, this third level of regime adaptation is almost entirely neglected within international relations. Yet, it is important in so far as we observe variation (or change) in outcomes even in the absence of variation (or change) at the levels of international bargaining or institutionalisation.

Explaining variation in implementation

Within the six case studies, both international bargaining and institutionalisation have been relatively constant across the cases. All of the states have signed and ratified 1951 Convention and its 1967 Protocol. All except for Yemen have also signed and ratified the OAU Refugee Convention of 1969. Yet despite a broadly common level of institutionalisation, the cases exhibit variation in the regime at the level of implementation. This begs the question of how we can explain that variation.

What has mattered in the case studies is the incentives on national elites in government to support more inclusive or exclusive recognition of survival migrants.[70] In the absence of clear or binding norms, national elites had discretion in their response to survival migrants who have fallen outside the 1951 Convention framework. How this discretion has been exercised has been shaped by interests. Where national elites have had positive international and domestic-level incentives to stretch the norm of 'who is a refugee', they have done so. Where they have had strong disincentives to do so, they have refrained. Meanwhile, UNHCR – present at the invitation of the government – has largely followed discretionary choice of government on the stretching of the regime, providing additional assistance where requested and able to do so. In other words, interests have mattered, defining the scope for old institutions to adapt to new challenges at the level of implementation.

Table 9.3 crudely illustrates positive (+), negative (–) and neutral (0) incentives on national elites for stretching, which emerge from the international system and from domestic politics. The table is not intended to represent a rigorous coding of the sets of incentives on host-state-ruling elites so much as a simplified abstraction of the qualitative empirical data outlined below. The zeros ('0') generally denote some kind of 'cancelling out' process, whereby both positive and negative incentives exist in countervailing directions. Table 9.3 illustrates that there is a correlation between the overall net incentives for stretching and the presence or absence of regime stretching.

Furthermore, the cases not only highlight how international and national incentives shape how the norm of 'who is a refugee' is implemented, but they also imply that whether or not UNHCR's own mandate has stretched has followed sequentially from the interests of the national elites in stretching or not stretching. Rather than autonomously stretching or not, the international organisation's own role has been correlated with the prior decision of national elites on whether to stretch the underlying norm. In other words, the international organisation's own role in stretching (or not) appears to have been epiphenomenal. The only exception to this has been in so far as UNHCR has – at the margins – been able to influence the government's own cost–benefit calculus by shaping the incentives for regime stretching (e.g. financial support).

Kenya – stretching

Kenya has had significant financial and diplomatic gains from hosting refugees. Given its porous border and the difficulty of forcibly excluding Somalis, its inclusive approach has enabled it to delegate responsibility directly to UNHCR, minimising the costs of hosting. In this context prima facie recognition has been cheaper and more efficient than individualised screening.[71] The international community has absorbed the costs of maintaining the refugee camps, and the refugees have been mainly confined to a particular area of the country. Moreover, refugee hosting gives Kenya a bargaining tool vis-à-vis the international community. For example, in its bilateral relationship with Denmark, it has used refugee hosting as a bargaining tool to attract additional development assistance.[72]

Domestically, there has been a mixed response to hosting Somalis. There is some xenophobia towards the Somali populations and historically there have been fears of secession. However, Somalis have been generally tolerated. Those in camps are geographically confined, while those in Nairobi contribute massively to the economy, with Somalis running one of the biggest market districts in Nairobi in the Eastleigh area of the city.

Table 9.3 Independent variables: international and domestic incentives on government elites to engage in regime stretching or not

Host state	Angola	Botswana	South Africa	Yemen	Tanzania	Kenya
reward (+)/ punishment (−) by international system	diamond mining investment (−)	limited external criticism (0)	international reputation (+) bilateral Zimbabwe (−)	pressure to protect (+) EU pressure to manage migration (−)	financial support (+)	financial support (+)
reward (+)/ punishment (−) by domestic politics	reducing UNITA support base (−)	xenophobia (−)	civil society activism (+) rising xenophobia (−)	integrated Somali diaspora (+) rising xenophobia (−)	tolerance (0)	tolerance (0)
overall net incentive	negative (−)	negative (−)	neutral (0)	neutral (0)	positive (+)	positive (+)

There has therefore been a net incentive for regime stretching and for maintaining a broadly inclusive approach. UNHCR has consequently also been able to be inclusive in its assistance and make use of prima facie status because of the response of the government. UNHCR appears to have had some influence in the original development of the Kenyan legislation that led to Kenya being the only state in Africa to recognise Somalis as prima facie refugees under the OAU Convention. However, it was arguably only able to do so in so far as incentives existed for Kenya to adopt that approach. Hence, sequentially, the government's interest in stretching the norm seems a precondition for the organisation to also stretch.

Tanzania – stretching

At an international level, Tanzania has historically derived significant financial and diplomatic gains from its inclusive refugee policies. This has gradually changed over time. It was once one of the most generous refugee-hosting states in Africa. However, democratisation and structural adjustment from the late 1980s made elected governments more accountable to their own citizens and created pressure – especially at local and regional levels – to reduce pressure on local resources. However, in spite of this, the government in Dar has persistently tried to temper pressure from regional and district commissioners to repatriate refugees.[73] This has partly been because of recognition of the links between refugee hosting and overseas development assistance and diplomatic status. For example, while Tanzania has actively promoted repatriation for a significant number of Burundians, it has not sought to return Congolese, instead taking the advice of UNHCR and valuing the legitimacy it appears to derive from refugee hosting.

Domestically, there has also not been significant xenophobia directed towards the Congolese who are generally tolerated by Tanzanians. In the Kigoma region, the Nyarugusu camp does not exert significant pressure on the local host population, and the presence of other Congolese immigrants as fishermen and traders along Lake Tanganyika is generally tolerated.[74] This is in contrast to Burundians, who were often seen as a potential security threat due to the spill-over of conflict and violence to the Burundian refugees camps.[75]

Overall, there has therefore been a net incentive to not forcibly repatriate the Congolese from South Kivu despite improved circumstances within South Kivu. This has allowed a degree of regime stretching to take place to protect de facto survival migrants, who might otherwise have been returned to South Kivu. UNHCR's role has followed this logic. In so far as the Tanzanian government has not exerted significant pressure to return the Congolese, UNHCR's country representation also been able to stretch to maintain the Nyarugusu camp. UNHCR staff admitted in interview that they hoped to maintain the camp because 'otherwise, we would be effectively packing up the [country] operation'.[76]

Yemen – intermediate response

The international incentives on Yemen to engage in regime stretching have also pulled in both directions. On the one hand, there has been international pressure, notably from UNHCR, not to return people to Somalia. On the other hand, though, there has been growing pressure to limit the onward movement of Somali migrants and asylum seekers to Europe, with the EU, the UK, Denmark and the Netherlands putting increasing resources into controlling Somali mixed migration 'in the region of origin'.[77] This shift has contributed to a change in the policy of the government, reducing incentives for regime stretching over time. This has been exemplified by EU money going into the development of a 'Mixed Migration Task Force' to triage 'refugees' from 'non-refugees' crossing the Gulf of Aden.[78]

Similarly, domestic incentives have gradually shifted over time from a position of tolerance and inclusivity towards growing hostility. There has historically been a sizeable and well-integrated Somali diaspora, which has had a significant role in the national economy, and sustaining economic and social ties with Somalia.[79] However, there has gradually been a shift towards increasing xenophobia, competition for resources and concern with terrorist links that has made the government concerned to more closely control who is on its territory.

At both the international and domestic levels, there have therefore traditionally been incentives for stretching. But, over time, countervailing pressures in both directions have emerged. Consequently, there has been a gradual move from regime stretching towards an intermediate and less coherent response. UNHCR's own position has followed this trend. It has traditionally been part of an inclusive response, but as the position of the government has changed, so too UNHCR has become involved in a move towards a more triage-based approach, becoming, for example, an active partner in the Mixed Migration Task Force.

South Africa – intermediate response

The international incentives on South Africa have pulled in both a positive and negative direction. In terms of incentives for non-stretching, the main one has been the bilateral relationship with Zimbabwe. The personal relationship between Mbeki and Mugabe for a long time stymied South African criticism of Zimbabwe and that has continued even since Jacob Zuma came to power in 2009.[80] The government acknowledges that its response to Zimbabwean survival migrants has been shaped significantly by the Department of Foreign Affairs not wishing the grant of status to Zimbabweans to be interpreted as condemnation of the Mugabe regime.[81] For example, when in March 2009, South Africa was considering some kind of temporary visa exemption status for all Zimbabweans in South Africa, it first discussed the issue with the Zimbabwean government at a meeting in Victoria Falls.[82] On the other hand, however, there has been a degree of countervailing international pressure that has tempered the impact of the bilateral relationship. In particular, the government has been susceptible to the international criticism it has received from a range of human rights organisations for its treatment of the Zimbabweans on its territory.

There has also been a similar, two-directional pull at the level of domestic incentives. On the one hand, there has been rising xenophobia within South Africa. In May 2008, in particular, there was severe xenophobic violence in the townships, in which Zimbabweans were among those targeted. Against the backdrop of economic recession, there has been increasing political pressure to move beyond pan-African open borders and towards increasing deportation for illegal immigrants.[83] On the other hand, tough, this shift has been partly offset by the role of a vibrant civil society in consistently condemning xenophobia, and upholding and litigating for the rights of immigrants.

At both the international and domestic levels, there have therefore been countervailing pressures in both directions. Hence the response has been an intermediate response. There has been some degree of tolerance of the Zimbabweans, but certainly not full stretching of the refugee norm to incorporate them. The result has been an ad hoc, incoherent and somewhat schizophrenic policy response. UNHCR's own role has sequentially followed this, being constrained in taking on a strong role but being able to do so in so far as ambiguities in government position opened up space to offer some assistance. For example, it has been able to offer some assistance in so far as all Zimbabweans are asylum seekers up until the point at which refugee status determination takes place, after which UNHCR has not taken any responsibility for those who have been rejected and liable for deportation.[84]

Botswana – no stretching

The international incentives on Botswana have been fairly neutral. It has not faced significant international pressure or incentives to stretch or not. Few arguments have been made to the government that it should recognise Zimbabweans. The international organisations in Gaborone, and especially UNHCR and the UN Resident Coordinator, have not criticised the government position, either privately or publicly.[85] Instead, they have been passive of and accepting of their own non-involvement in the issue and recognised the sovereign right of the government to detain and deport.

Meanwhile, there have been strong domestic incentives against regime stretching. The electorate has strongly favoured deportation, and there has been growing xenophobia towards the Zimbabweans. The numbers of Zimbabweans (40–100,000) have been high relative to the overall population (1.8 million), and Zimbabweans in Gaborone have been associated with crime and prostitution.[86] With pressure on the country's own resources and high HIV rates, the electorate has been reluctant to allocate rights to non-citizens. The country spends more on deportation than any other country in the region other than South Africa.[87]

The incentives on the government have therefore been neutral at the international level, but there have been strong domestic incentives against regime stretching. UNHCR's own role has followed the government's decision on non-stretching. In interviews, UNHCR staff have argued that the organisation's own work has been constrained by the government position and claimed that it could not get involved unless it was invited to do so by the government.

Angola – no stretching

The international incentives on Angola were strongly against regime stretching. From an international political economy perspective, the government had a strong incentive to remove Congolese migrants from the diamond-mining areas. After victory in the civil war in 2002, the MPLA government acquired control over the previously UNITA-controlled diamond-mining areas of the Lundas.[88] In attempting to develop the diamond industry as part of its national development strategy, it engaged in the privatisation of the mines, selling concessions to a range of multinational corporations with a strong interest in controlling and limiting diamond smuggling. When the deportations began in 2003, they were therefore conceived as an 'anti-diamond smuggling' operation to ensure exclusive access to mines for corporations rather than artisanal immigrant labour.[89] Aside from this set of economic incentives, there was almost no countervailing pressure from the international community to condemn Angola's human rights violations, mainly because the international community retained a vested interest in the diamond and oil industries.

In terms of domestic incentives, the timing of the main waves of deportations correlates closely with preparations for national and regional elections. The diamond-mining areas are traditionally a UNITA stronghold, and the Congolese have traditionally supported UNITA, which had tolerated their presence in the Lundas prior to 2002. After the MPLA government took control of those areas in 2002, however, the government sought to systematically remove Congolese from the region to prevent registering to vote in the build-up to regional and national elections, and bolstering UNITA's electoral support.[90]

There have therefore been strong incentives – both national and international – against regime stretching, based primarily on privatisation of diamond mines and elections in context of post-civil war era. Furthermore, the role of UNHCR in Angola has followed the government's non-stretching of the norm. Having not been invited by the government to engage in responding to the presence of the Congolese, it has had no clear basis for involvement and has consequently played no role in the Angolan side of the border.[91] On the DRC side of the border, it has also argued that responding to the needs of the expelled migrants has fallen outside its mandate.

Conclusion

The basis of the modern refugee regime was created in a very different era. It provided a legal–institutional identity of a 'refugee' as someone fleeing indi-vidualised persecution by their own government. Subsequently, a range of new drivers of cross-border displacement has emerged, including generalised violence, environmental change and food insecurity. The sociological reality of cross-border displacement no longer neatly aligns with the dominant legal category.

The concept of survival migration provides a way of highlighting the gap between these competing identities. It draws attention to people who look very much like refugees, crossing international borders as a last resort in order to get access to fundamental human rights, but who are often denied access to protection and assistance.

However, the concept of survival migration also helps make sense of another central question posed by Stevens and Kneebone (see Chapters 5–6 in this volume): how is it that the refugee definition is made, remade and given social and political meaning? It shows how, far from being static and global, 'who is a refugee' is defined by the interaction of international law with national and local politics. In different political and social contexts, the legal–institutional category of a 'refugee' can be ascribed with different meanings. These differences in meaning have radical consequences for the rights and assistance afforded to vulnerable populations. Populations fleeing similar types of human rights deprivations have been met with seemingly arbitrary differences in response, ranging from being protected as though they were refugees through to being rounded up, detained and deported.

By examining six different case studies, the chapter highlights significant variation in responses to survival migration. In some cases, the refugee regime has 'stretched' at the national level to address the new circumstances; in other cases it has failed to stretch, leaving important protection gaps. The explanation for this variation in responses can be found in the mechanisms through which international institutions adapt at the level of implementation. Across the cases, the interests of national government elites have mattered for defining the boundaries and scope of the legal–institutional category of a 'refugee'. Given normative ambiguity at the global level, interests at the domestic level will define national and, in turn, international responses.

Existing international relations scholarship has tended to focus on processes of international institutional change at the international level, to the neglect of a focus on how international institutions are translated and changed in their encounters with domestic law and politics. The chapter has shown how international regimes – in terms of both their norms and international organisations – can adapt at three different levels: (a) international bargaining; (b) institutionalisation; and (c) implementation. Even where international bargaining and institutionalisation are held constant, the way in which international institutions adapt at implementation can vary significantly across national contexts.

In trying to explain variation in the degree to which the refugee regime has sometimes stretched at implementation, this chapter has identified that the interests of national government elites matter. Where there have been significant positive incentives on elites, regime stretching has taken place. Where there have been negative incentives, regime stretching has not taken place. In other words, in the context of normative ambiguity at the global level, interests at the domestic level will define national and, in turn, international responses.

These findings have important practical implications. On the one hand, they highlight significant gaps in the existing international refugee protection regime. In different ways, all the case studies highlight how people fleeing fundamental human rights deprivations are sometimes deprived of protection and of the right not to be forcibly returned to their country of origin. This poses an immense challenge in terms of thinking through how the international community might most appropriately address that gap.

On the other hand, however, the chapter highlights how addressing gaps in existing international institutions can take place at three different levels. Rather than necessarily assuming that all gaps can only be addressed by immediately reverting to reform at the level of international bargaining, it may also be possible to address some gaps further downstream – at the levels of institutionalisation or implementation. It may make sense to begin by considering what can be changed at the level of implementation, and then the level of institutionalisation, before finally deciding on the need for change at the level of international bargaining. By showing the causal mechanisms through which international institutions adapt at the implementation stage and the role of elite interests within that process, the chapter highlights potential policy levers for influencing that process. In the absence of legal precision, incentives matter for how old institutions respond to new challenges.

Notes

1 Alexander Betts, *Survival Migration: Failed Governance and the Crisis of Displacement* (Cornell University Press, 2013).
2 Convention relating to the Status of Refugees, Geneva, 28 July 1951, 1989 UNTS 137, supplemented by the Protocol relating to the Status of Refugees, 31 January 1967, 19 UST 6223, 6257 ('1951 Refugee Convention').
3 Michelle Foster, *International Refugee Law and Socio-Economic Rights: Refuge from Deprivation* (Cambridge University Press, 2007).
4 Tamara Wood, 'Fragile States and Protection under the 1969 African Refugee Convention' (2013) *Forced Migration Review* 43.
5 Alexander Betts and Esra Kaytaz, 'National and International Responses to the Zimbabwean Exodus: Implications for the Refugee Protection Regime', *New Issues in Refugee Research*, Working Paper No. 175 (UNHCR, 2009).
6 Betts, above n. 1, 15–22; Jane McAdam, *Climate Change, Forced Migration, and International Law* (Oxford University Press, 2011).
7 Jeff Crisp, 'Beyond the Nexus: UNHCR's Evolving Perspective on Refugee Protection and International Migration', *New Issues in Refugee Research*, Working Paper No. 155 (UNHCR, 2008).
8 Betts, above n. 1; Alexander Betts, 'Survival Migration: A New Protection Framework' (2010) *Global Governance* 16, 361–82.
9 Anna Schmidt, 'Negotiating policy: refugees and security in Tanzania and Uganda', paper presented at ISA 49th Annual Convention, 2008.
10 A number of authors discuss the role and relevance of fieldwork and even ethnographic methodology within international relations. See, for example, Severine Auteserre, *The Trouble with Congo* (Cambridge University Press, 2010); Wanda Vastri, 'The Strange Case of Ethnography and International Relations' (2008) *Millennium* 37, 279–301.

11 Anthony Richmond, 'Reactive Migration: Sociological Perspectives on Refugee Movements' (1993) *Journal of Refugee Studies* 6, 7–24.

12 This term was used, for example, by UNHCR in the context of the International Conference on Refugees in Central America in the 1980s and 1990s.

13 Guy Goodwin-Gill, '*Non-refoulement* and the New Asylum Seekers' (1986) *Virginia Journal of International Law* 897.

14 Sarah Collinson, 'Globalisation and the Dynamics of International Migration: Implications for the Refugee Regime', *New Issues in Refugee Research*, Working Paper No. 1 (UNHCR, 1999).

15 Alexander Betts, 'Towards a Soft Law Framework for Protection of Vulnerable Irregular Migrants' (2010) *International Journal of Refugee Law* 22.

16 Andrew Shacknove, 'Who Is a Refugee?' (1985) *Ethics* 95, 274–84.

17 Jane McAdam, *Complementary Protection in International Refugee Law* (Oxford University Press, 2007).

18 See Article 1(2) of the 1969 OAU Convention Governing the Specific Aspects of Refugee Problems in Africa.

19 See Conclusion 3 of the 1984 Cartagena Declaration on Refugees.

20 See Article 15 of the Council Directive 2004/83/EC of 29 April 2004 on minimum standards for the qualification and status of third country nationals or stateless persons as refugees or as persons who otherwise need international protection and the content of the protection granted, 19 May 2004, 2004/83/EC.

21 Jeff Crisp and Esther Kiragu, 'Refugee Protection and International Migration: A Review of UNHCR's Role in Malawi, Mozambique and South Africa' (Geneva, UNHCR Policy Development and Evaluation Service, 2010).

22 Michelle Foster, '*Non-refoulement* on the Basis of Socio-Economic Deprivation: The Scope of Complementary Protection in International Human Rights Law' (2009) *New Zealand Law Review* 257. The decision in *R v. Secretary of State for the Home Department, ex parte Adam, Limbuela & Tesema* [2005] UKHL 66 (House of Lords) provides a good example of the application of the ECHR to cover economic and social rights. In that matter, the House of Lords held that an asylum applicant was subject to inhuman or degrading treatment when he was left without any support from the state because he failed to apply for asylum in the prescribed time period. Lord Bingham held that:

A general public duty to house the homeless or to provide for the destitute cannot be spelled out of article 3. But I have no doubt that the threshold may be crossed if a late applicant with no means and no alternative sources of support, unable to support himself, is, by the deliberate action of the state, denied shelter, food or the most basic necessities of life . . . When does the Secretary of State's duty . . . arise? The answer must in my opinion be: when it appears on a fair and objective assessment of all the relevant facts and circumstances that an individual applicant faces an imminent prospect of serious suffering caused or materially aggravated by denial of shelter, food or the most basic necessities of life.

(paras 7–8)

23 The idea of survival migration is not entirely new, and has been used in different contexts such as Oded Stark and Edward Taylors's work on the 'new economics of migration', in which they see migration as part of a household 'survival strategy'. However, this chapter's application of the concept to consider institutional questions of response to externally displaced people is new. See, for example, Oded Stark and Edward Taylor, 'Relative Deprivation and International Migration' (1989) *Demography* 26, 1–14.

24 James Hathaway, 'Forced Migration Studies: Could We Agree Just to "Date"?' (2007) 20 *Journal of Refugee Studies* 349.

25 Henry Shue, *Basic Rights* (Princeton University Press, 1996); Shacknove, above n. 16.

26 Unless one buys into the normative and negative rights violations to distinguish 'persecution' from other rights violations such as generalised violence then privileging basic security and basic liberty over basic subsistence is an arbitrary delineation. For the counter-argument, see Matthew Price, *Rethinking Asylum* (Cambridge University Press, 2009).

27 It is worth noting that this definition is not necessarily hugely expansive and need not necessarily imply permanent protection. Rather, it is intended to highlight the situations in which a fundamental set of rights is simply unavailable within the country of origin and can only be sort in another country – but in a way that does not arbitrarily exclude certain types of rights violations.

28 Adapted from Trygve G. Nordby, IFRC Special Envoy on Migration, Keynote Speech, High Commissioner's Dialogue on Protection Challenges, Geneva, 11–12 December 2007.

29 The justification for selecting the six cases is based on what the chapter is trying to explain: variation in the extent to which the refugee regime 'stretches' in particular national contexts to address survival migration. Selection on the dependent variable is twofold. First, it is justified by the purpose of the article being to explore why there is variation in the dependent variable, which requires the selection of cases in which there is variation in outcome. Second, the degree of bias introduced by this methodological choice is not especially significant because the chosen cases represent close to the full set of cases of non-refugee survival migration from failed states within Africa.

30 Betts and Kaytaz, above n. 5; Tara Polzer, 'Responding to Zimbabwean Migration in South Africa: Evaluating Options' (2008) 15 *South African Journal of International Affairs* 1.

31 CoRMSA, 'Protecting Refugees, Asylum Seekers and Migrants in South Africa', Johannesburg, 18 June 2008, 17.

32 Interview with Florencia Belvedere, Department of Home Affairs, Johannesburg, 30 March 2009.

33 Interview with Kajaal Ramjathan-Keogh, Head of Refugee and Migrant Rights Programme, LHR, Johannesburg, 18 March 2009.

34 For history of Zimbabwe, see Martin Meredith, *Robert Mugabe: Power, Plunder and Tyranny in Zimbabwe* (PublicAffairs, 2002); interview with Ambassador Simon K. Moyo, Zimbabwe House, Pretoria, 30 March 2009.

35 Interview with Florencia Belvedere, DHA, 30 March 2009.

36 IOM, 'Towards Tolerance, Law and Dignity: Addressing Violence against Foreign National in South Africa' (IOM, 2009).

37 Interviews with Zimbabwean migrants, Central Methodist Church, Johannesburg, 1 April 2009.

38 HRW, 'Neighbors in Need: Zimbabweans Seeking Refuge in South Africa' (2008) <www.hrw.org>; MSF, 'No Refuge, Access Denied: Medical and Humanitarian Needs of Zimbabweans in South Africa' (2009) <www.msf.org>.

39 Interview with Alice Mogwe, Director of Ditshwanelo, Gaborone, 25 March 2009.

40 Interview with Beleme Gelafele, UNHCR Botswana, Gaborone, 28 March 2009.

41 Interview with Gelafele.

42 Interview with Marcus Betts, UNICEF Deputy Representative to Botswana, Gaborone, 25 March 2009.

43 Monica Kiwanuka, *Zimbabwean Migration into Southern Africa: New Trends and Responses* (Wits, 2009).

44 Interview with Betts, above n. 42.

45 This is based on UNHCR statistics of the number of refugees and the proportion which are children. However, extrapolation from the refugee population to the undocumented migrant population is not unproblematic because the proportion of children may be higher in the refugee population, whereas undocumented migrants may be more likely to be individuals seeking employment than families.

46 Interview with Dr Lame Papys, MSF Belgium, Kinshasa, 9 November 2009.

47 OCHA, 'Point sur les expulses d'Angola au 15.10.09' (2009), on file with the author.

48 MSF, 'Women Tell of Their Angolan Ordeal' (2007) <http://www.doctorswith outborders.org/news/article.cfm?id=2232&cat=field-news>.

49 Dr Emmanuel Lampeart, MSF Belgium, Kinshasa, 9 November 2009.

50 Interview with Ebba Kalondo, Kinshasa, 11 November 2009.

51 Interview with Mohamed Toure, Assistant Regional Representative, UNHCR, Kinshasa, 10 November 2009.

52 Interview with Richard Guerra, Head of Coordination, OCHA, Kinshasa, 12 November 2009.

53 Interview with Toure.

54 Interview with Mr Chuleha, Assistant Zonal Coordinator, Department of Refugee Affairs, Kigoma, 15 September 2009.

55 Interview with Hans Hartmark, Protection Officer, UNHCR, Kigoma, 15 September 2009.

56 Interview with Mr Konecko, Head of UNHCR Field Office, Kasulu, 16 September 2009.

57 Interview with Konecko.

58 See, for example, James Milner, *Refugees, the State, and the Politics of Asylum in Africa* (Palgrave Macmillan, 2009).

59 Matthew Albert, 'Prima Facie Determination of Refugee Legal Status: An Overview of Its Legal Foundation', *RSC Working Paper* No. 55 (RSC, 2010).

60 Interview with Peter Klansoe, Regional Director, Danish Refugee Council, Nairobi, 14 May 2009.

61 Betts, above n. 1.

62 Stephen Krasner, 'International Regimes' (1982) *International Organization* 36.

63 Stephen Krasner – as author of the original regime definition – acknowledges in conversation that seeing regimes as norms and international organisations makes more sense, especially in empirical application. Other authors such as Gary Goertz have also argued for a more minimalist concept of a regime. Goertz states 'for my purposes, norms, principles, decision-making procedures, and rules can be seen as synonymous', arguing that the logical form of these norms is broadly reducible to the idea of a norm (as a single standard of behaviour) – although it may be useful to distinguish between those norms that define action and those that define organisational procedures (Gary Goertz, *International Norms and Decision Making: A Punctuated Equilibrium* (Rowman & Littlefield, 2003), 19).

64 These categories broadly follow Elinor Oostrom who has three levels of analysis: constitutional, directive and operational in looking at collective action (*Governing the Commons: The Evolution of Institutions for Collective Action* (Cambridge University Press, 1990)).

65 Vinod Aggarwal (ed.), *Institutional Design for a Complex World: Bargaining, Linkages and Networks* (Cornell University Press, 1998); Robert O. Keohane, 'The Demand for International Regimes' (1982) 36 *International Organization* 332; Harald Muller, 'Arguing, Bargaining and All That: Communicative Action, Rationalist Theory, and the Logic of Appropriateness in International Relations' (2004) 10 *European Journal of International Relations* 395.

66 There is a vast social constructivist literature on the institutionalisation of international norms. The literature on institutionalisation can be divided into two broadly chronological waves of scholarship: (a) institutionalisation as explained by international-level processes; (b) institutionalisation as explained by domestic-level processes. However, what these two waves have in common is that what they are trying to explain is institutionalisation, albeit that the definition of – and the 'line' where institutionalisation ends varies across the literature. That 'line' exists on a spectrum from signing and

ratifying international treaties, at one end of the spectrum, to the adoption of domestic legislation, policies and even standard operating procedures, at the other end of the spectrum. In contrast, this chapter contends that it is useful to analytically distinguish between two distinct processes: 'institutionalisation' as an *international process* and 'implementation' as a *domestic process*. This distinction is important because it enables us to clearly distinguish between two distinct phases of political contestation, and to recognise that even once a norm or international organisation mandate is formally institutionalised, it will be subject to a new phase of political contestation.

67 Margaret E. Keck and Kathryn A. Sikkink, *Activists beyond Borders: Advocacy Networks in International Politics* (Cornell University Press, 1998); Thomas Risse-Kappen, Stephen C. Ropp and Kathryn A. Sikkink, *The Power of Human Rights: International Norms and Domestic Change* (Cambridge University Press, 1999); Beth A. Simmons, *Mobilizing for Human Rights: International Law in Domestic Politics* (Cambridge University Press, 2009).

68 Adolf Berle and Gardiner Means, *The Modern Corporation and Private Property* (Harcourt, Brace and World, 1967, 2nd edn); Darren G. Hawkins, David A. Lake, Daniel L. Nielsen and Michael J. Tierney (eds), *Delegation and Agency in International Organizations* (Brigham Young University, 2006).

69 The concept of 'implementation' has been explored – implicitly or explicitly – in international relations in the work of: Wayne Sandholtz, 'Dynamics of International Norm Change: Rules against Wartime Plunder' (2008) 14 *European Journal of International Relations* 101; Carolyn Deere, *The Implementation Game: The TRIPS Agreement and the Global Politics of Intellectual Property* (Oxford University Press, 2009); Antje Wiener, 'Enacting Meaning in Use: Qualitative Research on Norms and International Relations' (2009) 35 *Review of International Studies* 175; David G. Victor, Kal Raustiala and Eugene B. Skolnikoff (eds), *The Implementation and Effectiveness of International Environmental Commitments: Theory and Practice* (MIT Press, 1998), but it still requires conceptual development.

70 The decision to frame the independent variable as the interests of 'national elites' rather than the 'state' is based on the recognition that in many states – including those examined in this chapter – the interests of the actors within government may not be in any way representative of a wider 'national interest'. See, for example: Mohammed Ayoob, *The Third World Security Predicament: State Making, Regional Conflict, and the International System* (Lynne Rienner, 1995); Christopher Clapham, *Africa and the International System* (Cambridge University Press, 1996); Robert Jackson, *Quasi-States: Sovereignty, International Relations and the Third World* (Cambridge University Press, 1990); Douglas Lemke, *Regions of War and Peace* (Cambridge University Press, 2002); Mancur Olson, *Power and Prosperity: Outgrowing Communist and Capitalist Dictatorships* (Basic Books, 2000), for a discussion of the distinction between the interests of the 'state' as an actor and the 'national elites in government'.

71 Matthew Albert, 'Prima Facie Determination of Refugee Legal Status: An Overview of Its Legal Foundation', *RSC Working Paper* No. 55 (Oxford, 2010).

72 Interview with Betina Gollander-Jensen, Counsellor, Danish Embassy to Kenya, Nairobi, 19 May 2009.

73 Milner, above n. 58.

74 Interview with Geoffrey Carliez, UNHCR Assistant External Relations Officer, Kigoma, Tanzania, 16 September 2009.

75 Interview with Geoffrey Carliez.

76 Interview with Hans Hartmark, Protection Officer, UNHCR, Kigoma, 15 September 2009.

77 Interview with Lily Sanya, IOM Technical Adviser to IGAD, Djibouti City, 26 May 2009.

78 See Mixed Migration Task Force website for details: <www.mmyemen.org>.

79 Reuters, 'Yemen getting tougher on Somalis', Reuters, 9 February 2010.

80 Interview with Ambassador Simon K. Moyo, Zimbabwe House, Pretoria, 30 March 2009.
81 Interview with Advocate Mashabane and Andreas Ousthuizen, Department of Foreign Affairs, Pretoria, 18 March 2009.
82 Interview with Burton Joseph, Department of Home Affairs, Pretoria, 19 March 2009.
83 IOM, above n. 36.
84 Interview with Sanda Kimbimbi, UNHCR Regional Representative, Pretoria, 17 March 2009.
85 Correspondence with Roy Hermann, former UNHCR Representative to Botswana; interview with Khin-Sandi Lwin, UNDP Representative (and UN Resident Coordinator), 24 March 2009.
86 Interview with Alice Mogwe, Director of Ditshwanelo, Gaborone, 25 March 2009.
87 Interview with Alice Mogwe.
88 Rafael Marques, *Lundas – The Stones of Death: Human Rights Abuses on the Lunda Provinces, 2004* (Apoios, 2005).
89 MSF, 'PUC Memo, W. Kasai to Antenne Kinshasa' 8/11/07 (MSF-Belgium).
90 MSF, 'RDC-Kasaï Occidental: violences sexuelles à l'égard des femmes congolaises refoulées de l'Angola', 11 December 2007–5 January 2008 (MSF-Belgium: Brussels).
91 Interview with Toure.

10 Transnational law and refugee identity: the worldwide effect of European norms

*Hélène Lambert**

Since the mid-twentieth century, the boundaries between the international and the domestic, and between state and non-state, have steadily eroded. This is not simply in terms of the proliferation of international rules with growing domestic effect, such as human rights law, it is also in terms of law and practice in one state shaping the laws and practice of other states through transnational connections. Horizontal links across state boundaries between legislators, regulators, judges and interest groups are increasingly shaping how laws are framed, interpreted and applied. This has led some international law scholars, working from the US liberal tradition, to declare the emergence of a new world order based on a complex web of trans-governmental networks.[1] The European Union (EU) is often held as a prime example of this development, and indeed of the future trajectory of this world order.

This chapter examines the global influence of European asylum law.[2] It discusses evidence of worldwide emulation of European asylum law through transnational and local actors, and considers the EU's normative power in refugee protection. It draws conclusions on the role of transnational processes in shaping the construction of refugee identity around the world. Essentially, it argues that, historically, refugee identity was rooted in Europe, in that both refugee law and human rights law are European constructs in origin. The 1951 Refugee Convention[3] was then emulated by states outside Europe, and what we may be witnessing today is a similar pattern of transnational diffusion of Western norms (the Common European Asylum System, or CEAS) encoded in the now internationalised Refugee Convention and other human rights treaties. This chapter further argues that Europe's normative power in refugee law is clearly at work in this transnationalism.

Just to clarify, a transnational approach to law invites attention to the actions of and links between non-state actors, and the trans-border effect of national and regional legal institutions. This chapter therefore challenges the traditional approaches to European law ('European integration') and international law (the 'vertical approach'), which treat states as the central players. It takes forward the research agenda first laid out by Goodwin-Gill and Lambert in *The Limits of Transnational Law: Refugee Law, Policy Harmonization and Judicial Dialogue in the European Union*.[1] The book examined the extent of transnational judicial dialogue within the EU and explained why there was less than might be expected. The empirical findings – that judges rarely use each other's decision on asylum within the EU, suggest that the transnational legal approach has limited applicability within the EU. In contrast, this chapter argues that the transnational legal approach is very relevant when we move outside of Europe. EU asylum law and protection practice is spreading and influencing countries around the world; transnational actors like UNHCR play an important role in this, but so do a variety of local actors. This chapter therefore continues the analysis in Chapter 5 on how refugee identities are constructed judicially and transnationally.

Global engagement with European asylum law

Europe has one of the most advanced regional refugee protection regimes in the world. The EU regime has emerged through a series of policy and legal agreement on asylum, and refugee law and human rights principles, aiming at achieving an ever-greater uniformity in the law and practice of its Member States. The second phase of the CEAS legislation has now concluded – this common legislation codifies over 20 years of state practice.[5] A regime covering 25 countries,[6] including some of the most developed and powerful in the world, is bound to exert considerable influence beyond Europe in matters of refugee law and practice.

The predicted impact of this body of EU norms has been widely identified in the academic literature as one of 'ripple effect' or 'trickling effect' beyond the EU.[7] However, very few studies have noted the fact that this regime has already influenced the law and practice of states around the world, for some time.[8] The implications of this are great in terms of understanding the transnational effect of European asylum law.

Approach: how to study worldwide emulation of Europe?

This section draws on scholarship from international relations, sociology and law to identify 'why' and 'how' European law and practice on refugee protection spreads and is being emulated worldwide. There exists a large body of literature on the possible global influence of the EU through transnational actors and processes, both in the socio-legal literature on the diffusion of law[9] and in the area of political science/political sociology of the EU.[10] Up to now, most European legal scholars have taken a 'European integration' approach to 'European asylum law' and have focused on EU institutional development and the effects of EU law on Member States.[11] At the same time, US scholars have for some time highlighted the global promise of European legal institutions.[12] International relations scholars too have long been working on diffusion theories in organisational structures.[13] The empirical data gathered by international relations scholars reveals that from the mid-twentieth century onward, growing similarity in organisational form and function within a range of specific policy areas, including public healthcare, education and managing the natural environment.[14] Such similarity constitutes a puzzle. Why is there such a degree of worldwide homogeneity in how societies organise themselves, given the great difference in local conditions and requirements?[15] Here, a particular school of international relations called constructivism is most useful in helping us understand this puzzle, as it seeks to explain how ideas spread across borders and take effect in national policy communities. Constructivists see a world that is substantially shaped by the identities of actors and the ideas they hold about how they should organise and act (i.e. norms). Thus, they emphasise the role of norm entrepreneurs and advocates in promoting new norms, and the role of transnational networks (e.g. professional, legal or advocacy) in diffusing norms.[16] Viewed through this lens, norm diffusion usually involves a process of *socialisation* and *internalisation*. Socialisation is where states (or policy communities within them) are pressured and/or persuaded to adopt the new norm. Internalisation is where the new norm is embedded in the laws, codes and practices of the adopting community.[17] Crucially, constructivists find that when states adopt certain norms in a selective process, these specific norms are often 'localised' in this process.[18] Much overlap exists between this body of work and socio-legal scholarship on the diffusion, reception or transplant of law. For instance, William Twining also emphasises the importance of local context. He explains that 'processes of diffusion are nearly always mediated through local actors'.[19] He too sees diffusion as 'typically a reciprocal rather than a one-way process', hence early influences of 'Western legal traditions lose their pre-eminence'.[20]

Drawing on this combined literature, two main drivers can be identified behind the spread of norms, and help us explain 'why' a non-EU state would look elsewhere for ideas relating to asylum law and protection practice. The first driver for emulation is new challenges and uncertainty. This emulation driver draws on rational processes and the need to succeed.[21] Where states are faced with new challenges and are uncertain about how to tackle them, they go fishing for ideas; emulation offers a practical solution to a real problem.[22] The second driver for emulation is normative and stems from reputation and the growing of transnational professional standards, through bilateral agreements with the EU, for instance. This emulation driver draws on social processes and the necessity to conform;[23] here the underlying motivation for emulation is its value.[24] In law, including refugee law, a transnational professional identity, composed of expertise and norms has developed that is shared by organisational actors the world over.[25] In the context of this chapter, the EU as a major source of new ideas and professional standards on refugee protection fulfils a leading role in this respect.

State emulation is also a process of norm diffusion: 'how' ideas travel and end being emulated. Here, the literature on constructivism points to three facilitating factors: the fit, the transmitter and the pusher. First, the fit; by this I mean the degree of fit between the foreign norm and local requirements, politics, laws and culture,[26] in other words, the 'context'.[27] The second is the transmitter, that is, the presence and role of transnational policy, legal or advocacy networks in 'transmitting' the foreign norms. The third facilitating factor is the role of advocacy groups and other stakeholders (e.g. local NGO, courts, academics, judges) in 'pushing' for normative change from within the country in question.[28]

Method: how to select norms when studying emulation of European asylum law?

It is notoriously difficult to trace the precise origin of a legislative rule.[29] To overcome this difficulty, one may instead concentrate on trends or 'patterns relating to law' (e.g. a set of restrictive or liberal rules, practices or ideas) as opposed to specific rules.[30] The substantive and procedural rules that currently form the CEAS are impaired by exceptions and derogations to existing international standards. While it is true that some of these rules and practices are still evolving, through recast instruments and judicial interpretation, we do have a clear sense of the existence of key norms of European refugee law, that originated over 20 years ago in state practice and asylum policies, and which are now squarely codified in the CEAS. Some of these are clearly positive, for instance, the recognition of a 'right to asylum' in the EU, which goes beyond protection from *refoulement*;[31] the recognition of non-state agents of persecution, and gender-based persecution; the codification of subsidiary protection and temporary protection. All of which are based on state practice and/or national legislation.[32]

Yet, significant gaps and shortcomings also characterise the CEAS, such as a tendency towards more exceptions and derogations to established standards (e.g. limitation of the application of the Refugee Convention definition to third-country nationals,[33] the internal flight alternative concept, the safe third country, first country of asylum and safe country of origin principles, manifestly unfounded applications);[34] restrictive access to international protection through delocalised migration control (e.g. discussions on extra-territorial processing);[35] the Dublin rule (according to which only one Member State is responsible for determining an asylum application and corresponding transfers) and the Aznar rule (according to which EU citizens are presumed not to be needing asylum);[36] increased securitisation (e.g. through detention, deportation and denaturalisation procedures),[37] and a tendency, in some countries, to resort to granting subsidiary protection rather than refugee status,[38] with the former still providing fewer rights than the latter.[39]

It is further *predicted* that other norms likely to spread worldwide are those which the Court of Justice of the European Union (CJEU) has ruled upon, particularly, where the ruling concerns a provision of EU law that enshrines a provision of the Refugee Convention (such as, cessation of refugee status[10] or exclusion from refugee status)[11] or a provision relating to subsidiary protection.[12] Indeed, once the CJEU answers a reference for a preliminary ruling in a judgment, this interpretation carries great weight as EU law. This pioneering role by the CJEU is further amplified by the fact that while the International Court of Justice is competent, it has never been used by states in this way (and is unlikely to ever be). While it is true that rulings of the CJEU are authoritative in respect of EU law only (in the sense of their binding legal force),[13] it is less true of their general authority (persuasive or not) as rulings from the first ever supranational court to have interpreted provisions of the Refugee Convention. These rulings will carry enormous weight in generally influencing the interpretation of the

Refugee Convention – that is, in promoting an interpretation of what is 'normal' interpretation in 27 of the 144 countries signatories to the Refugee Convention/ Protocol.

Most of the norms above pertain to who qualifies for asylum and under what conditions. In other words, these norms contribute to how a refugee is defined in the EU, as opposed to internationally. In so far as these norms have already and are likely to continue to spread beyond Europe, they will impact on the construction of refugee identity in other parts of the world. This has obvious implications for the 1951 Refugee Convention, which defines an international status for refugees. As they grow in influence around the world, European norms may compete with international rules on refugee status.

Findings: evidence of EU influence on refugee law worldwide

A recently completed empirical study finds evidence of the EU protection regime 'naturally' evolving transnationally and spreading internationally into the legal systems of non-EU countries.[14] The strength of evidence varies between countries. For example, EU law and practice on 'subsidiary protection' seems to have had an enormous influence on the codification of 'complementary protection' in Australia.[15] European influence can also be discerned with respect to the 'safe third country' concept, which has been borrowed in Australia. Both norms (complementary protection and safe third country) impact on state functions in granting refugee status, and therefore creating refugee identity.[16] Interestingly, other proposed practices considered 'bad' in the EU, such as those relating to 'transit processing centres', also failed in Australia under pressure from national and international criticism.[17] McAdam's discussion of these centres offers a striking illustration of the transnational phenomenon of refugee law-making. Indeed, there is clear evidence that Australia's Pacific Solution, created in 2001, was in fact a source of inspiration for the UK's proposal to create offshore processing centres in Europe, and the Pacific Solution was itself reminiscent of the US offshore processing of Cuban and Haitian asylum seekers in Guantánamo Bay in the 1990s. Another example is Canada, which for many years has imposed visa requirements on arrivals from the Czech Republic (and Hungary, to a lesser extent) as a means of deterring large numbers of Roma seeking asylum in Canada. However, in 2012, Canada introduced a new 'safe country of origin' provision in its revised refugee law, which acts as an alternative option to visa. This was motivated by Canada wishing to conclude a free-trade agreement with the EU and therefore having to withdraw imposing visa on all EU nationals. The new provision on safe country of origin is directly traceable to the 'white lists' of safe countries introduced by several European countries in the 1990s, including the UK, as well as, crucially, the Aznar Protocol.[18] In Africa, strong evidence of past, historical emulation of the 1951 Refugee Convention was found (but not present). The evidence is clear and 'can be traced back to an explicit objective of emulating the European approach in Africa' facilitated by the OAU and UNHCR. Since then, elements of contemporary regional, subregional and national refugee protection frameworks have been found to reflect European approaches, especially restrictive ones (such as 'safe third country', 'safe country of origin' and 'manifestly unfounded' asylum applications), but explicit evidence of this process is hard to find.[49]

Thus, the overall picture is one of EU norms being emulated; some are clearly restrictive (e.g. accelerated procedures, safe third country, safe first country, safe country of origin), others are of a more liberal tradition (e.g. the protection approach to actors of persecution, subsidiary protection). Overall, however, a broad trend of European restrictive practices appearing in the law and practice of countries and regions outside the EU can be said to be identifiable. At first sight, this would suggest a European refugee identity that is restrictive and in some aspects non-compliant with the 1951 Convention refugee. However, as will be discussed below, Europe's unique human rights legal framework is 'keeping refugee law "in line"' in that region.[50]

The general driver behind the spread of these norms appears to be 'new challenges and uncertainty'. For examples, Australia, Canada and Latin America found the challenges of having to cope with an increased number of mixed flows of refugees (be it from Africa, Asia or the Czech Republic) to be the principal reason for looking at the EU.[51] The EU, as a major source of new ideas in asylum law, was also found to fulfil a leading role in nudging states to emulate its norms through its formal agreements with Israel and Switzerland.[52] These agreements have led both countries to learn lessons from the EU, but the effect of these have been mostly of a restrictive kind.

The 'fit' or compatibility between the EU norm and the local context seems to be key in facilitating emulation. For example, the fit between Latin American and Spain in terms of legal systems and language has made Spain (an EU Member State since 1986) a direct source of inspiration in Latin America.[53] Other examples are the strong historical ties between the US and Europe and the cultural fit with the UK, and the shared common law tradition between Canada and the UK.[54] The role of UNHCR and senior political or judicial figures, as 'transmitter' for emulation, seems to be particularly important. For instance, in Australia, submissions by UNHCR before Parliament in Committee hearings during the development of legislation and policy on complementary protection were found to play an important role; so too concerning discussions between the Australian Minister for Immigration and his/her counterparts, which can have significant influence on the direction of Australian practice.[55] UNHCR was also found to be a strong mediating actor in Africa, Latin America and Israel. Finally, in all the countries/regions considered, the role of domestic courts, local NGOs, academics, judges have been identified as playing a crucial role in facilitating emulation of European norms. For instance, in Australia, note was made that 'influence stems from personal interactions between the Immigration Minister and his or her counterparts in EU Member States; from research by the Department of Immigration and Citizenship (Immigration Department) into comparative practices when formulating policy; from the interventions of academics and non-governmental organisations (NGOs) in parliamentary inquiries, and more generally through their advocacy and scholarly writings; and through consideration of European jurisprudence by the courts'.[56]

Yet, it is also the same domestic context or local requirements that are found to cause states to resist the influence of EU law and practice. Thus, in cases where emulation is occurring, this is never total; it can only be partial because the norms being emulated are deeply dependent on local conditions and requirements. As an example, in Australia, local conditions include the absence of a bill of rights or anything akin to a regional human rights treaty like the European Convention on Human Rights (ECHR), which means that emulation of EU norms can only be partial.[57] In Israel, local conditions or culture are powerful too, particularly the right of return for the Jewish diaspora and the 'Holocaust discourse'. This means that Israel has learned some lessons from the EU, but these have generally been of the restrictive kind.[58]

In sum, it is argued that a state's function in granting refugee status[59] is being shaped transnationally by European refugee law.

Europe's normative power in refugee law

While drivers and facilitators are useful in helping us understand the transnational movement of norms between different legal systems, their role is limited when it comes to explaining why the EU is such a source of inspiration. The idea that the EU may be setting world standards in normative terms is not new and has been explored in the writing of numerous scholars.[60] But what the empirical evidence suggests is that EU's normative power is clearly at work in the emulation of European norms of refugee protection. The long-standing commitments of the EU to peace, liberty, democracy, the rule of law, human rights, and its aspirations to social solidarity, anti-discrimination, sustainable development and good governance provide the EU with a broad normative basis.[61] In European refugee law more specifically, this normative basis is anchored in the 1951 Refugee Convention, the ECHR (now also the Charter of Fundamental Rights of the EU) and other human rights treaties. It is strengthened with a set of supranational institutions competent to legislate on refugee law and interpret provisions of refugee law. With this basis, the EU is able 'to define what passes for "normal"'[62] in refugee law and international protection. Thus, emulation of European refugee law involves more than a process of diffusion of an ideology or of a solution to a problem; it defines Europe's international identity in international protection and, it may also be argued, Europe's refugee identity. This power therefore challenges the view that 'the notion of "refugee" is internationalised precisely to ensure it is not captured by any one national or regional agenda or approach'.[63]

There are problems associated with this exercise in 'normality', such as, the logic underpinning the CEAS (which is based on mutual trust and freedom of movement between the Member States) and the resulting 'vanishing', at least in Europe, of the 1951 Convention refugee. As argued by Durieux, 'the EU concept of asylum induces the phenomenon of a "vanishing refugee", whereby the central character of the 1951 Convention regime, namely the refugee, is blurred, marginalised or ignored'.[64] The rules that are specific to the CEAS (e.g. Aznar Protocol and the rules on inclusion and exclusions in the EU Qualification Directive) are creating a refugee identity that is narrower in its scope (e.g. only applies to third-country nationals, from non-safe countries) than the 1951 Convention refugee. The risk of this new identity influencing countries outside the EU is far from academic. Indeed, Canada's motive for emulating the restrictive EU safe country of origin concept, as an alternative to a visa requirement (as mentioned above), has been identified as being EU's power and influence as an international actor.[65] Since the EU has set the standards (all EU Member States regard themselves as safe), it can hardly complain if Canada adopts the same (restrictive) ones. Another risk in emulation is that whereas the EU has a normative 'safety mechanism' in place, namely the ECHR, many other countries do not. No matter how restrictive the law might be in Europe, its application in practice is subject to a double-judicial check that is unique to Europe: one by the CJEU, and the other by the European Court of Human Rights. Furthermore, EU norms are constantly evolving, and many of them are becoming more liberal under the influence of this double-check. This is true of EU asylum legislation, which continues to be revised, and both courts (the CJEU and the European Court of Human Rights) play a key role in the enhancement of the standards set in the legislation. There is a danger of non-EU countries emulating some of Europe's restrictive rules, practices and ideas without the more liberal 'interpretation package' that comes with it in a European context. It has been argued elsewhere that the refugee protection regime (i.e. the 1951 Refugee Convention) 'is quite clear on the centrality it attaches to a legally endorsed status'; this is to be contrasted with the human rights movement that sees the human person first.[66] In this way, one effect that human rights law is having on refugee identify in the EU is to 'stand as a constant reminder that the status of "human persons" matters'.[67]

Conclusion: the role of transnational law in shaping refugee's identity across the world

This chapter has explored identity construction through transnational links between regions and countries. The approach it has used, to interrogate why and how certain norms of EU refugee protection are diffused worldwide and selectively adopted in countries outside the EU, is based on constructivist literature from international relations and socio-legal scholarship. The picture that emerges is of a natural diffusion of European norms around the world, mostly of a restrictive character, by a range of actors and for a number of motives. EU asylum law and protection practice is spreading. Transnational actors like UNHCR clearly play a key role but so do a variety of domestic actors. The importance of local requirements (context) is also important in understanding the extent to which states outside the EU emulate European law and practice in this area.

The refugee law regime, and human rights more generally, are historically European constructs in origin. The 1951 Refugee Convention may be viewed as a Western model of legal organisation that has been emulated by states outside

Europe, in the late modern period. This chapter argues that the CEAS may be seen in terms of similar pattern of worldwide diffusion of Western norms encoded in the Refugee Convention and other relevant human rights instruments through transnational processes and local actors. As some of these European norms concern the definition of a refugee and who qualifies for asylum, the transnational legal approach helps us develop a better understanding of how refugee identities are constructed in domestic law the world over.

Notes

*This chapter draws extensively on material published in Hélène Lambert, Jane McAdam and Maryellen Fullerton (eds), *The Global Reach of European Refugee Law* (Cambridge University Press, 2013).

1 Anne-Marie Slaughter, *A New World Order* (Princeton University Press, 2004).
2 In this chapter, I use the term 'law' in a normative sense, interchangeably with 'norm', that is, as principles beliefs about appropriate action, shared by a community, which are embedded in practice and codified in rules (i.e. law).
3 Convention relating to the Status of Refugees, Geneva, 28 July 1951, 1989 UNTS 137, supplemented by the Protocol relating to the Status of Refugees, 31 January 1967, 19 UST 6223, 6257 ('Refugee Convention').
4 (Cambridge University Press, 2010). See also, Hélène Lambert, 'Transnational Judicial Dialogue, Harmonization and the Common European Asylum System' (1999) 58 *International and Comparative Law Quarterly* 519–43.
5 Council of the European Union, 'Final steps towards a Common European Asylum System', Luxembourg 7 June 2013, 10411/13 PRESSE 230 <www.consilium.europa. eu/uedocs/cms_Data/docs/pressdata/en/jha/137420.pdf?>.
6 Denmark opted out entirely of the asylum package; both the UK and Ireland opted out of most of the second phase (recast) of EU legislation.
7 B. S. Chimni, 'Reforming the International Refugee Regime: A Dialogic Model' (2001) 14 *Journal of Refugee Studies* 151–68, 157; Volker Türk and Frances Nicholson, 'Refugee Protection in International Law: An Overall Perspective', in Erika Feller, Volker Türk and Frances Nicholson (eds), *Refugee Protection in International Law: UNHCR's Global Consultations on International Protection* (Cambridge University Press, 2003), 6; Catherine Dauvergne, *Making People Illegal* (Cambridge University Press, 2008), 150–3; Guy S. Goodwin-Gill, 'The Search for the One, True Meaning. . .', in Guy S. Goodwin-Gill and Hélène Lambert (eds), *The Limits of Transnational Law: Refugee Law, Policy Harmonization and Judicial Dialogue in the European Union* (Cambridge University Press, 2010), 238–9.
8 One such study to note this to be the case in Africa is Bonaventure Rutinwa, 'The End of Asylum: The Changing Nature of Refugee Policies in Africa' (2002) 21 *Refugee Survey Quarterly* 2–41, 33. See also, Jean-François Durieux, 'The Many Faces of "Prima Facie": Group-Based Evidence in Refugee Status Determination' (2008) 25 *Refuge* 151–63.
9 See, e.g., William Twining, *Globalisation and Legal Theory* (Cambridge University Press, 2000); see also 'Diffusion of Law: A Global Perspective' (2004) 49 *Journal of Legal Pluralism* 1–45; 'Social Science and Diffusion of Law' (2005) 32 *Journal of Law and Society* 203–40; 'Normative and Legal Pluralism: A Global Perspective' (2010) 20 *Duke Journal of Comparative & International Law* 473–517; Gunther Teubner, 'Legal Irritants: Good Faith in British Law or How Unifying Law Ends up in New Divergences' (1998) 61 *Modern Law Review* 11–32.
10 See e.g. Eiko Thielemann and Nadine El-Enany, 'Refugee Protection as a Collective Action Problem: Is the EU Shirking Its Responsibilities?' (2010) 19 *European Security* 209–29; Andrew Geddes, *Immigration and European Integration: Beyond Fortress Europe?* (2nd edn, Manchester University Press, 2008), 170–85; Ian Manners, 'Normative

Power Europe: A Contradiction in Terms?' (2002) 40 *Journal of Common Market Studies* 235–58.

11 See, e.g., Elspeth Guild and Carol Harlow (eds), *Implementing Amsterdam: Immigration and Asylum Rights in EC Law* (Hart, 2001); Anneliese Baldaccini, Elspeth Guild and Helen Toner (eds), *Whose Freedom, Security and Justice? EU Immigration and Asylum Law and Policy* (Hart, 2007).

12 Eric Stein, 'Lawyers, Judges, and the Making of a Transnational Constitution' (1981) 75 *American Journal of International Law* 1–27; Anne-Marie Burley and Walter Mattli, 'Europe before the Court: A Political Theory of Legal Integration' (1993) 47 *International Organization* 41–76; Anne-Marie Slaughter and William Burke-White, 'The Future of International Law Is Domestic (or, the European Way of Law)' (2006) 47 *Harvard International Law Journal* 327–52.

13 Emily Goldman and Leslie Eliason (eds), *The Diffusion of Military Technology and Ideas* (Stanford University Press, 2003); Alexander Betts (ed.), *Global Migration Governance* (Oxford University Press, 2011); Manners, above n. 10.

14 I am grateful to Theo Farrell for pointing me to this literature. John Meyer, David Frank, Ann Hironaka, Evan Schofer and Nancy Tuma, 'The Structuring of a World Environmental Regime, 1870–1990' (1997) 51 *International Organization* 623–51; Francisco Ramirez and John Meyer, 'Comparative Education: The Social Construction of the Modern World System' (1980) 6 *Annual Review of Sociology* 369–99.

15 Paul J. DiMaggio and Walter W. Powell, 'The Iron Cage Revisited: Institutionalism Isomorphism and Collective Rationality', in Powell and DiMaggio (eds), *The New Institutionalism in Organizational Analysis* (Chicago University Press, 1991), 63–82, 64.

16 Alexander Wendt, *Social Theory of International Politics* (Cambridge University Press, 1999); David Armstrong, Theo Farrell and Hélène Lambert, *International Law and International Relations* (2nd edn, Cambridge University Press, 2012), 100–10; Peter Haas, 'Epistemic Communities and International Policy Coordination' (1992) 41 *International Organization* 1–35; Thomas Risse, 'Ideas Do Not Float Freely: Transnational Coalitions, Domestic Structures, and the End of the Cold War' (1994) 48 *International Organization* 165–214; Preslava Stoeva, *New Norms and Knowledge in World Politics* (Routledge, 2010).

17 Martha Finnemore and Kathryn Sikkink, 'International Norm Dynamics and Political Change' (1998) 52 *International Organization* 887–917; Thomas Risse, Steven Ropp and Kathryn Sikkink, *The Power of Human Rights: International Norms and Domestic Change* (Cambridge University Press, 1999).

18 Amitav Acharya, 'How Ideas Spread: Whose Norms Matter? Norm Localization and Institutional Change in Asian Regionalism' (2004) 58 *International Organization* 239–75.

19 Twining, 'Diffusion of Law', above n. 9, 26. On the role of electoral mechanisms in shaping patterns of policy diffusion, see Katerina Linos, 'Diffusion through Democracy' (2011) 55 *American Journal of Political Science* 678–95.

20 Twining, 'Social Science and Diffusion of Law', above n. 9, 215–16, referring to the work of Patrick Glenn.

21 DiMaggio and Powell, above n. 15, 69–70.

22 Twining, 'Diffusion of Law', above n. 9, 30.

23 DiMaggio and Powell, above n. 15, 70–3.

24 Twining, 'Diffusion of Law', above n. 9, 30.

25 Alexander Betts, above n. 13.

26 Jeffrey Checkel, 'Norms, Institutions, and National Identity in Contemporary Europe' (1999) 50 *International Studies Quarterly* 83–111, 86–7; Andrew Cortell and James Davis, 'Understanding the Domestic Impact of International Norms: A Research Agenda' (2000) 2 *International Studies Review* 65–90.

27 Twining, 'Social Science and Diffusion of Law', above n. 9, 211 discussing the work of Otto Kahn-Freund. See also the discussion on 'fit' and 'proximity' in Katerina Linos, 'When Do Policy Innovations Spread? Lessons for Advocates of Lesson-Drawing'

(2006) 119 *Harvard Law Review* 1467–87. For different views on commonalities and distinctiveness between legal cultures, see, for instance, Roger Cotterrell, *Law, Culture and Society* (Ashgate, 2006); David Nelken, 'Puzzling Out Legal Cultures: A Comment on Blankenburg', in David Nelken (ed.), *Comparing Legal Cultures* (Ashgate, 1997), 58–88; Pierre Legrand, 'European Legal Systems Are not Converging' (1996) 45 *International and Comparative Law Quarterly* 52–81.

28 Anne-Marie Clarke, *Diplomacy of Conscience: Amnesty International and Changing Human Rights Norms* (Princeton University Press, 2002); Anne Klotz, *Norms in International Relations* (Cornell University Press, 1995).

29 Rosemary Byrne and Andrew Shacknove, 'The Safe Country Notion in European Asylum Law' (1996) 9 *Harvard Human Rights Journal* 185–228; Rosemary Byrne, Gregor Noll and Jens Vedsted-Hansen, 'Understanding Refugee Law in an Enlarged European Union' (2004) 15 *European Journal of International Law* 355–79.

30 Twining talks about 'patterns relating to law' in Twining, 'Diffusion of Law', above n. 9, 5.

31 Art. 18, Charter of Fundamental Rights of the European Union, and Recast Qualification Directive 2011/95/EU, Recital 16. See Maria-Teresa Gil-Bazo, 'The Charter of Fundamental Rights of the European Union and the Right to be Granted Asylum in the Union's Law' (2008) 27 *Refugee Survey Quarterly* 33–52; UNHCR's written observations in CJEU Joined Cases C-411/10 and C-493/10, para. 31.

32 Jane McAdam, *Complementary Protection in International Refugee Law* (Oxford University Press, 2007).

33 The Qualification Directive limits the scope of international protection to 'third country nationals and stateless persons' only. This led the House of Lords Select Committee on the EU to observe: 'for a major regional grouping of countries such as the Union to adopt a regime apparently limiting the scope of the Geneva Convention among themselves would set a most undesirable precedent in the wider international/global context' (House of Lords Select Committee on the EU, *Defining Refugee Status and Those in Need of International Protection* (Stationery Office, 2002), para. 54, cited in McAdam, above n. 32, 60).

34 Elspeth Guild, 'The Europeanisation of Europe's Asylum Policy' (2006) 18 *International Journal of Refugee Law* 630–51.

35 Thomas Gammeltoft-Hansen, *Access to Asylum: International Refugee Law and the Globalization of Migration Control* (Cambridge University Press, 2011); Madeline Garlick, 'The EU Discussions on Extraterritorial Processing: Solution or Conundrum' (2006) 18 *International Journal of Refugee Law* 601–29; Gregor Noll, 'Visions of the Exceptional: Legal and Theoretical Issues Raised by Transit Processing Centres and Protection Zones' (2003) 5 *European Journal of Migration and Law* 303–41.

36 Elspeth Guild, 'Seeking Asylum: Storm Clouds between International Commitments and EU Legislative Measures' (2004) 29 *European Law Review* 198–218; Guild, above n. 34.

37 Elspeth Guild, *Security and Migration in the 21st Century* (Polity, 2009).

38 This is the case, for instance, of Bulgaria, Italy, Cyprus, Malta, Poland, Slovakia, Finland and Sweden.

39 Directive 2011/95/EU. This recast Directive is a considerable improvement from the original Directive of 2004 but still today the right to residence permits (Art. 24) and the right to social welfare (Art. 29) remain unequally protected.

40 ECJ, Joined Cases C-175, 176, 178, 179/08, *Salahadin Abdulla and Others* v. *Germany*, ECR [2009] I-1493.

41 CJEU, Joined Cases C-57/09 and C-101/09, *Bundesrepublik Deutschland* v. *B and D*, judgment of 9 November 2010.

42 ECJ, Case C-465/07, *Mr and Mrs Elgafaji* v. *Dutch Secretary of State for Justice*, judgment of 17 February 2009; CJEU, Case C-285/12, *Aboubacar Diakité* v. *commissaire générale aux réfugiés et aux apatrides*, judgment of 30 January 2014.

43 As commented by Advocate General Eleanor Sharpston in her Opinion of 4 March 2010 in the Case C-31/09 *Bolbol* v. *Bevándorlási es Állampolgársági Hivatal (Hungarian Office for Immigration and Citizenship)*.

44 Hélène Lambert, Jane McAdam and Maryellen Fullerton (eds), *The Global Reach of European Refugee Law* (Cambridge University Press, 2013).

45 Jane McAdam, 'Migrating Laws? The "Plagiaristic Dialogue" between Europe and Australia', ibid., 25–70.

46 Colin Harvey, 'Is Humanity Enough? Refugees, Asylum Seekers and the Rights Regime', in Satvinder Juss and Colin Harvey (eds), *Contemporary Issues in International Refugee Law* (Edward Elgar, 2013), 68–88.

47 McAdam, above n. 45.

48 Audrey Macklin, 'A Safe Country to Emulate? Canada and the European Refugee', in Lambert *et al.* (eds), above n. 44, 99–131.

49 Marina Sharpe, 'The Impact of European Refugee Law on the Regional, Subregional and National Planes in Africa', ibid., 178–200.

50 Harvey, above n. 46, 88.

51 McAdam, above n. 45; Macklin, above n. 48; David Cantor, 'European Influence on Asylum Practices in Latin America: Accelerated Procedures in Colombia, Ecuador, Panama and Venezuela', in Lambert *et al.* (eds), above n. 44, 71–98.

52 Dallal Stevens, 'Between East and West: The Case of Israel', in Lambert *et al.* (eds), above n. 44, 132–55; Vincent Chetail and Céline Bauloz, 'Is Switzerland an EU Member State? Asylum Law Harmonization through the Backdoor', ibid., 156–77.

53 Cantor, above n. 51.

54 Maryellen Fullerton, 'Stealth Emulation: The United States and European Protection Norms', in Lambert *et al.* (eds), above n. 44, 201–24; Macklin, above n. 48.

55 McAdam, above n. 45.

56 Ibid., 28.

57 Ibid.

58 Stevens, above n. 52.

59 To read more on this state's function, see Harvey, above n. 46.

60 For a review of this literature, see Manners, above n. 10, 235–58.

61 Ibid., 242–4.

62 Manners argues that '[T]he ability to define what passes for 'normal' in world politics is, ultimately, the greatest power of all' (ibid., 253).

63 Harvey, above n. 46, 72.

64 Jean-François Durieux, 'The Vanishing Refugee: How EU Asylum Law Blurs the Specificity of Refugee Protection', in Lambert *et al.* (eds), above n. 44, 225–57, at 228.

65 Macklin, above n. 48.

66 Harvey, above n. 46, 72.

67 Ibid., 88.

Part IV

Refugee identities and protection: micro, social and individual perspectives

11 Ambivalent policies, uncertain identities: asylum-seeking families in Sweden

Ulla Björnberg

Introduction

This chapter addresses the well-being of children who, at the time of this study, were in Sweden with their families as asylum seekers awaiting a decision regarding their residence permit.[1] At a general level, the overarching goal of the Swedish policy towards asylum seekers and refugees is to promote their integration into the host society as soon as possible following their arrival in the country. The waiting period during the asylum process is to be made as constructive as possible, while also preparing the asylum seekers for the eventuality of having to return to their country of origin. While this stage is intended to strengthen asylum seekers' self-reliance, it also maintains the threat of forced return, doing little to alleviate the emotional tensions and anxieties created by the circumstances that led the asylum seekers to leave their country of origin in the first place.

The first section of this chapter provides a brief contextualisation of asylum policies in Sweden, outlining the relevant policy changes in the country over the last two decades. The second section describes the in-depth empirical study of asylum-seeking families in Sweden from which the interviews used for this study are drawn. The third section introduces the theoretical concepts guiding the analysis of these interviews in this chapter. Thereafter the results of this study are presented, with sense of recognition, sense of belonging, emotional support and transnational kin relationships emerging as the main themes from the findings. The chapter concludes with a discussion of the main findings and their significance, followed by suggestions for concrete measures to support asylum-seeking families and their children to foster their well-being.

The many amendments made to the Swedish Aliens Act over the last two years reflect an ambition to formalise the entry process for heterogeneous categories of asylum seekers. I argue that the changes introduced to better manage the large number of asylum seekers who arrive with varying motives for their entry, both deter and protect asylum seekers and their children. In its current form, the country's asylum policy aims at promoting asylum seekers' integration and self-reliance, while at the same time preparing them for the eventuality of having to return to their country of origin. This double aim, as I will show, gives rise to certain ambivalence in the policy, causing, in many cases, psychological problems and uncertain identities in asylum seekers. Overall, the waiting period can be said to create dependency and loss of control over everyday life among asylum seekers, a situation that, moreover, also fosters a sense of guilt in the family. As a consequence, the possibilities for sustaining and creating helpful social networks in such circumstances remain limited.

Refugee policy in Sweden

Following the economic crisis of the 1970s, labour migration to Sweden was restricted, with the country's migration policy becoming more focused on refugees. In the 1990s, the influx of refugees, however, grew significantly, mainly owing to the wars in the former Yugoslavia and in Iraq. The problems the new situation caused to the country's migration authority strained its management capabilities, prompting much criticism of the prevailing migration policy in public debates. As a result, the need for policy reform was deemed urgent. The greatly increased number of asylum applicants had excessively prolonged the application-processing periods, leaving applicants waiting for a final decision on their case even for years. Also the number of residence permit application denials had rapidly increased, leaving many asylum seekers with uncertainty about their future and even their personal fate. In 1994 and 1995, a temporary law was passed that gave families with children, in particular, the right to have their applications assessed promptly and without delays. In direct consequence, a large majority of the then-applicants were quickly issued residence permits on humanitarian grounds. That the law could be so quickly enacted was due to the special circumstances surrounding its birth, but owed also much to a great wave of public protests taking place in Sweden at the time that targeted the country's refugee policy, claiming it had resulted in too many cases being denied protection.[2]

A decade later, in 2004–5, alarming reports began to surface about asylum-seeking children suffering from severe withdrawal symptoms, provoking intense discussions about the possible causes of the phenomenon. The speculations went as far as to suggest, as proposed by a few individual professionals, that parents had deliberately poisoned their children in order to influence the assessment process and secure a positive decision from it. The discourse became polarised between, on the one hand, those expressing distrust in the reasons and explanations given by the asylum-seeking families and, on the other hand, those arguing against an inhuman asylum policy incapable or unwilling to recognise the past experiences of children. As research would later verify, though, the psychological symptoms of the refugee children most likely resulted from the combination of their past (pre-departure) experiences and their present uncertainty about their future.[3] Another temporary law then opened up the possibility of a new examination of the asylum applications of those persons who had remained in the country after their initial application had been turned down, particularly benefiting families with children.[1]

Following the intense debates around these issues, the country's refugee policy then underwent several rounds of reform, targeting both asylum application procedures and the social rights of asylum seekers, with special attention given to children and children's need for protection in accordance with the United Nations Convention on the Rights of the Child.[5] An amended Aliens Act was introduced in 2006, with the aim of speeding up the handling of applications, creating a more transparent procedure and ensuring due process for all applicants. The procedure for assessing the merit of individual residence permit applications was made more formalised based on stricter legal criteria, and exerting political influence on the decision making was made more difficult. In addition, special migration courts were set up, not only enabling the possibility of appealing the decisions of the country's migration authority, the Swedish Migration Board, but also allowing, through trial-type procedures, recourse to oral proceedings in increasing numbers of cases. In a similar fashion, the Migration Board itself, as the country's first point of contact for examining and deciding on applications for a residence permit, was instructed to act more strictly in accordance with the 1951 Refugee Convention[6] and other applicable instruments providing criteria for assessing individuals' need for protection. Issuing a residence permit on humanitarian grounds was made assessment based, on the verification of the presence of 'particularly distressing circumstances'. As a general rule, the examination of the right to protection was now to be strictly based on individual factors and circumstances. However, in subsequent years, the law was amended several times, bringing the total number of revisions to approximately 25 in the first three years following the introduction of the Act in 2006. Several of these revisions were aimed at harmonising the Swedish law on migration and asylum policy with the directives of the European Union.[7] In 2011, the Act was then revised once more, to clarify the application of the rules regarding 'particularly distressing circumstances'.[8]

During the same time period, and in contrast to many other European Union member countries, some of the asylum seekers' social rights were expanded while others were limited.[9] The rights that were expanded primarily involved children, regarded as a particularly vulnerable group. Primary and secondary school education and preschool (day care, after-school programmes) were now to be offered free of charge to all asylum-seeking children, and were to be provided to them no later than one month after their arrival in the country. Healthcare was to be offered to them on the same terms and conditions as to resident children. Adult asylum seekers also became entitled to medical and dental care, although this concerned emergency care only and was to be offered for a (low) fee. All asylum seekers, in fact, would from now on receive a free medical examination, even if recent information suggests that it is in practice offered to few individuals only. The right to free healthcare has subsequently been extended to also cover undocumented children, while undocumented adults would only be able to receive medical care for a fee or by voluntary clinics. The Migration Board is also required to provide organised daytime activities for asylum seekers, such as language classes. As concerns their ability to work, asylum seekers can today take up employment without a separate work permit if their asylum application is estimated to take longer than four months.[10]

At the same time, however, some restrictions were also introduced. The financial assistance that the Migration Board offers to asylum seekers in the form of daily allowances, for instance, continues to be given at benefit levels clearly lower than those applied to the country's citizens, and is regarded as temporary only. These levels have repeatedly been pointed out as being too low, given that they have remained unchanged since 1994.[11] While additional one-time allowances for special reasons, such as warmer clothing during winter, can be applied for and granted, on the whole the right to economic assistance remains restricted. 'Disciplinary' measures such as reduction in social assistance benefits can, moreover, be taken, if the applicant is deemed uncooperative, for instance by hiding information or not attending language classes or other organised activities offered by the Migration Board. Furthermore, those preferring to arrange their housing independently, rather than accepting the accommodation offered them by the Migration Board, are no longer (since 2005) eligible for a separate housing allowance, in order to reduce possibilities for overcrowded living arrangements with friends and relatives in the big cities. In the lodging provided by the Migration Board, however, families often have to share their apartment with asylum-seeking individuals unfamiliar to them.[12]

In a 2009 government report, it was, however, suggested that the procedures used by the Migration Board were not sufficiently transparent for the applicants, given that approximately 90 per cent of all the negative decisions on asylum applications were appealed to the country's Migration Courts.[13] As a result of this, the waiting periods for final decisions on individual cases had only become longer and longer. A review of the impact that the Convention on the Rights of the Child had on the country's asylum application procedures concluded that, while the best interest of the child could now indeed be better taken into account, the state's interest in regulating immigration still took priority.[14] The Aliens Act is a general law that allows for a broad scope of interpretation at the local offices of the Migration Board. For instance, asylum-seeking children's right to be heard and have their own grounds for asylum examined was applied differently in different parts of the country.[15] Similarly, the granting of residence permits to children had become subject to criticism for being too exclusively focused on the presence of 'particularly distressing circumstances' such as the applicant's poor state of health, while leaving the children's other reasons and personal grounds for refugee status without adequate consideration.[16]

In the public debates, much attention has been paid to the rights of refugees who have been denied their residence permit but have remained in the country living under difficult circumstances. While children in these families today have access to education and healthcare, the implementation efforts overall, especially in recent times, have become more focused on quicker and smoother deportation of these individuals and families to the home country, prompting heated public protests against, among other things, the methods used by the police in enforcing the policy (such as identity checks in public). The toughening policy has brought increased uncertainty not just to those directly targeted by it on the street, but to all asylum seekers waiting for the decisions on their residence permit applications.

Taken as a whole, the many amendments made to the Swedish Aliens Act over the last decades reflect an overall ambiguity in the country's asylum policy, one which law-makers have attempted to do something about. While policy makers have striven for an application procedure that is based on clear rules and rational principles, the expectation has been that it also be efficiently managed and quick. And while there has been a desire to make the reception of asylum seekers humane as well as capable of ensuring the adequate provision of their basic needs, in terms of things like housing, subsistence income and safety, the expectation has also been that the families should contribute by following the prescribed rules.

In 2012, approximately 44,000 asylum applications were submitted in Sweden. The same year 12,400 positive decisions were made and refugee status was granted to about 30 per cent of these decisions. All in all, three in every four protection status applications approved annually within the European Union are submitted in France, Germany, Italy, the Netherlands, Sweden and the United Kingdom.[17]

Researching asylum-seeking families and children

This chapter is based on a study undertaken in 2005–10 on the health and well-being of asylum-seeking children and their families in Sweden.[18] A special focus in the study was placed on the interactions between local practices in the implementation of policies regarding the reception of children. The health and well-being of children were assessed both in the context of their immediate living conditions such as the family, the school, the material conditions and the local environment, looking at these in relation to different policy levels. In view of the many aspects of the research problem, a multidisciplinary approach was adopted to enable analysis of the way in which general structures influence actors nationally and locally, along with the children themselves.

The examination and analysis that follow draw in particular on one sub-study of the overall research project, consisting of qualitative interviews with seventeen asylum-seeking families. At the time of the interviews, the families had been waiting for the decision on their residence permit for several months or even years. The children in the families were aged between 9 and 18. Eight of them were in their upper teens (aged 14 to 18), five in their lower teens (aged 12 to 13), while three were 9 years old. The interviewed families came from Afghanistan, countries of the Middle East, Iraq, Iran and Uzbekistan. The interviews with the parents and the children were conducted separately, each lasting two hours and taking place on two separate occasions. A total of approximately four hours of interviews were recorded per individual and eight hours per family. Two interviewers were present for each of the families: one for the parent and another for the child.[19] With few exceptions, accredited and experienced interpreters were used. The interviews were open-ended, covering experiences before, during and after the arrival in Sweden.

Some theoretical considerations

One of the main objectives of the study was to identify elements in the conditions of the children that contribute to their sense of well-being. The research into this question was informed by Article 24 of the Convention on the Rights of the Child, which emphasises the right of children to protective conditions fostering their health. The main focus in the investigation was on how children and parents coped with adversity during the waiting period, adversity that was linked to the circumstances during the trial period. Of particular interest in this research was how the Swedish policy of recognition and the construction of a social identity among parents and children perhaps influenced each other. 'Identity' here referred to the construction of self in social relationships under circumstances brought about by the processes and system of reception of asylum-seeking families. The reception system was taken to include the general procedures for assessing asylum applications and the relationships between asylum seekers and case officers in charge of supporting asylum applicants through provision of accommodation, financial assistance, healthcare services, schooling, training and the like. Within this context of the asylum reception system, asylum seekers' social identities are shaped in reciprocal social relationships between them and their case officers. In the formation of asylum seekers' social identity, coping and managing various life circumstances thus come to play an essential role.

The coping process during the period of transition extends from the time of departing from the home country to the time when the residence permit or a deportation order is issued. Transition in these cases means moving to a new set of conditions characterised by low predictability and high uncertainty. The transitional process itself can be described as a social state or phase of great ambiguity in which one's position, identity and social belonging are no longer clearly defined. It is marked by experiences of social exclusion in the homeland, often accompanied by encounters with physical and psychological violence and significant circumscription of one's civil and economic rights. The tension between these experiences of exclusion and the expectations of improvement directed at asylum seekers after their arrival in the host country forms the framework in which strategies for dealing with their life situation have been studied.

In the following analysis, concepts such as trust, social recognition, social capital and resilience are used to better understand coping among asylum seekers. Given the ambiguity marking the situation of asylum-seeking children, trust or the absence of it, forms an important element to focus on when examining their everyday life. Indeed, both trust and social recognition are of special significance as necessary preconditions for the cultivation and shaping of social interaction and social capital. *Trust* can be characterised as the set of:

> socially learned and socially confirmed expectations that people have of each other, of the organizations and institutions in which they live, and of the natural and moral social orders that set the fundamental understandings for

their lives. In social interaction, a sense of normality is constructed through some tacit understanding of rules that make our world predictable, reliable and legible.[20]

To feel comfortable and safe, one needs to minimise irregularity and follow the rules of interaction recognised by those involved in the social interaction. Trust plays an essential role in determining how individuals interpret the social interaction that they are part of.[21] It is therefore an essential element of any social interaction capable of creating a sense of predictability and normality: having trust in a person means confidence that those with whom one interacts will follow shared norms. In more formal contexts, trust thus implies that the applied rules are transparent and fair. The ability to trust the process is quite clearly of vital importance in the special situation faced by asylum-seeking adults and children.

Another aspect of trust concerns risk management in one's choice of action. Luhmann has defined risk in terms of the extent to which our present behaviour impacts future possibilities: 'Risks ... emerge only as a component of decision and actions. They do not exist by themselves. If you refrain from action you run no risk. It is a purely *internal* calculation of *external* conditions which creates risk.'[22] The presence of trust, in reducing the risk related to situational uncertainty, is thus a necessary condition for building social relationships and social capital.

Trust is also connected to *social recognition* among the persons involved in the social interaction. Social recognition takes place when the individual is met with symbols, gestures or talk signifying positive value and an invitation to reciprocity. It is about being made visible, and thus the opposite of being made invisible for example by harmless inattention or general lack of interest by others who may see the person as socially insignificant. At the same time, to avoid the risk of being held in negative regard, the individual can also make a conscious choice to remain socially invisible.[23]

Social recognition is closely connected to self-esteem and social identity. It is to act while attributing positive value to others. What this implies is that the subject commits to acting in a moral way, showing regard for others. In socially recognising the other in the interaction, the subject thus no longer ignores or neglects the other party. Through this process, social recognition becomes part of the project of building trust. Trust and social recognition thus become elements of emotional capital that can be drawn upon in social interaction. In its basic form, trust means having confidence in one's own ability to anticipate the actions of those with whom one interacts; it is a matter of double confidence – confidence in others and in oneself.[24]

As the present study of asylum-seeking families demonstrated, trust and social recognition come about as a result of one's experiences of social interaction. At the same time, they are also a condition for one's desire to interact. It is therefore of vital importance that the question of trust and recognition be properly addressed by those in charge of processing and deciding on asylum applications and by those first coming into contact with asylum seekers – and not only to be able to better identify reasons for granting asylum in deserving cases, but also to demonstrate to asylum seekers, especially when they are children, that they are socially recognised as individuals in their own right. Asylum seekers need to appear trustworthy in their interactions with the reception officers, caseworkers, and handling officers, but also with local and state authorities on whom they depend for provision of services and benefits. They find themselves in a situation where they must be able to present convincing asylum claims while the criteria for the acceptance of these claims often remain unclear to them. Both the children and the adults studied for this chapter stressed the need to have their reasons for migration believed. Yet, since case officers must carefully scrutinise all the information and testimonies provided in support of the asylum application, the process cannot but take on some elements of apparent distrust. The perception of not being regarded as trustworthy then gives rise to insecurity and lack of predictability in social relationships, both in the everyday interaction with others and in the more formal interaction with authorities.

Resilience concerns the capacity of individuals and their families to resist adversities they experience as harmful to their psychological well-being. It is promoted by resources that increase one's operational capacity in the environment, most importantly social relationships. A supportive environment fosters greater resilience in individuals, which in turn contributes to improved capacity to cope with and master stress. While resilience is developed primarily in the family context, within the family system, it must also be analysed in the context of institutional rights and options availed to asylum seekers in the host country.[25] As argued by Morrow[26] and others, the extent to which children feel embedded in social networks, neighbourhoods, schools and other formal organisations in their everyday lives is related to their sense of recognition and well-being.

The trauma of return

The transition period for the asylum-seeking families and children included in this study was fraught with different kinds of adversity. It meant the loss of resources, social capital, and trust that they were accustomed to relying on in the home country. Nevertheless, both parents and children expressed that their arrival in Sweden had brought a sense of security and relief. The children described feelings of freedom and a release from the anxiety and stress that had marked their experience of the constraining and threatening living conditions at home.

The sense of insecurity linked to events in their previous life diminished after a while, but in the course of the protracted asylum process the newly found sense of security was eventually replaced by feelings of uncertainty and unpredictability regarding the future. In the research literature, this transformation is often connected to 'the trauma of return':[27] for many refugees, the prospect of having to return home causes the future to be identified with past, often traumatic, experiences. The threat of being forced to return blocks the motivation to manage the new circumstances of their everyday life in the host country. At the same time, they remain outside of the new society without rights to work, with limited access to healthcare, and, not least, without an official social security or personal identification number enabling them to assume an active role in the host society.[28] The trauma of return was highly present in the everyday concerns of both parents and children in the study.

Sense of social recognition

Asylum-seeking parents and children in Sweden are under the authority of the Swedish Migration Board and the lawyers assisting them with their asylum application. These institutional actors basically decide the future of the families they work with. Contacts with officers and caseworkers at the Swedish Migration Board and the lawyers upon whom they were highly dependent for their accommodation and financial support were thus, obviously, of major significance for the lives of the asylum-seeking families studied for this chapter.

Once the asylum seekers' applications were accepted for processing, they were each appointed a lawyer by the Migration Board. Having then explained their case to their lawyers in the presence of an interpreter, the applicants were interviewed by a case officer. Normally, the applicants meet with their lawyer no more than once. The professional qualifications of these legal representatives can vary, and not all of them are practising lawyers. Also the interpreters (who ordinarily, however, are accredited) can differ in their qualifications and in terms of how professionally they approach their task.[29]

Almost all of the families studied for this chapter experienced material deprivation. The children had lived in economically deprived circumstances for prolonged periods, given the length of time they had been waiting for their asylum cases to be decided. This, in turn, meant that their possibilities for expanding their range of social activities had remained restricted, with the children unable to afford spending free time with friends. As a result, they expressed a sense of otherness in many dimensions of daily life. Overcrowded living conditions and the necessity to repeatedly change accommodation were common experiences that added to the difficulties of making friends and socialising.

The children's own and their parents' experiences of dealing with the Swedish Migration Board, in turn, gave them a sense of being mistrusted about their reasons for wanting to stay in the country. The effect of such experiences, however, is often mitigated when the children start attending school. In the school environment, children can develop a sense of being included, taking part in activities that normalise, and bring structure to, their everyday life. All of the children in the study spoke appreciatively about being at school, commenting positively about teachers and how teaching and learning differed from what they were used to in their home country. When asked about their experiences of school, most of the children mentioned that the teachers were kind, that they did not use physical punishment as occurred in schools at home and that they explained things instead of forcing pupils to learn them by heart. The different school system, however, was also a source of worry among parents and children, in view of the possibility of having to return to the home country and the risk of lagging behind in what was expected of pupils back there.

Among the parents in the study, there were several examples of constraints experienced in managing their parental role during the transition period. Almost all of the parents identified their worries about the future of their children and about their ability to protect their children as the main reasons for their decision to leave their home country. In Sweden, however, they experienced a contradiction between their parental responsibility and their dependence on authorities for support, sometimes entirely unable to control their own life. This had given rise among them to a sense of guilt and shame, about themselves, about family members and kin left behind, and about their inability to adequately take care of their children on their own. While the set of emotions involved in this kind of sense is always complex, part of it, in the case of these parents, was linked to unclear information given to them about their rights, for instance regarding financial support beyond normal social assistance entitlements. Similarly, the information they had received about how long they would have to wait for their asylum decisions was often unclear, as was that about whether they had supplied all the necessary information to enable the processing of their applications in the first place.

The asylum seekers' descriptions of their relationships with their Migration Board case officers conveyed a sense of uncertainty and lack of control, something that they experienced in their interactions with authorities even more broadly. This experience was exacerbated by the long waiting periods and a lack of transparency regarding the relevant rules and rights. The asylum seekers found their contacts with the officers in charge of their individual cases to be frequently ambiguous, causing insecurity and mistrust.

Mistrust in particular seemed to be an inherent feature of the asylum process. The asylum seekers often felt they had to convince the authorities of the merit of their asylum claim and of their need and qualification for support and benefits. Mistrust and lack of recognition on the authorities' side was also a recurrent theme in the parents' reports about their difficulties in managing their basic needs, such as when requesting a change of accommodation or extra economic support to, for instance, buy clothes and eyeglasses for children. Negotiations in these cases could turn humiliating when such needs were questioned or when the decision took a long time to make. Indeed, the impression we had in several cases was that of ad hoc implementation of the rules.

Several concrete examples of this kind of lack of trust from the authorities' side could be mentioned. Robin, for instance, wanted to move his family to another place because of harassment they were experiencing, but at first received no response to his questions about such a possibility.[30] He, furthermore, had to wait for a long time before being contacted by his appointed lawyer about the matter. In addition, he also felt unsatisfied with the interpreter helping him with his request. Altogether, his problems in these respects then added to his worries about when his family's case would be decided. Gradually, all the family members became depressed because of this lack of information about their rights as asylum seekers, which contributed to their sense of not being able to control their immediate life circumstances. When asked about his own trust in the case officers in charge of helping him and his family, Robin replied:

> Yes, [I trust in them,] but some things go amiss because we don't know all the rules and our rights. The laws, those we don't know, but for instance just today we found out that our children can get financial support to buy winter clothes, so we handed in our application about that. Information about such things they could give us in a simple format, in some single piece of paper. Where we now got this information was from the school.

Similar stories were told by other interviewees, indicating that what was most disturbing for them was the uncertainty about what their lawyers were there for, why they were not given any information about the reasons for delays, and why it was so difficult to communicate with their case officers and lawyers. Another problem brought up by some of the parents related to the interview methods used by the Migration Board case officers when talking to their children. The parents reported several of their children to have been upset by the questions they had been posed about what the parents had stated, leaving the children with a feeling that they had to confirm the stories told by their parents. Leila, for example, explained that her daughter had had to answer questions like: 'Your father said this and that – is that correct? What will you do if we send you back to the Middle East?' Yet, the most difficult thing for her to give a detailed account of had been how she and her family had been physically attacked in their home.

Another interviewee, Fatima, talked about how difficult it had been for her to describe how she had been abused and assaulted by her (drug addict) husband prior to her leaving her country. Both her case officer and her interpreter were men, and she had felt unable to talk to them about all the circumstances and details pertaining to her case when offered the opportunity to do so during her asylum interview, at which, moreover, her son had been present. Coming from a strict Muslim family background, her only escape from her misery had been to leave the country, and she had simply expected this fact alone, together with her life situation at home, to be sufficient grounds for being granted a residence permit in Sweden. Her appointed lawyer she had met only once, despite her repeated efforts to book further appointments.

These examples show that, while the emotional dynamics characterising the social situation of asylum seekers may be rooted in very different circumstances, the absence of a sense of control in that situation fosters mistrust and a sense of lack of social recognition of their situation. The common emotions expressed during the interviews with the study participants were feelings of guilt and shame. These feelings often then combined with well-founded fears about how the future might unfold, leaving the asylum applicants and their families in an emotionally stressful, even paralysing situation.

On the other hand, the Migration Board was also perceived as helpful for the asylum seekers. Some of the interviewed parents spoke appreciatively of the support they had received, although the availability and quality of this support seemed to depend on the individual case officer or lawyer assigned to their case. Also church-based organisations were described as very helpful; they had assisted several of the asylum-seeking families studied by donating food and clothing. In contrast to the authorities, the people working for these organisations were perceived to have time for the individual asylum seekers, and in general seemed to have shown a more supportive attitude.

Sense of belonging

As already noted, trust is an important dimension in a salutogenic perspective, forming a necessary condition for establishing social contacts and a sense of safety while waiting for the asylum verdict. Social networking with schoolmates may be regarded as a particularly influential factor in this regard. Among the asylum-seeking children studied, however, there seemed to be little evidence of expanding social relations among the classmates. Judging from their own descriptions of the social landscape at school, there seemed to be small cliques of individuals keeping to themselves, with no more than occasional socialisation between them. Many asylum-seeking children in Sweden are first enrolled in a preparatory class where they learn Swedish and receive some basic education on other fundamental topics; these classes also serve as an introduction to the Swedish school system. Class sizes are very small and the children attending the classes all share the same basic life situation. This more intimate context made it easier for the asylum-seeking children in this study to make friends; as they themselves reported, these classes were the most important social context for them in which to make friends. Laila (aged 15), for instance, who had one close friend at school, stated that: 'If we had first met in a normal class, we might not have become such close friends, because we both felt marginalized. Here [in Sweden] you have to trust people more; to have someone to trust is very important.' All the asylum-seeking children attending the preparatory class had similar experiences even when they were not from the same country. They all talked about the important role the preparatory class at school played in terms of their ability to make friends; friends, moreover, with whom they were able to stay close and continue being friends even later when moving on to a regular class.

The children also reported spending time primarily with other immigrant children at school, regardless of whether they were from the same country or not. As Kaden (aged 15), for example, described:

> My school is an immigrant school. There are some Swedes there, too, but I don't have any contact with them. Sometimes it happens that some Swedes come along [with us] . . . but still there is no real contact. I feel better with other immigrants . . . The Swedish guys seem so cold towards one another.

Statements like Laila's and Kaden's indicate that asylum-seeking children, and immigrant children more generally, may have very little trust in others. Both

Laila and Kaden felt anxious about making mistakes, about not speaking properly and not wearing the right clothes. Laila, moreover, claimed that she did not, in fact, need any more acquaintances, since, in her view, these could also be potential enemies: 'At first I wanted to have more friends, but now I feel happy with how things are. I try not to make more enemies.' She mentioned that she was careful not to be involved in conflicts with other children at school, explaining her deliberate strategy: 'If you stay calm and don't aggravate things, you avoid conflicts.' According to her, she socialised with a few other children with whom she always hung out at school. In general, everybody was nice, nobody was mean, and nobody had a higher status, in her opinion, 'even when they think they have a higher status'. This 'high status', for her, was displayed by the fashionable clothes worn. The cases of Laila and Kaden illustrate the important role that risk management has in regulating social interaction: by avoiding interaction beyond a narrow circle of trusted friends, they both strived to limit their risk of being held in negative regard.

The social contacts that the asylum-seeking children in this study cultivated at school did not, however, extend to free time and leisure activities. Moreover, most of the children had hardly any friends and acquaintances in the neighbourhoods where they lived. One reason they mentioned for this was the absence of suitable local places or venues where they could make friends outside school. In addition, their own attitudes towards their neighbourhoods were markedly suspicious or indifferent. There was ambivalence about how to relate to people living in their area that had its roots in the children's experiences as asylum seekers. For some, this experience translated into feelings of outright mistrust. Kaden was one example: in both his own and his parents' view, the youths living in their neighbourhood were 'drug users'. His sense of embeddedness in the local neighbourhood was fairly weak, suggesting itself as both a cause and a consequence of this situation.

The lonely children in the study group also had lonely parents. It was typical of both the mothers and the fathers participating in the study that they tended to just wait out their time in the place where they lived, without venturing to create social contacts there. Alternatively, they remained openly suspicious or even afraid of people familiar with their situation, should they be forced to remain as undocumented refugees.

As the above examples show, lack of trust and fears about negative recognition were thus significant factors contributing to the asylum-seeking children's aversion to forming new friendships in their local environment. Lack of social contacts was, however, compensated for by transnational contacts using internet and other equipment. A recurrent theme in the interviewed children's stories was the children's relationships with their extended families that were generally quite attenuated. Some of the children maintained some form of contact with their cousins living in Sweden, while most of them had only sparse contact with relatives back home. Also the parents in the study tended to have few or infrequent transnational family contacts. This situation may, however, have been temporary, coming about as a result of factors such as guilt for having left close kin, problems linked to the uncertainties of the future, and practical difficulties encountered while waiting for the asylum decision. The general impression gained from the interviews was nevertheless that the children followed a pattern similar to their parents, while they were also constrained by limited access to means of communication.

Emotion management

Asylum-seeking families thus find themselves having to cope with several significant forms of adversity while waiting for a decision on their residence permit. For the families in this study, the trauma of return, material deprivation, temporary and, in most cases, overcrowded housing, lack of social relationships, parents' anxiety, lack of transparent rules regulating their rights to economic and social support, and lack of information about the status of their asylum application represented perhaps the most important sources of these. All of these circumstances bring with them emotions that then need to be managed.

The research for this chapter clearly showed the most important source of resilience for the asylum-seeking children and their parents to be the family. In the interviews, the strong interdependency relations that the study participants described to be there within their families were expressed in different ways. The parents talked about their great responsibility to protect their children from worries about lack of resources in everyday life: freeing children from the burden of such concerns was perceived as their main parental task in the circumstances.[31] The children believed their parents to know what was best for them and that the parents' decisions were for their own good. At the same time, the children, for their part, tended to feel responsible for the well-being of their parents. Some of them had a close relationship with their parents, claiming to be able to talk with them about their worries and concerns. In those cases, they could find temporary relief from their thoughts and feelings of exclusion at not being able to socialise on equal terms with their classmates. Laila, for example, had great trust in her mother and her close friend. She could talk openly with both of them about matters that caused her anxiety. She talked with her mother about her fears about having to return to her home country, but also about missing it deeply. It helped her to talk about such things, although, as she herself put it, 'it is like taking a pill: it calms you down but after a while the worries return'. Sometimes she was struck by a sudden fear that she would lose her mother; her mother thought this was probably owing to the fact that they were so alone in the new country. Hardly any of their relatives were there with them; they were all scattered around the world. Attending school had nevertheless helped alleviate this fear of Laila.

On the whole, the children were unwilling to talk to others about the problematic situation of their families. One stated reason for this was that talking, by bringing fears out in the open, only heightened their anxieties by making the problem seem more formidable and real. Another reason, according to the interviewed children, was that parents (usually mothers) should be protected from their children's problems. Jemina (aged 15), for instance, whose family was in a particularly vulnerable situation, stated that she felt unable to talk to anyone about her worries and problems, whether it be her mother or her close friend. Instead, she kept everything to herself without even wanting to talk about her feelings and concerns. When asked whether this was because she thought that her mother was already encumbered by so many worries and she did not want to disturb her even more, or whether it was because she simply did not like to talk about her feelings or worries in general, Jemina responded: 'It's both; I just think that it's best for me not to talk.' Her reluctance to share her feelings and thoughts was not, however, because she thought she would not find a sympathetic ear. On the contrary, she believed that her mother actually wanted her to talk about them; she simply preferred to keep it all inside herself. In addition to her mother, her sister and grandparents who lived with the family, she also had a brother, none of whom she wanted to open up to. She did, however, express that she would have liked to have someone to share her thoughts with. When asked how she managed this inner conflict of hers, she explained: 'I write, at nights' (she suffered from sleeping problems and stomach aches). Her wish was to learn music or acting, as she thought she could then act out her problems instead: 'I want to get it out of me', she confessed.

Among the asylum-seeking children in this study, Sonia had a similar dilemma. She did not speak with anyone in her family about their situation. While she did much to support her mother, she nevertheless felt unable to open up to her; like Jemina, she simply preferred not to talk. There was also a school nurse whom she said she trusted and knew she could visit anytime, even if she only went to see her once. Both Jemina's and Sonia's families were in a precarious situation, and they both feared that talking about their problems might only make them seem bigger. Yet, what also lay behind their unwillingness to talk was a basic problem of trust – or, rather, insecurity about the extent to which they could trust others. Sonia and the other children in the more vulnerable families studied were highly sensitive to the difficult situation faced by their mothers who were lonely, very worried about their future and frequently depressed. The children were aware of their mothers' dependency on them, which inspired deep loyalty in them. In order to be more supportive to their mothers, they then discounted their own needs. Yet, when asked about it, they spoke of their positive expectations for the future, with an immediate future that promised to deliver their much-longed-for residence permits. At the same time, they all tried to avoid thinking and talking about their past and future, opting instead to make themselves invisible to reduce the risk of being held in negative regard. Among the many bystanders failing to recognise this situation of theirs were the authorities at the Swedish Migration Board: only a few of the children in this study had ever been interviewed or directly addressed by any of them.

Conclusions

Based on the interviews conducted for this study, mistrust appears to be a built-in part of the organisation of the asylum process, and is mostly associated with the intrusive nature of the asylum determination procedure. The asylum seekers' position is frequently one of dependency, where the absence of trust by others and lack of social recognition influence their sense of self-confidence. Needs testing in particular is often associated with a feeling of negative social recognition, especially when the rules are not transparent and are applied differently from case to case.

The period of transition in which the asylum-seeking families were caught at the time of this study brought with it uncertainties, ambivalence, and asymmetric dependencies affecting their lives. To engage in reciprocal exchange of resources presupposes that they can expect a more balanced exchange to develop within a certain time-frame. In this situation, it is thus important for both parties to be able to prove self-reliance and independence.

This study indicates that there is a basic lack of trust among asylum-seeking adults and children, which prevents them from building social capital during the transition period to refugee status. Not cultivating social relationships, however, can also be looked upon as a matter of self-protection. Keeping a low profile functions as a resilience strategy, helping to reduce the risk of experiencing shame and humiliation in the difficult economic circumstances and poor housing conditions typical of the asylum seekers' situation upon arrival in the host country. Both the children and the parents in this study kept a low social profile, expressing an attitude that, in their situation, this was 'better' for them. This attitude can be interpreted as linked to the asylum seekers' lack of a sense of trust and to the uncertainty they felt about their status, reflecting in turn their ambiguous situation as individuals caught in between two statuses.

Among the asylum-seeking families studied, family bonding provided a strong source of resilience for both the parents and the children, in particular in families with many adversities to cope with. Uncertainty about the future was usually accompanied by a desire to appear independent and self-reliant vis-à-vis the environment. The mothers' commitment to their children provided them with emotional capital that they could draw upon in everyday life, translating into an atmosphere of protection and a sense of safety and belonging. Building emotional capital within the family was thus used by mothers as a way to develop resources for coping with past insecurity and uncertainty about the future. The high degree of dependency and reliance on the family as a source of resilience nevertheless put new pressure on family members, given how keen they were to protect one another from their worries and how responsible they felt for each other's well-being. Worries, psychologically straining memories, and closure against the environment could then combine to create a vicious circle. While parents and children felt responsible for each other's well-being, the ambiguous interdependency that this sentiment gave rise to could be experienced as a burden by the children, who often felt a need to suppress their own needs of emotional support vis-à-vis their mothers or friends, thus compromising their own well-being. The findings of the study thus suggest a close link between emotional capital and social capital, but also the complexity of this linkage: while giving emotional support might bring relief to both the support giver and the support receiver, the reciprocity of emotional support can also give rise to mutual dependencies that entail significant emotional costs.

Another important observation is that the dynamics of the social interactions discussed above can create a vicious circle, aggravating a socially exposed position to the point of social exclusion. Both in the context of the migration policy in Sweden and more broadly, the findings from this study highlight the importance of finding new ways to support asylum-seeking families and their children. The strategy of integration into the host society during the waiting period should be made more responsive to the applicants' needs. One concrete way to do this could be by improving communication about the school system.[32] In addition, making it possible for children to take part in leisure activities would predictably have important effects in improving their general well-being, thus helping to reduce stress in their families as well.

Notes

1 Some informants were living in hiding after having had their applications rejected. These informants expected to renew their applications at a later date.

2 Gerhard Wikrén and Håkan Sandesjö, *Utlänningslagen med kommentarer* (9th edn, Norstedts Juridik, 2010).

3 Göran Bodegård, 'Pervasive Loss of Function Progressing to Devitalization: An Earlier Unknown Life Threatening Stress Reaction Seen in Asylum-Seeking Children in Sweden', in Hans E. Andersson *et al.* (eds), *The Asylum-Seeking Child in Europe* (Centre for European Research at the University of Gothenburg, 2005), ch. 12, 135; Gellert Tamas, *De apatiska. Om makt, myter och manipulation* (Natur och Kultur, 2009).

4 Marita Eastmond and Henry Ascher, 'In the Best Interest of the Child? The Politics of Vulnerability and Negotiations for Asylum in Sweden' (2011) 37 *Journal of Ethnic and Migration Studies* 1185; Swedish Migration Board, *Arbetet med den tillfälliga utlänningslagstiftningen 2005–2006. Slutrapport* (report, Swedish Migration Board, 2007).

5 Hans E. Andersson and Susanne Nilsson, 'Asylum Seekers and Undocumented Migrants' Increased Social Rights in Sweden' (2011) 11 *International Migration* 167; Eva Nilsson, 'A Child Perspective in the Swedish Asylum Process: Rhetoric and Practice', in Hans E. Andersson *et al.* (eds), *The Asylum-Seeking Child in Europe* (Centre for European Research at the University of Gothenburg, 2005), 73; Wikrén and Sandesjö, above n. 2.

6 Convention relating to the Status of Refugees, Geneva, 28 July 1951, 1989 UNTS 137, supplemented by the Protocol relating to the Status of Refugees, 31 January 1967, 19 UST 6223, 6257 ('1951 Refugee Convention').

7 Wikrén and Sandesjö, above n. 2.

8 Ministry of Justice, Government Offices of Sweden, *Synnerligen ömmande ömständigheter och verkställighetshinder – en kartläggning av tillämpningen*, Memorandum No. DS 2011:14 (2011).

9 Andersson and Nilsson, above n. 5.

10 Ibid.

11 See, e.g., Swedish Government Official Reports, *Den nya migrationsprocessen*, Report No. SOU 2009:56 (2009).

12 See, e.g., Boverket – The Swedish National Board of Housing, Building and Planning, *Asylsökandes eget boende, EBO – en kartläggning*, Report (2008).

13 Swedish Government Official Reports, above n. 11, 22.

14 Hans E. Andersson, 'Spänningen mellan barnkonventionen och den reglerade invandringen', in Hans E. Andersson *et al.* (eds), *Mellan det förflutna och framtiden.*

Asylsökande barns välfärd, hälsa och välbefinnande (Centre for European Research at the University of Gothenburg, 2010), 39.

15 Eva Nilsson, *Barn i rättens gränsland. Om barnperspektiv vid prövning av uppehållstillstånd* (Justus, 2007); Lisa Ottoson, '"Barntänk" ur ett tjänstemanaperspektiv. En intervjustudie med barnhandläggare vid Migrationsverket', in Hans E. Andersson *et al.* (eds), *Mellan det förflutna och framtiden. Asylsökande barns välfärd, hälsa och välbefinnande* (Centre for European Research at the University of Gothenburg, 2010), 63.

16 Eastmond and Ascher, above n. 4.

17 European Commission (2012) *Europe in Figures – Eurostat Yearbook*, Eurostat <http://epp. eurostat.ec.europa.eu/statistics_explained/index.php/Europe_in_figures_-_Eurostat_yearbook>.

18 The study was funded by the European Refugee Fund in Sweden.

19 The interviews were conducted by the author and Dr Mirzet Tursunovic.

20 Bernard Barber, *The Logic and Limits of Trust* (Rutgers University Press, 1983), 164–5.

21 Barbara A. Misztal, *Trust in Modern Societies: The Search for the Bases of Social Order* (Polity, 1996).

22 Niklas Luhmann, 'Familiarity, Confidence, Trust: Problems and Alternatives', in D. Gambetta (ed.), *Trust: Making and Breaking Cooperative Relations* (Basil Blackwell, 1988) 94, 100 (emphasis in original).

23 See Carl-Gören Heidegren, *Erkännande* (Liber, 2009).

24 Jack Barbalet, 'Tillitens emotionella bas och dess följder', in Åsa Wettergren, Bengt Starrin and Gerd Lindgren (eds), *Det sociala livets emotionella grunder* (Liber, 2008), 57.

25 Michael Ungar, 'Resilience across Cultures' (2008) 38 *British Journal of Social Work* 212.

26 Virginia Morrow, 'Conceptualising Social Capital in Relation to the Well-Being of Children and Young People: A Critical Review' (1999) 47 *Sociological Review* 744.

27 Jan-Paul Brekke, *While We Are Waiting: Uncertainty and Empowerment among Asylum-Seekers in Sweden*, Report No. 2004:010 (Institute for Social Research, 2004).

28 Ibid.

29 Olga Keselman *et al.*, 'Mediated Communication with Minors in Asylum-Seeking Hearings' (2008) 21 *Journal of Refugee Studies* 103.

30 All interviewee names have been changed to protect confidentiality.

31 See Marita Eastmond, 'Gäster i välfärden? Föräldraskap i asylprocessen', in Hans E. Andersson *et al.* (eds), *Mellan det förflutna och framtiden. Asylsökande barns välfärd, hälsa och välbefinnande* (Centre for European Research at the University of Gothenburg, 2010), 87.

32 See Mirzet Tursunovic, 'Skolan i de asylsökande barnens vardag', in Hans E. Andersson *et al.* (eds), *Mellan det förflutna och framtiden. Asylsökande barns välfärd, hälsa och välbefinnande* (Centre for European Research at the University of Gothenburg, 2010), 141.

12 Better than our fears? Refugees in Italy: between rhetorics of exclusion and local projects of inclusion

Maurizio Ambrosini

The reception of refugees in the last two decades has become a major issue on the political agendas of developed countries. Approximately 80 per cent of refugees are welcomed in countries of the Global South, 10 per cent more than ten years ago, with Pakistan and Iran heading the list of receiving countries (UNHCR, *Displacement*, 2013). However, public opinion in the Global North tends to view asylum seekers as freeloaders on diminishing welfare provisions, whose applications require more stringent examination, and who should receive fewer benefits once they have been accepted. Even European Union documents refer to the need to 'prevent the abuse of asylum applications that undermines the credibility of the system and constitutes an additional administrative and financial burden on Member States'.[1] On the other hand, armed conflict, persecutions of minorities, political instability and natural disasters have forced states to introduce new forms of international protection and new categories of beneficiaries, together with new rules for reception.[2] Among these, to be mentioned in particular is the provision of the Dublin conventions, which obliges asylum seekers to apply for asylum in the first safe country that they are able to enter.

This innovation, together with the recurrent political and humanitarian crises that have erupted in the Middle East and Africa, has brought the countries of Southern Europe to the front line; countries that previously were not significantly involved in the flow of refugees. This function as the gatekeepers of Europe has become a crucial issue since 2011, as a consequence of the North-African Spring, the turmoil in the region, and the new flows of asylum seekers. Italy occupies a leading position among the Southern European countries because of its size, geographical location, and historical and political ties with the other side of the Mediterranean Sea.

In this new gateway for asylum seekers, the controversy surrounding the image of the would-be refugees, their motivations and aspirations, and the treatment that they should receive is particularly heated. In recent years, political forces and the media have waged fierce campaigns for border closures. Other social forces and civil society organisations, on the other hand, have defended refugees and sought to improve their circumstances. The refugees themselves, rather than simply being subject to top-down policies and to internal disputes within the host society, seek ways to integrate, redefining their identities in ways that cause less political and social resistance.

The Italian case is the subject of this chapter, which is divided into three parts. The first part deals with the evolution of Italian policies of asylum. The second presents the real processes of social integration of refugees. Finally, the third part refers to the present scenario. It first describes the contradictory management of the new emergency caused by the arrivals from the African coast in 2011–12, and then presents the innovations resulting from some local projects that seemingly open up new prospects.

Italian policies towards refugees

Italy still lacks a domestic law regarding the reception of refugees, although it has signed international treaties and conventions and is party to European Union law relating to applicants for international protection,[3] including the 1951 Refugee Convention,[1] that oblige it to recognise the right of asylum. It has long put itself on the margins of the routes of asylum seekers. When Italy signed the Refugee Convention, it entered a 'geographical reservation clause': until 1989, Italy only recognised refugee flows from Eastern Europe. The reason was obvious: Italy had to deal with the strongest communist party in Western Europe. Refugees from the Eastern bloc, who were members of cultural and professional elites, represented a potential political asset. Those who arrived from third countries, however, were of no interest.

Exceptions to this rule were put in place during particularly serious events on the international scene. The first was the advent of the military dictatorships in Chile and Argentina in the 1970s, which provoked the arrival of thousands of persecuted people in Italy, several of whom were of Italian origin. Left-wing parties, trade unions and associations close to them took action to find accommodation and work (mainly skilled) for the newcomers. The second event, a few years later, was the arrival of thousands of 'boat people' from Vietnam and Cambodia. In the latter case it was mainly Catholic organisations that took it upon themselves to help them. These were always considered exceptional measures taken reluctantly by the fragile governments of the time under pressure from advocacy campaigns. In the 1980s other political dissidents began to arrive in dribs and drabs, but generally they were not recognised as such. They came, for example, from Eritrea, Iran and the occupied Palestinian territories; and usually as students, thanks to entry procedures that were rather liberal for the time.

Meanwhile, Italy was becoming a new destination for international migration, but political institutions took cognisance of the fact quite late, and with some reluctance. Since the mid-1980s, Italian immigration policies have had two constants which have proved quite insensitive to changes of governments. First, the recognition in retrospect of settlement that has already happened, through acts of regularisation, which are presented as exceptional but have actually been recurrent (7 in 25 years, in addition to the hidden amnesties of decree-flows).

Second, the reference to employment as the pivotal element in legitimising immigrants' presence in Italy.[5] It is no coincidence that all the most recent amnesties have given employers the right to regulate the immigrants working for them, and hence the power to grant or deny the possibility of emerging from social invisibility (see also the Chapter 11 in this volume). The unauthorised immigrant is not directly recognised as the holder of a right.

It was only with the Immigration Act of 1989 (known as the Martelli Law) that the clause on geographical reservation was dropped, although the Act did not include any specific provision relating to refugees. At the time of the subsequent Balkan wars, provisional reception measures were introduced in the form of temporary residence permits on humanitarian grounds. After a brief period of acceptance (three months), supported by state funding, the refugees (in total the official figure was 77,000)[6] were in fact given the same status as economic migrants, having obtained a renewable residence permit of one year that allowed them to work. But they had to find their own means to live independently, negotiating their way through the black economy, which was certainly prevalent in the early stages, and the formal economy. Many of them had opportunities to regularise their positions through the amnesty measures in the years to follow.

For the other aspiring refugees, as a standard practice, the Italian authorities unofficially let them pass through the country, silently helping them on their way to other countries where they had relatives and friends, and where national policies were more open to reception. Even today (2011 data),[7] Italy hosts some 58,000 refugees in all, compared with 572,000 in Germany, 210,000 in France and 194,000 in the UK. In other words, until recently it was difficult for an asylum seeker to be recognised as a refugee in Italy, but it was usually easier to pass through the country, or in the case of those who decided to stay, to find work and be regularised as economic migrants. I shall return to this point later.

Over the past decade, partly as a result of the new rules introduced by the two conventions in Dublin, the countries of Mediterranean Europe, located at the southern borders of the Union, have come under increasing pressure from people seeking safety from war and persecution.[8] This is particularly the case for Italy and Greece: in 2011, the latter registered a significant growth in the reception of refugees (11,500 people), despite the economic crisis of the country. Also to be noted is that small Euro-Mediterranean countries like Malta and Cyprus respectively hosted about 7,000 and 3,500 refugees in 2012.[9]

As for Italy, for a period, more controls and restrictions produced a lower number of applications (20 per cent in 2009 in comparison with 2008). In the Italian case, the majority of asylum seekers arrive by sea, looking for a better life by undertaking very dangerous and often fatal journeys. They land mostly on the small island of Lampedusa, the Italian territory closest to the African coast. Lampedusa has thus become the symbol of unwanted immigration, and for many Italians it represents the entrance for invasion of the country by hordes of desperate people. With the Arab Spring of 2011, the arrivals by boat have restarted, and with them a high number of fatal accidents: 2,160 casualties in 2011, 409 in 2012, 1,050 in 2013 (end of October), without taking into account the accidents of which no traces have remained. The most recent tragedies, at the beginning of October, saw the death of almost 500 people.

The Italian governments of the period 2008–11 gradually tightened controls on entries, increased vigilance on the coasts, and sought to involve the countries of the southern Mediterranean in surveillance of the departure ports. These measures were also partly in response to the Schengen agreements and the growing European involvement in the fight against unauthorised immigration.[10] This strategy produced different and controversial results. It was successful in fighting arrivals by sea from Albania, a very common practice in the 1990s and which has now almost disappeared, while in the case of arrivals from North Africa the tendency was less linear. Studies on the topic have noted that following the closure of some routes there was a search for new routes and entry points. In addition, the strengthening of surveillance led to increasing levels of criminal human-smuggling organisations, with a parallel growth in the costs and risks for migrants trying to enter by sea, especially for those with fewer resources.[11] As in the German case discussed by Friedrich Heckmann,[12] a sort of 'arms race' could be seen in the Mediterranean area between institutions responsible for border control, which became increasingly better organised, and smugglers, who in their turn resorted to more sophisticated means and became ever more skilled, specialised and indifferent to the destiny of their passengers.

Indeed, for some years the number of asylum applications on Italian territory increased, reaching a peak of 31,100 applications in 2008, in direct proportion to landings from the sea. In that year, about three-quarters of the people who landed applied for protection, and about half of them were later recognised as being entitled to some form of international protection. At the same time, however, there developed in the country a vehement campaign against immigration defined in no uncertain terms as 'illegal' or even 'clandestine'; and the fragile Prodi government, which fell in early 2008, showed evident difficulties in dealing with the security demand expressed by the public and fuelled by most of the mass media, as well as by opposition parties.

Security and the fight against illegal immigration were among the key issues of the election campaign mounted by right-wing forces during the elections of spring 2008. The apparent harmony between the political platform of the coalition led by Mr Berlusconi and the expectations of the public on these issues was one of the main reasons for the overwhelming electoral victory of the centre-right. Furthermore, the success of the populist formation of the Northern League can be explained to a certain extent by the wide following that it acquired through the anti-immigration rhetoric of its leaders.[13] A tightening of immigration rules followed, especially in regard to persons with an irregular immigration status, which led to, among other things, the criminalisation of unauthorised residence. In this context, in 2009 the Italian government reached new and more stringent agreements with Libya, turning away sea vessels carrying a total of about 800 migrants, despite protests from the UN and the European Union.[14] This action was partly motivated by the fact that Libya did not have reception struc-tures for asylum seekers and had not signed international conventions protecting them. The case brought to light the dramatic tension between national sovereignty and the 'liberal constraint' which influences, or should influence, the policies of states on sensitive matters such as respect for human rights and the right to apply for asylum.[15]

The Italian policy of closure nevertheless resulted in a marked drop in coastal landings, as well as in the number of refugees accepted in Italy (which fell from more than 31,000 in 2008 to just over 17,000 in 2009), emphasising the correlation between the two phenomena: a halt to the invasion of 'illegal' immigrants had been announced, but also many people entitled to humanitarian assistance sanctioned by international law were refused entry or were persuaded not to depart from their country of origin. The UNHCR, and then the Court of Strasbourg strongly condemned Italy's agreements with Libya, and in particular its practice of turning boats back towards an unsafe country like Libya. Laura Boldrini, spokesperson for UNHCR in Italy, actively fought against the Italian government's policy, arguing that, while the Italian government had declared it would stop the irregular immigration flows from Libya, it had actually prevented many people in need of international protection from seeking political asylum in the country.[16] The Italian government rejected these accusations, but the controversy significantly damaged the relationship between the Italian authorities and the UNHCR.[17] For probably the first time since the founding of the UNO, the Italian government came into direct conflict with the United Nations.

While the streets began to be festooned with posters depicting boats full of immigrants, accompanied by the words 'we have stopped the invasion', in the summer of 2009 the Italian government passed an amnesty for immigrants employed in households as domestic workers or carers of the elderly. This resulted in 294,000 applications. Compared with the deportations carried out in the same year (about 14,000, a decrease compared with 18,000 in 2008),[18] and while accounting for a number of rejected applications, these figures show that for every person deported, nearly 20 irregular migrants settled in Italy. The story was repeated with little variation – at the beginning – with the new wave of emergency landings (spring 2011). The national government, closely followed by the media, used the term 'emergency' to describe a situation that was fully expected, i.e. the spontaneous arrival of migrants and asylum seekers from North Africa as a result of political change, and the resulting conflicts and socio-economic instability. Prime Minister Berlusconi spoke of a 'human tsunami'[19] and several leading figures in the Lega Nord party also described the arrivals in the most violent terms (the Lega Nord's leader Umberto Bossi: 'immigrants, get out of here'),[20] while some proposed opening fire on the approaching fragile boats.

The sea passengers (23,000 in early April; more than 50,000 at the end of the year) were initially left out in the open on the island of Lampedusa, and fed thanks to the spontaneous solidarity of the local people. They were then moved elsewhere, housed in tents or in other temporary accommodation. After a few days, notwithstanding a rhetoric that spoke of illegal immigrants and immediate rejections, and despite new agreements with Tunisia for the control of departures, the government granted migrants who arrived by sea before 5 April a temporary residence permit issued on humanitarian grounds for a period of three months.

The Italian government made little secret of the fact that the granting of the temporary permit would allow the refugees to reach France, where many had relatives and acquaintances. A severe political crisis ensued with France, which objected and set up check points with expulsions.[21] The Italian government also tried to involve the European Union, citing the recent European Directive No. 55 on temporary protection in the event of a massive influx of persons fleeing from wars or violations of fundamental rights, but without having previously made this appeal, and not after having unilaterally granted temporary permits. The existence of the circumstances required to apply the directive, however, was denied by the European partners, thereby politically isolating the Italian government. The reputation of the Italian government of the time was worsened even further by its refusal to ratify three European directives on immigration.

With subsequent arrivals, the Italian government finally showed a better capacity to deal with the situation. Since 2011, arrivals at Lampedusa are welcomed, fed, if necessary given medical treatment, then transferred to other reception centres (see below). Italian policies of immigration and asylum reverted to their consolidated approach, although burdened by a hostile and aggressive public rhetoric towards the new residents. Asylum seekers are conflated with unauthorised immigrants and therefore criminalised; an emphasis is placed on external border controls, even at the risk of undermining international conventions and human rights norms. In contrast, little surveillance is exercised on the labour market resulting in abusive working conditions; at the end of the day, regularisations *a posteriori* of immigrants (and in the case of refugees) working in the huge underground economy are enacted, in particular for domestic workers in Italian families.[22] Moreover, Italy showed more blatant closure to immigration with widespread demands for protection against the arrival and settlement of immigrants and refugees, differential treatment, and redefinition of social membership in terms of more extreme demarcation of boundaries between 'us' and 'them'. All of these processes were favoured by representatives of political institutions at central and often local levels too.

Integration without reception?

In an article published more than ten years ago, Maja Korac,[23] on comparing the apparently more generous formal reception of refugees from the former Yugoslavia in Northern Europe with the totally inadequate reception given to them in Italy, reached a conclusion that at first sight may seem surprising: refugees accommodated in reception centres in Northern European countries were left for years in a state of inactivity, brooding over their circumstances, and resentful of the wrongs and the violence they had suffered. In contrast, those who arrived in Italy had to adapt to harsh living conditions and were forced to immediately seek work in the informal economy to survive, with mostly limited and informal forms of help from networks of fellow countrypeople and civil society organisations.

They were subjected to social downgrading, and found only menial manual occupations; they were victims of unfair treatment and outright deceit.

However, with time the Italian arrivals were also better integrated than their counterparts in Northern Europe. While formal, institutional reception was not forthcoming, the initial temporary permits and then amnesties for immigrant workers allowed the issue of residence permits to be resolved, and integration from below, despite its limitations, yielded better results than regulated protection, with its ambiguous and exclusionary tendencies. The former Yugoslav refugees in Rome usually even refused to use assistance facilities for the poor such as canteens, which they considered degrading. For many of them, self-sufficiency came at a high price, because they were forced to enter the niches at the lower end of the employment system (housework and care work for women; the construction industry and low-skilled urban services for men), from which it is difficult to escape and find better jobs.[24] However, being able to work was good for their well-being and helped them overcome the trauma of war and uprooting.

These spontaneous processes of integration also worked in women's favour, who often found welcome and work within a few days in domestic services, in part through mediation by the Catholic Church. These processes also favoured refugees with better skills and greater initiative, who were free from family responsibilities, compared with older refugees or those accompanied by children; or ones belonging to majority groups, compared with the minority of Roma refugees coming from the same countries.[25] Like other non-regulated social processes, these confirmed and consolidated initial social differences.

The pathways to integration into Italian society have been characterised by minimal interventions on the part of public institutions, and have featured the use of two main resources: social networks and non-governmental organisations, especially those related to the Catholic Church. As a result, refugees tend to resemble economic migrants, in the sense that social networks are their main means to finding employment, and civil society organisations are a point of reference for many needs, especially in the early stages of settlement, or at other critical junctures, such as loss of work, health problems or family reunification procedures.[26]

The results of Maja Korac's research can be generalised. The Italian State has never been outstanding in terms of its level of hospitality and initiative towards refugees, but over the last 20 years the Italian economy has needed labour, having created many low-skilled jobs. People fleeing persecution and conflict, who have rarely found protection under the rules of international law, have often been confused with economic migrants and have followed the paths typical of the latter: upon entry, there begins a phase of irregular employment and social invisibility; then comes their emergence from the underground economy through an explicit or masked amnesty aimed at regularising foreign workers who have found a job in Italy. Employment and work have legitimised their settlement on national territory more than humanitarian reasons have. It can be said that in Italy it is easier to obtain regular employment status through the economic route of irregular work than through the political route of applying for asylum. The combination of economic and political motivations often observed among refugees, with the alleged difficulty of distinguishing 'real refugees' from economic migrants, is an endemic feature in the Italian case, one that is even favoured by immigration control policies.

As well as the positive stories of success concerning at least relative economic integration, there are also stories without happy endings. As reported by the UNHCR,[27] in several Italian cities (Rome, Milan, Turin, Florence, Bari, Naples and Palermo), groups of Somali, Eritrean, Afghan and homeless refugees circulate 'deprived of the dignity that the right to asylum should return them'.[28] They find precarious refuge in abandoned buildings, squats without basic facilities. They are seen by local communities as a source of illegality, urban decay and a risk to the safety of residents. They do not have the means to provide for their own housing needs, nor can they access reception centres or public housing facilities. Local authorities deny them residence, and therefore access to basic services, such as the ability to obtain an identity document, register with employment services, or access the National Health Service.

The North African Spring and the new arrivals

The North African crisis has exacerbated this precarious situation. More than 50,000 people arrived by sea during 2011, with an average of around 1,500 landings per week between January and September,[29] as well as a difficult-to-quantify number of lives lost during the crossing (around 2,000, according to Hein de Haas and Nando Sigona).[30] But the landings were only partly followed by applications for asylum (37,350). In the end, the number of applicants was greater than that of the two previous years (19,090 in 2009, 12,121 in 2010) but not much larger than that of 2008 (31,723). In 2013, new arrivals by sea mainly comprised people who applied for international protection. By October, they numbered 35,085 people including 9,805 from Syria; 8,443 from Eritrea; 3,140 from Somalia; 1,058 from Mali and 879 from Afghanistan. It has been estimated that 73 per cent could qualify for asylum rights.

The arrivals of 2011–13 galvanised public attention with their drama, concentration in space and time, and links with the Arab Spring and the conflict in Libya and in Syria. But they also did so because of the initial unpreparedness of the institutions, political alarmism and blanket media coverage. After an initial negative reaction by the majority of local governments, with the activation of the Civil Defence Department and definition of an agreement with the local authorities in April 2011, the distribution of refugees across the country began, although it was haphazard and lacked an overall strategy for integration. The forms of reception, initially based on the extraordinary opening of large reception centres and the erection of tent cities, and then of dispersion among often isolated and unsuitable locations devoid of supporting services, raised serious questions.[31] The central government allocated funds for reception on the basis of per-capita quotas, but it did not adequately monitor the activities of administrators in regard to training and accompanying schemes. Facilities without the necessary preparation and suitable staff – for example numerous hotels and holiday camps

– were also involved in the reception system. The status itself of the refugees was indefinite and uncertain, with humanitarian stay permits being renewed every three months, precluding the possibility to work legally; while, at the same time, the economic recession reduced opportunities for employment in the underground economy.

Local institutions and non-profit organisations took action. In some cases they set up more structured projects which included training, socialisation and leisure activities, and employment counselling. However, the overall situation was highly uneven and generally unsatisfactory. Many refugees were left to their own devices for months, at times for almost two years. While their basic needs were satisfied, they were excluded from economic and social participation, and consequently anxious and frustrated in regard to their future prospects. The fear of potential rejection, especially for Tunisians, with the forced repatriation of some of them, heightened the uncertainty.

Eventually, after various uncertainties and delays, at the end of March 2013 the reception centres for refugees who arrived in 2011 (the so-called ENA, North African Emergency) were officially closed. Except in particular cases of persons who continue to receive assistance from municipalities (families with small children, the sick, pregnant women), refugees have been issued with stay permits for humanitarian reasons and given an entry grant of €500, in some circumstances supplemented with other local contributions. But they have then been left to themselves. Some have sought their fortune outside Italy; others have found jobs, especially in the small and medium-sized towns of central-northern Italy; some have found hospitality with friends and relatives, yet there are also those who have swelled the homeless population that wanders among the large Italian cities and is forced to rely on the institutions furnishing basic assistance to the most impoverished.

Different approaches, different visions of forced migrations

I will now try to put the Italian case into an international perspective. I think we can identify four political approaches to the complex issue of forced migration. All four are to be found in the Italian experience, though they can be detected on a much larger scale. Different images and representations of asylum seekers come into play in this articulation of policies.

The first approach can be described as *passive tolerance*, and consists of choosing to ignore the phenomenon, a lack of political will to establish rules for recognition and reception centres, and an emphasis on efforts to facilitate the transit of asylum seekers to other destinations. Here, the refugees are seen simply as a problem to be avoided, and attempts are made to pass the problem on to other countries.

The second is *closure without alternative*, a sort of 'zero option' on refugees, which is not only the motto of various xenophobic European movements, but may also represent the direction in which the protection systems of most developed countries are shifting. In this case, refugees are seen in a more hostile way as deceitful invaders, as unscrupulous exploiters of the generous welfare states of receiving countries and of their dedication to human rights. This has been the prevailing view in Italy in the past decade, but it is not an isolated phenomenon.

The third strategy is *protection without integration*, and it is emerging as the more practical choice when it is not possible to reject asylum seekers or keep them in close proximity to their homes. This means temporary and purely humanitarian reception measures, where efforts are focused on the preservation of life, but no investments are planned to stabilise those refugees who are accepted, but who are explicitly excluded by the governments of the receiving countries. This was the predominant approach in Italy during the recent coastal landings from Libya, as we have seen: minimal protection was guaranteed, for a limited time only, without clear integration projects. In this instance, there is a widespread vision of asylum seekers as victims, to whom help cannot be denied, but it is intertwined with the suspicion that they actually intend to profit from their condition, thus falling into the previous category.

The fourth strategy, which is traceable in Italian history though never actually theorised as such, may be termed *integration without protection*. Whenever it has no longer been possible to pursue the first strategy, this solution has been used on forced migrants (or at least on the lucky ones) who have landed in Italy. In fact, apart from facilitating their transit to other, more generous countries, their existence on the margins of society and their integration in the economy has been tolerated, leaving the task of providing for their needs to ethnic networks, poor sectors of the labour market and solidarity organisations. The periodic amnesties have allowed forced migrants to come out into the open, along with many undocumented migrants who have found jobs in the meantime. Here the refugees are in practice treated the same as economic migrants, considered to be manpower for the labour market. Employers and the socio-economic forces (e.g. the trade unions) become the main actors responsible for the immigrants' reception. The refugees themselves, however, can to some extent achieve personal autonomy and a chance to work towards their integration into the host society.

A possible alternative

Some local experiences in recent years, however, make it possible to identify a fifth possibility: that of a 'merger' between humanitarian reception and integration programmes in the receiving society. The projects supported by SPRAR (Protection System for Asylum Seekers and Refugees), with the involvement of the ANCI (National Association of Italian Municipalities), municipal governments and local NGOs have worked along these lines.[32] In 2009/2010, 123 local authorities were part of the SPRAR network and 138 projects were active, with a total of 3,000 places, while in all (2008 data) 8,400 refugees were accepted by the SPRAR. The refugees included in SPRAR projects are therefore only a minority, compared with the total number of people to whom the Italian state has granted humanitarian protection, but they still amount to several thousands of people. In local projects, municipalities contribute at least 20 per cent to the financing, while the remainder is covered by central government. NGOs on the other hand have the role of project managers. Projects pursue an integrated accommodation plan for small groups of beneficiaries (on average 22 per project), addressing not only the basic needs of food and lodging, but also offering social counselling and individual pathways of employment insertion.

A study prepared by the agencies involved in various ways in the reception network[33] highlights that activated in more robust projects are other local resources, such as institutions furnishing vocational training (Padua, Udine), local agencies involved in finding housing for vulnerable social groups (Turin), employment services (Modena), and so on. In the best cases, local networks have been formed around accommodation projects for refugees undertaken jointly by public and non-governmental actors. This collaboration between local authorities and NGOs tends to emphasise a strength of Italian social policies, especially in their more innovative aspects: the central government's delays and weaknesses are often offset by the activism of local actors. Also, in the recent reception of asylum seekers from North Africa, several local projects have developed good practices of networking and empowerment.

We can, however, identify various combinations between the actions of local public authorities and the role of NGOs. The position of the former varies from total delegation to playing a leading role, which leaves the NGOs very little autonomy; the latter also differ, ranging from well-structured organisations, looser organisations, and associations with more difficulty in providing project continuity because they are mainly based on the deployment of volunteers. An interesting aspect is the involvement of even small municipalities. Here SPRAR projects have sometimes been opportunities for the innovation of local social policies; for example, when services for immigrants have not yet been activated. On other occasions, they have encouraged the development of more collaborative relationships between the various institutions involved. In some cases, such as that of the small town of Riace, in the southern region of Calabria, the arrival of refugees and their families has helped to prevent the closure of the town's school and to revitalise the economy of the old town with the development of small workshops. According to research conducted by the Cittalia Foundation[34] on small municipalities, the results were differentiated: according to the persons in charge, nearly 50 per cent of beneficiaries found a job. The recession that followed, however, caused people to move away again and created problems in situations that seemed well established.

In some marginal small towns affected by depopulation, the arrival of families with children has been well accepted, and seen as an opportunity for the rebirth of the village. In others, when groups of young men have been admitted, the local community has behaved with greater mistrust and closure. In yet others, especially in situations of territorial isolation and deprivation in terms of social relationships, many of the refugees have preferred to abandon the reception projects.

Other projects have been developed locally, independently from SPRAR. In Turin a reception project alternative to the SPRAR one was led by a local NGO (Coop. ORSO), with the participation of 30 associations brought together into one committee. With the support of European funds, and then also of the local authorities (province and region), a network was established among more than 25 municipalities in the region, linked to various charities and associations. More than 200 refugees who had occupied an abandoned clinic living in very precarious conditions were accepted and incorporated into the local society, where they quickly found homes and jobs, without conflict with local communities, thanks to the mediation and support of social workers and volunteers and the active participation of beneficiaries.[35]

Among local networks of integrated reception there is also the 'Cittadini possibili' (Possible Citizens) project, developed in Lombardy by a network of organisations and coordinated by the 'Farsi Prossimo' Consortium sponsored by the Caritas Ambrosiana. This project, aimed at welcoming and integrating one hundred refugees of various origins into local society, has involved NGOs, local authorities and a bank foundation (Cariplo) as the financial supporter, and it has provided coordinated measures for housing assistance, the teaching of Italian, vocational training and support for work entry.

Between anti-proactive protection and an indolent pseudo-tolerance, which really means a lack of institutional responsibility and social neglect, there have arisen support processes and initiatives towards independence. In this way, and within a reasonable timeframe, the asylum seekers who arrived in need of protection have become able to meet their own needs, to contribute with their work to the development of the places that have welcomed them, to enrich the cultural life of local communities with their history and their vision of the world. The zero-sum game between the interests of native citizens and those of asylum seekers has been overcome, since with appropriate investments in personalised integration pathways, the refugees, like many immigrants, have also become a resource for the receiving societies.[36]

The success of a programme of this type depends on two factors. The first is the activation of positive approaches on the part of the public institutions, as well as within local civil societies, with their various voluntary organisations and associations, and with regard to companies, employers and the labour market. The second factor is the relationship with the beneficiaries of the project, more precisely the balance achieved between support and promotion of the autonomy of those admitted. Freeing refugees from dependence on welfare, without abandoning them to themselves, requires developing the capacity to provide significant support, insisting on the acquisition of knowledge and tools that can help the beneficiaries make progress in redesigning and rebuilding their lives in the new context despite the trauma and the initial displacement.

A dimension that has proved crucial is the tension between the expectations of refugees and the employment and social status opportunities that the market and local companies can offer. When the refugees have skills and qualifications, a serious problem is that they expect to be given greater consideration by the receiving society than that reserved for 'normal' economic migrants. Their expectations, however, collide with an environment that gives foreign immigrants almost exclusively low-level jobs and rarely recognises their qualifications, and which does not provide any particular favourable treatment for refugees. This is a problem also observed in national contexts with greater traditions of humanitarian hospitality and with fewer language barriers.[37] Since 2009, the recession has aggravated the situation, making it more difficult to find low-skilled jobs and causing a return to applications for assistance by immigrants who, after having entered the labour market, have since lost their jobs. The support provided by the 'Cittadini possibili' project is directed mainly at reducing the expectations of the beneficiaries and their adaptation to market opportunities. This is a more realistic approach, considering the constraints of the context and of the required timeline for job placements of those concerned. This problem of employment qualifications, however, remains a weakness in hospitality projects, and it highlights the need to involve economic actors, starting with the social economy, in identifying opportunities for refugees with appropriate skills.

Conclusions: an unresolved tension between fear and reception

In recent years, the international scenario of the experience of refugees has not offered many reasons to be optimistic. The protection accorded tends to become more selective, more fragmented into diverse categories and overall less generous. In this situation, the countries of Mediterranean Europe have found themselves in the front line, given their location on the southern border of the European Union, towards which most streams of asylum seekers will likely head in the coming years. The upheavals of recent years in the countries of North Africa and the Middle East seem to confirm these fears.

Within the area, Italy represents an important case, not only for its size and large migrant population (more than 4 million regular sojourners in 2011),[38] but also for the political positions it has taken in the last decade. It is perhaps the European country where the public anti-immigrant and anti-refugee rhetoric has reached its highest levels in recent years. It is the only case in which the representatives of a political formation that makes hostility towards immigrants a focal point of its political agenda for many years formed part of the government, in key positions of responsibility such as the Home Office. Regulations were tightened, and controversial agreements were reached with Libya in 2009. These agreements considerably reduced the flow of refugees until the new wave of arrivals by sea in the spring of 2011. For many years, Italy had no systematic policy for the reception of refugees. In recent years, three different visions of the identity of refugees have coexisted in Italy. The main, publicly declared view of refugees has confused them with illegal migrants and considered them a threat to national security or a burden on the welfare state.[39] The second, and more covert, vision adopted at micro-social level treats refugees like economic migrants, quietly absorbed by the labour market, and if necessary authorised to stay through the repeated regularisations of undocumented migrants. More recently, in the case of asylum seekers from the conflict in Libya, in Syria and from other African wars, a vision of refugees as victims has arisen, so that they have become the receivers of temporary and limited humanitarian protection, but to whom no clear commitment is made in terms of their being fully accepted and successfully integrated into Italian society.

Viewed more closely, however, Italy does not exhibit only attitudes of closure or indifference to those in need of humanitarian protection. Different actors express different representations of asylum seekers: national political authorities, followed by the most important mass media, have built up a rhetoric of invasion; economic actors have actually treated immigrants and refugees as a flexible and inexpensive resource for the lower strata of the labour market; the NGOs have tried to present them as human beings in need, sometimes stressing an image of them as victims; local political authorities have sometimes taken the opportunity to present a liberal image of themselves, as champions of human rights, presenting refugees as the beneficiaries of socially advanced projects and, in some cases, as a resource for local economies. In this framework, the projects involving NGOs and local authorities reveal that it is possible to design supporting programmes that combine reception, integration and empowerment by connecting different local institutions, social forces and organised solidarity networks. The tension between the public rhetoric of exclusion and local practices of inclusion, however, remains high, and it has been exacerbated by the recent coastal landings of more than 100,000 people (2011–October 2013). This is not only an Italian problem, but in the peninsula it reaches particularly high levels. The country has difficulty in realising that it is better than its fears suggest.

Notes

1 European Commission, 'Transposition of the Asylum Procedures Directive' (press release, MEMO/07/538, 3 December 2007) <http://europa.eu/rapid/pressReleases Action.do?reference=MEMO/07/538&format=HTML&aged=1&language=EN& guiLanguage=en> cited in Liza Schuster, 'Dublino II ed Eurodac: esame delle conseguenze (in)attese' (2009) 3 *Mondi Migranti* 37.

2 Stephen Castles, *New Issues in Refugee Research Working Paper No. 70: Environmental Change and Forced Migration: Making Sense of the Debate* (UNHCR, 2002); Chiara Marchetti, 'Blurring Boundaries: "Refugee" Definitions in Policies, Law and Social Discourse in Italy' (2007) 11 *Mediterranean Journal of Human Rights* 71; Roger Zetter, 'More Labels, Fewer Refugees: Remaking the Refugee Label in the Era of Globalization' (2007) 20 *Journal of Refugee Studies* 172–92.

3 Including: European Commission, EC Qualification Directive, Council Directive 2004/83/EC on minimum standards for the qualification and status of third country nationals or stateless persons as refugees or as persons who otherwise need international protection and the content of the protection granted, OJ 2004 No. L304/12; European Commission, EC Qualification Directive, Council Directive 2011/95/EU of the European Parliament and of the Council of 13 December 2011 on standards for the qualification of third-country nationals or stateless persons as beneficiaries of international protection, for a uniform status for refugees or for persons eligible for subsidiary protection, and for the content of the protection granted (recast), OJ 2011 No. L337/9; European Council, 6 February 2003, Council Directive 2003/9/EC of 27 January 2003 laying down minimum standards for the reception of asylum seekers,

OJ 2003 L31/18 ('Reception Conditions Directive') <http://eur-lex.europa. eu/LexUriServ/LexUriServ.do?uri=OJ:L:2003:031:0018:0025:EN:PDF>; Council of the European Union, 26 June 2013, Directive 2013/33/EU of the European Parliament and of the Council of 26 June 2013 laying down standards for the reception of applicants for international protection (recast), OJ 2013 L180/96 <http:// eur-lex.europa.eu/smartapi/cgi/sga_doc?smartapi!celexplus!prod!CELEX numdoc&lg=EN&numdoc=32013L0033>.

4 Convention relating to the Status of Refugees, Geneva, 28 July 1951, 1989 UNTS 137, supplemented by the Protocol relating to the Status of Refugees, 31 January 1967, 19 UST 6223, 6257 ('1951 Refugee Convention').

5 Maurizio Ambrosini, 'Immigration in Italy: Between Economic Acceptance and Political Rejection' (2013) 14 *Journal of International Migration and Integration* 175.

6 Maja Korac, 'Politiche, agency e dialogo interculturale. Esperienze dei rifugiati dei conflitti jugoslavi in Italia' (2009) 3 *Mondi migranti* 127.

7 UNHCR, 'Richiedenti asilo e rifugiati nel mondo e in Italia', in Caritas-Migrantes, *Immigrazione. Dossier statistico 2012* (Idos, 2012).

8 Chiara Marchetti, 'Rifugiati e richiedenti asilo: introduzione' (2009) 3 *Mondi migranti* 29.

9 UNHCR, above n. 7.

10 Anna Triandafyllidou and Maurizio Ambrosini, 'Irregular Immigration Control in Italy and Greece: Strong Fencing and Weak Gate-Keeping Serving the Labour Market' (2011) 13 *European Journal of Migration and Law* 251.

11 Paola Monzini, Ferruccio Pastore and Giuseppe Sciortino, 'L'Italia promessa. Geopolitica e dinamiche organizzative del traffico di migranti verso l'Italia, Roma', *CESPI (Centro Studi Politica Internazionale Working Papers) No. 9* (2004).

12 Friedrich Heckmann, 'Illegal Migration: What Can We Know and What Can We Explain? The Case of Germany' (2004) 38 *International Migration Review* 1103.

13 Anna Cento Bull, 'Addressing Contradictory Needs: The Lega Nord and Italian Immigration Policy' (2010) 44 *Patterns of Prejudice* 411.

14 Chiara Marchetti, 'The Expanded Border. Policies and Practices of Preventive Refoulement in Italy', in Martin Geiger and Antoine Pécoud (eds), *The New Politics of Mobility. Discourses, Actors and Practices of Migration Management* (Palgrave Macmillan, 2010).

15 See, e.g., Christina Boswell, 'Theorizing Migration Policy: Is There a Third Way?' (2007) 41 *International Migration Review* 75; cf. Martin Schain, 'The State Strikes Back: Immigration Policy in the European Union' (2009) 20 *European Journal of International Law* 93.

16 Laura Boldrini, *Tutti indietro* (Rizzoli, 2010).

17 The Secretary of State for Defence, La Russa, commented on the UNHCR thus: '[it is] one of those organizations that nobody cares about until the press decides that they are important' (Maria Antonietta Calabrò, 'Immigrati, affondo di La Russa: Il commissariato Onu non conta', *Corriere della Sera* (online), 17 May 2009 <http://archiv iostorico.corriere.it/2009/maggio/17/Immigrati_affondo_Russa_commissariato_ Onu_co_8_090517023.shtml>). The head of the Senate group of the governing PdL party, Gasparri, added on the following day: 'We do not understand who this Ms Boldrini is and in whose name she is speaking. To echo the words of my colleague La Russa, we do not care [what she says]' (Giuliano Gallo, 'Frattini sul caso Unhcr: sbaglia ma va rispettato. La Russa smorza i toni', *Corriere della Sera* (online), 18 May 2009), <http://archiviostorico.corriere.it/2009/maggio/18/Frattini_sul_caso_Unhcr_ sbaglia_co_8_090518020.shtml>).

18 Caritas-Migrantes, above, n. 7.

19 Lorenzo Fuccaro, 'Cento milioni per fermare lo "tsunami umano"', *Corriere della Sera* (online), 2 April 2011 <http://archiviostorico.corriere.it/2011/aprile/02/Cento_milioni_per_ fermare_tsunami_co_8_110402006.shtml>.

20 Anonymous, 'Bossi: "Immigrati föra da i ball". Berlusconi arriva sull'isola', *La Repubblica* (online), 29 March 2011 <http://www.repubblica.it/politica/2011/03/29/news/bossi_immigrati_fora_da_i_ball-14227475/?ref=search>.

21 Actually, many refugees who landed in Italy have managed to reach France, Germany, Sweden or other European countries. The political management of asylum by national states conflicts with Schengen agreements and open borders between the signature states.

22 Maurizio Ambrosini, *Irregular Immigration and Invisible Welfare* (Palgrave Macmillan, 2013).

23 Maja Korac, 'Cross-Ethnic Networks, Self-Reception System, and Functional Integration of Refugees from the Former Yugoslavia in Rome' (2001) 2 *Journal of International Migration and Integration* 1.

24 See Emilio Reyneri and Giovanna Fullin, 'Labour Market Penalties of New Immigrants in New and Old Receiving West European Countries' (2010) 49 *International Migration* 31.

25 Maja Korac, *Remaking Home: Reconstructing Life, Place and Identity in Rome and Amsterdam* (Berghahn, 2009).

26 Maurizio Ambrosini, 'Immigration in Italy: Between Economic Acceptance and Political Rejection' (2013) 14 *Journal of International Migration and Integration* 175.

27 UNHCR, above n. 7.

28 Ibid., 498.

29 Oliviero Forti and Santino Tornesi, 'Emergenza Nord Africa: verso un nuovo sistema d'accoglienza?' in Caritas-Migrantes, above n. 7, ch. 9, 140.

30 Hein de Haas and Nando Sigona, 'Migration and Revolution' (2012) 39 *Forced Migration Review* 4.

31 Chiara Marchetti, 'Assistiti o segregati? I grandi centri per richiedenti asilo in Italia' (2012) 41 *La società degli individui* 57.

32 Cittalia Foundation, *I volti dell'integrazione. Il ruolo delle comunità locali, dei cittadini e dei mass media nei processi di inclusione dei rifugiati in Italia* (ANCI, 2010).

33 ARCI, Caritas Italiana and CIR, *Un Team per l'integrazione: viaggio nel mondo dell'asilo* ('Team integrazione' Report Project, 2010).

34 Cittalia Foundation , above n. 32.

35 Michele Manocchi, *Richiedenti asilo e rifugiati politici. Percorsi di ricostruzione identitaria: il caso torinese* (FrancoAngeli, 2012).

36 Maurizio Ambrosini and Chiara Marchetti (eds), *Cittadini possibili. Un nuovo approccio all'accoglienza e all'integrazione dei rifugiati* (FrancoAngeli, 2008).

37 Alastair Ager and Alison Strang, 'Understanding Integration: A Conceptual Framework' (2008) 21 *Journal of Refugee Studies* 166.

38 Caritas-Migrantes, above n. 7.

39 Maurizio Ambrosini, '"We Are against a Multi-ethnic Society": Policies of Exclusion at the Urban Level in Italy' (2013) 36 *Ethnic and Racial Studies* 136.

13 Moving beyond protection space: developing a law of asylum in South-East Asia

Martin Jones[1]

Introduction

This book, and indeed much of the refugee law literature, takes as its starting point that the cornerstone of refugee identity is the legal and normative framework of protection enshrined in the Convention Relating to the Status of Refugees of 1951 ('1951 Refugee Convention').[2] As such, it explores 'how that identity has been made, remade and given social and political meaning'[3] by the institutions and processes which transform the 1951 Refugee Convention into lived reality. This starting point is deeply problematic when our examination turns to the meaning of refugeehood in South-East Asia, a region that has been traditionally understood as having 'rejected' the 1951 Refugee Convention.

This chapter examines the approach of UNHCR and other actors in the international refugee regime to refugee protection in South-East Asia and argues that, unlike in other regions, the approach relies less on the legal cornerstone of the 1951 Refugee Convention and more on a negotiated humanitarian 'protection space'.[4] It argues that such an approach privileges international interests, fora and UNHCR as the negotiator, and that it belies a developing bedrock of legal norms that offers protection to refugees in the region. It argues that there is a developing 'law of asylum' in the region based on human rights instruments and emerging national and regional institutions. In this way, it can be seen that the identity of refugees in the region is shifting from a person who is the object of the exercise of sovereign discretion as a 'humanitarian entrant', to one who is the bearer of rights.

The problem of refugee law in Asia

The Asian region is home to a majority of the world's refugees.[5] Notwithstanding the large numbers of refugees in Asia, the 'rejection' of refugee law by Asian states has become a touchstone of refugee law scholarship. Asia has been described as 'a region not known for its formal adherence to refugee law'.[6] Subregions of Asia have been characterised in similar terms: 'The whole of South Asia is devoid of any standards and norms on any dimension of refugee reception, determination and protection.'[7] While it is conceded that the policies of Asian states towards refugees have frequently met international standards, such achievements are seen as being built on an unstable foundation:

> Despite the low number of accessions to the Convention and Protocol, Southeast Asia has produced important developments in the treatment of refugees. However, because these developments usually have no basis in law and have been formed in response to specific refugee caseloads, the regime for the protection of refugees in Asia remains fragile.[8]

Davies provides the most elaborate exposition of the rejection hypothesis in a collection of work, including two articles,[9] a book chapter[10] and a book[11] on the topic. As the titles of her article and her book – respectively 'The Asian Rejection?' and *Legitimizing Rejection* – indicate, her work puts forward the Asian rejection hypothesis. Focusing on the South-East Asian subregion, Davies writes of 'the persistent rejection of international refugee law by the large majority of South East Asian states',[12] characterising Asian states as being reluctant to accept 'the promotion of refugee norms as part of becoming law-abiding members of the international community'[13] and ultimately asks, rhetorically, 'why most Southeast Asian states have not acceded to international refugee law?'.[14] In a similar vein, Chimni pointedly notes that 'it may come as a surprise to some that no country in South Asia is party to the 1951 Refugee Convention'.[15]

The so-called 'rejection' of refugee law by the states of Asia, and in particular South-East Asia, places UNHCR in an exceedingly difficult position. Since its inception, one of the primary roles of UNHCR has been '[p]romoting the conclusion and ratification of international conventions for the protection of refugees, supervising their application and proposing amendments thereto'.[16] As a result of the perceived 'rejection' of refugee law by the states of Asia, the operations of UNHCR in the region are characterised by an appeal to the value of 'humanitarianism' and its assumed role as negotiator of 'protection space'. Focusing on the subregion of South-East Asia, which in many respects is the archetype for the Asian 'rejection', this chapter seeks to interrogate one of the principal consequences of the rejection proposition: the adoption of a humanitarian approach which relies upon the political negotiation of 'protection space'.

This chapter outlines and critiques the protection space approach. It raises three concerns about the approach that are inherent in it: the international fora and international (UNHCR) negotiators that are privileged by it; its devaluation of the normative strength of obligations towards refugees; and its shifting of the underlying responsibility for the provision of refugee protection from the state to UNHCR. As an alternative, this chapter proposes a re-examination of the legal obligations of states towards refugees notwithstanding that they may not be party to the treaties of international refugee law, including the 1951 Refugee Convention. Even in a region as relatively deficient in human rights obligations as South-East Asia, there is an assemblage of obligations that provides a framework for the development of a 'law of asylum'. Such a focus on the legal foundation of refugee protection shifts the fora and actors involved in refugee protection and provides a revitalised role for human rights institutions, the legal profession and civil society. A corollary of this shift is that the underlying proposition that refugee law has been rejected is in need of re-examination, and along with it our conceptions of refugee identity.

This chapter proceeds by providing background to refugee protection in South-East Asia. It then sets out the elements of the 'humanitarian' or 'protection space' approach and provides a critique based upon the three reasons outlined above. It then proceeds to set out an alternative legalistic approach and assesses the extent to which a nascent law of asylum exists in the region. After revisiting the utility of the proposition that South-East Asia has rejected refugee law, the chapter concludes by trying to set out how a shift from humanitarianism ('protection space') to legalism ('law of asylum') might occur – a shift that is, in fact, already occurring.

For reasons of space, throughout this chapter the primary focus within South-East Asia will be Malaysia although reference will be made to examples from elsewhere in the region. Malaysia has been selected both because it provides a very explicit example of some of the perils of humanitarianism and because the legal environment of Malaysia is one of the most challenging in the region. In so far as the argument made in the chapter is true of refugee protection in Malaysia, it is true elsewhere in the region if only to the extent that Malaysia is representative of the region.[17]

Background to the South-East Asian region

The South-East Asian region is conventionally defined as collinear with the ten states of the Association of Southeast Asian States (ASEAN) regional organisation: the Philippines, Vietnam, Laos, Cambodia, Thailand, Malaysia, Brunei, Singapore, Burma and Indonesia.[18] Although ASEAN began as a small grouping of geopolitically fractious states, it is increasingly unifying, both politically and economically, an otherwise diverse region.[19]

Only two of the states of the region (Cambodia and the Philippines) are party to the 1951 Refugee Convention. Although Indonesia has signalled it anticipates becoming a party to the 1951 Refugee Convention, it has on several occasions postponed becoming a state party.[20] Only Thailand (since 1979) and the Philippines (since 1991) are members of UNHCR's Executive Committee. The states of the region are also less likely than those of other regions to be party to major international human rights treaties.

Although the exact number of refugees in the region is much contested, it is certainly home to at least 200,000 refugees.[21] Almost all of these refugees originate from within the region, with Myanmar being the country of origin for the overwhelming majority. The plight of Myanmarese refugees is a protracted refugee situation although such a characterisation should not obscure the change over time in the size, composition and distribution of the population. The most significant extra regional populations are from Afghanistan, Iraq, Sri Lanka and various African states.[22] In the past two years, refugees from the conflict in Syria have also begun to appear in the region. The region is also a transit point for refugees with the most notable example of this being largely extra-regional refugees travelling by boat to Australia. Refugees in transit through the region have increasingly drawn the attention of policy makers within and outside of the region.[23]

There are also significant stateless and internally displaced populations in the region. The former often overlaps with the refugee population and includes the Rohingya of Bangladesh and Myanmar; members of the various hill tribes of the Indochinese peninsula; and the Filipinos of East Malaysia.[24] The latter include the significant populations of internally displaced persons in Myanmar, Indonesia and the Philippines.[25]

Many of the refugees and stateless persons reside in border regions or contested territories; their presence in these areas often exacerbates tensions between neighbouring states. While refugee camps persist, particularly in Thailand, and remain the archetype to the general public of refugee protection in the region, there are increasingly large numbers of self-settled urban refugees.

Refugee protection in South-East Asia as the negotiation of 'protection space'

The determination of the obligations towards refugees owed by a state is, in a word, complicated. This is nowhere else truer than in South-East Asia. As noted earlier, most of the states of the region have not expressed a legally binding commitment to the international treaties protecting refugees. In the absence of such commitments, refugee protection in the region is often understood as negotiated: a politically contested commodity that is expressed as a 'humanitarian' gesture towards refugees in need or, more recently and now much more commonly articulated, as creating 'protection space' for refugees. This section of this chapter will first set out what is meant by the 'protection space' approach and then, in turn, flesh out a critique.

The protection space approach in South-East Asia and elsewhere

The 'protection space' approach has a contested etymology, though there is a general consensus that it derives from the related, though similarly etymologically disputed, term of 'humanitarian space'.[26] Some trace the roots of the latter to 'éspace humanitaire' coined by Médecins Sans Frontières (MSF) president Rony Brauman, who described it in the mid-1990s as 'a space of freedom in which we are free to evaluate needs, free to monitor the distribution and use of relief goods, and free to have a dialogue with the people'.[27] Others attribute the term to Latin American activists 'who have used their presence to create and gradually expand [humanitarian] "space" in areas previously closed off to agencies, through confidence-building measures which have involved local authorities, local military commanders and the local population'.[28] There is also a legal etymology that can be traced to international humanitarian law and is particular to the activities of the Red Cross movement.[29]

UNHCR's early usage of the term 'protection space' is most in keeping with the aforementioned operational etymology of the term (linked to MSF and other humanitarian organisations) as opposed to the normative or legal usage.[30] One of the earliest usages by UNHCR was in its description of its new 'comprehensive approach'[31] to refugee protection in the early 1990s. It described 'humanitarian space' in relation to its then recent successes in Latin America as being the discussion of refugee protection 'within a sensitive political dialogue at both the regional and national levels'.[32] As the subsequent General Assembly resolution endorsing a comprehensive approach states, the creation of humanitarian space is achieved by 'consulting with states' concerning 'possibilities for additional measures and initiatives'.[33] More recently, Erika Feller has said the following about humanitarian space, the related concept of 'protection space' and UNHCR's understanding of the terms:

> For UNHCR, the concept of humanitarian space is closely linked to the related notion of protection space, which we understand to equate with an environment sympathetic to international protection principles and enabling their implementation to the benefit of all those entitled to protection.[34]

The use of the term 'protection space' is of more recent origin than humanitarian space, with public usage by UNHCR no earlier than the turn of the millennium.[35] Notwithstanding its recent provenance, the use of protection space as a term is now relatively common – though far from widespread – with its use in more than 100 different UNHCR documents since 2001. It is most prominent in UNHCR's long awaited 'urban policy', which devotes an entire section to 'protection space'.[36] What is particularly interesting about its usage is that it occurs most frequently in the country operations plans of UNHCR in states that are not a party to the 1951 Refugee Convention, most notably in South-East Asia and also in the Middle East.[37]

The understanding of UNHCR's obligations towards refugees as the negotiation of protection space is very explicit in the operational reports and policy evaluations of UNHCR concerning the Asian region. Common usage of the term in describing UNHCR's operations in Asia dates back to shortly after the term was coined. While there is no institutional definition of the term, from UNHCR's usage, various components of the meaning of 'protection space' can be discerned.[38] 'Protection space' as employed by UNHCR is a variable, negotiated and operationally focused state of affairs. The following explanation of the definition provides a brief sketch of the usage of 'protection space' in the South-East Asian context; each element of the definition will be further elaborated upon in the following critique of its use as an approach to refugee protection in the region.

First, protection space is variable over time and between contexts. Protection space both expands and contracts. Thus, in Malaysia, UNHCR noted that the installation of Najib Abdul Razak as Prime Minister in April 2009 brought with it '[a] sense of openness on the part of the new Government' and 'provided an opportunity to expand the boundaries of the protection space in the country'.[39] Conversely, more recently in Thailand, UNHCR has been challenged by 'a marked erosion of the protection space for all groups of concern over the past two years'.[40]

Second, protection space is pragmatic not normative; it does not have 'a legal definition' and rather simply describes the ease of UNHCR's operations on behalf of refugees.[41] Thus, protection space is an environment 'within which the prospect of providing protection is optimized'[42] or, as stated in UNHCR's urban policy, 'it is a concept employed by the Office to denote the extent to which a conducive environment exists'.[43]

Third, protection space is the result of negotiation. UNHCR's 2007 plan for Malaysia describes the task as follows:

> In terms of the overall implementation strategy, UNHCR will need to main-
> tain a process of interactive participation with the Malaysian Government, at
> different levels, as well as its implementing, operational and other partners
> in order to promote a shared vision in addressing the needs of, and durable
> solutions for, the various refugee and stateless groups in Malaysia.[44]

Even more recently, similar language can be found in UNHCR's regional plan for South-East Asia:

> In South-East Asia, UNHCR will engage relevant actors to support policy
> changes aimed at finding durable solutions for refugees and increasing
> protection space.[45]

Similar usage of the term 'protection space' to describe UNHCR's approach can be found in all the operational plans for the region and in many of the general policy documents originating in the region. Up until very recently, only when UNHCR discusses its work in the Middle East did it show a similarly high level of usage of the protection space approach.[46]

Finally, there is a slightly different usage of the term that bears mentioning. Although much of the usage of the term speaks of the negotiation of protection space as UNHCR's project in a particular state, there is also use of the term to describe the outcomes (read failure) of negotiations. In this respect the term has an insidious usage as a euphemism for the violation of refugee rights. In this sense, 'shrinking protection space' is code for refugees suffering violations of their rights, including having been arbitrarily arrested, indefinitely imprisoned and *refouled* to persecution. For example, in a speech in 2010, the term 'shrinking protection space' was used to refer to events in South-East Asia – where within the six weeks previously 4,000 Hmong had been *refouled* to Laos and 20 Uigurs had been *refouled* to China.[17] It is also not a coincidence that the term protection space, as in 'the shrinking of protection space in Asia', is usually employed in the passive voice. State accountability – and also UNHCR accountability – can often be lost in the phrasing.

First critique of the protection space approach: privileging of international actors, fora and interests

The adoption of the language of 'protection space' to describe the task to be performed in countries that have not signed the 1951 Refugee Convention raises concerns based upon how it privileges international interests, fora and UNHCR as the negotiator; devalues the normative strength of obligations towards refugees; and allows the underlying responsibility for the provision of refugee protection to drift from the state to UNHCR. This is not to say that the negotiation of protection space does not achieve at least short-term results; rather it is to suggest that notwithstanding any results which are achieved there are structural concerns which bias the types of short-term results which are achieved and which undermine the achievement of long-term results.

The first issue raised by the protection space approach is, as its etymology suggests, that it privileges international actors, including UNHCR, as the negotiators of protection space. This necessarily means that it also privileges the fora in which these actors operate and their interests.

With respect to the privileging of international actors, it is significant that all of UNHCR's usage of the term concerns its own negotiation of protection space. Notwithstanding the early and somewhat dissonant Latin American usage noted earlier, protection space is never negotiated by regional actors, other states, civil society or refugees themselves. This is not to suggest that in a revised protection space approach that this would be impossible but rather to highlight that in its current usage protection space is the negotiated outcome achieved by the international community, and in particular by UNHCR. Protection space is negotiated with states, involves a political discussion, and results in typically ad hoc arrangements. This brokered approach relies upon a broker – entrenching and reinforcing the institutional mandate of UNHCR.

With respect to the privileging of international fora, the negotiation of protection space occurs during UNHCR–state dialogues. These typically occur in dialogues (both formal and informal) between in-country UNHCR international staff and government officials or in discussions on the sidelines of more formalised consultations such as at the meetings of the Executive Committee of the High Commissioner's Programme (ExCom) or during the present year's celebrations of the 60th anniversary of the 1951 Refugee Convention. The negotiations are often private, privilege actors able to operate in these fora, and are often only tangentially concerned with the protection issues at hand; the accords about protection space can often be only deduced indirectly and confirmed unofficially. Both the processes and the results of negotiations in these fora are opaque. With respect to the privileging of international interests, it is significant that the early usage of humanitarian space concerned negotiating literal space in which international NGOs such as MSF could operate during times of conflict. Thus when UNHCR speaks of protection space, it speaks of the needs (and the security) of its staff. UNHCR in Malaysia uses it to describe their fear that their office will be closed by the government if it performs various types of activities. As stated in UNHCR's recent 'urban policy':

> The extent to which 'protection space' exists in a refugee situation can also be assessed in terms of the circumstances in which UNHCR and its humanitarian partners are able to work. In simple terms, the protection space can be regarded as relatively broad in situations where the Office has few restrictions placed upon its movements and activities, is able to make direct contact with refugees, has the freedom to choose its own implementing partners and enjoys a constructive dialogue with both national or municipal authorities.[48]

Not surprisingly, the needs of the negotiators of protection space are prominent: the need for physical space from which to operate, the need for the means of entrance and egress to the locations in which assistance is to be offered, and the need for the safety of their staff and the security of their possessions. These needs are neither inconsequential nor are they without foundation in state obligation in the case of the needs of UNHCR. The Charter of the UN, the Statute of UNHCR and the various GA resolutions which authorise its operations all call on – require – states to cooperate with UNHCR in the fulfilment of its mandate. However, while 'protection space' for UNHCR is important it is neither a necessary nor a sufficient condition for the enjoyment of rights by refugees. As stated by Abild, drawing upon Foucault's arguments about discursive power, with respect to humanitarian space

> by characterizing [it] solely as an operating environment for humanitarian agencies, it is these agencies themselves who end up controlling the understanding of this space. Agencies often hold information relating to a given situation and suggest how it should be solved, they do the actual operations and they evaluate them.[49]

As UNHCR itself points out, ultimately only states can truly redeem the rights of refugees and this aspect of the term shifts the focus away from that singular necessary and sufficient condition.

The protection space approach necessarily privileges institutional interests and, as a direct result, sidelines the rights of refugees. The rights of refugees are not always absent, as for example in the urban refugee policy where protection space is defined in terms of refugees enjoying various rights,[50] but they are subsidiary to the demands of the institutions through which, and the fora in which, the negotiation occurs.

Second critique of the protection space approach: undermining of the normative strength of obligations towards refugees of both states and UNHCR

As noted in the first critique, protection space is negotiated. These negotiations also make, implicitly, the granting or the refusal of protection space, a matter of state discretion. As such, the negotiations undermine the normative strength of obligations towards refugees owed by both the states with which UNHCR enters negotiations – and even those owed by UNHCR itself.

As will be further developed later, notwithstanding that most states in the region have not become party to the 1951 Refugee Convention, they nonetheless have obligations towards refugees. The negotiated approach of UNHCR risks undermining the normative strength of these obligations and makes them contingent upon negotiated benefits. For example, the 'strategic' use of resettlement to forestall *refoulement* makes a state's (arguably peremptory and increasingly accepted as customary)[51] obligations not to *refoule* refugees contingent upon the resettlement of refugees from its territory by other states as brokered by UNHCR. The linkage between compliance with obligations and other benefits has been made explicit in the cases of Malaysia and Indonesia. In the former case, the Malaysian response to the recent marine arrival in the region of numerous Rohingya has been met with explicit threats of 'push-backs' unless resettlement is provided.[52] Similarly, in a less pointed way, Indonesia's recent regulation which legalises asylum seekers puts a time limit on its obligation of *non-refoulement* – implicitly making it contingent upon resettlement of legalised refugees to other states within a reasonable period.

Arguably the coerced performance of obligations by states will always result in, at least initially, incomplete performance; even the 'soft' coercion of negotiated protection space will have this drawback.[53] However, it is less the incomplete performance of obligation that is concerning and more the way in which the negotiations legitimise it. Implicit in these negotiations is most often the understanding that UNHCR will not critique the incomplete performance of obligations by the state. In neither of the former examples from Indonesia and Malaysia, has UNHCR publicly criticised the shortcomings of the policies adopted by the respective governments.[54] In this respect, this critique of the protection spaces approach is closely related to the earlier critique that it privileged particular fora, marked by opaque process and not publicly known outcomes.

But if the brokering process of negotiations risks undermining state obligation, it poses an even greater risk to the obligations of UNHCR. According to the terms of its statute and its various operational directives, UNHCR has various legal obligations towards refugees. The process of negotiating protection space risks UNHCR 'agreeing' to a negotiated outcome that prevents it from fulfilling these obligations.

An extremely troubling example of the conflict between negotiated agreement and obligation concerns UNHCR's operations in Malaysia. From 2004 to 2008,

UNHCR maintained a count of between 35,000 to 47,000 asylum seekers and refugees in Peninsular Malaysia.[55] Notwithstanding that refugees in Malaysia benefited (and continue to benefit) from a significant resettlement operation, at the end of every year the number of refugees remained almost completely constant: with the number of refugees being resettled being, over time, equivalent to those newly registered. UNHCR effectively 'capped' its recognition of refugees in Malaysia at 47,000.[56] This decision was reached notwithstanding a plethora of UNHCR internal guidance, public statements by the High Commissioner, and obligations under its statute to the contrary. Notwithstanding this conflict with obligations, this cap was also consistent with the interests of the local UNHCR office which was grossly under-resourced to deal with the 'true' number of refugees in Malaysia and with the hostility of the Malaysian government of the period towards refugees and other 'illegal migrants'. Although this policy has been revised after increasingly vocal criticism by local civil society, refugees in Peninsular Malaysia continue to complain that refugee registration (which has now risen to around 100,000)[57] has occurred for only a minority of refugees in Malaysia.[58] The cap represented a tacit and agreed – even if likely never explicitly stated – understanding between the Malaysian government and UNHCR of the limit on protection in Malaysia for refugees.

During the 'capped' period, UNHCR did not dispute the existence of the 'true' population of (largely unregistered) refugees; rather, its negotiated cap compelled it to deny or otherwise limit its obligation for the registration of refugees. This is an example of the process of negotiations, and the compromise it entails, undermining the normative strength of obligations.

Third critique of the protection space approach: shifting of the underlying responsibility for the provision of refugee protection from the state to UNHCR

The third critique of the protection space approach is that it has shifted the underlying responsibility for the protection of refugees from states to UNHCR. As the negotiator for refugee protection, UNHCR implicitly takes on an operational obligation to the provision of various forms of support to refugees, including schooling, healthcare and basic subsistence financial support. While all of these obligations directly benefit refugees, none of them is explicitly referenced in UNHCR's founding statute.[59]

Examples of this problem are more difficult to locate, in part because the shift is much more subtle and in part because UNHCR's operational role is so well established.[60] Civil society advocates in the Asia Pacific region note the reluctance of UNHCR to make more than a pro forma push for ratification by the states of South-East Asia and its reluctance to push for the transfer of refugee status determination responsibilities to the states of the region.[61]

This shift has been noted elsewhere and has not always been seen as a negative development.[62] However, even such commentators suggest that this is an approach of 'last resort'.[63]

An alternative 'legalistic' approach in South-East Asia

If the argument is that the protection space approach has problems embedded within it, then the question becomes: what is the alternative? Necessity is the primary defence of negotiated protection space, its proponents would argue. Its utility therefore hinges on the existence of (or lack thereof) an alternative.

The alternative that I will suggest is to shift the debate and analysis from the terrain of negotiated humanitarian space to legal obligations (and access to justice). Now, as previously acknowledged, these are terms not completely absent from some of the usage of 'protection space', nor are they new concepts to advocates for refugee rights. However, by shifting the stated approach to these terms, even in a landscape seen as hostile to both concepts, it will be my argument that refugee protection in regions such as South-East Asia becomes disencumbered from the constraints associated with a protection space approach.

A precondition for my argument is the existence of relevant legal obligations in the group of states which are our focus, the states of South-East Asia. As noted previously, only two (and possibly soon three) of the states in question have ratified the 1951 Refugee Convention. While the 1951 Refugee Convention is often described as the cornerstone of international refugee law, it is not the only source of international legal obligation towards refugees. This part of the chapter will set out an alternate legal framework for the protection of refugees in the region and the preconditions for the relevance of this framework.

An alternate legalistic approach: the framework of a 'law of asylum'

There are both international and domestic legal obligations relevant to refugee protection in the region. The former international legal obligations include both treaty obligations under various human rights treaties concerning various subsets of migrants (if not refugees, per se) and customary obligations. The latter domestic legal obligations include constitutional, statutory and common law or customary obligations. While the assemblage of a law of asylum may be validly criticised as 'an inadequate response to the scale of the problem',[61] it nonetheless provides a mandatory framework for the protection of refugees even in a region as underdeveloped in terms of human rights obligations as South-East Asia.

There is an international legal framework for the protection of refugees in the region notwithstanding that most states are not party to the 1951 Refugee Convention. While the 1951 Refugee Convention has been described as the 'cornerstone' of international refugee law, it is not the exclusive source of state obligations towards refugees. International human rights law guarantees refugees various rights. In addition, international labour law, customary international law and recent international developments to combat transnational crime[65] supplement international human rights law to provide a collection of rights almost equivalent to those provided by international refugee law. This alternate international legal framework of protection can be understood as a 'law of asylum' particularly as it guarantees rights to individuals other than refugees.

International legal obligations towards refugees arise from both other conventional international law provisions and customary international law. With respect to the former, the major human rights treaties guarantee many of the civil and political rights provided in the 1951 Refugee Convention. Furthermore, most of the civil and political rights provided in the 1951 Refugee Convention are subject to reservation – a possibility that is frequently acted upon.[66] Of the rights of the 1951 Refugee Convention, only a handful is not found explicitly in the other major international human rights treaties. The exceptions include the exemptions from reciprocity and exceptional measures; administrative assistance; identity and travel papers; fiscal charges. The majority of these rights are seldom invoked by refugees. They also include non-punishment for illegal entry; and non-*refoulement*, which are very significant to the protection of refugees. However, even these rights have support in other human rights treaties. The Human Rights Committee has interpreted the right to life and prohibition on torture to prohibit certain types of *refoulement*.[67] Furthermore, Article 3 of the Convention Against Torture and Other Cruel, Inhuman or Degrading Treatment or Punishment[68] of 1984 prohibits *refoulement* to torture. As the jurisprudence and policy developments in Hong Kong since the case of *Prabakhar*[69] have shown, Article 3 of the CAT provides refugees with a significant amount of protection against *refoulement*. Non-punishment for illegal entry is slightly more difficult and will be the subject of further discussion below.

Needless to say, the domestic legal obligations of states towards refugees vary from state to state. In some states of the region, advocates have argued convincingly that nearly all of the obligations of the state towards refugees in the 1951 Refugee Convention can be found in existing domestic law.[70] In other states, the lack of constitutional or statutory attention makes the assemblage of the law of asylum much weaker.

As the term 'assemblage' suggests, the strength and extent of the law of asylum in each state of the region will vary and it is beyond the scope of this chapter to exhaustively detail all of the assemblages other than to briefly take the example of punishment for irregular entry and explore the extent to which the substance of the obligation can be mapped to obligations other than that found in the 1951 Refugee Convention.

The prohibition on punishment for irregular entry is, in many respects, the epitome of Hathaway's note that there is a category of rights in the 1951 Refugee Convention that are specific to refugees.[71] It is suggested that such a right would arguably be the hardest to locate elsewhere because of this characteristic. However, recent legislation and case law in Malaysia suggests that the principle of non-punishment (if not non-liability) can be found within the principles of local administrative and common law. With respect to the former, the Attorney General's Chambers has issued a directive that registered refugees should neither be convicted nor punished for irregular entry into Malaysia.[72] With respect to the latter, recent jurisprudence applied domestic common-law principles that at least some refugees should not be punished for irregular entry:

> This court is therefore of the firm opinion that asylum seekers and refugees, if they have not committed acts of violence or brutality or are habitual offenders or have threatened our public order, should not be punished with whipping.[73]

While this application of common-law principles provides incomplete protection, it nonetheless is remarkable in an environment where refugees are routinely convicted and ordered whipped by lower court (sessions court) judges.

Similar judgments have been issued by Malaysian courts with respect to the other area of refugee rights most incomplete in international human rights instruments and domestic frameworks: the right to work. The Malaysian Court of Appeal in the matter of *Sukatno v. Lee Seng Kee & another* recently recognised the ability of an irregular migrant (albeit not a refugee) to claim damages for the loss of future earnings as a result of a motor vehicle accident, provided his earnings could be legitimised in law.[74]

I have focused the discussion on 'difficult' rights to incorporate into the assemblage of the law of asylum. At the very least, the evidence indicates that there is the potential for an, albeit incomplete, law of asylum even in the relatively hostile to human rights legal environment of South-East Asia. In this respect, the focus on Malaysia is apt for the region. It is party to only two international human rights treaties, the Palermo Convention and its protocols, and 14 of the International Labour Organization's conventions.[75] Constructing a law of asylum to protect refugees in Malaysia is a difficult task that can never be wholly satisfactory.

Notwithstanding this difficulty, the discussion of the law of asylum has both resonances in the situation of and implications for the broader Asian region. Similar developments have been occurring elsewhere in the broader region. As a result of a series of litigation victories by refugee advocates, Hong Kong SAR has introduced a formal administrative screening process for individuals fearing *refoulement* to torture and is moving towards a unified system of risk assessment, including refugee status determination; other litigation has resulted in restrictions on detention and the provision of financial support to indigent asylum seekers. In South Korea and Japan, there is a growing body of jurisprudence that increasingly makes reference to international and comparative legal sources. The turn to an alternate legalistic approach is not to deny the political realities of operationally providing protection to refugees in the region. As Hathaway states, legalism 'does not take anything away from the resort to the political process as one mechanism to promote respect for human dignity', rather it simply ensures that 'at least in some circumstances a rule based alternative can be invoked in support of human rights'.[76]

An alternate legalistic approach: the preconditions for the relevance of this framework

The existence of obligations under the law of asylum approach is insufficient to provide a way forward for the protection of refugees. In addition to the normative basis for argument on behalf of refugees, fora and processes for the enforcement of these obligations is required. The law of asylum approach relies upon a set of largely domestic institutions and understandings concerning the role of legal obligations. In short, the law of asylum approach relies upon the rule of law and access to justice in the states of South-East Asia.

The states of ASEAN enjoy the rule of law to varying extent. Myanmar, Vietnam, Laos and Cambodia have all been criticised by local and regional actors and by international human rights institutions for their lack of the rule of law. However, the main hosts of refugees in the region (Malaysia, Thailand and Indonesia) provide a somewhat different picture. Although the rule of law, including principally judicial independence, is under challenge in all three states, as implied previously in the citation of Malaysian jurisprudence, both the courts and the legal professions in all three states have a capacity to argue and adjudicate claims concerning obligations owed to refugees.

Developing a law of asylum in South-East Asia

The project of shifting the approach to the development of a law of asylum from one in which protection space is negotiated would return UNHCR to a project that has long been part of its mandate. In 1999, Erika Feller encouraged the judges of Asia to get involved in the development of protection in the region:

> UNHCR sees an urgent need to revitalise the legal principles and ethical values that underpin asylum and refugee protection. The law in this area cannot remain static if it is to meet the contemporary needs of forcibly displaced people, it must be allowed constantly to evolve. By the same token, this process of evolution must remain principled and true to its real object and purpose – the protection of people. It is here that the Judiciary and Bar in each country will have a key role to play.[77]

Nor would it be a project incompatible with wider trends in the region. In recent years, South-East Asia has seen the rapid development of regional human rights institutions. ASEAN now has a working human rights institution: the ASEAN Intergovernmental Commission on Human Rights (AICHR). While the AICHR has a much narrower mandate and fewer powers than other regional human rights bodies, its very existence marks a milestone in the region. Furthermore, amongst its first charges is the investigation of migration, including asylum seeking populations. Members of the AICHR have also expressed an interest in investigating the issue of statelessness in the region, which as noted earlier has a significant overlap with refugee populations in the region.

Furthermore, at a national level, many of the states of the region have developed national human rights institutions (NHRIs), which meet international standards.[78] There have also been recent efforts to cooperate in the investigation of issues concerning refugees, including on the topic of the arbitrary arrest and indefinite detention of refugees. Both the growing number of and stronger links between human rights institutions in the region are developments that must be incorporated into strategies for refugee protection. The building of capacity by lawyers and judges on refugee law and by lawyers on the litigation of a law of asylum is a project that has already begun in the region.[79]

Finally, in closing, the larger context of the practice of negotiating protection space cannot be avoided. The difficulties which lead to the negotiation of protection space can be directly attributed to the reality that capacities and obligations with respect to the protection of refugees are not distributed equally; developed nations of the North accept relatively small asylum burdens while most refugees remain in the Global South. As Amy Slaughter and Jeff Crisp explain, host governments in the Global South often argue 'that they would only admit and refrain from *refoulement* of refugees if the needs of such populations were fully met by the international community'.[80]

However, the solution to this fundamental problem is not to negotiate (necessarily downward and ad infinitum) the protection of refugees. Rather, it is to support the development of local standards and capacities that ensure that the refugees in all situations, even in the non-signatory states of South-East Asia, are afforded their rights. This new approach does not foreclose a role for UNHCR; indeed, the active participation of UNHCR in developing a law of asylum is needed. Its vast experience gained in developing refugee law provides it with an organisational expertise and experience-base that is unparalleled. Thus, the project for the present and future is to constantly challenge the rejection of refugee law by the states of Asia and to engage them in a manner that develops a law of asylum in the region that offers refugees within the states of the region an opportunity to live their lives with greater dignity.

Notes

1 The author would like to thank the participants in the workshop at Prato, and especially the editors of this volume, for their comments and feedback on earlier versions of this chapter.
2 Convention relating to the Status of Refugees, Geneva, 28 July 1951, 1989 UNTS 137, supplemented by the Protocol relating to the Status of Refugees, 31 January 1967, 19 UST 6223, 6257 ('1951 Refugee Convention').
3 This phrase is taken from Roger Zetter's chapter in this volume (see Chapter 2).
4 The Middle East is perhaps the exception to this proposition and most analogous to South-East Asia. However, even in the Middle East, major states of asylum, including Turkey, Iran, Egypt and, increasingly, Israel, are party to the 1951 Refugee Convention.
5 Of the world's 8.8 million 4.4 million live in the UN-defined region of 'Asia', a vast region stretching from Turkey eastward but excluding the states of Australia and the Pacific (Oceania). If UNHCR regional bureaux are used, then 2.7 million refugees live

in 'Asia and the Pacific' (this time including Oceania, with the remainder of the 'Asian' refugees being allocated to the bureau responsible for the Middle East and North Africa).

6 Pia Oberoi, 'Regional Initiatives on Refugee Protection in South Asia' (1999) 11 *International Journal of Refugee Law* 193, 193.

7 Prabodh Saxena, 'Creating Legal Space for Refugees in India: The Milestones Crossed and the Roadmap for the Future' (2007) 19 *International Journal of Refugee Law* 246, 246 (quote taken from abstract). In fairness to Saxena, he follows this absolute observation with an analysis of the progress that India has made in establishing norms and standards.

8 Fernando Chang-Muy, 'International Refugee Law in Asia' (1991–1992) 24 *New York University Journal of International Law and Policy* 1171, 1177.

9 Sara Davies, 'The Asian Rejection? International Refugee Law in Asia' (2006) 52 *Australian Journal of Politics and History* 562.

10 Sara Davies, 'Seeking Security for Refugees', in Anthony Burke and Matt Macdonald (eds), *Critical Security in the Asia Pacific* (Manchester University Press, 2007), 152.

11 Sara Davies, *Legitimising Rejection: International Refugee Law in Southeast Asia* (Martinus Nijhoff, 2008).

12 Ibid., 5.

13 Sara Davies, 'Redundant or Essential? How Politics Shaped the Outcome of the 1967 Protocol' (2007) 19 *International Journal of Refugee Law* 703, 718.

14 Davies, above n. 11, 5–6.

15 B. S. Chimni, 'The Birth of a 'Discipline': From Refugee to Forced Migration Studies' (2009) 22 *Journal of Refugee Studies* 11, 16. In the same article, Chimni also critiques the 'legal fetishism' of centring refugee protection on legal categories; this is a critique to which we will return below.

16 UNHCR Statute, para. 8(a). See also the provisions of Article 35 of the 1951 Refugee Convention, which recognises the UNHCR's role in 'supervising the application of the provisions of this Convention'.

17 This proposition is not uncontroversial. Malaysia is a democratic, post-colonial, largely common-law jurisdiction with a relatively strong tradition of the rule of law and a well-developed legal profession. At the opposite end of the spectrum of legal and political environments in the region, Vietnam is an autocratic, communist jurisdiction with no recent tradition of the rule of law and a very weak legal profession. Having said this, the overwhelming majority (>95 per cent) of refugees in the region are hosted by, in addition to Malaysia, the Philippines, Thailand and Indonesia all of which arguably bear more similarity to Malaysia than Vietnam. The extent to which the legal environments of ASEAN (or other groups of Asian) states can be understood as a 'region' – and compared – to each other is well addressed in Penelope Nicholson and Sarah Biddulph (eds), *Examining Practice, Interrogating Theory: Comparative Legal Studies in Asia* (Martinus Nijhoff, 2008). See also the (at times self-serving) report of ASEAN's Human Rights Resource Center entitled *Rule of Law for Human Rights in the ASEAN Region* (HRRC, May 2011) which concludes that there is an 'increasing' convergence by states in the region with respect to the rule of law and other features of the legal environment relevant to human rights protection.

18 At least two other states may claim membership in an 'expanded' notion of South-East Asia: East Timor and Papua New Guinea. The former is currently pursuing admission to ASEAN (with a formal application filed in March 2011). The latter has at least a geographic claim to being a part of the region, sharing the island of New Guinea with Indonesia (though it has been relegated to an 'observer' to ASEAN since 1976).

19 ASEAN began as a grouping of Malaysia, Singapore, the Philippines, Thailand and Indonesia. At the time of its founding, fears of communist influence in the region were

at their peak, border disputes plagued three of its members and there were competing hopes for ASEAN with respect to influencing the status of Indonesia as the region's hegemon. See Rodolfo Severino, 'ASEAN beyond Forty: Towards Political and Economic Integration' (2007) 29 *Contemporary Southeast Asia: A Journal of International and Strategic Affairs* 406.

20 Indonesia's National Plan of Action of Human Rights (2004–9) listed the 1951 Refugee Convention and 1967 Protocol Relating to the Status of Refugees as international human rights instruments to which Indonesia would accede.

21 Based upon UNHCR statistics, Thailand (with 105,000) and Malaysia (with 94,400) are the principal hosts of refugees in the region. Vietnam has a shrinking number (2,357) of Cambodian refugees and Indonesia has 798 refugees (but a growing number of asylum seekers). The other states in the region have fewer than 200 recognised refugees each. Many NGOs and refugee CBOs allege that the numbers of refugees recognised by the UNHCR in both Thailand and Malaysia grossly underestimate the size of the refugee populations in both states.

22 None of these extra-regional refugees meets the UNHCR's threshold of 5,000 refugees from a country of origin in a single state to merit statistical reporting.

23 Australia has recently implemented a policy of expelling refugees who arrive by boat to Malaysia, various Pacific Islands and Papua New Guinea. The discussion of refugee protection in the region has increasingly been focused on the development of a 'regional protection framework' which would, not coincidentally, serve to reduce the number of refugees in transit to Australia (and to allow for easier expulsion back to the region of these refugees by Australia).

24 The Rohingya include both de jure and de facto stateless individuals. The other two populations are largely de facto stateless.

25 The number of IDPs in Myanmar and Indonesia is estimated by the Internal Displacement Monitoring Centre as, respectively, about 500,000 and 200,000. There are small IDP populations in Lao and the Philippines.

26 Although not discussed in this chapter for reasons of space, an alternate etymology would derive protection space from the term 'asylum space', a term used from the 1990s onwards mainly in the European context to describe the creation of what would later be termed the Common European Asylum Policy. The term 'asylum space' is occasionally used as a synonym for protection space in UNHCR documents' discussions of South-East Asia (see for example its use in *UNHCR Global Report 2009* (UNHCR, June 2010), 'Thailand', at 239).

27 Anne Evans Barnes, 'New Issues in Refugee Research, Research Paper 167: Realizing protection space for Iraqi refugees: UNHCR in Syria, Jordan and Lebanon' (UNHCR, January 2009), 11.

28 Report of the Representative of the Secretary-General, Mr Francis M. Deng, submitted pursuant to Commission on Human Rights Resolutions 1993/95 and 1994/68, UN Document E/CN.4/1995/50 (2 February 1995), [231]. Erik Abild in his 'New Issues in Refugee Research: Research Paper 184: Creating Humanitarian Space: a Case Study of Somalia' (UNHCR, December 2009), 2, cites Gil Loescher as authoring the first academic usage of 'humanitarian space' in discussion of refugee protection in Latin America in his 'Working Paper 86: Humanitarianism and Politics in Central America' (Kellogg Institute for International Studies, University of Notre Dame, 1986).

29 For example, relief action – 'which is humanitarian and impartial in character and conducted without any adverse distinction' – may be undertaken pursuant to Article 70(1) of the 1977 Additional Protocol I and Article 18(2) of the 1977 Additional Protocol II.

30 The tension between the operational and normative/legal usage of humanitarian space will be returned to and, it will be suggested, provides hope for its rehabilitation.

31 See the October 1993 Excom A/AC.96/821, para. 19(n) and subsequent General Assembly Res. 48/116.

32 UNHCR, *Comprehensive and Regional Approaches to Refugee Problems*, UN Document EC/1994/SCP/CRP. 3 (3 May 1994).

33 Para. 15 of UNGA Res. 48/116.

34 Erika Feller, 'Protecting people in conflict and crisis – responding to the challenges of a changing world' (opening address at the Humanitarian Space conference at the Refugee Studies Centre, Oxford, October 2009), 5.

35 The earliest usage in describing UNHCR operations is in the 2001 Country Operations Plan for Egypt. The earliest usage in reference to an Asian state is in the 2002 Country Operations Plan for Malaysia (see below).

36 UNHCR, *UNHCR Policy on Refugee Protection and Solutions in Urban Areas* (September 2009), §II (paras. 14–22).

37 This aspect of its usage is noted by Barnes, above n. 27, 11 relying upon email correspondence with the director of UNHCR's Middle East and North Africa Bureau.

38 The lack of definition is admitted by Barnes, ibid., 11.

39 UNHCR, *UNHCR Global Report 2009* (June 2010), see 'Malaysia', 245.

40 Ibid., see 'Thailand', 236.

41 UNHCR, above n. 36, para. 20.

42 Barnes, above n. 27, 12.

43 UNHCR, above n. 36, para. 20.

44 UNHCR, *UNHCR Country Operation Plan: Malaysia* (UNHCR, 2007), 8.

45 UNHCR, UNHCR *Global Appeal 2010–2011* (2010).

46 An often-quoted example is from Barnes's report on the protection of Iraqi refugees: 'Carving out protection space is not without its obstacles; for in addition to meeting the protection needs of refugees, UNHCR must simultaneously meet the concerns of states' (above n. 27, 1).

47 Erika Feller, 'Refugee Protection: Challenges and Opportunities in the Australian Region and Beyond' (UNHCR, 18 February 2010).

48 UNHCR, above n. 36, para. 22.

49 Abild, above n. 28, 5.

50 See also the usage in Barnes, above n. 27: 'Carving out protection space is not without its obstacles; for in addition to meeting the protection needs of refugees, UNHCR must simultaneously meet the concerns of states' (1).

51 *C et al. v. Director of Immigration and Secretary for Security* Civil Appeal 132-7/2008 (Hong Kong Court of Appeal, 21 July 2011).

52 In an interview with the *Bangkok Post*, Prime Minister Abdullah Badawi stated: 'Well they are very concerned and at times they are critical of actions taken by governments. But if we cannot be firm we cannot deal with this problem. We have to be firm at all borders. We have to turn them back. If they (international groups) help we will be very happy' (Pichai Chuensuksawad, 'Full text of the interview with Malaysian Prime Minister Abdullah', *Bangkok Post* (27 February 2009)).

53 Eric Neumayer, 'Do International Human Rights Treaties Improve Respect for Human Rights?' (2005) 49 *Journal of Conflict Resolution* 925–53.

54 Arguably, UNHCR's at first explicit and later more quiet support of the Australia–Malaysia Agreement to swap asylum seekers for resettled refugees is a continuation of this approach.

55 In 2004, UNHCR recorded 24,900 recognised refugees and 10,322 asylum seekers. The numbers in subsequent years were 33,693 and 10,838 (2005); 37,170 and 9,186 (2006); 32,243 and 6,851 (2007); and 36,088 and 9,323 (2008).

56 This assertion is based upon discussions with refugee community leaders, civil society activists and both local and international UNHCR staff based in Malaysia during the period in question.

57 It was 94,400 as of May 2011.

58 Refugee community leaders in conversation and public discussions frequently cite the ratio '1 in 3' as the proportion of their communities who have been registered with UNHCR.

59 The closest reference to such operational tasks comes in para. 8(c) of the statute: '[UNHCR shall provide for the protection of refugees falling under the competence of his Office by] [a]ssisting governmental and private efforts to promote voluntary repatriation or assimilation within new national communities.' Arguably, the coordination responsibilities of para. 8(g) (h) and (i) may include some of these operational obligations (though not necessarily in the form of the direct provision of services).

60 To say that UNHCR's operational role is well established is not to suggest it has not itself been the subject of much commentary and critique, the latter most notably in the context of its refugee status determination operations.

61 The former arose as part of discussions between the APPRN civil society network and UNHCR around the commemorations of the 60th anniversary of the 1951 Refugee Convention and an example of the latter most recently occurred in Hong Kong during the tripartite (UNHCR–Hong Kong SAR–Hong Kong Law Society) negotiations surrounding the creation of a domestic Convention Against Torture screening process.

62 See, in particular, Mike Kagan's recent work on UNHCR as a surrogate state based upon his experiences in Egypt and the Middle East ('New Issues in Refugee Research, Research Paper 201: The UN Surrogate State and Refugee Policy in the Middle East' (UNHCR, February 2011)).

63 'To be clear, I do not argue that state-to-UN responsibility shift is an ideal arrangement. There are some essential components of refugee protection that only a sovereign state may deliver . . . Responsibility shift, when used, must be limited and defined, so that lines of accountability are clear and expectations realistic' (ibid., 2).

64 See Chapter 9 in this volume.

65 The Palermo Convention and its protocols concerning trafficking and smuggling are the notable recent developments in this regard. This is not to suggest that the framing of the issue as one of combating transnational crime is not without problems in so far as it perpetuates the association of refugees with 'criminals' (or, at the very least, somewhat helpless 'victims') and runs the risk of criminalising (and encouraging the prosecution of) actions in practice necessary to refugee protection (for example the irregular crossing of borders to escape persecution).

66 Employment rights, for example, have been noted to be the subject of frequent reservation.

67 United Nations Human Rights Committee, 26 May 2004, General Comment No. 31 [80] The Nature of the Legal Obligation Imposed on State Parties to the Covenant, CCPR/C/21/Rev.1/Add.13, adopted on 29 March 2004, para. 12. For further discussion of the interpretation of Articles 6 and 7 of the ICCPR, see Kees Wouters, *International Legal Standards for the Protection from Non-Refoulement* (Intersentia, 2009), ch. 4.

68 Convention Against Torture and Other Cruel, Inhuman or Degrading Treatment or Punishment, opened for signature 10 December 1984, 1465 UNTS 85 (entered into force 26 June 1987) ('CAT').

69 *Secretary for Security* v. *Prabakar* Final Appeal No. 16 of 2003 (Civil) (Hong Kong Court of Final Appeal, 8 June 2004). *Prabakar* established that, *inter alia*, decisions as to whether or not it is safe to return an individual who claims he or she would be subject to torture require high standards of procedural fairness. This has led to the establishment of a state-funded system of legal aid for CAT claimants and a formal process of application, hearing and appeal. For more information, see Mark Daly, 'Refugee Law in Hong Kong: Building the Legal Infrastructure' *Hong Kong Lawyer* (September 2009), 14–30.

70 See the submission of LBHI (the national legal aid provider) to the government of Indonesia on the process required for the ratification of the 1951 Refugee Convention (2010) (unpublished, on file with author).
71 James Hathaway, *The Rights of Refugees under International Law* (Cambridge University Press, 2006), 121.
72 It is this directive that makes the above-mentioned debate over (non)registration all the more important. Refugees who are not registered are otherwise technically liable to punishment for irregular entry, including a fine (up to 10,000 RM or more than €2,000), imprisonment (up to five years) and whipping (up to six lashes of the rattan), under s. 6 Immigration Act 1959/1963.
73 *Tun Naing Oo* v. *Public Prosecutor* (High Court of Malaya, Shah Alam, Yeoh Wee Siam, JC) (File number 43-9-2009; 24 March 2009), at para. 34 (reviewing the decision of a lower court to impose whipping).
74 (Court of Appeal, James Foong, JCA, Abdul Malik Ishak, JCA and Abu Samah Nordin, JCA) (File number A-04-76-2008; 2 January 2009). The decision itself is quite complicated and not an entirely satisfactory decision. However, it rejected the principle of *ex turpi causa* that precluded irregular migrants from previously recovering lost or unpaid wages.
75 Including five of the ILO's eight fundamental conventions. To underscore Malaysia's reluctance to make international commitments, it ratified and subsequently denounced one of the ILO's core conventions (Convention No. 105 on the Abolition of Forced Labour).
76 Hathaway, above, n. 71, 33.
77 Erika Feller, Address by Ms Erika Feller, Director of the Department of International Protection, UNHCR, at the South Asia Regional Judicial Symposium on Refugee Protection (New Delhi, 13–14 November 1999), 14 November <www.unhcr.org/refworld/docid/42a00d932.html> (accessed 30 April 2011).
78 While there are still gaps in the NHRI framework, the major hosts of refugees in the region (and also the signatories of the 1951 Refugee Convention) now have strong NHRIs. The development of strong NHRIs has been contentious; the threat by the international community to downgrade the status of Malaysia's NHRI (SUHAKAM) because of, *inter alia*, its lack of institutional independence is a notable example of the struggle that has occurred.
79 With respect to the latter, the Asian Refugee Legal Aid Networks project (of which the author was the co-director) held three regional seminars to build litigation and legal argument capacity in local refugee legal aid organisations.
80 Amy Slaughter and Jeff Crisp, 'A Surrogate State? The Role of UNHCR in Protracted Refugee Situations', in Gil Loescher *et al.* (eds), *Protracted Refugee Situations* (United Nations University Press, 2008), 123, 128.

Part V

14 Law, identity and protection: concluding reflections

Dallal Stevens, Susan Kneebone and Loretta Baldassar

In this volume, we have considered the role of law and policy in making and unmaking the refugee category through an interdisciplinary lens. Our starting point is that the cornerstone of refugee identity is the legal and normative framework of protection enshrined in the Refugee Convention,[1] and that refugee identity is shaped by the particular legal, political and social processes that surround asylum-seeking. Our aim is to examine what we term 'the paradox of protection' – that is, the protection afforded by the Refugee Convention definition creates conflicting identities conferred through such processes. The role of law, legal policy and the legal process has played a central role within our analysis. Of particular concern is the power of law and its institutions in describing and making refugee identity, and the consequent implications for protection. Not only is such power ever present in the increasing global and regional securitisation of asylum and migration (see, for example, Zetter, Chapter 2; Guild, Chapter 8), but it is very evident in governmental attempts to directly or indirectly alter state responsibilities to asylum seekers and refugees (Galloway, Chapter 3; Björnberg, Chapter 11; Ambrosini, Chapter 12). We are also interested in the dialectical process at play in which the law not only influences but is itself influenced by individuals, communities, society, politics and government. A final concern is the meaning and content of protection itself, and the interconnection between the development of a (legal) concept of protection and refugee identity.

In addressing these issues of immediate concern, this concluding chapter revisits the central questions that have shaped the volume and summarises some of the arguments raised by our contributors:

- 60 years after the creation of the Refugee Convention, is refugee law fulfilling the protection needs of the world's refugees?
- How have refugee identities and protection changed in this period?
- What are the macro and state perspectives on law, power and refugee identity?
- How do micro, social and individual perspectives affect identity construction and protection?

Refugee law and protection: fit for purpose 60 years on?

The question posed by Part I is based on the title of the chapter by Erika Feller, former Assistant High Commissioner for Protection: 'The Refugee Convention at 60: Still Fit for Purpose?' (Chapter 4). In her chapter, Feller explains the centrality of the Refugee Convention definition to the international refugee law regime and examines its continuing relevance to current global protection challenges. Feller addresses global developments in relation to four, potentially overlapping, displacement 'situations' to determine whether the Convention, as a 'protection tool' meets the 'protection needs' of each of the situations she identifies:

1   the 'classical' persecution-driven movement where refugees, individually or in small groups, flee state or non-state persecution, including that comprising deliberately targeted acts of violence;
2   the mass-influx situations where large-scale displacement is provoked by danger or violence accompanying conflicts or civil disturbance and which overwhelms receiving state apparatuses;
3   cross-border displacement provoked by natural disasters or human-made calamities, such as nuclear disasters; and
4   mixed flows of persons moving as an integral and often indistinguishable part of an asylum/migration movement.[2]

Another way of looking at the issues raised is to consider how far the Convention definition of a refugee – the legal identity it creates – is adequate to meet contemporary migration flows. Feller concludes that it is essential to 'recognise and reaffirm [the Convention's] enduring strengths but also to buttress it when it comes to the "refugee problem" in all its dimensions, where these are understood to include asylum–migration nexus issues and new drivers of displacement' described above.[3]

The Refugee Convention, which provides a legal identity for the refugee, is an obvious focus for our analysis. This identity is expected to be 'declared' by state parties to the Convention through the conduct of refugee status determination (RSD),[4] or by the UNHCR where it has assumed responsibility for RSD. Zetter reminds us, nonetheless, that the consequences of conducting RSD – assumed to be a positive institutional act – can be much greater than anticipated by the legal mind (Chapter 2). In fact, it may not be wholly accurate to speak of a legal identity as such, since the ascribed identity is the *product* rather than being constitutive of definitional interpretation; thus, it is flexible and subject to the whim of decision maker or judge, a fact that emerges in a number of chapters. In Zetter's words, the Convention 'did not make an "identity" but it framed the parameters of an identity in terms of specific social membership (the five grounds of persecution), spatial displacement (across an international border), and a claim (protection)'.[5]

As we have shown throughout the collection, the manifestation of an identity through law is only the starting point. The attribution of 'refugee' to an individual can result in further societal and personal identities, with implications for both the individual, their families and communities, and the host state as well as to the legal and social category of 'refugee'. Recent developments in international migration, securitisation and the increased criminalisation of the asylum seeker have influenced the legal identity of the refugee in complex and myriad ways. An example in the domestic context is provided by Galloway in his description of how the legal concept of a refugee, and the associated protection, can be undermined by legislation if government is so inclined (Chapter 3). Reflecting on the implications of recent changes to Canadian law on the designation of countries and individuals,[6] Galloway arrives at the radical position that 'the status determination hearing is no longer conceived as a remedial forum offering an opportunity for the vindication of rights. It is now reshaped as a public investigation into the possibility of persecution.'[7] As a consequence, refugees are increasingly denied status as rights-holder.[8]

These three chapters highlight two fundamental concerns with the Convention, which challenge its enduring relevance and fitness for purpose. The nature of mass displacement, as Feller clearly outlines, often creates a problem for a Convention that is framed with the individual in mind, rather than groups or categories of refugees. This discord between the aim of the Convention and the reality of forced migration has been exacerbated in the last 60 years by the apparent divergence between the state and the UNHCR in approaches to the 'refugee problem'. While the UNCHR often has to handle the consequences of mass flight and is consequently very much solution focused (Feller), state parties, by contrast, either suspend RSD and use an ad hoc status,[9] or they cling to the so-called individualised legal definition of the refugee in the Convention, which enables them to limit entitlement to refugee status in their territories. Thus, even where individual RSD is undertaken, governments, decision makers and the courts have undermined the protective power of the definition through restrictive policies and interpretation. The unfortunate outcome of the state *versus* UNHCR paradigm is a hierarchy of refugee identities, where the Convention status is deemed the 'gold-standard' with its hope of full implementation of Convention rights and a durable solution to the refugee's plight.

Refugee identities and protection: historical shifts

By outlining the changes in (forced) global migration in recent years, Feller's chapter is an effective link to Part II of the volume in which we consider refugee identity and protection in a historical perspective. There is recurring reference in the contributions to Part I, and indeed in Feller's own chapter, to the individual–group refugee identity dichotomy. As explained in Chapter 1, the refugee definition contained in the Convention, and in paragraph 6 of the UNHCR Statute, focuses on the individual applicant. Such a legal regime struggles to protect the reality of many contemporary refugee movements – namely large-scale or group-based displacement – as shown very clearly by a number of authors: (Feller, Chapter 4; Betts in relation to Africa, Chapter 9; Stevens in the Middle Eastern context, Chapter 5; and, generally, Kneebone, Chapter 6).

In addition to the individual refugee definition, the UNHCR Statute of 1950 recognised the need for the work of the High Commissioner to relate to 'groups and categories of refugees'.[10] This inherent tension between individual or group identity remains both problematic for refugee identity and contested.[11] Within a few years of its statute entering into force, the UNHCR sought expansion of its mandate beyond the initial intentions of either the Convention or statute. A new form of refugee – or 'person of concern' – was born. With the existence of regional definitions of the refugee, we are today confronted with numerous refugee identities, which can create confusion. Thus, for example, a 'refugee' is not merely someone who meets the criteria of Article 1A(2) but is also a person recognised by UNHCR as:

> outside [her] country of origin or habitual residence and unable to return there owing to serious and indiscriminate threats to life, physical integrity or freedom resulting from generalised violence or event seriously disturbing public order.[12]

Furthermore, recourse is made by the UNHCR (and some states) to determination of refugee status in circumstances where it is difficult to conduct an individual assessment. In such situations, each member of the population in question can be deemed to be a prima facie refugee, and may be resettled if the state in question is willing to accept him or her without the need for separate 1A(2) determination.[13] Each of these definitions – individual, group or prima facie – is based on different attributes – or, in the words of Zetter, an identity – that of 'refugee' – is ascribed through RSD or under UNHCR guidance, if certain conditions are met. Further, the broadening of the 'legal identity' of a refugee, to address novel and unforeseen migrations across borders, is reconceptualised by Betts as 'regime stretching' and seen as a necessity if protection is to be effective (Chapter 9). From a historical perspective, it is particularly striking to note that the pre-Second World War regime – based on national group identity – appears in many respects better suited to the majority of today's forced migrations en masse than the largely individualised approach of the Refugee Convention.[14]

As Kneebone explains, the 'individualistic' refugee definition implies three shifting refugee identities which she terms the 'political, legal and cosmopolitan'. In her discussion of surrogate protection she explains how refugee identity has shifted over time from the group to the 'individualistic' (Chapter 6). From Kneebone we learn how legal interpretation of the Convention definition of the refugee can lead to diminishing international protection, that is protection outside of the state of origin, for persons in need. The contrast with the Middle East is stark. In her chapter, Stevens outlines the shifting concepts of refugee identity within the European (Convention-based) and Middle Eastern (non-Convention-based) contexts and considers the implications for protection (Chapter 5). The conclusions are intriguing. Recent protection seekers in the Middle East, where few states are party to the Convention, are assigned alternative labels, such as, *inter alia*, asylum seeker, guest, Arab brother. From a state perspective, the label/ identity 'refugee' denotes 'Palestinian' and is to be resisted (at least until the recent arrival of Syrians). Nonetheless, many of the countries in the region have adopted much more generous protection policies without recourse to refugee law than their European counterparts. Ambrosini, too, draws out the issue of multiple and alternating identities in the case of Italy. Sometimes perceived as illegal migrant, sometimes as national security threat or welfare 'scrounger', the asylum seeker's latest manifestation, following the conflict in North Africa of 2011, is as victim deserving of (albeit temporary) humanitarian protection (Chapter 12).

Law, power and refugee identity: macro and state perspectives

In Part III of the book, we examine the power behind law. The Foucauldian analysis employed by Guild to examine European Union asylum policy highlights how the mechanism of power operates within the EU and between the EU institutions and Member States (Chapter 8). The rule of law, as a form of governance, works effectively in Foucault's three modes of thinking about power – sovereignty, discipline and biopolitics.[15] The asylum seeker arriving at the shores of the EU poses a problem for Member States. Is she entitled to protection? Is she just 'lucky or devious'? Should she be disciplined?[16] Such questions arise because, as Guild asserts, '[s]tate authorities will not tolerate complex identities';[17] those asylum claimants who manage to emerge from the so-called mixed migration flows are consequently forced to provide coherent and consistent versions of their lives to meet the expectations of the law, or those who administer it (Guild, Chapter 8; Galloway, Chapter 3). Any of those who do not pass the test become 'failed asylum seekers', a linguistic euphemism for 'bogus' or 'cheat'. The possibility that the *asylum system* has failed is seldom admitted by government or countenanced by a wider public, frequently influenced by the tabloid press. The outcome of negative stereotyping is extremely serious: as Galloway suggests, the refugee is being reclassified as 'illegal'.[18] In some senses, one can regard this construction of illegality as a new form of group identity, the aim of which is to bar access to territory, to RSD and hence protection. It would appear that protection of rights and freedoms is no longer regarded as priority.

Even in circumstances where asylum seekers and refugees are not deemed 'illegal', state power has encouraged a re-imagining or re-identification of such groups. This may occur either through the law, as discussed by a number of contributors to this volume, or through politicisation of the asylum issue. O'Sullivan addresses this issue directly in relation to Australia, which appears to lead the way in designating asylum seekers as 'good' (or, at least, acceptable) – 'the resettled' – or as 'bad' – the 'offshore entry person' (Chapter 7) for political reasons.[19] Thus, the public are encouraged to regard those who arrive by sea as 'bad' and 'illegal', while the 'good' are 'legals' who use the 'correct' channels and patiently await their turn in camps. This approach is strikingly reminiscent of the United Kingdom's Aliens Act 1905, which sought to divide new arrivals into 'undesirable immigrants' and, one must presume, desirables (or, again, those deemed acceptable). As in the present case of Australia, such division was based on the mode of arrival – by sea – and was inherently illogical and discriminatory.[20]

Refugee identities and protection: micro, social and individual perspectives

In Chapter 2, Zetter argued that:

> Like other groups ... refugees negotiate within a framework of legal designation, state practice, and political and everyday language, on the one hand, and their own accounts, on the other. It is the interplay between the formation of the narrated identity of the group and the situated identity produced by institutional and bureaucratic power that is the central concern here.[21]

Part IV of the volume focuses on some of the tensions that arise from the narrated–situated multiplicity of refugee identity. Empirical, sociological and anthropological research helps us to appreciate the impact of the exercise of power on the individual and her own identity – whether through law, institutions or governance. Björnberg poignantly describes the unintended consequences of an established, and in many ways progressive, domestic asylum regime through a case study of asylum-seeking families in Sweden (Chapter 11). Ambrosini reveals how Italian state policy has rarely distinguished asylum seekers and refugees from economic migrants (Chapter 12). While there might be more formal processes of integration of asylum seekers in Sweden than in Italy, the suffering endured by the individual is similar. The psychological implications of, *inter alia*, the experiences of shame, humiliation, lack of trust, fear of the future and diminishing confidence, inherent within the asylum system, are immense. In Italy, it is the failure to process asylum seekers appropriately that gives rise to insecurity. Not only do the labels of asylum seeker or refugee bring with them the risk of marginalisation and exclusion, but they are transformative of the individual, and her self-perception. Thus, the asylum process has the capacity to be both constructive of an externally ascribed identity and destructive of an internally ascribed identity.

Jones, by contrast, considers a region – South-East Asia – in which the majority of states are not party to the Convention, and which also have rather dubious human rights records (Chapter 13). As in the case of the Middle East (Stevens, Chapter 5), the UNHCR and NGOs in South-East Asia are keen to 'protect rights' through the negotiation of the so-called 'humanitarian protection space'. And, similar to the Middle East, there is wide rejection of substantive refugee law. A shift in protective responsibility from the state towards the UNHCR has taken place. Following a critique of the protection space approach, Jones proposes an alternative – 'the law of asylum' – which he describes as follows:

> International human rights law guarantees refugees various rights. In addition, international labour law, customary international law and recent international development to combat transnational crime supplement international human rights law to provide a collection of rights almost equivalent to those provided by international refugee law.[22]

So, for Jones, with a focus on achieving concrete protection, the crucial identity is not so much that of 'refugee' but that of 'human' being and 'rights-bearer'. It is only through such an approach that one can mitigate the power of law in ascribing refugee identities that influence other processes and policies, such as integration, employment, housing, welfare and education. The irony is that the legal process has the power to bestow refugee status/identity as well as the power to erase the subject by rendering the individual an 'object' of asylum law policy. In so doing, the asylum seeker is robbed of agency, self-ascribed identity, integrity and trustworthiness. Ultimately, she is denied her humanity.

Intended and unintended consequences

We return now to the question with which the volume opened and which is its focus: is refugee protection fit for purpose after more than 60 years of the Refugee Convention? We seek to answer this apparently simple question by outlining what we have termed 'the intended and unintended consequences of refugee identity'. As the contributions have revealed, the process of claiming protection under the Refugee Convention requires asylum seekers to construct or 'narrate' their 'identity' as victims of persecution on one of the five Convention grounds; yet the basis for claiming protection may in turn lead to unintended consequences and discrimination in countries of refuge because of such identity. In considering 'intended' and 'unintended consequences', we mean intended or unintended from the perspective of the individual and the original drafters who participated in creating the Convention in 1951, not from the receiving states many of which now clearly intend to restrict access to protection, often through the arm of the law.

Intended consequences

In identifying the intended consequences of refugee identity, it is helpful to reflect on the original impetus for the Refugee Convention. The Final Act of the UN Conference of Plenipotentiaries on the Status of Refugees and Stateless Persons is a helpful source; it stated:

The Conference,

Considering that many persons still leave their country of origin for reasons of persecution and are entitled to special protection on account of their position,

Recommends that Governments continue to receive refugees in their territories and that they act in concert in a true spirit of international cooperation in order that these refugees find asylum and the possibility of resettlement.[23]

. . .

Expresses the hope that the Convention relating to the Status of Refugees will have value as an example exceeding its contractual scope and that all nations will be guided by it in granting so far as possible to persons in their territory as refugees and who would not be covered by the terms of the Convention, the treatment for which it provides.[24]

This, together with the Preamble to the Refugee Convention, is a clear expression of the intended unique position of refugees under international law, of their entitlement to protection, and the importance of fundamental rights for all refugees, in particular the right to be free from discrimination.[25] In addition, states were encouraged to act in a humanitarian manner towards non-refugees in their territory within the spirit of the Convention. It was recognised that without international cooperation, a solution to the 'problem' of refugees would be difficult to achieve. Arguably, that 'solution' is still far from reach.

Some of the ambitious aims of the Conference and Convention – which might be termed the intended consequences – have been met in part: 147 states are now party to either the Refugee Convention or the 1967 Protocol.[26] Although there was some hesitation in 1951 to have an open-ended commitment to future refugees, which gave rise to the inclusion of a temporal limitation in the Convention, states subsequently recognised the need to address new refugee situations; agreement was therefore reached in 1967 to extend the benefit of the Convention to all refugees covered by the definition in the Convention, irrespective of the date line of 1 January 1951. Despite concerns about the continued relevance of the Convention to contemporary forced migrations, states have continued to remain party to the Convention and have endorsed its enduring significance – perhaps the most apposite being the Declaration of States Parties adopted in December 2001 as part of the 50th anniversary celebrations of the Convention.[27] Broadly, then, states continue to recognise the need to cooperate and assist one another in the face of mass movements of peoples, and to this extent the spirit – and intention – of the 1950s lives on.

This spirit of generosity encouraged in 1951 is further evidenced by a teleological approach to protection, adopted in particular by the courts, which have succeeded in expanding certain categories or identities of refugees. The most notable examples are provided by the inclusion of gender-based discrimination within the ground of 'membership of a particular social group' in Article 1A(2), and by the growing acceptance that deprivation of social and economic rights can give rise to a successful refugee claim.[28] States have also played their role in developing alternative forms of protection – subsidiary or complementary – for those who fail to meet the high threshold of the Refugee Convention; these are considered in some quarters to be a positive development and an appropriate consequence of the advancement of protection as an important principle. Certainly, complementary protection as employed in the European Union can be regarded as meeting the aspirations of both the League of Nations and the United Nations that the 'problem' of 'unprotected persons' is a matter of concern to the international community and should be resolved through international cooperation and agreement.[29]

Unintended consequences

While there are undoubtedly intended consequences flowing from making a claim for asylum, the discussion in this collection demonstrates clearly the complexity surrounding the concomitant issues of the role of law, refugee protection and identity/identities; a complexity that has arguably increased over the past 60 years and given rise to numerous unintended consequences, some of which we now highlight:

- A particularly striking feature of the current regime is the extent to which the perception of the legally constructed concept of 'refugee' has shifted from an individual *in need of* state or international protection to a figure seen as a threat and *against which* the state itself seeks protection; or, in the case of the associated 'asylum seeker', to a figure which the state may wish to discipline (see, for example, Galloway, O'Sullivan, Guild, Ambrosini).
- Changes in state attitudes towards asylum seekers and refugees have resulted in the creation of very evident barriers to access to asylum, which are *contra* the aims of the international refugee law regime established in the 1950s (O'Sullivan; Galloway; Stevens). These barriers can take the form of legal impediments – such as the imposition of higher standards of proof (Guild; Kneebone); the growing use of credibility criteria; and the creation and legalisation of invidious practices, such as safe third-country removal or 'white listing' of countries of origin (Galloway); or the barriers may simply relate to institutionalised mistrust of protection seekers by both state and public (Ambrosini; Björnberg).
- Similarly, the interpretation of the definition of a 'refugee' in Article 1A(2) of the Refugee Convention has arguably moved away from the original protective intention of the Conference of Plenipotentiaries; the surrogate protection approach employed by a number of states is a prime example of a move away from a collective obligation to protect to a focus on the individual and his or her home state (Kneebone; O'Sullivan). A crucial associated issue, outlined by Lambert, is the extent to which restrictive or progressive norms are disseminated globally through 'transnational conversations', be it at the judicial or institutional level, and whether the 'refugee' has become 'blurred, marginalised or ignored'.[30]
- The minimum standard of protection provided by the Refugee Convention is the *non-refoulement* principle, the 'negative' right *not* to be returned to the frontiers of a territory where 'life or freedom would be threatened'.[31] Yet,

many contributions question whether this fundamental principle is being respected, whether through the development of the concept of 'surrogate protection' by states or through measures that result in refusals, return or *non-entrée* (see, for examples, Kneebone; Galloway; O'Sullivan).

- In the last 20 years, it has become very noticeable that states have modified their approach to the protection to which refugees are entitled. Whereas in the past refugees were frequently granted permanent residence, in support of the important objective of achieving an early durable solution, the current preference is for a form of temporary protection (see O'Sullivan, for example). Government rhetoric frequently stresses temporality and legislation is passed to sanction limited residence. Australia was an early supporter of time-limited humanitarian protection with the introduction of temporary protection visas in 1999. The EU has followed suit with its Qualification Directive under which refugees are guaranteed a minimum three-year stay.[32] This has forced a rethinking within UNHCR. Feller argues that 'the time has come to work with states to develop an internationally agreed doctrine of temporary protection, which would ensure the availability of interim protection to people in temporary need'.[33]

- Temporary protection is one aspect of shifting attitudes leading to new identity construction; another is what might be termed 'a race to the bottom' in terms of protection standards (Feller; Galloway; Betts; Stevens; Jones). The paradox here is that the protection provided by state parties to the Refugee Convention may not differ widely from non-parties (Stevens); indeed, some regions of the world – for example, the Middle East and Africa – accept refugees on a more permanent basis than their richer and more developed counterparts in the North (Betts; Stevens). The spirit of humanitarianism underlying the international refugee regime is not necessarily dependent on strict legal compliance.

- The Convention was a product of state recognition that international cooperation was needed to avoid the grant of asylum placing unduly heavy burdens on certain countries. In many areas of the world, a shift in responsibility is occurring from state cooperation[34] to UNHCR/civil society cooperation, without consideration of the implications of these changes for refugees (Jones; Stevens; Ambrosini). Interestingly, the change in many states' willingness to assume responsibility, or permit refugees access to the rights to which they are entitled, is not necessarily dependent on whether they are party to the Convention (Stevens; Jones). Both state and non-state parties are increasingly loath to accept refugees on a long-term basis.

- The drafters of the Convention did not anticipate that the system of international protection they created would, over the next six decades, be augmented or influenced by a range of regional instruments, human rights instruments, humanitarian law treaties and international criminal law – described recently as 'other relevant norms of international law'.[35] While some would argue that this enhances protection, and is to be lauded, such a development results in a refugee identity that is subject to change to accommodate or dismiss new notions of harm and reasons for flight; this can be destabilising for both the individual asylum seeker and the protection framework as a whole.

- Legal processes focus on stabilising and pinpointing and refining legal status as a fixed unchanging identity. But social life requires flexible, dynamic identities that permit ambiguities and transformation. This can lead to surprising outcomes: in Sweden, which is arguably more compassionate than many countries, the policies create significant stress and social problems for the individual through the (legalised) delivery of refugee status and identity (Björnberg); Italy, by contrast, fails to process asylum seekers and deliver formal status, and is a very negative system in comparison to Sweden; yet, it actually delivers a level of ambiguity and flexibility that can be seen to help asylum seekers to fare better than their Swedish counterparts (Ambrosini).
- The Refugee Convention was borne out of international recognition that 'human beings [should] enjoy fundamental rights and freedoms without discrimination', and that refugees should be assured 'the widest possible exercise of . . . fundamental rights and freedoms'.[36] However, this still remains an aspiration.[37] For it to become a reality, the law needs to shift direction somewhat. The full enjoyment of rights and freedoms cannot simply be enforced by law; it also requires respect for the agency of refugees; it involves greater trust, a concept that is often inimical to legal processes, but which is central to sociological and anthropological approaches to refugee studies.
- The final, but highly significant, unintended consequence we wish to highlight is the emergence of law as an instrument of power (Guild; Zetter). The paradox here is that the desire in 1951 to use law as a tool for good – the creation of an internationally recognised legal identity for the refugee, with associated rights – has slowly been replaced by an equally fervent wish on the part of states to employ law to retreat from obligations now widely perceived as too onerous.

Conclusion

While the construction or application of identity is arguably a fundamental feature of refugee law and policy, it has not, to date, received sufficient academic enquiry. Similarly, the link between identity and protection calls for further exploration. This book has sought to address the gaps in the literature, by offering an interdisciplinary approach to the issues of identity, refugee protection and the role of law. From a sociological perspective, a legal approach appears not to consider sufficiently the way in which legal processes directly impact on the intimate and everyday life experiences of individuals and their families and communities – often referred to as the 'lived experiences'. Similarly, sociological accounts tend to focus on such 'lived experiences', often without a sophisticated understanding of the legal processes at play. In our volume, we seek to do both – to consider the intimate and myriad ways in which the legal processes are actually experienced by people and how they are so influential to the most central and compelling aspects of social life: the development and construction of identity. It is rare for state or UNHCR officials to reflect on the potential unintended consequences of their laws and policies. Although they may be working in good faith to provide effective protection, insufficient attention to the muted processes of identity formation can result in the legal processes falling far short of their intended consequences. This book is a call to make the legal apparatus more nuanced and more aware of the implications of its power. Identity is a compelling and productive prism through which to achieve this.

Notes

1 Convention relating to the Status of Refugees, Geneva, 28 July 1951, 1989 UNTS 137, supplemented by the Protocol relating to the Status of Refugees, 31 January 1967, 19 UST 6223, 6257 ('Refugee Convention').
2 Chapter 4, pp. 58.
3 Ibid., pp. 67.
4 UNHCR, *Handbook on Procedures and Criteria for Determining Refugee Status*, January 1988, para. 28.
5 Chapter 2, pp. 26.
6 This refers to the policy widely adopted in the EU of designating countries of origin as 'safe'; Canada has introduced a new category of 'designated foreign national' for those identified to be part of a group that is itself designated as arriving irregularly (see Chapter 3, pp. 40–1).
7 Ibid., pp. 49.
8 Ibid., pp. 52.
9 Jean-François Durieux and Jane McAdam, '*Non-refoulement* through Time: The Case for a Derogation Clause to the Refugee Convention in Mass Influx Emergencies' (2004) 16 *International Journal of Refugee Law* 4–24, 8.
10 Para. 2.
11 See Introduction for further discussion of this point. Jean-François Durieux disputes the 'highly individualistic' approach to Article 1A(2) citing the US Asylum Regulations of 1990 in support – 'fear of persecution upon return can be considered reasonable where "the applicant can show a pattern or practice of persecution of a group of persons similarly situated and his or her own inclusion in, and identification with, such a group of persons"' ('The Many Faces of "prima facie": Group-based Evidence in Refugee Status Determination' (2008) 25 *Refuge* 151–63, 153); Durieux and McAdam, above n. 9.
12 UNHCR, *UNHCR Resettlement Handbook: Chapter 3 – Refugee Status and Resettlement*, para. 3.2.2. The debt owed by this broad definition to the OAU Convention and the Cartagena Declaration is very apparent: OAU Convention governing the aspects of refugee problems in Africa, 1969; Cartagena Declaration on Refugees, Colloquium on the International Protection of Refugees in Central America, Mexico and Panama, 1984.
13 See Matthew Albert, 'Governance and prima facie Refugee Status Determination: Clarifying the Boundaries of Temporary Protection, Group Determination, and Mass Influx' (2010) 29 *Refugee Survey Quarterly* 61–91; Albert focuses on the misconceptions and misunderstandings surrounding prima facie refugee status (determination) and concludes that it is a 'unique procedure that leads to a unique legal status' (ibid., 90).
14 It should be stressed however that an applicant can be determined to be a refugee under Article 1A(2) where he or she is a proven member of a persecuted group or persecuted for reasons of membership of a particular social group. See for further discussion Durieux, above n. 11.

15 Chapter 8, pp. 156.
16 Ibid., pp. 159.
17 Ibid., pp. 160.
18 Ibid., Chapter 3, pp. 53.
19 Chapter 7, pp. 123–4.
20 The Act only applied to ships carrying more than 20 alien steerage passengers, i.e. first- and second-class passengers were exempted, s. 8(1) Aliens Act 1905. See for discussion of the Act, Helena Wray, 'The Aliens Act 1905 and the Immigration Dilemma' (2006) *33 Journal of Law and Society* 302–23.
21 Chapter 2, pp. 25.
22 Chapter 13, pp. 261.
23 Recommendation D of the Final Act.
24 Recommendation E of the Final Act.
25 Preamble to Refugee Convention: 'Considering that the Charter of the United Nations and the Universal Declaration of Human Rights . . . have affirmed the principle that human beings shall enjoy fundamental rights and freedoms without discrimination.'
26 As at 1 April 2011 <www.unhcr.org/3b73b0d63.html> (accessed 2 January 2014).
27 In an effort to courage greater compliance with the Convention, and in recognition of its ongoing relevance, the UNHCR initiated the Global Consultations on International Protection and the Agenda for Protection as part of these celebrations. See UNHCR, *Agenda for Protection* (October 2003) <www.unhcr.org/3e637b194.html> (accessed 3 January 2014).
28 See Michelle Foster, *International Refugee Law and Socio-Economic Rights* (Cambridge University Press, 2007).
29 See Stevens, Chapter 5 in this volume.
30 Jean-François Durieux, 'The Vanishing Refugee: How EU Asylum Law Blurs the Specificity of Refugee Protection', in Hélène Lambert, Jane McAdam and Maryellen Fullerton (eds), *The Global Reach of European Refugee Law* (Cambridge University Press, 2013), 228.
31 Refugee Convention, Article 33.
32 Directive 2011/95/EU of the European Parliament and of the Council of 13 December 2011 on standards for the qualification of third-country nationals or stateless persons as beneficiaries of international protection, for a uniform status for refugees or for persons eligible for subsidiary protection, and for the content of the protection granted (recast), OJ L337/9 20.12.2011, Art. 24.
33 Chapter 4, pp. 64.
34 Refugee Convention, Preamble.
35 Andreas Zimmermann (ed.), *The 1951 Convention Relating to the Status of Refugees and Its 1967 Protocol: A Commentary* (Oxford University Press, 2010), 259.
36 Refugee Convention, Preamble.
37 See for example James C. Hathaway, *The Rights of Refugees under International Law* (Cambridge University Press, 2005).

Bibliography

Secondary sources

Abou-El-Wafa, Ahmed, *The Right to Asylum, between Islamic Shariah and International Law* (UNHCR, 2009).

Acharya, Amitav, 'How Ideas Spread: Whose Norms Matter? Norm Localization and Institutional Change in Asian Regionalism' (2004) 58 *International Organization* 239–75.

Agamben, Giorgio, *Homo Sacer; Sovereign Power and Bare Life* (Stanford University Press, 1998).

Ager, Alastair and Alison Strang, 'Understanding Integration: A Conceptual Framework' (2008) 21 *Journal of Refugee Studies* 166.

Akram, Susan, 'Palestinian Refugees and Their Legal Status: Rights, Politics and Implications for a Just Solution' (2002) 31 *Journal of Palestine Studies* 36–52.

Albert, Matthew, 'Governance and Prima Facie Refugee Status Determination: Clarifying the Boundaries of Temporary Protection, Group Determination and Mass Influx' (2010) 29 *International Refugee Law Journal* 61–91.

Albert, Matthew, 'Prima Facie Determination of Refugee Legal Status: An Overview of Its Legal Foundation', *Refugee Studies Centre Working Paper Series No. 55* (University of Oxford, 2010).

Aleinikoff, T. Alexander, 'State-centered Refugee Law: From Resettlement to Containment' (1992–3) 14 *Michigan Journal of International* 120.

Alter, Karen and Sophie Meunier (2009), 'The Politics of International Regime Complexity' (2009) 9 *Perspectives on Politics* 13–24.

Ambrosini, Maurizio, 'Immigration in Italy: Between Economic Acceptance and Political Rejection' (2013) 14 *Journal of International Migration and Integration* 175.

Ambrosini, Maurizio, *Irregular Immigration and Invisible Welfare* (Palgrave Macmillan, 2013).

Ambrosini, Maurizio, '"We Are against a Multi-ethnic Society": Policies of Exclusion at the Urban Level in Italy' (2013) 36 *Ethnic and Racial Studies* 136.

Ambrosini, Maurizio and Chiara Marchetti (eds), *Cittadini possibili. Un nuovo approccio all'accoglienza e all'integrazione dei rifugiati* (FrancoAngeli, 2008).

Andersson, Hans E., 'Spänningen mellan barnkonventionen och den reglerade invandringen', in H. E. Andersson *et al.* (eds), *Mellan det förflutna och framtiden. Asylsökande barns välfärd, hälsa och välbefinnande* (Centre for European Research at the University of Gothenburg, 2010).

Andersson, Hans E. and Susanne Nilsson, 'Asylum Seekers and Undocumented Migrants' Increased Social Rights in Sweden' (2011) 11 *International Migration* 167.

Anker, Deborah, 'Refugee Law, Gender, and the Human Rights Paradigm' (2002) 15 *Harvard Human Rights Journal* 133.

anonymous, 'Bossi: "Immigrati föra da i ball". Berlusconi arriva sull'isola', *La Repubblica* (online), 29 March 2011 <www.repubblica.it/politica/2011/03/29/news/bossi_immigrati_fora_da_i_ball-14227475/?ref=search>.

Arboleda, Eduardo and Ian Hoy, 'The Convention Refugee Definition in the West: Disharmony of Interpretation and Application' (1993) 5 *International Journal of Refugee Law* 69.

Arnaout, Ghassan, *Asylum in the Arab-Islamic Tradition* (UNHCR/Institute of Humanitarian Law, 1987).

Arendt, Hannah, *The Origins of Totalitarianism* (Harcourt Brace, 1951).

Arendt, Hannah, *The Human Condition* (Chicago University Press, 1958).

Armstrong, David, Theo Farrell and Hélène Lambert, *International Law and International Relations* (2nd edn, Cambridge University Press, 2012).

Auteserre, Severine, 'Hobbes and the Congo: Frames, Local Violence, and International. Intervention' (2009) 63 *International Organization* 249–80.

Auteserre, Severine, *The Trouble with Congo* (Cambridge University Press, 2010).

Ayoob, Mohammed, *The Third World Security Predicament: State Making, Regional Conflict and the International System* (Lynne Rienner, 1995).

Baldaccini, Anneliese, Elspeth Guild and Helen Toner (eds), *Whose Freedom, Security and Justice? EU Immigration and Asylum Law and Policy* (Hart, 2007).

Barbalet, Jack, 'Tillitens emotionella bas och dess följder', in Åsa Wettergren, Bengt Starrin and Gerd Lindgren (eds), *Det sociala livets emotionella grunder* (Liber, 2008).

Barber, Bernard, *The Logic and Limits of Trust* (Rutgers University Press, 1983).

Barnett, Laura, 'Global Governance and the Evolution of the International Refugee Regime' (2002) 14 *International Journal of Refugee Law* 238.

Barnett, Michael and Martha Finnemore, 'The Politics, Power, and Pathologies of International Organizations' (1999) 53 *International Organization* 699–732.

Barnett, Michael and Martha Finnemore, *Rules for the World: International Organizations in Global Politics* (Cornell University Press, 2004).

Bethlehem, Daniel, 'The End of Geography' (Comments on the Keynote Address at the Biennial Conference of the European Society of International Law, Cambridge, 2–4 September 2010).

Betts, Alexander, 'Survival Migration: A New Protection Framework' (2010) 16 *Global Governance* 361–382.

Betts, Alexander (ed.), *Global Migration Governance* (Oxford University Press, 2011).

Betts, Alexander, *Survival Migration: Failed Governance and the Crisis of Displacement* (Cornell University Press, 2013).

Bigo, Didier, 'The birth of ban-opticon: detention of foreigners in (il)liberal regimes', paper presented at the annual meeting of the International Studies Association, Hilton Hawaiian Village, Honolulu, Hawaii, 1–5 March 2005.

Bigo, Didier, 'Security: A Field Left Fallow', in Michael Dillon and Andrew Neal (eds), *Foucault on Politics, Security and War* (Palgrave Macmillan, 2008), 93–114.

Bloch, Alice, Nando Sigona and Roger Zetter, *No Right to Dream: The Social and Economic Lives of Young Undocumented Migrants in Britain* (Paul Hamlyn Foundation, 2009) <www.jrf.org.uk/publications/immigration-social-cohesion-and-social-capital-what-are-links>.

Bodegård, Göran, 'Pervasive Loss of Function Progressing to Devitalization: An Earlier Unknown Life Threatening Stress Reaction Seen in Asylum-Seeking Children in Sweden', in Hans E. Andersson *et al.* (eds), *The Asylum-Seeking Child in Europe* (Centre for European Research at the University of Gothenburg, 2005), ch. 12.

Boldrini, Laura, *Tutti indietro* (Rizzoli, 2010).

Boswell, Christina, *European Migration Policies in Flux: Changing Patterns of Inclusion and Exclusion* (Wiley-Blackwell, 2003).

Boswell, Christina, 'Theorizing Migration Policy: Is There a Third Way?' (2007) 41 *International Migration Review* 75.

Bosworth, Mary and Elspeth Guild, 'Governing through Migration Control: Security and Citizenship in Britain' (2008) 48 *British Journal of Criminology* 703–19.

Brekke, Jan-Paul, *While We Are Waiting: Uncertainty and Empowerment Among Asylum-Seekers in Sweden* (Report No. 2004:010) (Institute for Social Research, 2004).

Brubaker, Rogers, 'Aftermaths of Empire and the Unmixing of Peoples: Historical and Comparative Perspectives' (1995) 18 *Ethnic and Racial Studies* 189–218.

Burchell, Graham, 'Liberal Government and Techniques of the Self', in Andrew Barry, Thomas Osborne and Nikolas Rose (eds), *Foucault and Political Reason, Liberalism, Neo-Liberalism and Rationalities of Government* (University of Chicago Press, 1996), ch. 1.

Burley, Anne-Marie and Walter Mattli, 'Europe before the Court: A Political Theory of Legal Integration' (1993) 47 *International Organization* 41–76.

Busby, Joshua, 'Bono Made Jesse Helms Cry: Jubilee 2000, Debt Relief, and Moral Action in International Politics' (2007) 51 *International Studies Quarterly* 247–308.

Butler, Judith, *Gender Trouble: Feminism and the Subversion of Identity* (Routledge, 1999).

Buzan, Barry, Ole Weaver and Jaap De Wilde, *Security: A New Framework for Analysis* (Lynne Rienner, 1998).

Byrne, Rosemary and Andrew Shacknove, 'The Safe Country Notion in European Asylum Law' (1996) 9 *Harvard Human Rights Journal* 185–228.

Byrne, Rosemary, Gregor Noll and Jens Vedsted-Hansen, 'Understanding Refugee Law in an Enlarged European Union' (2004) 15 *European Journal of International Law* 355–79.

Caporaso, James A., 'Regional Integration Theory: Understanding Our Past and Anticipating Our Future', in Wayne Sandholtz and Alec Stone Sweet (eds), *European Integration and Supranational Governance* (Oxford University Press, 1998), ch. 12.

Castells, Manuel, *The Rise of the Network Society* (Blackwell, 1996).

Castles, Stephen, 'Towards a Sociology of Forced Migration and Transformation' (2003) 37 *Sociology* 13–34.

Castles, Stephen and Mark J. Miller, *The Age of Migration: International Population Movements in the Modern World* (4th edn, Palgrave Macmillan, 2006).

Cento Bull, Anna, 'Addressing Contradictory Needs: The Lega Nord and Italian Immigration Policy' (2010) 44 *Patterns of Prejudice* 411.

Chang-Muy, Fernando, 'International Refugee Law in Asia' (1991–2) 24 *New York University Journal of International Law and Policy* 1171.

Chase, Steven, 'New Fast-track Rules See Big Drop in Refugee Asylum Claims', *Globe and Mail*, 21 February 2013 <www.theglobeandmail.com/news/politics/new-fast-track-rules-see-big-drop-in-refugee-asylum-claims/article8961268/>.

Chatty, Dawn, *Displacement and Dispossession in the Modern Middle East* (Cambridge University Press, 2010).

Checkel, Jeffrey T., 'Norms, Institutions, and National Identity in Contemporary Europe' (1999) 43 *International Studies Quarterly* 83–114.

Chimni, B. S., 'Reforming the International Refugee Regime: A Dialogic Model' (2001) 14 *Journal of Refugee Studies* 151–68.

Chimni, B. S., 'The Birth of a 'Discipline: From Refugee to Forced Migration Studies' (2009) 22 *Journal of Refugee Studies* 11.

Chuensuksawad, Pichai, 'Full Text of the Interview with Malaysian Prime Minister Abdullah', *Bangkok Post* (Bangkok, 27 February 2009).

Clapham, Christopher, *Africa and the International System* (Cambridge University Press 1996).

Clarke, Anne-Marie, *Diplomacy of Conscience: Amnesty International and Changing Human Right Norms* (Princeton University Press, 2002).

Cortell, Andrew P. and James W. Davis Jr, 'Understanding the Domestic Impac of International Norms: A Research Agenda' (2000) 2 *International Studies Review* 65–87.

Cotterrell, Roger, *Law, Culture and Society* (Ashgate, 2006).

Crawley, Heaven, *Refugees and Gender: Law and Process* (Jordans, 2001).

Daly, Mark, 'Refugee Law in Hong Kong: Building the Legal Infrastructure', *Hong Kong Lawyer* (September 2009), 14–30.

Dauvergne, Catherine, *Making People Illegal* (Cambridge University Press, 2008).

Davies, Sara, 'Redundant or Essential? How Politics Shaped the Outcome of the 1967 Protocol' (2007) 19 *International Journal of Refugee Law* 703.

Davies, Sara, 'Seeking Security for Refugees', in Anthony Burke and Matt Macdonald (eds), *Critical Security in the Asia Pacific* (Manchester University Press, 2007).

Davies, Sara, 'The Asian Rejection? International Refugee Law in Asia' (2006) 52 *Australian Journal of Politics and History* 562.

Davies, Sara, *Legitimising Rejection: International Refugee Law in Southeast Asia* (Martinus Nijhoff, 2008).

de Haas, Hein and Nando Sigona, 'Migration and Revolution' (2012) 39 *Forced Migration Review* 4.

Dean, Mitchell, *Critical and Effective Histories: Foucault's Methods and Historical Sociology* (Routledge, 1994).

Dean, Mitchell, *Governmentality* (2nd edn, Sage, 2009).

Deere, Carolyn, *The Implementation Game: The TRIPS Agreement and the Global Politics of Intellectual Property Reform in Developing Countries* (Oxford University Press, 2009).

Derrida, Jacques, *Of Hospitality*, trans. Rachel Bowlby (Stanford University Press, 2000).

Diehl, Paul F., Charlotte Ku and Daniel Zamora, 'The Dynamics of International Law: The Interaction of Normative and Operating Systems' (2003) 57 *International Organization* 43–75.

Dillon, Mitchell and Andrew Neal (eds), *Foucault on Politics, Security and War* (Palgrave Macmillan, 2008).

DiMaggio, Paul and Walter Powell, 'The Iron Cage Revisited: Institutionalism Isomorphism and Collective Rationality', in W. Powell and P. DiMaggio (eds), *The New Institutionalism in Organizational Analysis* (Chicago University Press, 1991), ch. 3, 63–82.

Drezner, Daniel, *All Politics is Global* (Princeton University Press, 2007).

Dumper, Michael, 'Palestinian Refugees', in Gil Loescher, James Milner, Edward Newman and Gary Troeller (eds), *Protracted Refugee Situations – Political, Human Rights and Security Implications* (UN University Press, 2008).

Dumper, Michael (ed.), *Palestinian Refugee Repatriation: Global Perspectives* (Routledge, 2006).

Dumper, Michael, *The Future for Palestinian Refugees: Towards Equity and Peace* (Lynne Rienner, 2007).

Durieux, Jean-François, 'The Many Faces of "Prima Facie": Group-Based Evidence in Refugee Status Determination' (2008) 25 *Refuge* 151–63.

Durieux, Jean-François, 'The Vanishing Refugee: How EU Asylum Law Blurs the Specificity of Refugee Protection', in Hélène Lambert, Jane McAdam and Maryellen Fullerton (eds), *The Global Reach of European Refugee Law* (Cambridge University Press, 2013), 228.

Eastmond, Marita, 'Gäster i välfärden? Föräldraskap i asylprocessen', in Hans E. Andersson *et al.* (eds), *Mellan det förflutna och framtiden. Asylsökande barns välfärd, hälsa och välbefinnande* (Centre for European Research at the University of Gothenburg, 2010), ch. 3.

Eastmond, Marita and Henry Ascher, 'In the Best Interest of the Child? The Politics of Vulnerability and Negotiations for Asylum in Sweden' (2011) 37 *Journal of Ethnic and Migration Studies* 1185.

Edwards, Alice, 'Symposium: Territory without Boundaries: Immigration beyond Territory: Human Security and the Rights of Refugees: Transcending Territorial and Disciplinary Borders' (2009) 30 *Michigan Journal of International Law* 763.

Einarsen, Terje, 'Drafting History of the 1951 Convention and the 1967 Protocol', in Andreas Zimmermann (ed.), *The 1951 Convention Relating to the Status of Refugees and Its 1967 Protocol* (Oxford University Press, 2011).

Elmadmad, Khadija, 'An Arab Convention on Forced Migration: Desirability and Possibilities' (1991) 3 *International Journal of Refugee Law* 461–481.

Feller, Erika, Volker Türk and Frances Nicholson (eds), *Refugee Protection in International Law: UNHCR's Global Consultations on International Protection* (Cambridge University Press, 2003).

Finnemore, Martha and Kathryn Sikkink, 'International Norm Dynamics and Political Change' (1998) 52 *International Organization* 887–917.

Fortin, Antonio, 'The Meaning of "Protection" in the Refugee Definition' (2001) 12 *International Journal of Refugee Law* 548.

Foster, Michelle, *International Refugee Law and Socio-Economic Rights* (Cambridge University Press, 2007).

Foster, Michelle, 'Protection Elsewhere: The Legal Implications of Requiring Refugees to Seek Protection in Another State' (2007) 28 *Michigan Journal of International Law* 223.

Foucault, Michel, 'The Political Technology of Individuals', in Luther H. Martin, Huck Gutman and Patrick H. Hutton (eds), *Technologies of the Self: A Seminar with Michel Foucault* (University of Massachusetts Press, 1988), 16–49.

Foucault, Michel, 'Governmentality', in Graham Burchell, Collin Gordon and Peter Miller (eds), *The Foucault Effect: Studies in Governmentality* (University of Chicago Press, 1991), ch. 4.

Foucault, Michel, *Discipline and Punish: The Birth of the Prison* (Vintage, 1995).

Foucault, Michel, *Society Must Be Defended: Lectures at the Collège de France 1975–76* (Palgrave Macmillan, 2003).

Foucault, Michel, *The Birth of Biopolitics: Lectures at the Collège de France 1978–1979* (Palgrave Macmillan, 2008).

Foucault, Michel, *Security, Territory, Population: Lectures at the Collège de France 1977–1978* (Palgrave Macmillan, 2009).

Franck, Thomas M., *The Power of Legitimacy among Nations* (Oxford University Press, 1990).

Franck, Thomas M., 'The Power of Legitimacy and the Legitimacy of Power: International Law in an Age of Power Disequilibrium' (2006) 100 *American Journal of International Law* 88–106.

Fuller, Lon L., 'The Forms and Limits of Adjudication' (1978) 92 *Harvard Law Review* 353.

Gammeltoft-Hansen, Thomas, *Access to Asylum: International Refugee Law and the Globalization of Migration Control* (Cambridge University Press, 2011).

Garlick, Madeline, 'The EU Discussions on Extraterritorial Processing: Solution or Conundrum' (2006) 18 *International Journal of Refugee Law* 601–29.

Geddes, Andrew, *Immigration and European Integration – Beyond Fortress Europe?* (2nd edn, Manchester University Press, 2008).

Geddes, Andrew, *Immigration and European Integration: Towards Fortress Europe?* (Manchester University Press, 2000).

Geddes, Andrew, *The Politics of Migration and Immigration in Europe* (Sage, 2003).

Geddes, John, 'Kenney Assertive on Roma Refugees, but Critics Argue the Details', *Maclean's* 14 December 2012 <www2.macleans.ca/2012/12/14/kenney-assertive-on-roma-refugees-but-critics-argue-the-details/>.

Gelber, Katharine, 'A Fair Queue? Australian Public Discourse on Refugees and Immigration' (2003) 27 *Journal of Australian Studies* 23.

Gibney, Matthew J., *The Ethics and Politics of Asylum: Liberal Democracy and the Response to Refugees* (Cambridge University Press, 2004).

Gibney, Matthew J. and Randall Hansen (eds), *Immigration and Asylum: From 1900 to the Present*, Vol. I (ABC CLIO, 2005).

Gil-Bazo, Maria-Teresa, 'The Charter of Fundamental Rights of the European Union and the Right to be Granted Asylum in the Union's Law' (2008) 27 *Refugee Survey Quarterly* 33–52.

Goertz, Gary, *International Norms and Decision Making: A Punctuated Equilibrium* (Rowman and Littlefield, 2003).

Goffman, Erving, *Stigma: Notes on the Management of Spoiled Identity* (Penguin, 1963).

Goffman, Erving, *Asylums* (Penguin, 1982).

Goldman, Emily and Leslie Eliason (eds), *The Diffusion of Military Technology and Ideas* (Stanford University Press, 2003).

Goodwin-Gill, Guy and Jane McAdam, *The Refugee in International Law* (3rd edn, Oxford University Press, 2007).

Goodwin-Gill, Guy S. and Hélène Lambert (eds), *The Limits of Transnational Law: Refugee Law, Policy Harmonization and Judicial Dialogue in the European Union* (Cambridge University Press, 2010).

Gordkenker, Leon, *Refugees in International Politics* (Columbia University Press, 1987).

Gordon, Thomas E., 'The Problems of the Middle East' (March 1900) 47 *Nineteenth Century*, 413–24.

Gorlick, Brian, 'Common Burdens and Standards: Legal Elements in Assessing Claims to Refugee Status' (2003) 15 *International Journal of Refugee Law* 357.

Grahl-Madsen, Atle, *The Status of Refugees in International Law*, Vol. I (AW Sijthoff-Leiden, 1972).

Gros, Frédéric, *États de violence: Essai sur la fin de la guerre* (Gallimard, 2006).

Guild, Elspeth, 'Exceptionalism and Transnationalism: UK Judicial Control of the Detention of Foreign "International terrorists"' (2003) 28 *Alternatives: Global, Local, Political* 491–515.

Guild, Elspeth, 'Seeking Asylum: Storm Clouds between International Commitments and EU Legislative Measures' (2004) 29 *European Law Review* 198–218.

Guild, Elspeth, 'The Europeanisation of Europe's Asylum Policy' (2006) 18 *International Journal of Refugee Law* 630–51.

Guild, Elspeth, *Security and Migration in the 21st Century* (Polity, 2009).

Guild, Elspeth and Carol Harlow (eds), *Implementing Amsterdam: Immigration and Asylum Rights in EC Law* (Hart, 2001).

Haas, Ernst, *The Uniting of Europe* (Stanford University Press, 1958).

Haas, Ernst, 'Why Collaborate? Issue-Linkage and International Regimes' (1980) 32 *World Politics* 357–405.

Haas, Peter, 'Epistemic Communities and International Policy Coordination' (1992) 41 *International Organization* 1–35.

Hacker, Jacob, 'Privatizing Risk without Privatizing the Welfare State' (2004) 98 *American Political Science Review* 243–260.

Haddad, Emma, *The Refugee in International Society: Between Sovereigns* (Cambridge University Press, 2008).

Hall, Peter and Kathleen Thelen, 'Institutional Change in Varieties of Capitalism' (2009) 7 *Socio-Economic Review* 7–34.

Harper, Andrew, 'Iraq's Refugees: Ignored and Unwanted' (2008) 90 *International Review of the Red Cross* 169–90.

Harvey, Colin, 'Is Humanity Enough? Refugees, Asylum Seekers and the Rights Regime', in Satvinder Juss and Colin Harvey (eds), *Contemporary Issues in International Refugee Law* (Edward Elgar, 2013), 68–88.

Hasenclever, Andreas, Stefan Meyer and Volker Rittberger, *Theories of International Regimes* (Cambridge University Press, 1997).

Hathaway, James C., 'The Evolution of Refugee Status in International Law: 1920–1950' (1984) 33 *International and Comparative Law Quarterly* 348.

Hathaway, James C., 'A Reconsideration of the Underlying Premise of Refugee Law' (1990) 31 *Harvard International Law Journal* 129.

Hathaway, James C., 'Reconceiving Refugee Law and Human Rights Protection' (1991) 4 *Journal of Refugee Studies* 113.

Hathaway, James C., *The Law of Refugee Status* (Butterworths, 1991).

Hathaway, James C., *The Rights of Refugees under International Law* (Cambridge University Press, 2005).

Hathaway, James C., 'Forced Migration Studies: Could We Agree Just to "Date"?' (2007) 20 *Journal of Refugee Studies* 349.

Hathaway, James C. and R. Alexander Neve, 'Making International Refugee Law Relevant Again: A Proposal for Collectivised and Solution-Oriented Protection' (1997) 10 *Harvard Human Rights Journal* 115.

Hawkins, Darren *et al.* (eds), *Delegation and Agency in International Organizations* (Cambridge University Press, 2006).

Hayden, Bridget, 'What's in a Name? The Nature of the Individual in Refugee Studies' (2006) 19 *Journal of Refugee Studies* 471–87.

Heckmann, Friedrich, 'Illegal Migration: What Can We Know and What Can We Explain? The Case of Germany' (2004) 38 *International Migration Review* 1103.

Heidegren, Carl-Gören, *Erkännande* (Liber, 2009).

Herlihy, Jane and Stuart W. Turner, 'The Psychology of Seeking Protection' (2009) 21 *International Journal of Refugee Law* 171.

Hilal, Leila and Shahira Samy, *Asylum and Migration on the Mashrek – Asylum and Migration Country Fact Sheet: Syria* (Euro-Mediterranean Human Rights Network, 2008).

Hindess, Barry, 'Government and Discipline' (2008) 2 *International Political Sociology* 268–270.

Human Security Report Project, *Human Security Backgrounder* (Simon Fraser University School for International Studies, 2005) <www.humansecurityreport.info/index.php?option=content&task=view&id=24&Itemid=59>.

Hurd, Ian, 'Strategic Use of Liberal Internationalism: Libya and the UN Sanctions' (2005) 59 *International Organization* 495–526.

Hurd, Ian, *After Anarchy: Legitimacy and Power in the United Nations Security Council* (Princeton University Press, 2008).

Hyndman, Jennifer, 'Introduction: the Feminist Politics of Refugee Migration' (2010) 17 *Gender, Place and Culture* 453–59.

Jackson, Ivor, *The Refugee Concept in Group Situations* (Kluwer Law International, 1999).

Jackson, Robert, *Quasi-States: Sovereignty, International Relations and the Third World* (Cambridge University Press, 1990).

Jayasinghe, Udara and Sasha Baglay, 'Protecting Victims of Human Rights within a "Non-Refoulement" Framework: Is Complementary Protection an Effective Alternative in Canada and Australia?' (2011) 23 *International Journal of Refugee Law* 489.

Jepperson, Ronald, Alexander Wendt and Peter Katzenstein, 'Norms, Identity and Culture in National Security', in Peter J. Katzenstein (ed.), *The Culture of National Security: Norms and Identities in World Politics* (Columbia University Press, 1996), ch. 2.

Joerges, Christian, 'Deliberative Political Processes Revisited: What Have We learned about the Legitimacy of Supranational Decision Making' (2006) 44 *Journal of Common Market Studies* 779–812.

Joly, Daniéle (ed.) *Global Changes in Asylum Regimes* (Palgrave Macmillan, 2002).

Joppke, Christian, 'Asylum and State Sovereignty' (1997) 30 *Comparative Political Studies* 259.

Kagan, Michael, 'The Beleaguered Gatekeeper: Protection Challenges Posed by UNHCR Refugee Status Determination' (2006) 18 *International Journal of Refugee Law* 1–29.

Kalin, Walter, 'Non-State Agents of Persecution and the Inability of the State to Protect' (2001) 15 *Georgetown Immigration Law Journal* 415.

Karpat, Kemal, *Studies on Ottoman Social and Political History: Selected Articles and Essays* (Brill, 2002).

Karpat, Kemal, 'The Transformation of the Ottoman State, 1789–1908' (1972) *International Journal of Middle East Studies* 243–81.

Keck, Margaret E. and Kathryn Sikkink, *Activists beyond Borders: Advocacy Networks in International Politics* (Cornell University Press, 1999).

Keohane, Robert O., 'The Demand for International Regimes' (1982) 36 *International Organization* 332–355.

Kesby, Alison, *The Right to Have Rights: Citizenship, Humanity and International Law* (Oxford University Press, 2012).

Keselman, Olga *et al.*, 'Mediated Communication with Minors in Asylum-Seeking Hearings' (2008) 21 *Journal of Refugee Studies* 103.

King, Gary, Robert Keohane and Sidney Verba, *Designing Social Enquiry: Scientific Inference in Qualitative Research* (Princeton University Press, 1994).

Klotz, Anne, *Norms in International Relations* (Cornell University Press, 1995).

Kneebone, Susan, 'Moving beyond the State: Refugees, Accountability and Protection', in Susan Kneebone (ed.), *The Refugees Convention 50 Years on: Globalisation and International Law* (Ashgate, 2003), ch. 11.

Kneebone, Susan, 'Strangers at the Gate: Refugees, Citizenship and Nationality' (2004) 10 *Australian Journal of Human Rights* 33.

Kneebone, Susan, 'What We *Have* Done with the Refugees Convention: The Australian Way' (2005) 22 *Law in Context 83*.

Kneebone, Susan (ed.), *Refugees, Asylum Seekers and the Rule of Law: Comparative Perspectives* (Cambridge University Press, 2009).

Kneebone, Susan, 'Refugees and Displaced Persons: The Refugee Definition and "Humanitarian" Protection', in Sarah Joseph and Adam McBeth (eds), *Research Handbook on International Human Rights Law* (Edward Elgar, 2010), ch. 9.

Kneebone, Susan, 'The Refugee–Trafficking Nexus: Making Good (the) Connections' (2010) 29 *Refugee Survey Quarterly* 137.

Kneebone, Susan, 'Outing Offshore Processing: The High Court of Australia Defines the Role of the Refugee Convention' (2012) 26 *Immigration, Asylum and Nationality Law* 156.

Kneebone, Susan, 'Protecting Trafficked Persons from *Refoulement*: Re-examining the Nexus', in Satvinder Juss and Colin Harvey (eds), *Contemporary Issues in International Refugee Law* (Edward Elgar, 2013), ch. 5.

Kneebone, Susan and Maria O'Sullivan, 'Commentary on Art. 1C of the Refugee Convention', in Andreas Zimmerman (ed.), *The 1951 Convention Relating to the Status of Refugees and Its 1967 Protocol: A Commentary* (Oxford University Press, 2011), ch. 23.

Kneebone, Susan and Felicity Rawlings-Sanaei (eds), *New Regionalism and Asylum Seekers: Challenges Ahead* (Berghahn, 2007).

Koh, Harold Hongju, 'Why Do Nations Obey International Law?' (1997) 106 *Yale Law Journal* 2599–659.

Koppes, Clayton R., 'Captain Mahan, General Gordon, and the Origins of the Term Middle East' (1976) 12(1) *Middle Eastern* Studies 95–98.

Korac, Maja, 'Cross-Ethnic Networks, Self-Reception System, and Functional Integration of Refugees from the Former Yugoslavia in Rome' (2001) 2 *Journal of International Migration and Integration* 1.

Korac, Maja, 'Politiche, agency e dialogo interculturale. Esperienze dei rifugiati dei conflitti jugoslavi in Italia' (2009) 3 *Mondi migranti* 127.

Korac, Maja, *Remaking Home: Reconstructing Life, Place and Identity in Rome and Amsterdam* (Berghahn, 2009).

Koser, Khalid and Charles Pinkerton, *The Social Networks of Asylum Seekers and the Dissemination of Information about Countries of Asylum* (Home Office, 2002).

Koslowski, Rey and David Kyle, *Global Human Smuggling* (John Hopkins University Press, 2001).

Krasner, Steve, *Sovereignty: Organized Hypocrisy* (Princeton University Press, 1999).

Laessing, Ulf, 'Yemen getting tougher on Somalis on Qaeda fears' (Reuters, 9 February 2010).

Lambert, Hélène, 'Transnational Judicial Dialogue, Harmonization and the Common European Asylum System' (1999) 58 *International and Comparative Law Quarterly* 519–43.

Lambert, Hélène, 'Transnational Law, Judges and Refugees in the European Union', in Guy S. Goodwin-Gill and Hélène Lambert (eds), *The Limits of Transnational Law: Refugee Law, Policy Harmonization and Judicial Dialogue in the European Union* (Cambridge University Press, 2010), ch. 1.

Lambert, Hélène, Jane McAdam and Maryellen Fullerton (eds), *The Global Reach of European Refugee Law* (Cambridge University Press, 2013).

Lavenex, Sandra, *The Europeanisation of Refugee Policies: Between Human Rights and Internal Security* (Ashgate, 2001).

Lavenex, Sandra and Emek M. Uçarer (eds), *Migration and the Externalities of European Integration* (Lexington Books, 2003).

Lebanese Centre for Human Rights, *Asylum Seekers and Refugees: Languishing in Injustice* (2011).

'Legality *vs* Legitimacy: Detention of Refugees and Asylum Seekers in Lebanon' (Beirut: Frontiers Association, 2006).

Legomsky, Stephen, 'Secondary Refugee Movements and the Return of Asylum Seekers to Third Countries: The Meaning of Effective Protection' (2003) 15 *International Journal of Refugee Law* 567.

Legrand, Pierre, 'European Legal Systems are not Converging' (1996) 45 *International and Comparative Law Quarterly* 52–81.

Legro, Jeffrey W., 'Which Norms Matter? Revisiting the "Failure" of Internationalism' (1997) 51 *International Organization* 31–63.

Lemke, Douglas, *Regions of War and Peace* (Cambridge University Press, 2002).

Levitz, Stephanie, 'Israel, Mexico added to list of "safe" countries for refugee claimants', *Globe and Mail*, 14 February 2013 <www.theglobeandmail.com/news/politics/israel-mexico-added-to-list-of-safe-countries-for-refugee-claimants/article8677347/>.

Lieberman, Robert, 'Ideas, Institutions and Political Order: Explaining Political Change' (2002) 96 *American Political Science Review* 697–712.

Linos, Katerina, 'When Do Policy Innovations Spread? Lessons for Advocates of Lesson-Drawing' (2006) 119 *Harvard Law Review* 1467–87.

Linos, Katerina, 'Diffusion through Democracy' (2011) 55 *American Journal of Political Science* 678–95.

Loescher, Gil, *UNHCR in World Politics: A Perilous Path* (Oxford University Press, 2001).

Long, Katy, 'When Refugees Stopped Being Migrants: Movement, Labour and Humanitarian Protection' (2013) 1 *Migration Studies* 4–26.

Löwenheim, Oded, 'The Responsibility to Responsibilize: Foreign Offices and the Issuing of Travel Warnings' (2007) 1 *International Political Sociology* 203–21.

Luhmann, Niklas, 'Familiarity, Confidence, Trust: Problems and Alternatives', in Diego Gambetta (ed.), *Trust: Making and Breaking Cooperative Relations* (Basil Blackwell, 1988).

Lui, Robyn Nicole, 'State Sovereignty and International Refugee Protection', in Trudy Jacobsen, Charles Sampford and Ramesh Thakur (eds), *Re-envisioning Sovereignty: The End of Westphalia?* (Ashgate, 2008).

McAdam, Jane, *Complementary Protection in International Refugee Law* (Oxford University Press, 2007).

McAdam, Jane, 'The Refugee Convention as a Rights Blueprint for Persons in Need of International Protection', in Jane McAdam (ed.), *Moving On: Forced Migration and Human Rights* (Hart, 2008).

McAdam, Jane, *Climate Change, Forced Migration, and International Law* (Oxford University Press, 2011).

McCarthy, Justin, *The Ottoman Peoples and the End of Empire* (Arnold, 2001).

Macklin, Audrey, 'A Safe Country to Emulate? Canada and the European Refugee', in Hélène Lambert *et al.* (eds), *The Global Reach of European Refugee Law* (Cambridge University Press, 2013), ch. 4.

McCleod, Fiona *et al.*, '"AIDS Assassins": Australian Media's Portrayal of HIV-Positive Refugees Who Deliberately Infect Others' (2011) 9 *Journal of Immigration and Refugee Studies* 20.

McCleod, Fiona, Samantha Thomas and Susan Kneebone, '"It Would Be Okay If They Came through the Proper Channels": Community Perceptions and Attitudes toward Asylum Seekers in Australia' (2012) 25 *Journal of Refugee Studies* 113.

Mahan, Alfred Thayer, 'The Persian Gulf and International Relations' (September 1902) *National Review* 40, 39.

Mahoney, James and Kathleen Thelen, 'A Theory of Gradual Institutional Change', in James Mahoney and Kathleen Thelen (eds), *Explaining Institutional Change: Ambiguity, Agency and Power* (Cambridge University Press, 2010), 1–37.

Malkki, Liisa, *Purity and Exile: Violence, Memory and National Cosmology Among Hutu Refugees in Tanzania* (Chicago University Press, 1995).

Manners, Ian, 'Normative Power Europe: A Contradiction in Terms?' (2002) 40 *Journal of Common Market Studies* 235–58.

Manocchi, Michele, *Richiedenti asilo e rifugiati politici. Percorsi di ricostruzione identitaria: il caso torinese* (FrancoAngeli, 2012).

Marchetti, Chiara, 'Blurring Boundaries: "Refugee" Definitions in Policies, Law and Social Discourse in Italy' (2007) 11 *Mediterranean Journal of Human Rights* 71.

Marchetti, Chiara, 'Rifugiati e richiedenti asilo: introduzione' (2009) 3 *Mondi migranti* 29.

Marchetti, Chiara, 'The Expanded Border. Policies and Practices of Preventive Refoulement in Italy', in Martin Geiger and Antoine Pécoud (eds), *The New Politics of Mobility: Discourses, Actors and Practices of Migration Management* (Palgrave Macmillan, 2010).

Marchetti, Chiara, 'Assistiti o segregati? I grandi centri per richiedenti asilo in Italia' (2012) 41 *La società degli individui* 57.

Marques, Rafael, *Lundas: The Stones of Death, Angola's Deadly Diamonds: Human Rights Abuses in the Lunda Provinces, 2004* (Apoios, 2005).

Marrus, Michael, *The Unwanted* (Temple University Press, 2002).

Meredith, Martin, *Robert Mugabe: Power, Plunder and Tyranny in Zimbabwe* (Jonathan Ball, 2002).

Mertus, Julie, 'The State and the Post-Cold War Refugee Regime: New Models, New Questions' (1998) 10 *International Journal of Refugee Law* 321.

Meyer, James, 'Immigration, Return, and the Politics of Citizenship: Russian Muslims in the Ottoman Empire, 1860–1914' (2007) 39 *International Journal of Middle East Studies* 15–32.

Meyer, John *et al.*, 'The Structuring of a World Environmental Regime, 1870–1990' (1997) 51 *International Organization* 623–51.

Milner, James, *Refugees, The State and the Politics of Asylum in Africa* (Palgrave Macmillan, 2009).

Misztal, Barbara A., *Trust in Modern Societies: The Search for the Bases of Social Order* (Polity, 1996).

Moravcsik, Andrew, 'Preferences and Power in the European Community: A Liberal Intergovernmentalist Approach' (1993) 31 *Journal of Common Market Studies* 473–524.

Moravcsik, Andrew, 'Taking Preferences Seriously: A Liberal Theory of International Relations' 1997 (51) *International Organization* 513–53.

Moreno-Lax, Violeta, 'Must EU Borders Have Doors for Refugees? On the Compatibility of Schengen Visas and Carriers' Sanctions with EU Member States' Obligations to Provide International Protection to Refugees' (2008) 10 *European Journal of Migration and Law* 315–64.

Morrow, Virginia, 'Conceptualising Social Capital in Relation to the Well-Being of Children and Young People: A Critical Review' (1999) 47 *Sociological Review* 744.

Muller, Harald, 'Arguing, Bargaining and All That: Communicative Action, Rationalist Theory, and the Logic of Appropriateness in International Relations' (2004) 10 *European Journal of International Relations* 395–435.

Nathwani, Niraj, 'The Purpose of Asylum' (2001) 12 *International Journal of Refugee Law* 354.

Neal, Andrew, 'Goodbye War on Terror? Foucault and Butler on Discourses of Law, War and Exceptionalism', in Michael Dillon and Andrew Neal (eds), *Foucault on Politics, Security and War* (Palgrave Macmillan, 2008), 43–64.

Nelken, David (ed.), *Comparing Legal Cultures* (Ashgate, 1997).

Neumayer, Eric, 'Do International Human Rights Treaties Improve Respect for Human Rights?' (2005) 49 *Journal of Conflict Resolution* 925–953.

Nicholson, Philippa and Sarah Biddulph (eds), *Examining Practice, Interrogating Theory: Comparative Legal Studies in Asia* (Martinus Nijhoff, 2008).

Nilsson, Eva, 'A Child Perspective in the Swedish Asylum Process: Rhetoric and Practice', in Hans E. Andersson *et al.* (eds), *The Asylum-Seeking Child in Europe* (Centre for European Research at the University of Gothenburg, 2005), ch. 7.

Nilsson, Eva, *Barn i rättens gränsland. Om barnperspektiv vid prövning av uppehållstillstånd* (Justus, 2007).

Noll, Gregor, 'Visions of the Exceptional: Legal and Theoretical Issues Raised by Transit Processing Centres and Protection Zones' (2003) 5 *European Journal of Migration and Law* 303–41.

Oberoi, Pia, 'Regional Initiatives on Refugee Protection in South Asia' (1999) 11 *International Journal of Refugee Law* 193.

Oestreich, Joel, *Power and Principle: Human Rights Programming in International Organizations* (Georgetown University Press, 2007).

Olson, Mancur, *Power and Prosperity: Outgrowing Communist and Capitalist Dictatorships* (Oxford University Press, 2000).

Ostrom, Elinor, *Governing the Commons: The Evolution of Institutions for Collective Action* (Cambridge University Press, 1990).

O'Sullivan, Maria, 'Acting the Part: Can Non-State Entities Provide Protection under International Refugee Law?' (2012) 24 *International Journal of Refugee Law* 85.

Ottosson, Lisa, '"Barntänk" ur ett tjänstemanaperspektiv. En intervjustudie med barnhandläggare vid Migrationsverket', in Hans E. Andersson *et al.* (eds), *Mellan det förflutna och framtiden. Asylsökande barns välfärd, hälsa och välbefinnande* (Centre for European Research at the University of Gothenburg, 2010), ch. 2.

Park, Susan, 'Theorizing Norm Diffusion Within International Organizations' (2006) 43 *International Politics* 342–61.

Percy, Sarah V., 'Mercenaries: Strong Norm, Weak Law' (2007) 61 *International Organization* 367–97.

Pierson, Paul, *Politics in Time: History, Institutions, and Social Analysis* (Princeton University Press, 2004).

Pierson, Paul, 'The Study of Policy Development' (2005) 17 *Journal of Policy History* 34–51.

Polzer Ngwato, Tara, 'Responding to Zimbabwean Migration in South Africa: Evaluating Options' (2008) 15 *South African Journal of International Affairs* 1–15.

Ramirez, Francisco and John Meyer, 'Comparative Education: The Social Construction of the Modern World System' (1980) 6 *Annual Review of Sociology* 369–99.

Raustiala, Kal and Anne-Marie Slaughter, 'International Law, International Relations and Compliance', in Walter Carlnaes, Thomas Risse and Beth Simmons (eds), *The Handbook of International Relations* (Sage, 2002).

Reyneri, Emilio and Giovanna Fullin, 'Labour Market Penalties of New Immigrants in New and Old Receiving West European Countries' (2010) 49 *International Migration* 31.

Rijpma, Jorrit J., *Frontex: Successful Blame Shifting of the Member States?* (ARI) Real Instituto Elcano, Madrid, Spain, 13 April 2010 <www.realinstitutoelcano.org/wps/wcm/conne ct/391e6a00421a96f98d66ef8b6be8b54b/ARI692010_Rijpma_Frontex_Memeber_ State_European_Union.pdf?MOD=AJPERES&CACHEID=391e6a00421a96f98d6 6ef8b6be8b54b>.

Risse, Thomas, Steven Ropp and Kathryn Sikkink, *The Power of Human Rights: International Norms and Domestic Change* (Cambridge University Press, 1999).

Risse-Kappen, Thomas, 'Ideas Do Not Float Freely: Transnational Coalitions, Domestic Structures, and the End of the Cold War' (1994) 48 *International Organization* 165–214.

Risse-Kappen, Thomas, *Bringing Transnational Relations Back in: Non-state Actors, Domestic Structures, and International Institutions* (Cambridge University Press, 1995).

Rose, Nikolas and Peter Miller, *Governing the Present: Administering Economic, Social and Personal Life* (Polity, 2008).

Rousseau, Cecile, Francois Crepeau, Patricia Foxe and France Houle, 'The Complexity of Determining Refugeehood: A Multidisciplinary Analysis of the Decision-making Process of the Canadian Immigration and Refugee Board' (2002) 15 *Journal of Refugee Studies* 43.

Ruelle, Charles, 'Population, milieu et normes: Note sur l'enracinement biologique de la biopolitique de Foucault' (2005) 22 *Labyrinthe* 27–36.

Ruhs, Martin and Bridget Anderson, 'Semi-Compliance in the Labour Market', *COMPAS Working Paper No. 30* (COMPAS, 2006).

Rutinwa, Bonaventure, 'The End of Asylum: The Changing Nature of Refugee Policies in Africa' (2002) 21 *Refugee Survey Quarterly* 2–41.

Ryan, Bernard and Mitsilegas Valsamis (eds), *Extraterritorial Immigration Control: Legal Challenges* (Martinus Nijhoff, 2010) <http://nijhoffonline.nl/book?id=nij97890041 72333_nij9789004172333_i-441>.

Saxena, Prabodh, 'Creating Legal Space for Refugees in India: the Milestones Crossed and the Roadmap for the Future' (2007) 19 *International Journal of Refugee Law* 246.

Schain, Martin, 'The State Strikes Back: Immigration Policy in the European Union' (2009) 20 *The European Journal of International Law* 93.

Schuster, Liza, 'Dublino II ed Eurodac: esame delle conseguenze (in)attese' (2009) 3 *Mondi Migranti* 37.

Severino, Rudolfo, 'ASEAN Beyond Forty: Towards Political and Economic Integration' (2007) 29 *Contemporary Southeast Asia: A Journal of International and Strategic Affairs* 406.

Shacknove, Andrew E., 'Who Is a Refugee?' (1985) 95 *Ethics* 274–84.

Shaw, S. and E. K. Shaw, *Ottoman Empire and Modern Turkey, Volume II: Reform, Revolution and Republic* (Cambridge University Press, 1977).

Shoukri, Arafat Madi, *Refugee Status in Islam* (IB Tauris, 2011).

Simmons, Beth, *Mobilizing for Human Rights* (Cambridge University Press, 2009).

Simpson, Jeffery, 'Refugee reform: give Kenney's Plan a Chance to Work', *Globe and Mail*, 23 January 2013 <www.theglobeandmail.com/commentary/refugee-reform-give-kenneys-plan-a-chance-to-work/article7623935/>.

Sjöberg, Tommie, *The Powers and the Persecuted* (Lund University Press, 1991).

Skran, Claudena, *Refugees in Inter-War Europe* (Clarendon Press, 1998).

Slaughter, Anne-Marie, *A New World Order* (Princeton University Press, 2004).

Slaughter, Anne-Marie and William Burke-White, 'The Future of International Law is Domestic (or, the European Way of Law)' (2006) 47 *Harvard International Law Journal* 327–52.

Slaughter, Amy and Jeff Crisp, 'A Surrogate State? The Role of UNHCR in Protracted Refugee Situations', in G. Loescher *et al.* (eds), *Protracted Refugee Situations* (United Nations University Press, 2008) 123–40.

Smadi, Khair, 'Towards Adopting a Legal System for Asylum in Jordan' (January 2011) 11 *Fahamu Refugee Legal Aid Newsletter* 11.

Spijkerboer, Thomas, *Gender and Refugee Status* (Ashgate, 2000).

Squire, Victoria, *The Exclusionary Politics of Asylum* (Palgrave Macmillan, 2009).

Statham, Paul, 'Understanding Anti-alien Rhetoric: Restrictive Politics or Racist Publics' (2003) 74 *Political Quarterly* 163.

Stein, Eric, 'Lawyers, Judges, and the Making of a Transnational Constitution' (1981) 75 *American Journal of International Law* 1–27.

Steinbock, Daniel J., 'The Refugee Definition as Law: Issues of Interpretation', in Frances Nicholson and Patrick Twomey (eds), *Refugee Rights and Realities: Evolving International Concepts and Regimes* (Cambridge University Press, 1999), ch. 1.

Stevens, Dallal, *UK Asylum Law and Policy* (Sweet & Maxwell, 2004).

Stevens, Dallal, 'Between East and West – the Case of Israel', in Hélène Lambert, Jane McAdam and Maryellen Fullerton (eds), *The Global Reach of European Refugee Law* (Cambridge University Press, 2013).

Stevens, Dallal, 'Legal Status, Labelling and Protection: The Case of Iraqi "Refugees" in Jordan' (2013) 25 *International Journal of Refugee Law* 1–38.

Stevens, Dallal, 'What Do We Mean by Protection?' (2013) 20 *International Journal on Minority and Group Rights* 233.

Stoeva, Preslava, *New Norms and Knowledge in World Politics* (Routledge, 2010).

Sundstrom, Lisa McIntosh, 'Foreign Assistance, International Norms, and NGO Development: Lessons from the Russian Campaign' (2005) 59 *International Organization* 419–49.

Takkenberg, Lex, *The Status of Palestinian Refugees in International Law* (Clarendon Press, 1998).

Tamas, Gellert, *De apatiska. Om makt, myter och manipulation* (Natur och Kultur, 2009).

Teubner, Gunther, 'Legal Irritants: Good Faith in British Law or How Unifying Law Ends up in New Divergences' (1998) 61 *Modern Law Review* 11–32.

Thielemann, Eiko and Nadine El-Enany, 'Refugee Protection as a Collective Action Problem: Is the EU Shirking Its Responsibilities?' (2010) 19 *European Security* 209–29.

Triandafyllidou, Anna and Maurizio Ambrosini, 'Irregular Immigration Control in Italy and Greece: Strong Fencing and Weak Gate-Keeping Serving the Labour Market' (2011) 13 *European Journal of Migration and Law* 251.

Tsebelis, George, *Veto Players: How Political Institutions Work* (Princeton University Press, 2002).

Tuitt, Patricia, *False Images: Law's Construction of the Refugee* (Pluto, 1996).

Tursunovic, Mirzet, 'Skolan i de asylsökande barnens vardag', in Hans E. Andersson *et al.* (eds), *Mellan det förflutna och framtiden. Asylsökande barns välfärd, hälsa och välbefinnande* (Centre for European Research at the University of Gothenburg, 2010).

Turton, David, 'Who Is a Forced Migrant?', in Chris de Wet (ed.), *Development-Induced Displacement: Problems, Policies and People* (Berghahn, 2006), ch. 2.

Twining, William, *Globalisation and Legal Theory* (Cambridge University Press, 2000).

Twining, William, 'Diffusion of Law: A Global Perspective' (2004) 49 *Journal of Legal Pluralism* 1–45.

Twining, William, 'Social Science and Diffusion of Law' (2005) 32 *Journal of Law and Society* 203–40.

Twining, William, 'Normative and Legal Pluralism: A Global Perspective' (2010) 20 *Duke Journal of Comparative & International Law* 473–517.

United Nations News Centre, *UN calls Italy to Ensure Better Conditions for Tunisian Migrants on Italian Island*, 22 March 2011 <www.un.org/apps/news/story.asp?NewsID=37849&Cr=tunisia&Cr1=#.Ua6inhp--M8>.

Ungar, Michael, 'Resilience across Cultures' (2008) 38 *British Journal of Social Work* 212.

Valverde, Mariana, 'Law versus History: Foucault's Genealogy of Modern Sovereignty', in Michael Dillon and Andrew Neal (eds), *Foucault on Politics, Security and War* (Palgrave, 2008), 135–50.

Van Kersbergen, Kees and Bertjan Verbeek, 'The Politics of International Norms: Subsidiarity and the Imperfect Competence Regime of the European Union' (2007) 13 *European Journal of International Relations* 217.

Vastri, Wanda, 'The Strange Case of Ethnography and International Relations' (2008) 37 *Millennium* 279–301.

Victor, David G. and Kal Raustiala, 'The Regime Complex for Plant Genetic Resources' (2004) 58 *International Organization* 277–309.

Victor, David G., Kal Raustiala and Eugene B. Skolnikoff, *The Implementation and Effectiveness of International Environmental Commitments: Theory and Practice* (MIT Press, 1998).

Walker, R. B. J., *Inside/Outside: International Relations as International Theory* (Cambridge University Press, 1993).

Walker, R. B. J., *After the Globe, Before the World* (Routledge, 2009).

Warner, Daniel, 'Voluntary Repatriation and the Meaning of a Return to Home' (1994) 7 *Journal of Refugee Studies* 160–74.

Warner, Daniel, 'The Refugee State and State Protection', in Frances Nicholson and Patrick Twomey (eds), *Refugee Rights and Realities* (Cambridge University Press, 1999), ch. 12.

Wendt, Alexander, *Social Theory of International Politics* (Cambridge University Press, 1999).

West, Ed, 'It's not the Home Office's fault – the UN Convention on Refugees is not fit for purpose', *The Telegraph*, 11 January 2011.

Weyland, Kurt, 'Toward a New Theory of Institutional Change' (2008) 60 *World Politics* 281–314.

Wiener, Antje, 'Enacting Meaning-in-use: Qualitative Research on Norms and International Relations' (2009) 35 *Review of International Studies* 175–93.

Wiener, Antje, 'Cultural Validation: Examining the Familiarity Deficit in Global Governance', in Corneliu Bjola and Markus Korrnprobst (eds), *Arguing Global Governance* (Routledge, 2010).

Wikrén, Gerhard and Håkan Sandesjö, *Utlänningslagen med kommentarer* (9th edn, Norstedts Juridik, 2010).

Wood, Tamara and Jane McAdam, 'Australian Asylum Policy all at Sea: An Analysis of *Plaintiff M70/2011 v. Minister for Immigration and Citizenship* and the Australia–Malaysia Arrangement' (2012) 61 *International and Comparative Law Quarterly* 274.

Young, Oran, *Institutional Dynamics* (MIT Press, 2010).

Zaat, Kirsten, *The Protection of Forced Migrants in Islamic Law* (UNHCR, New Issues in Refugee Research, Research Paper No. 146, 2007).

Zambelli, Pia, 'Problematic Trends in the Analysis of State Protection and Article 1F(a) Exclusion in Canadian Refugee Law' (2011) 23 *International Journal of Refugee Law* 252.

Zetter, Roger, 'Labelling Refugees: Forming and Transforming a Refugee Identity' (1991) 4 *Journal of Refugee Studies* 39–62.

Zetter, Roger, 'More Labels, Fewer Refugees: Remaking the Refugee Label in the Era of Globalization' (2007) 20 *Journal of Refugee Studies* 172–92.

Zetter, Roger, David Griffiths and Nando Sigona, 'Social Capital or Social Exclusion? The Impact of Asylum Seeker Dispersal on Refugee Community Organisations' (2005) 40 *Community Development Journal* 169–81.

Zetter, Roger *et al.*, *Immigration, Social Cohesion and Social Capital: What Are the Links?* (Joseph Rowntree Foundation, 2006) <www.jrf.org.uk/publications/immigration-social-cohesion-and-social-capital-what-are-links>.

Zimmerman, Andreas (ed.), *The 1951 Convention Relating to the Status of Refugees and Its 1967 Protocol: A Commentary* (Oxford University Press, 2011).

Zolberg, Arstide, Astri Suhrke, and Sergio Aguayo, *Escape from Violence – Conflict and the Refugee Crisis in the Developing World* (Oxford University Press, 1989).

Official publications

Abild, Erik, 'New Issues in Refugee Research: Research Paper 184: Creating Humanitarian Space: A Case Study of Somalia' (UNHCR, December 2009).

African Union Convention for the Protection and Assistance of Internally Displaced Persons in Africa (adopted by the Special Summit of the Union held in Kampala, Uganda, 22 October 2009).

ALEF/IKV Pax Christi, *Two Years On: Syrian Refugees in Lebanon*, September 2013.

Arab Convention on Regulating Status of Refugees in the Arab Countries, 1994.

ARCI, Caritas Italiana and CIR, *Un Team per l'integrazione: viaggio nel mondo dell'asilo* ('Team integrazione' Report Project, 2010).

Arrangement with Regard to the issue of Certificates of Identity to Russian Refugees, signed at Geneva July 5, 1922 LNTS 13 No. 355, 237–42.

Arrangement of 12 May 1926 relating to the Issue of Identity Certificates to Russian and Armenian Refugees, Supplementing and amending the previous Arrangements dated 5 July 1922 and 31 May 1924, LNTS 89 No. 2004, 47–52.

Arrangement concerning the Extension to other Categories of Refugees of certain Measures taken in favour of Russian and Armenian Refugee, LNTS 89 No. 2006, 63–7.

Barnes, Anne Evans, 'New Issues in Refugee Research, Research Paper 167: Realizing Protection Space for Iraqi Refugees: UNHCR in Syria, Jordan and Lebanon' (UNHCR, January 2009).

Betts, Alexander and Esra Kaytaz, 'National and International Responses to the Zimbabwean Exodus: Implications for the Refugee Protection Regime', *New Issues in Refugee Research Working Paper No. 175* (UNHCR, 2009).

Boverket – The Swedish National Board of Housing, Building and Planning, *Asylsökandes eget boende, EBO – en kartläggning* (report, 2008).

Bulletin de législation libanaise (Journal Officiel), No. 28–1962, 10 July 1962.

Cairo Declaration on Human Rights in Islam, Organization of the Islamic Conference (OIC), 5 August 1990.

Cairo Declaration on Protection of Refugees and Displaced Peoples, 19 November 1992.

Calabrò, Maria Antonietta, 'Immigrati, affondo di La Russa: Il commissariato Onu non conta', *Corriere della Sera* (online), 17 May 2009 <http://archiviostorico.corriere.it/2009/maggio/17/Immigrati_affondo_Russa_commissariato_Onu_co_8_0905 17023.shtml>.

(Canada) Legal Services, Immigration and Refugee Board, *Interpretation of the Convention Refugee Definition in the Case Law: Key Points* (1999).

Canadian Council for Refugees, *Refugee Reform – Bill C-31 Changes to the Refugee Determination System* <https://ccrweb.ca/en/refugee-reform>.

Caritas-Migrantes, *Immigrazione. Dossier Statistico 2010* (Idos, 2010).

Caritas-Migrantes, *Immigrazione. Dossier Statistico 2012* (Idos, 2012).

Charter of Fundamental Rights of the European Union: OJ 2000 No. C364/01.

Cittalia Foundation, *I volti dell'integrazione. Il ruolo delle comunità locali, dei cittadini e dei mass media nei processi di inclusione dei rifugiati in Italia* (ANCI, 2010).

Convention against Torture and Other Cruel, Inhuman or Degrading Treatment or Punishment, opened for signature 10 December 1984, 1465 UNTS 85 (entered into force 26 June 1987).

Convention for the Protection of Human Rights and Fundamental Freedoms 1950, ETS No. 005.

Convention Relating to the Status of Refugees, opened for signature 28 July 1951, 189 UNTS 150 (entered into force 22 April 1954).

Consortium for Refugees and Migrants in South Africa (CoRMSA), 'Protecting Refugees, Asylum Seekers and Migrants in South Africa' (CoRMSA, 18 June 2008).

Costello, Cathryn, 'The European Asylum Procedures Directive in Legal Contest', *UNHCR Research Paper 134*, November 2006 <www.refworld.org/pdfid/4ff14e932.pdf>.

Constitution on the International Refugee Organization, 15 December 1946, 18 UNTS 3, Annex 1, Section A, para. 1.

Convention relating to the International Status of Refugees, 28 October 1933, LNTS 159 No. 3663, Art. 1.

Convention concerning the Status of Refugees coming from Germany, 10 February 1938, LNTS 92 No. 4461, 59.

Council of Europe, Commissioner for Human Rights, 28 September 2008, *It Is Wrong to Criminalize Migration* <www.refworld.org/docid/48e34d8a2.html>.

Council of Europe Parliamentary Assembly, Committee on Migration, Refugees and Population, 'The Image of Asylum-seekers, Migrants and Refugees in the Media', Doc. 11011, 10 July 2006.

Council of the European Union, 25 February 2003, Council Regulation (EC) No. 343/2003 of 18 February 2003 establishing the criteria and mechanisms for determining the member state responsible for examining an asylum application lodged in one of the member states by a third-country national, OJ L50/1 <http://eur-lex.europa.eu/LexUriServ/LexUriServ.do?uri=OJ:L:2003:050:0001:0010:EN:PDF>.

Council of the European Union, 3 October 2003, Council Directive 2003/86/EC of 22 September 2003 on the right to family reunification, OJ L251, 3 <http://eur-lex.europa.eu/LexUriServ/LexUriServ.do?uri=OJ:L:2003:251:0012:0018:en:PDF>.

Council of the European Union, 13 December 2005, Council Directive 2005/85/EC of 1 December 2005 on minimum standards on procedures in member states for granting and withdrawing refugee status, OJ L326/13 <http://eur-lex.europa.eu/LexUriServ/LexUriServ.do?uri=OJ:L:2005:326:0013:0034:EN:PDF>.

Council of the European Union, 24 December 2008, Council Directive 2008/115/EC of the European Parliament and of the Council of 16 December 2008 on common grounds and procedures in members states for returning illegally staying third-country nationals, OJ L348/98 <http://eur-lex.europa.eu/LexUriServ/LexUriServ.do?uri=OJ:L:2008:348:0098:0107:EN:pdf>.

Council of the European Union, 20 December 2011, Council Directive 2011/95/EU of the European Parliament and of the Council of 13 December 2011 on standards for the qualification of third-country nationals or stateless persons as beneficiaries of international protection, for a uniform status for refugees or for persons eligible for subsidiary protection, and for the content of the protection Granted (recast), OJ L337 <http://eurlex.europa.eu/LexUriServ/LexUriServ.do?uri=OJ:L:2011:337:0009:0026:EN:PDF>.

Council of the European Union, 26 June 2013, Council Directive 2013/32/EU of the European Parliament and of the Council of 26 June 2013 on common procedures for granting and withdrawing international protection (recast), OJ L160/60 <http://eurlex.europa.eu/LexUriServ/LexUriServ.do?uri=OJ:L:2013:180:0060:0095:EN:PDF>.

Council of the European Union, 26 June 2013, Directive 2013/33/EU of the European Parliament and of the Council of 26 June 2013 laying down standards for the reception of applicants for international protection (recast), OJ 2013 No. L180/96

<http://eur-lex.europa.eu/smartapi/cgi/sga_doc?smartapi!celexplus!prod!CELEXn umdoc&lg=EN&numdoc=32013L0033>.

Castles, Stephen, *New Issues in Refugee Research Working Paper No. 70: Environmental Change and Forced Migration: Making Sense of the Debate* (UNHCR, 2002).

Crisp, Jeff, *New Issues in Refugee Research Paper No. 155: Beyond the Nexus: UNHCR's Revolving Perspective on Refugee Protection and International Migration* (UNHCR, April 2008).

Crisp, Jeff and Esther Kiragu, 'Refugee Protection and International Migration: A Review of UNHCR's Role in Malawi, Mozambique and South Africa' (UNHCR Policy Development and Evaluation Service (PDES), 2010).

Deng, Francis M, *Report of the Representative of the Secretary-General, Mr. Francis M. Deng, submitted pursuant to Commission on Human Rights Resolutions 1993/95 and 1994/68*, UN Document E/CN.4/1995/50 (2 February 1995).

Edwards, Alice, *Back to Basics: The Right to Liberty and Security of Person and 'Alternatives to Detention' of Refugees, Asylum-Seekers, Stateless Persons and Other Migrants* (UNHCR, PPLA/2011/01.Rev.1, April 2011) <http://www.unhcr.org/refworld/docid/4dc935fd2.html>.

Expert Panel on Asylum Seekers (Australia), 13 August 2012, *The Report of the Expert Panel on Asylum Seekers* <http://expertpanelonasylumseekers.dpmc.gov.au/report>.

European Commission, 31 January 2001, *Unity, Solidarity, Diversity in Europe, Its People and Its Territory*, Second Report on Economic and Social Cohesion Adopted by the European Commission on 31 January 2001 <www.inforegio.cec.eu.int/wbdoc/docoffic/official/reports/conclu32_en.htm>.

European Commission, EC Qualification Directive, Council Directive 2004/83/EC on minimum standards for the qualification and status of third country nationals or stateless persons as refugees or as persons who otherwise need international protection and the content of the protection granted OJ 2004 No. L304/12.

European Commission, 'Transposition of the Asylum Procedures Directive' (press release, MEMO/07/538, 3 December 2007) <http://europa.eu/rapid/pressReleasesAction.do?reference=MEMO/07/538&format=HTML&aged=1&language=EN&guiLanguage=en>.

European Commission, 13 February 2008, Examining the Creation of a European Border Surveillance System, COM(2008) 68 final <http://eur-lex.europa.eu/LexUriServ/LexUriServ.do?uri=COM:2008:0068:FIN:EN:PDF>.

European Commission, 17 June 2008, *Policy Plan on Asylum: An Integrated Approach to Protection Across the EU*, COM(2008) 360 <http://eurlex.europa.eu/LexUriServ/LexUriServ.do?uri=COM:2008:0360:FIN:EN:PDF>

European Commission, 21 October 2009, Proposal for a directive of the European Parliament and of the Council on minimum standards on procedures in member states for granting and withdrawing international protection (recast), COM(2009) 554 final <http://eur-lex.europa.eu/LexUriServ/LexUriServ.do?uri=COM:2009:0554:FIN:EN:PDF>.

European Commission, EC Qualification Directive, Council Directive 2011/95/EU of the European Parliament and of the Council of 13 December 2011 on standards for the qualification of third-country nationals or stateless persons as beneficiaries of international protection, for a uniform status for refugees or for persons eligible for subsidiary protection, and for the content of the protection granted (recast), OJ 2011 No. L337/9.

European Commission, *Europe in Figures – Eurostat Yearbook*, Eurostat, 2012 <http://epp.eurostat.ec.europa.eu/statistics_explained/index.php/Europe_in_figures_-_Eurostat_yearbook>.

European Council, 6 February 2003, Council Directive 2003/9/EC of 27 January 2003 laying down minimum standards for the reception of asylum seekers, OJ 2003 L31/18 <http://eur-lex.europa.eu/LexUriServ/LexUriServ.do?uri=OJ:L:2003:031:0 018:0025:EN:PDF>.

European Council, 13 December 2005, Council Directive 2005/85/EC of 1 December 2005 on minimum standards on procedures in member states for granting and withdrawing refugee status, OJ 2005 L326/13 <http://eur-lex.europa.eu/LexUriServ/ LexUriServ.do?uri=OJ:L:2005:326:0013:0034:EN:PDF>.

European Parliament and of the Council of the European Union, 20 December 2011, European Directive 2011/95/EU of the European Parliament and of the Council, OJ 2011 L337/9 (recast 2011 Qualification Directive) <http://eurlex.europa.eu/ LexUriServ/LexUriServ.do?uri=OJ:L:2011:337:0009:0026:EN:PDF>.

EUROSTAT, *Asylum Statistics* (data from August 2012) <http://epp.eurostat.ec.europa.eu/ statistics_explained/index.php/Asylum_statistics>.

Feller, Erika, address by Ms Erika Feller, Director of the Department of International Protection, UNHCR, at the South Asia Regional Judicial Symposium on Refugee Protection (New Delhi, 13–14 November 1999), 14 November.

Feller, Erika, 'Protecting people in conflict and crisis – responding to the challenges of a changing world', opening address at the Humanitarian Space Conference at the Refugee Studies Centre, Oxford (October 2009).

Feller, Erika, 'Refugee Protection: Challenges and Opportunities in the Australian Region and beyond' (UNHCR, 18 February 2010).

Forti, Oliviero and Santino Tornesi, 'Emergenza Nord Africa: verso un nuovo sistema d'accoglienza?', in Caritas-Migrantes, *Immigrazione. Dossier statistico 2012* (Idos, 2012).

Fuccaro, Lorenzo, 'Cento milioni per fermare lo "tsunami umano"', *Corriere della Sera* (online), 2 April 2011 <http://archiviostorico.corriere.it/2011/aprile/02/Cento_ milioni_per_fermare_tsunami_co_8_110402006.shtml>.

Gallo, Giuliano, 'Frattini sul caso Unhcr: Sbaglia ma va rispettato. La Russa smorza i toni', *Corriere della Sera* (online), 18 May 2009 <http://archiviostorico.corriere.it/2009/ maggio/18/Frattini_sul_caso_Unhcr_sbaglia_co_8_090518020.shtml>.

Gomez, Margarita Puerto and Asger Christensen, 'The Impacts of Refugees on Neighboring Countries: A Development Challenge' (World Development Report 2011 Background Note, World Bank, 29 July 2010).

Goodwin-Gill, Guy, *High Commissioner's Dialogue on Protection Challenges*, 2 December 2010.

Government of Canada, news release, 'Harper government takes action against human smuggling', 5 December 2012 <http://news.gc.ca/web/article-eng.do?nid=710859>.

Government of Canada, Citizenship and Immigration Canada, 30 March 2010, speaking notes – remarks by the Honourable Jason Kenney <www.cic.gc.ca/english/department/ media/speeches/2010/2010-03-30.asp>.

Government of Canada, Citizenship and Immigration Canada, 16 February 2012, 'Backgrounder – Designated Countries of Origin' <www.cic.gc.ca/english/department/ media/backgrounders/2012/2012-02-16i.asp>.

Government of Canada, Citizenship and Immigration Canada, Summary of Changes to Canada's Refugee System in the Protecting Canada's Immigration System Act, 16 February 2012 <www.cic.gc.ca/english/department/media/backgrounders/2012/ 2012-02-16f.asp>.

Government of Canada, Citizenship and Immigration Canada, speaking notes for the Honorable Jason Kenney, PC, MP Minister of Citizenship, Immigration and Multiculturalism – at a news conference following the tabling of Bill C-31, Protecting

Canada's Immigration System Act, 16 February 2012 <www.cic.gc.ca/EnGlish/department/media/speeches/2012/2012-02-16.asp>.

Government of Canada, Citizenship and Immigration Canada, news release, 'Canada's new asylum system a success', 22 February 2013 <www.cic.gc.ca/english/department/media/releases/2013/2013-02-22.asp>.

Government of Canada, Citizenship and Immigration Canada, 27 February 2013, Preliminary tables – Permanent and temporary residents, 2012 <www.cic.gc.ca/english/resources/statistics/facts2012-preliminary/01.asp>.

Government of Canada, Citizenship and Immigration Canada, 'Overview: Ending the Abuse of Canada's Immigration System by Human Smugglers', 29 June 2012 <www.cic.gc.ca/english/department/media/backgrounders/2012/2012-06-29i.asp>.

Hazaimeh, Hani, 'Syrian army defectors came as individuals to Jordan', *Jordan Times*, 25 November 2011.

Home Office Statistics, *Asylum Statistics United Kingdom 2007*, 21 August 2008 <http://webarchive.nationalarchives.gov.uk/20110218135832/rds.homeoffice.gov.uk/rds/pdfs08/hosb1108.pdf>.

House of Lords Select Committee on the EU, *Defining Refugee Status and Those in Need of International Protection* (London: Stationery Office, 2002).

HumanCareSyria, *Statistic Report December 2013* <www.humancaresyria.org/images/uploads/documents/Syria-StatisticalReport-December2013.pdf>.

Human Rights Resource Center, *Rule of Law for Human Rights in the ASEAN Region* (HRRC: Jakarta, May 2011).

Human Rights Watch, 21 September 2009, *Pushed Back, Pushed Around: Italy's Forced Return of Boat Migrants and Asylum Seekers and Libya's Mistreatment of Migrants and Asylum Seekers* <www.hrw.org/sites/default/files/reports/italy0909webwcover_0.pdf>.

Human Rights Watch, 'Egypt: Syria refugees detained, coerced to return' <www.hrw.org/news/2013/11/10/egypt-syria-refugees-detained-coerced-return>.

Integrated Regional Information Networks (IRIN), 'Yemen–Somalia: bracing for a fresh influx of Somali refugees', September 2009 <www.irinnews.org/Report.aspx?ReportId=85943>.

International Conference on Indo-Chinese Refugees, Geneva, 13–14 June 1989; *Declaration and Comprehensive Plan of Action*, UN Doc. A/CONF.148/2, 13 June 1989.

International Convention on the Protection of the Rights of All Migrant Workers and Members of Their Families (ICRMW), opened for signature 18 December 1990, GA Res. 45/158 (entered into force 1 July 2003).

International Covenant on Civil and Political Rights, 999 UNTS 171, 16 December 1966.

International Covenant on Economic, Social and Cultural Rights, 993 UNTS 3, 16 December 1966.

International Federation of Red Cross and Red Crescent Societies (IFRC), *World Disasters Report 2012, Focus on Forced Migration*, 2012 <www.ifrc.org/wdr>.

International Organization for Migration, *Towards Tolerance, Law and Dignity: Addressing Violence against Foreign National in South Africa* (IOM, 2009).

Kagan, Michael, 'New Issues in Refugee Research, Research Paper 201: The UN Surrogate State and Refugee Policy in the Middle East' (UNHCR, February 2011).

Kagan, Michael, '"We Live in a Country of UNHCR": The UN Surrogate State and Refugee Policy in the Middle East' (UNHCR, New Issues in Refugee Research, Research Paper No. 201, February 2011).

Kumin, Judith, remarks to the Cross-Dimensional Corfu Meeting, Organization for Security and Co-operation in Europe (OSCE), Vienna, 28 May 2010 <www.unhcr.org/4c03cf106.html>.

Lebanese Centre for Human Rights, *Asylum Seekers and Refugees: Languishing in Injustice* (2011).

Legislative Decree No. 29 of 15 January 1970 – The Entry and Exit of Aliens to and from the Syrian Arab Republic and their Residence therein; Ministry of Interior Decision No. 1350 of 15 August 1948 (Lebanon).

Letter of Understanding signed between the Government of the Hashemite Kingdom of Jordan and the Office of the United High Commissioner for Refugees, 15 April 2003.

Médecins Sans Frontiérs, 2007, *Ten Women Tell of Their Angolan Ordeal*, MSF-Belgium <http://doctorswithoutborders.org/news/article.cfm?id=2232&cat=field-news>.

Médecins Sans Frontiérs, 'PUC Memo, W. Kasai to Antenne Kinshasa' (MSF-Belgium, 8 November 2007).

Médecins Sans Frontiérs, 'RDC-Kasaï Occidental: violences sexuelles à l'égard des femmes congolaises refoulées de l'Angola', 11 December 2007–5 January 2008 (MSF-Belgium: Brussels).

Memorandum of Understanding signed between the Government of the Hashemite Kingdom of Jordan and the Office of the United High Commissioner for Refugees, 5 April 1998.

Memorandum of Understanding between the Directorate of the General Security and the United Nations High Commissioner for Refugees concerning the processing of asylum seekers applying for refugee status, 9 September 2003.

Ministry of Interior, Population Immigration and Border Authority, Procedure for Handling Political Asylum Seekers in Israel, entered into force 2 January 2011.

Ministry of Justice, Government Offices of Sweden, *Synnerligen ömmande ömständigheter och verkställighetshinder – en kartläggning av tillämpningen*, Memorandum No. DS 2011:14 (2011).

Monzini, Paola, Ferruccio Pastore and Giuseppe Sciortino, 'L'Italia promessa. Geopolitica e dinamiche organizzative del traffico di migranti verso l'Italia, Roma', CESPI (Centro Studi Politica Internazionale Working Papers No. 9 (2004).

Morrison, Scott, 'A Real Solution: An International, Regional and Domestic Approach to Asylum Policy' (Speech to the Lowey Institute, Sydney, 30 November 2010).

MRT–RRT, *A Guide to Refugee Law in Australia* (Legal Services RRT 2013) 8–6 <http://www.mrt-rrt.gov.au/Conduct-of-reviews/Guide-to-refugee-law.aspx>.

Neumann, Klaus, 'Whatever happened to the right of asylum' (address to the Law and History Conference, Melbourne, 13 December 2010).

Office for the Coordination of Humanitarian Affairs (OCHA), 'Point sur les expulses d'Angola au 15.10.09' (2009), on file with the author.

Principles Concerning Treatment of Refugees as adopted by the Asian–African Legal Consultative Committee at its Eighth Session, Bangkok, August, 1966; reproduced in Eberhard Jahn, 'The Work of Asian–African Legal Consultative Committee on the Legal Status of Refugees' 1967 Max-Planck-Institut <www.zaoerv.de/27_1967/27_19 67_1_2_b_122_138.pdf>.

Reliefweb, 'Legal status of individuals fleeing Syria', June 2013 <http://reliefweb.int/sites/reliefweb.int/files/resources/legal_status_of_individuals_fleeing_syria.pdf>.

Report of the Representative of the Secretary-General, Mr Francis M. Deng, submitted pursuant to Commission resolution 1997/39, Addendum, *Guiding Principles on Internal Displacement*, E/CN.4/1998/53/Add.2 (11 February 1998).

Resolution on the Problem of Refugees in the Muslim World, No. 15/10-P (IS), Adopted by the Tenth Session of the Islamic Summit Conference Putrajaya, Malaysia, 16–17 October 2003.

Sen, Amartya, June 2000, 'Social Exclusion: Concept, Application, and Scrutiny', *Social Development Papers No. 1* (Office of Environment and Social Development, Asian Development Bank), 10 <http://housingforall.org/Social_exclusion.pdf>.

Statement by Volker Türk, Director of International Protection to the 64th Session of the Executive Committee of the High Commissioner's Programme, 3 October 2013.

Statute of the Office of the UN High Commissioner for Refugees, UNGA Res. 428(v), 14 December 1950.

Strik, Tineke, 5 April 2012, 'Lives Lost in the Mediterranean Sea: Who Is Responsible', *Report from the Committee on Migration, Refugees and Displaced Persons*, Doc. 12895 <http://assembly.coe.int/ASP/Doc/XrefViewPDF.asp?FileID=18095>.

Swedish Government Official Reports, *Den nya migrationsprocessen*, Report No. SOU 2009:56 (2009).

Swedish Migration Board, *Arbetet med den tillfälliga utlänningslagstiftningen 2005–2006. Slutrapport* (report, Swedish Migration Board, 2007).

Travaux préparatoires, 25 July 1951 <www.refworld.org/docid/40a8a7394.html>.

United Nations, *Rapport de la Mission Inter-Agences d'Evaluation des Besoins Humanitaires des Populations des 2ZS du Territoire de Kahemba* (September 2007).

United Nations Development Programme, *Human Development Report 2010* (2010).

United Nations General Assembly, Resolution 217 A(III), 10 December 1948.

United Nations General Assembly, Resolution 319(IV), 3 December 1949.

United Nations General Assembly, Resolution 428(V), Annex, 14 December 1950.

United Nations High Commissioner for Refugees, *Handbook on Procedures and Criteria for Determining Refugee Status under the 1951 Convention and the 1967 Protocol Relating to the Status of Refugees*, HCR/IP/4/Rev.1, 1979, re-edited, Geneva, January 1992.

United Nations High Commissioner for Refugees, *Comprehensive and Regional Approaches to Refugee Problems*, UN Document EC/1994/SCP/CRP. 3, 3 May 1994.

United Nations High Commissioner for Refugees, *Annotated Comments on the EC Council Directive 2004/83/EC of 29 April 2004 on Minimum Standards for the Qualification and Status of Third Country Nationals or Stateless Persons as Refugees or as Persons who otherwise need International Protection and the Content of the Protection granted*, OJ 2004 No. L304/12.

United Nations High Commissioner for Refugees, *UNHCR Country Operation Plan: Malaysia* (2007).

United Nations High Commissioner for Refugees, *Refugee Protection and Durable Solutions in the Context of International Migration*, UNHCR/DPC/2007/Doc. 02, 19 November 2007.

United Nations High Commissioner for Refugees, *2009: Global Trends* <www.unhcr.org/4c11f0be9.html>.

UNHCR, *Country Operations Plan 2008–09, Hashemite Kingdom of Jordan* <www.unhcr.org/49cb98a42.html>.

United Nations High Commissioner for Refugees, *UNHCR Policy on Refugee Protection and Solutions in Urban Areas* (September 2009).

United Nations High Commissioner for Refugees, December 2009, *Some 74,000 Africans Cross Gulf of Aden to Yemen in Record-Breaking Year* <www.unhcr.org/4b2bac179.html>.

United Nations High Commissioner for Refugees, 'Richiedenti asilo e rifugiati nel mondo e in Italia', in Caritas-Migrantes, *Immigrazione. Dossier statistico 2010* (Idos, 2010).

United Nations High Commissioner for Refugees, *UNHCR Global Appeal 2010–2011* (2010).

United Nations High Commissioner for Refugees, 2010, *Yemen: Global Needs Assessment* <www.unhcr.org/pages/49e486ba6.html>.

United Nations High Commissioner for Refugees, *Asylum Levels and Trends in Industrialized Countries 2009* (23 March 2010).

United Nations High Commissioner for Refugees, 21 May 2010, *UNHCR Statement on the Right to an Effective Remedy in Relation to Accelerated Asylum Procedures* <www.unhcr.org/4deccc639.pdf>.

United Nations High Commissioner for Refugees, *UNHCR Global Report 2009* (June 2010).

United Nations High Commissioner for Refugees, 'Table 12 – Asylum Applications and Refugee Status Determination by Origin and Country/Territory of Asylum', *Statistical Yearbook 2011*, 2011 <www.unhcr.org/51628f589.html>.

United Nations High Commissioner for Refugees, Written observations in *NS* v. *Secretary of State for the Home Department* and *ME and Others* v. *Refugee Applications Commissioner and Minister for Justice, Equality and Law Reform*, Joined Cases C-411/10 and C-493/10, 1 February 2011.

United Nations High Commissioner for Refugees, July 2011, *Global Roundtable on Alternatives to Detention of Asylum-Seekers, Refugees, Migrants and Stateless Persons: Summary Conclusions* <www.refworld.org/cgi-bin/texis/vtx/rwmain?docid=4e315b882>.

United Nations High Commissioner for Refugees, *A Year Of Crisis. UNHCR Global Trends 2011* (2012).

United Nations High Commissioner for Refugees, 'Richiedenti asilo e rifugiati nel mondo e in Italia', in Caritas-Migrantes, *Immigrazione. Dossier statistico 2012* (Idos, 2012).

United Nations High Commissioner for Refugees, 'UNHCR promotes Innovation and Self-sufficiency at Annual NGO Meet', 3 July 2012 <www.unhcr.org/4ff300320.html>.

United Nations High Commissioner for Refugees, 'Egypt: UNHCR concerned over detention of Syrian refugees amid anti-Syrian sentiment', 26 July 2013 <www.unhcr.org/51f242c59.html>.

United Nations High Commissioner for Refugees, *Displacement: The New 21st Century Challenge. UNHCR global trends 2012* (2013).

United Nations High Commissioner for Refugees, *International Protection Considerations with regard to people fleeing the Syrian Arab Republic, Update II*, 22 October 2013.

United Nations High Commissioner for Refugees *2014 Syria Regional Response Plan – Strategic Overview* <www.unhcr.org/syriarrp6/docs/Syria-rrp6-full-report.pdf>.

United Nations Human Rights Committee, 26 May 2004, *General Comment No. 31 [80] The Nature of the Legal Obligation Imposed on State Parties to the Covenant*, CCPR/C/21/Rev.1/Add.13, adopted on 29 March 2004.

Universal Islamic Declaration on Human Rights, 21 Dhul Qaidah 1401, 19 September 1981.

Cases

Adam and others v. *The Knesset and others (7146/12); Doe and others* v. *Ministry of Interior and others (1192/13); Tahangas and others* v. *Ministry of Interior (1247/13)*, 7146/12, 1192/13, 1247/13, 16 September 2013.

Bundesrepublik Deutschland v. *B and D*, Court of Justice of the European Union (C-57/09 and C-101/09) [2010] ECR I-000.

C et al. v. *Director of Immigration and Secretary for Security* Civil Appeal 132–137/2008 (Hong Kong Court of Appeal, 21 July 2011).

Canada (Attorney General) v. *Ward* [1993]2 SCR 689, [1993] SCJ No. 74.

Carrillo v. *Canada (Minister of Citizenship and Immigration)* 2008 FCA 94.

Elgafaji v. *Staatssecretaris van Justitie* (C-465/07) [2009] ECR 1-921 (17 February 2009).

Horvath v. *Secretary of State* [2001] 1 AC 489.

Husan v. *Secretary of State* [2005] EWHC 189 (Admin).

Islam v. *Home Department; R* v. *Immigration Appeal Tribunal, ex parte Shah* [1999] 2 AC 629.

Mari Cruz Hernandez Fuentes v. *(Minister of Citizenship and Immigration)* 2010 FC 457 (29 April 2010).

Minister of Employment and Immigration v. *Satiacum* [1989] FCJ No. 505, 99 NR 171 (FCA).

Minister for Immigration & Multicultural Affairs v. *Respondents S152* (2004) 222 CLR 1.

Mosilhy v. *Canada (Minister of Citizenship and Immigration)* 2007 FC 1302.

Oscar Leonard Perez Mendoza v *Canada (Minister of Citizenship and Immigration)* 2010 FC 119.

R v. *Appulonappa* 2013 BCSC 31, [2013] BCJ No. 35.

Refugee Appeal No. 74665/03 [2005] NZAR 60.

Refugee Appeal No. 76044 [2008] NZAR 719.

Salah Sheekh v. *Netherlands* ECtHR 11 January 2007, Application no. 1948/04.

Salahadin Abdulla and Others v. *Germany* (C-175, 176, 178, 179/08) [2009] ECR I-1493.

Samuel v. *Canada (Minister for Citizenship and Immigration)* 2008 FC 762.

Secretary for Security v. *Prabakar* Final Appeal No. 16 of 2003 (Civil) (Hong Kong Court of Final Appeal, 8 June 2004).

Secretary of State for the Home Department, ex parte Bagdanavicius [2005] UKHL 38 (26 May 2005).

Singh v. *Minister of Employment and Immigration* [1985]1 SCR 177, [1985] SCJ No. 11.

Tun Naing Oo v. *Public Prosecutor* (Court of Appeal, James Foong, JCA, Abdul Malik Ishak, JCA, and Abu Samah Nordin, JCA) (File number A-04-76-2008; 2 January 2009).

Tun Naing Oo v. *Public Prosecutor* (High Court of Malaya, Shah Alam, Yeoh Wee Siam, JC) (File number 43-9-2009; 24 March 2009).

Index

Lightning Source UK Ltd.
Milton Keynes UK
UKOW05n0747160415

249756UK00008B/118/P